THE MEDIEVAL RISK-REWARD SOCIETY

COURTS, ADVENTURE, AND LOVE IN THE EUROPEAN MIDDLE AGES

Will Hasty

THE OHIO STATE UNIVERSITY PRESS · COLUMBUS

Copyright © 2016 by The Ohio State University.
All rights reserved.

Library of Congress Cataloging-in-Publication Data
Names: Hasty, Will, author.
Title: The medieval risk-reward society : courts, adventure, and love in the European Middle Ages / Will Hasty.
Other titles: Interventions (Columbus, Ohio)
Description: Columbus : The Ohio State University Press, [2016] | "2016" | Series: Interventions: new studies in medieval culture | Includes bibliographical references and index.
Identifiers: LCCN 2015045866| ISBN 9780814213032 (cloth ; alk. paper) | ISBN 0814213030 (cloth ; alk. paper)
Subjects: LCSH: Literature, Medieval—History and criticism. | Love in literature. | Courtly love—History. | Courts and courtiers. | Aristocracy (Social class)
Classification: LCC PN671 .H37 2016 | DDC 809/.02—dc23
LC record available at http://lccn.loc.gov/2015045866

Cover design by Lisa Force
Text design by Juliet Williams
Type set in Adobe Minion Pro
Printed by Thomson-Shore, Inc.

Cover image: Cod. Pal. germ. 848, Große Heidelberger Liederhandschrift (Codex Manesse), 52r. Used with permission of the Universitätsbibliothek Heidelberg.

♾ The paper used in this publication meets the minimum requirements of the American National Standard for Information Sciences—Permanence of Paper for Printed Library Materials. ANSI Z39.48-1992.

9 8 7 6 5 4 3 2 1

IN LOVING MEMORY OF PATRICIA JANE HASTY

CONTENTS

Acknowledgments   vii

Introduction   1

1   The Cultural Action   8
    Toward a Cultural Game Theory   8
    The New Medieval Move   13
    A Race of Four Cities: Troy, Jericho, Rome, and Jerusalem   16

2   The Medieval Self as Bankroll   34
    The City of God: Otherness as a Global Parameter of Action   34
    The City of God: Sameness as a Global Parameter of Action   39
    Loss, Reiteration, Growth   46
    The New Medieval Move Exemplified   50

3   Rules of the House   57
    Courtly Representation as Aristocratic Competition   57
    Investitures: A Diachronic View of the Political Action   72

4   The Poetic Action   79
    Wars, Tournaments, Verses: The Place of Poetry at Court   79
    Benchmarks of Performance   85
    The Vernacular as Poetic Resource   89
    Stars in Competition   95

5	Adventure as a Cultural Wager	118
	Dynamics of Adventure	118
	Highlights from Chrétien de Troyes's *Érec et Énide*	139
	Highlights from Wolfram von Eschenbach's *Parzival*	149
6	Love as a Cultural Wager	161
	Dynamics of Love	161
	Highlights from Marie de France's *Lanval*	176
	Highlights from Gottfried von Strassburg's *Tristan*	188
7	The Modern Self in Play	205
	The Global as Individual	205
	Reformation Moves	208
	Enlightenment Moves	219
	A Gilded-Age Connecticut Yankee Adventures for High Stakes	230
	Emancipation, Totalitarianism, and the (Post)Modern Cultural Action	239
	Bibliography	245
	Index	255

ACKNOWLEDGMENTS

I FINISHED AN INITIAL DRAFT of this study during a year-long research leave in the academic year 2009–10. For that indispensable time to think, write, and get critical momentum behind this book project, I would like to thank the University of Florida's College of Liberal Arts and Sciences. It is perhaps worthy of mention, as a remoter kind of acknowledgment, that this research leave followed shortly after the dissolution of my former Department of Germanic and Slavic Studies in 2008 for cost-cutting reasons, and the merging of GSS faculty into my current department, a larger Department of Languages, Literatures, and Cultures. In my new department, I have had the opportunity to be involved in discussions with non-European medievalists and to begin to think about what a *global* medieval studies might look like, which has done much to offset the sense of loss stemming from the dissolution of my former department. The year of my research leave in which this study first took form was shaped to a large degree, both positively and negatively, by the events of the preceding years. Having taken to heart that some academic departments in our day and age, especially on the Humanities end of the spectrum, as it seems, can be considered expendable, I remember during that year being preoccupied by a basic question: what is medieval poetry and the study of it *worth*? For better or worse, this question and the events of the previous years that led to it also doubtless played a role in shaping the concerns of this book.

With this study, I return to research topics and authors that have often occupied me in the past, though a glance at the title of this book should make clear that I endeavor to place them in a different context. Some of my earlier ruminations that have played a role in the new context of the present study have appeared in print in the more or less distant past: "Theorizing German Romance: The Excursus on Enite's Horse and Saddle in Hartmann von Aue's *Erec*," *Seminar* 43:3 (2007): 253–64; "Luther's Bible as Artwork: The Singularity of Aura and the Artistry of Translation," *Monatshefte für deutschsprachige Literatur und Kultur* 101:4 (2009): 457–68; "Bullish on Love and Adventure: Chivalry as Speculation in the German Arthurian Romances," *Arthuriana* 20:3 (2010): 65–80; and "Revolutions and Final Solutions: On Enlightenment and its Dialectic in Mark Twain's *A Connecticut Yankee in King Arthur's Court*," *Arthuriana* 24:2 (2014): 21–42. According to my view in this book, a critical moment of poetic, social, and cultural transition is visible in the Old French and Middle High German romance poetry of the latter twelfth and early thirteenth centuries, in which the French poets make initial pioneering poetic moves that are picked up and varied by the later German poets. What is important to me is the drive toward innovation and cultural growth that is common to all these poets. My greater professional experience by far has been with the German poets and the Holy Roman imperial cultural situation from the Middle Ages onward, which shapes my overall presentation, but I endeavor to do full justice to the cutting edge accomplishments of *all* the poets whom I consider. My approach leads me to be interested in competitions among *individual* medieval poets, and I isolate only a moment—though I believe a crucial one—in these contests, but I *call the action* as neutrally as I can.

Many colleagues at the University of Florida have helped me along with my work on this book. I would like particularly to thank Franz Futterknecht for generously sharing his thoughts and ideas with me in our many discussions, which have helped me place the Middle Ages in relation to broader cultural developments (more recently, particularly of the digital kind) and encouraged me to try to think outside the disciplinary box. I would like to thank Mary Watt for her unabated encouragement as I worked on this book and for sharing the vision of a global medieval studies. Beyond my own university, I would like to thank Francis Gentry for his willingness to look over the manuscript and for his helpful assessment of it, which led me to provide additional context for and—hopefully—precision to the presentation of my case. I would like, finally, to thank the many other colleagues with whom I have had the privilege to work over the last decade or so, especially in connection to the activities of the Society for Medieval Germanic Studies at the annual International Medieval Congresses at Kalamazoo, and the activities of the Arthurian Comparative Literary and Cultural Studies Group at the annual Conventions of the Modern Language Association. This book has been shaped by these and many other helpful voices and influences and would not have been possible without them. My expressions of gratitude go to the Universitätsbibliothek Heidelberg for permission to use images (of Walther von Klingen on the cover and Gottfried von Strassburg in chapter 4) reproduced from the Manesse Codex, the Bibliothéque Nationale de France (via Art Resource, NY) for permission to employ the image of Marie de France at work (in chapter 4), and my own Department of Languages, Literatures, and Cultures for assisting me with the acquisition of these permissions. Finally, I would like to express thanks to Eugene O'Connor, Acquisitions Editor for The Ohio State University Press, and to Ethan Knapp, editor of the Interventions series, for their kind consideration of my manuscript.

Above all, I thank my wife, Barbara, and my daughters Isabel and Natalie for their love, patience, and support during the many hours I spent working on this book over the past years. You have been, as ever, my strongest and truest inspiration.

INTRODUCTION

Omnis substantia singularis in perfecta notione sua involvit totum universum
—Gottfried Wilhelm Leibniz[1]

THE BEGINNING POINT of this study was an observation about the disposition of ladies and knights in courtly romance poetry of the late twelfth and early thirteenth centuries, composed by authors such as Marie de France, Chrétien de Troyes, Wolfram von Eschenbach, and Gottfried von Strassburg. Imaginary courtiers are able and willing in adventure and love—the principal concerns of this poetry—to dedicate themselves to transitory things *entirely*. This disposition of self is very much in the foreground of the poetry, eludes not even the most casual reader, and thus perhaps seems self-evident. Yet there is something extraordinary about it that seems to call for elucidation on its own *absolute* terms. Ladies and knights in court poetry, who manifestly regard themselves as Christians, are dedicating themselves *as such* to concerns that are understood to be passing. They are reiterating the Christian attitude of absolute dedication, but by directing this dedication to something mutable, they act in a manner different from, if not opposed to, the value placed by Christians in things everlasting, the "unchangeable life," the *vita incommutabilis* as St. Augustine puts it (*Doctrina Christiana*, I.VIII, 8). Coupled with the

---

1. From *Opuscules et fragments inédits de Leibniz: Extraits des manuscrits de la Bibliothèque royale de Hanovre*, 521 (edited by Louis Couturat. Paris: F. Alcan, 1903, https://archive.org/details/opusculesetfragoobibgoog [accessed July 1, 2015]).

observation of what seems to be new kinds of absolute dedication of self in the romances was the related observation that adventure and love are, as well, frequently if not typically depicted as games or contests, as if they needed to be understood as efforts or *moves* on which success or failure, growth or diminishment, happiness or sorrow depend.

The absolute disposition of self in adventure and love toward the transitory and mutable, toward something closer to chance than providence or fate, which is rendered as a contest or game: the implications of this observation formed the original kernel and forms the current nucleus of the present study. As an apparent reorientation in and of medieval Christian culture, I have assumed that this disposition is extraordinary enough to warrant being regarded as *cultural* and not only poetic in its import, even if poetry may be its most indelible specific marker. This is to say, one must try to provide a context for seeing how the complete, universal, or what I shall also call the *global* integration and mobilization of the resources of self that is supposed to be occurring in medieval Christian culture *continues,* even as it is drastically *reoriented* in adventure and love. The present study is my endeavor to provide such a context and to do justice to the observation that this cultural reorientation is occurring as games or contests—hence my concept of *cultural action* and the chapter headings I have chosen. In order to illustrate how Christianity can be regarded as a global orientation of self that is in turn reoriented in adventure and love, I take a correspondingly global approach and consider source texts by pagan and Israelite predecessors (and later rivals) of Christianity, as well as seminal Christian texts: Homer's Iliad, Virgil's Aeneid, biblical verses from the Old and New Testaments, and writings of St. Augustine—as indicated in the overview of my study below.

Following from my observation that adventure and love occur as games or contests, I develop and elaborate an approach to cultural production as structured competitions involving the element of chance in my study's first two chapters, "The Cultural Action" and "The Medieval Self as Bankroll." In emulation of the analytic posture of systematic studies of the dynamics of games and athletic contests, I take a *descriptive* approach to the competitions in religion, politics, and poetry that I see as constitutive of medieval culture. In my consideration of these competitions, I undertake descriptions of *culture as action* based on the assumptions that culture is always happening, that it happens as competitions for rewards, and that chance or indeterminacy is a describable aspect of these competitions, as it is of any competitions in which the action remains ongoing (as in "repeated games"). In these initial chapters, I approach cultural action in terms of different dispositions of self, which in turn are indicative of different overall dispositions of cultural resources, be these spiritual, intellectual, or physical-material. We observe that the cultural action of pagan peoples in antiquity and the Middle Ages is shaped by sacrificial practices in discrete cultural domains over which local deities and spirits preside. In the pagan sacrificial cultural action as rendered by Homer and Virgil, for example, people seek optimal outcomes with sacrifices according to the local logics of such discrete cultural domains. Outcomes in this action are local and immediate, and the statuses of selves and cultural resources are relatively fixed or determinate, having been decided at higher levels by fate and capricious deities. By contrast, the *global* cultural action of Christianity, as defined by St. Paul and elaborated and given imperial Roman dimensions by St. Augustine, articulates cultural domains universally in the name of Christ and in competition with the cultural action as assessed by pagan and Jewish rivals. Freed by Christ's sacrifice from the sacrificial practices of numerous different discrete cultural domains, as well as from the laws of the Israelites (though emerging competitively from these), the Christian self disposes of resources globally in a cultural action of greater indeterminacy. Based on Augustine's *City of God*, we observe that cultural *moves* have only to be made in a Christian sense. As long as the self loves God and neighbor, as long as it manages cultural resources globally in dying to the world in emulation of Christ as it makes its way toward its heavenly reward, the widest latitude remains for exploiting cultural resources in the interest of growth. Such exploitation is what happens in the Middle Ages, particularly in the twelfth and thirteenth centuries as court poetry shows, for which reason I propose the view of the medieval self as a "bankroll."

In my third chapter, "Rules of the House," I regard competitions among the households of secular and ecclesiastical princes as constitutive of medieval court society and as setting an imperial tone for the cultural action at court, from the highest *principes* to the lowest squires and servants. An imperial, global view of the competitive action at and among medieval courts is consistent with Jürgen Habermas's understanding of the "structural transformation of the public sphere" (*Strukturwandel der Öffentlichkeit*), according to which a "culture of representation" (*repräsentative Öffentlichkeit*) is characteristic of the Middle Ages. In the cultural action at courts in the High Middle Ages, in which there is as yet no private sphere juxtaposed to a public one, everything is *on the table*. Following through my global and imperial view of the medieval cultural action, in a manner consistent with Habermas's understanding of medieval society as based on a *representational* "public," I describe some of the principal competitions that establish the relative stature of princes and their courts. These representational events at court range from the sponsorship of poetry to warfare and feuds, from the rivalries of ambitious courtiers to the global moves made by emperors and popes in the interest of imperial ascendancy.

My fourth chapter, "The Poetic Action," brings us closer to the medieval romances by focusing on the literary performances of poets as competitors. The contests in poetry are consistent with the dynamics of rivalries among princes and their respective households, as the latter were seen in the previous chapter, and with competitions in other domains of courtly culture (such as chivalric tournaments). Based on passages that underscore poetry as competitive effort, I observe that the value of a poetic performance has much to do with rendering things better than one's competitors, past and present. Finding the competitive edge vis-à-vis one's rivals drives the innovation characteristic of poetic developments, including tapping the potential of the vernacular languages and their associated narrative traditions and concerns. In the poetic action, poet-performers make their best moves before critical audiences that deal out praise and shame, decide winners and losers. As in the political competitions among princes, in the global action of Christianity outlined in the initial chapters, and in the imaginary action involving adventure and love to be examined in the following chapters, we also observe in the poetic action that joy or pain is at stake—a growth or diminishment of self that is experienced collectively and individually.

Adventure and love are viewed in the fifth and sixth chapters, respectively, as related "cultural wagers." In these chapters, I describe the competitions in which knights and ladies are involved in the interest of stature in the eyes of their peers (honor) and in the interest of the dedicated devotion of another (love), as these competitions are rendered in the imaginary action of the courtly romances. The imaginary action is *real*, as I observe with the help of fMRI-based research into physiological responses to fictional narratives, which demonstrates neurological simulations of narrative events and suggests these simulations rehearse different kinds of social experience. In the imaginary competitive action involving the concerns of adventure and love, the Christian self, which is described in the initial chapters of this study as globally mobilized in the interest of its heavenly prize, puts itself into play *again*, in a specifically medieval way. In an expanding, increasingly indeterminate cultural action, the courtly chivalric self speculates it will experience growth by investing itself absolutely in the temporal, perishable goods associated with adventure and love, without foregoing the play for its timeless heavenly reward. In this medieval poetic reiteration of the absolute investment of self, now in the interest of temporal goods, *we observe a culture of wagers and investments emerge from and begin to replace a culture based on sacrifice.* Correspondingly, the examples from the court poetry surveyed in these chapters show the competitive action of adventure and love to be rendered as games, particularly games of chance, in which ladies and knights put themselves into play absolutely. The imaginary moves of knights and ladies in romance poetry and the outcomes of these moves—which creatively build upon and vary the moves visible in patristic literature and saints lives—are concretely demonstrative of the cultural innovation and growth occurring in the European High Middle Ages.

My final chapter and conclusion, "The Modern Self in Play," follows through my approach to the cultural action and considers ways in which the modern individual self takes over the imperial parameters of the medieval City of God (i.e., the Roman *ecclesia*) as the new principal locus of indeterminacy in the European risk-reward society. I look first at the Reformation and early writings of Martin Luther, in which this later cultural moment of transition is made manifest in religious terms. I then focus on a few culturally significant *individualizations of the universal* during the Age of Enlightenment, including Gottfried Leibniz's Christian cosmological understanding of monads and binary numbers and Immanuel Kant's dualistic and identifiably Lutheran conception of Enlightenment in his famous definitive essay of this movement, *An Answer to the Question: What Is Enlightenment?* Finally, I survey the imaginary cultural action depicted in Mark Twain's *A Connecticut Yankee in King Arthur's Court*. This action follows from the Reformation and Enlightenment moves already observed in this chapter; brings us back to our concerns with courts, adventure, and love; and widens our focus to include Europe and North America, the industrial revolution, and totalitarianism in the nineteenth and twentieth centuries. With the help of Twain, Hannah Arendt (*The Origins of Totalitarianism, The Human Condition*), and others, I conclude with the open-ended, *global* observation that modernity is not so much a break with the Middle Ages as it is an expansion and acceleration of the medieval cultural action.

Adventure and love as I understand them involve significant moments of transition in European cultural history. I do not differentiate strictly between the modern terms and their medieval versions—*avanture, âventiure, amor, minne*—because the specifically medieval moment of cultural transition designated by these terms has modern ramifications. In this study, more interesting and consequential than such terminological differentiations is how the medieval terms and what is designated by them prepare the way for the modern ones and what is designated by them. The *alterity* of the rapidly increasing cultural dynamism that we observe in the High Middle Ages pertains to the still primarily communal rather than individual parameters of action. We shall observe that medieval ladies and knights are not yet positioned to claim the *courtly* concerns of adventure and love for themselves alone. The findings of my study are in this way consistent with cultural developments—particularly regarding the early modern emergence of autonomous subjectivity—as understood by the above-mentioned Jürgen Habermas, whose writings on antiquity, the Middle Ages, and modernity corroborate findings of my study and provide important signposts for it.

In the foreground of this study will be the medieval transition from a culture of sacrifice to a culture of wagers and investments. A more specific associated contribution that I hope my study of the medieval risk-reward society brings to scholarly discussions of cultural developments, particularly to the understanding of the above-mentioned dynamism observable in the High Middle Ages, is the finding that adventure and love involve an absolute wager on or investment in the mutable, perishable individual self that occurs even as the still predominantly communal (i.e., religious and imperial) parameters of medieval culture are maintained. As such, the absolute valuation of the individual self that is posited in adventure and love may be considered an auspicious cultural *precedent,* a first significant and perhaps indispensable *move* in the direction of subjectivity and individual autonomy as hallmark features of the cultural action of modernity. This specific finding—involving what I call *individualizations of the universal* or the apprehension of modern subjectivity as a contingency of medieval communal absolutes—is achieved by way of an approach to the source texts that I hope will be considered a contribution in its own right, possibly as a step in the direction of a *cultural game theory.* My view of culture is shaped to the degree possible by the *global parameters* set forth in and by the source texts themselves, and by nothing else other than the *action* I endeavor to describe. This approach and the associated hope concerning its productiveness carry over to my positions vis-à-vis past scholarly discussions of the various texts and topics examined in the different chapters of this study.

Adventure and love as considered in this study are *trendsetting* cultural moves in a European risk-reward society that extends from the High Middle Ages to the present. I concur with the gist of Zygmunt Bauman's observation below—though we observe already in the High Middle Ages much of what he describes here. Europe, according to Bauman, is an "unfinished adventure":

> Adventure? According to the Oxford English Dictionary, in Middle English that word meant anything that happened without design—a chance, hap, luck. It also meant a happening pregnant with danger or a threat of loss: risk, jeopardy; a hazardous enterprise or hapless performance. Later, closer to our own modern times, "adventure" came to mean putting one's chances to the

test: a venture, or experiment—a novel or exciting endeavor as yet untried. At the same time, a derivative was born: the *adventurer*—a highly ambivalent noun, whispering in one breath of blind fate and cunning, of craftiness and providence, of aimlessness and determination. We may surmise that the shifts in meaning followed the maturation of the European spirit: its coming to terms with its own "essence."[2]

Correspondingly, my approach to the risk-reward society in the following pages is also self-consciously European and by this extension also North American, a limitation that I hope may help to place the cultural developments as I describe them in a fruitful transcultural context.

---

2. *Europe*, 1–2.

CHAPTER 1

The Cultural Action

TOWARD A CULTURAL GAME THEORY

In this study of courts, adventure, and love in the European Middle Ages, I endeavor to describe European cultural history as action.[1] The various literary sources employed for this description—poetic, theological, political, philosophical, and historical—are regarded as records of the ongoing cultural action in the past. The descriptive apprehension of culture as action shows itself to be especially appropriate and useful for European developments generally and for the European Middle Ages in particular. During the twelfth and thirteenth centuries, we witness a moment in the European cultural action when a *baton* is passed from Greco-Roman, Judeo-Christian antiquity to the modern world as shaped by European peoples and their cultural descendants. Especially noteworthy about the moment when the baton is passed is the degree to which medieval European people actually understand themselves

---

1. What I call *cultural action* involves the indeterminate status of culture between continuity and change that is referenced by Zygmunt Bauman in his book *Culture as Praxis*: "The work of culture does not consist so much in its self-perpetuation as in securing the conditions for further experimentation and change. Or, rather, culture 'self-perpetuates' in as far as not the pattern, but the urge to modify it, to alter and replace it with another pattern, stays viable and potent over time" (xx).

to be in a *race*. Following through the athletic analogy, medieval people are like competitors running a leg in a relay, competing with runners on the same team—trying to be as fast or faster so as to avoid being considered a weaker link—as well as against the opposing runners on the other tracks. The medieval action that becomes visible in the sources examined in this study is one in which people are newly keen to compete with the great cultural performers of the past and among themselves. While the cultural action becomes tangible in the sources as interrelated competitive performances of different kinds, there is also an observable shift in the cultural loci of the self-investments and the experiences of success and failure involved in these competitions. From the twelfth century, individual striving at the courts of households of nobility has ever more to do with this temporal, mutable world. At these courts, the cultural action is increasingly about the full and accurate assessment and exploitation of *perishable goods,* as a fixed or determinate culture based on sacrifice gives way to an ever more indeterminate culture of wagers and investments.[2] With the help of the literary sources, the subsequent chapters of this book describe how a European society of risk and reward emerges in the High Middle Ages.[3] In the present chapter and the next, I focus on basic parameters of cultural action and on significant moments in the action that precede and prepare the way for my medieval topics.

My approach to culture as action combines a traditionally humanist, close textual analysis with a descriptive posture modeled on the systematic consideration of games and athletic contests.[4] Considering the religious, political, and poetic cultural action at high medieval courts in a manner analogous to games and contests is consistent, as we shall observe in later chapters, with competitions for ascendancy among households of nobility, among top poets in literary performances, and among knights and ladies in their imaginary adventures and loves. My view of culture as action seeks to extend descriptive

---

2. The transition from a culture of sacrifice to a culture of wagers and investments needs to be regarded not as inevitable or *essential* (i.e., *given* in the nature of things), but rather as a shift in the preponderance of certain kinds of moves in the action.

3. "Literary scholars [...] use the phrase 'High Middle Ages' for the entire courtly age which began with the emergence in the twelfth century of the courts of the secular princes as the new centers of literature, and which lasted to the end of the thirteenth century" (Bumke, *Courtly Culture,* 18).

4. My approach to culture as action involves games in the broadest sense and works against the dualistic thinking to which Eric Dunning draws attention, with specific reference to sports, in the preface of his coauthored (with Norbert Elias) collection of essays, *Quest for Excitement*: "Sport appears to have been ignored as an object for sociological reflection and research because it is seen as falling on the negatively valued side of the complex of overlapping dichotomies which are conventionally perceived, such as those between 'work' and 'leisure,' 'mind' and 'body,' 'seriousness' and 'pleasure,' 'economic' and 'non-economic' phenomena" (4).

analyses of the dynamics of games that have provided insights into language, politics, social phenomena, economics, and natural sciences.[5] A basic assumption in the consideration of different cultural domains as games or contests is that their dynamics can be modeled or described, and possible outcomes in them anticipated to some degree, but that one cannot know *with certainty* how any specific future outcome will be decided. Games are understood to be indeterminate in view of outcomes that have yet to be decided, as well as in view of the time and space within them for players to pursue their various different strategies individually or collectively. Motivated and inspired by its medieval subject matter, the present study extrapolates the indeterminacy of games and athletic contests to cultural developments. Accordingly, the literary sources are approached not as containing or referring to truths that have yet to be discovered or unveiled, but rather as records of the parameters according to which cultural action is occurring. Chapter titles suggestive of games of chance have been selected, because these reveal chance in its greatest relief and transparency, and are also one of the preferred manners of courtiers in romance poetry to express their own wagers of self.

For the purpose of describing the indeterminacy of cultural action, the above-referenced *race* needs to be qualified as one of myriad possible analogies. The descriptive terminology and imagery employed in this study draws from numerous different endeavors—games of chance, individual and team sports, business and financial markets, and so on[6]—in which the element of chance and the dynamics of competitive performance are common denominators. In contravention of the conventional decorum of academic writing, I will occasionally avail myself of colloquial speech and idioms when these seem especially adept at bringing the dynamics of a crucial moment in the cultural action to the fore. What matters in the cultural action is what matters in games: strategies, skills, training, and poise under pressure, combined with

---

5. See, for example, Eichberger, *Game Theory*; Hamburger, *Games as Models*; McCarty and Meirowitz, *Political Game Theory*; Pietarinen, *Game Theory*; and Samuelson, *Evolutionary Games*.

6. Johan Huizinga, in his *Homo Ludens*, argues that a stark distinction between wagers and investments, in the specific case of financial markets, is questionable: "The hazy borderline between play and seriousness is illustrated very tellingly by the use of the words 'playing' or 'gambling' for the machinations on the Stock Exchange. The gambler at the roulette table will readily concede that he is playing; the stock-jobber will not. He will maintain that buying and selling on the off-chance of prices rising or falling is part of the serious business of life, at least of business life, and that it is an economic function of society. In both cases the operative factor is the hope of gain; but whereas in the former the pure fortuitousness of the thing is generally admitted (all 'systems' notwithstanding), in the latter the player deludes himself with the fancy that he can calculate the future trends of the market. At any rate the difference of mentality is exceedingly small" (52).

innate or acquired personal characteristics, such as mental acuity, athleticism, endurance, a certain *competitive edge*. As in "repeated games," outcomes in the cultural action typically do not mark absolute beginnings and ends, but occur as significant structuring moments of an action that remains ongoing. In the ongoing action, players are able to adjust their strategies based on previous outcomes and the reputations players have gained for themselves.[7] As one might expect, it seems crucial for players in the cultural action to know or at least have a good idea about the track records and preferred strategies of others—to be able to "put themselves in the other person's shoes."[8]

The sources surveyed in this study show that the indeterminacy of the European cultural action is shaped by a recurring pattern that indicates what is at stake in the action and how outcomes in it are marked. Tapping into the various innate and acquired resources at their disposal, players venture themselves in the action with an exertion that manifests pain, corresponding to the status of a self and its resources placed at risk of decrease or loss. This pain is comingled to varying degrees with anticipatory happiness, corresponding to the prospects of success. The other significant moment punctuating the cultural action is the experience of joy accompanying rewards in the event of success and victory, or conversely, pain-magnified, shame, ignominy in the event of failure and defeat. Thus, victory joyfully increases self and its resources, defeat painfully decreases them. In the cultural action, self is a resource and stake in ongoing competitions in which, overall, the resources of some tend to be increasing or decreasing relative to those of others. In the European cultural action beginning with the court societies based on risk and reward that emerge in the twelfth century, we observe that it becomes ever more difficult *not* to be a player. The sources that we shall examine demonstrate a culturally *bullish* principle of action to be increasingly valid at medieval courts.[9] Holding oneself and one's resources in reserve, standing pat, resting on one's laurels is too risky because one misses out on the possibility of increase and finds oneself relatively behind. One must accept that the world is a risky place of competition for limited and fickle resources, and venture oneself. In the medieval world, no longer viewed primarily as a "vale of tears" (Ps 83:7), but rather as a *field of play,* one increasingly recognizes that it is better to try to improve one's chances with an interested, strategic approach to the mutability of things.

---

7. See Mailath and Samuelson, *Repeated Games.*
8. Dixit and Nalebuff, *Art of Strategy,* 5.
9. This seems an appropriate point to reference my 2010 article "Bullish on Love and Adventure," a preliminary look at some of the concerns that are developed more fully in the fifth and sixth chapters of this study.

Mathematics has been the primary descriptive language for the apprehension of the indeterminacy of the action of games and by extension the action of other complex cultural domains. But even mathematically oriented game theorists have suggested there are aspects of games that might best be approached with other, non-mathematical analytic and descriptive tools.[10] The present study of the European cultural action is humanist and philological in its approach and bases itself on the written records of the action preserved in languages of antiquity, the Middle Ages, and modernity. I regard traditionally humanist domains—such as religion, literature and the arts, and philosophy—and the array of associated human capacities, ranging from spiritual-intellectual to physical-material, all as being *in play*.[11] An influential humanist manner of apprehending the indeterminacy of the European cultural action is provided by the modern philosophical discussion of subjective identity. The following view of subjectivity, excerpted from a commentary on Hegel by the philosopher Jürgen Habermas, might be seen to have a broader applicability to the cultural action of European modernity:

> The question arises as to whether the principle of subjectivity and the structure of self-consciousness residing in it suffice as the source of normative orientations—whether they suffice not only for "providing foundations" for science, morality, and art in general but also for stabilizing a historical formation that has been set loose from all historical obligations.[12]

The question posed by Habermas in this context draws attention to subjectivity and to the cultural action in the cultural domains shaped by subjectivity (i.e., modernity), as something indeterminate. The modern subject is disengaged from history and tradition. Instead of being a fixed figure in a determined world, the subject—along with all the cultural domains based on

---

10. For example, see Dixit and Nalebuff: "Many mathematical game theorists dislike the dependence of an outcome on historical, cultural, or linguistic aspects of the game or on purely arbitrary devices like round numbers; they would prefer the solution be determined purely by the abstract mathematical facts about the game—the numbers of players, the strategies available to each, and the payoffs to each in relation to the strategy choices of all. We disagree. We think it entirely appropriate that the outcome of a game played by humans interacting in a society should depend on the social and psychological aspects of the game" (*Art of Strategy*, 114).

11. In keeping with my global view of the cultural action, I employ the terms *spiritual, intellectual, physical,* and *material* to describe the range of cultural resources available to people. I also occasionally juxtapose the terms *spiritual-intellectual* and *physical-material* in order to describe different ways in which cultural resources are organized along dualist lines, beginning with the religion of the Israelites discussed later in this chapter.

12. Habermas, *Philosophical Discourse*, 20. I return to these considerations in later chapters of this study.

or driven by it—is "set loose" from the past and rolls, somewhat like dice, indeterminately into the future. The philosophical discourse of modernity, as elaborated here by Habermas, is largely about working out the possibility of "stabilizing" subjectivity, developing some normative orientations that would not be forced upon it. While this endeavor is ongoing, elsewhere in philosophy it has been suggested that the indeterminate status of subjectivity and modernity with all its implications might rather be accepted as such. Richard Rorty's observation here provides a philosophical underpinning for my own view of the European cultural action:

> The line of thought common to Blumenberg, Nietzsche, Freud, and Davidson suggests that we try to get to the point where we no longer worship anything, where we treat nothing as a quasi-divinity, where we treat everything—our language, our conscience, our community—as a product of time and chance. To reach this point would be, in Freud's words, to "treat chance as worthy of determining our fate."[13]

In this study, I try to make moves consistent with Rorty's line of thought. I speculate that the cultural indeterminacy of the modern subject—even as philosophical attempts to stabilize or determine it continue—might eventually be comprehended as congruent with the dynamics of games or contests involving the element of chance.[14] Correspondingly, with my approach to culture as action, as outlined on the pages above and elaborated in this study, I hope to contribute useful humanist perspectives to the possible future development of a cultural game theory.

THE NEW MEDIEVAL MOVE

The philosophical discussion of Habermas referenced above offers a view of modern (European) culture as shaped throughout by the indeterminate dynamics of subjectivity. The self-positing and self-reflective subject with all

---

13. Rorty, *Contingency*, 22.

14. The social scientist Gerda Reith makes consistent points in her book *The Age of Chance*: "In the late twentieth century, chance is understood as a constituent part of the world, codified in the rules of probability theory and, in the branches of quantum mechanics and chaos theory, an irreducible feature of modern science." Reith goes on to place the emergence of chance in modernity in a broader sociocultural context that is consistent with the findings of the present study: "However, this theoretical perspective is a recent development and represents the apogee of a long historical process that culminated in the separation of 'chance' or random phenomena from broadly religious notions of divine providence and fate" (13).

its unresolved questions is involved in all cultural domains—"science, morality, and art in general"—and provides the most encompassing and appropriate descriptor of (the indeterminacy of) the cultural action. Looking back to the twelfth century as the beginning point of a European society based on risk and reward, this study will observe that we did *not* reach a point—at the end of the Middle Ages and the dawn of subjectivity and modernity—when the cultural action more or less suddenly began to become indeterminate. The sources examined in this study will show that the medieval cultural action was *already* indeterminate in ways that later began to be reconfigured and technologically enhanced and accelerated. While this study differs from the assumption, whether overt or implicit, that the cultural action of the Middle Ages has to be viewed as fixed or determinate in some basic or essential way (vis-à-vis the dynamics of subjectivity), it reiterates a move of Habermas and other philosophers in assuming that certain parameters can be regarded as apt descriptors of the (indeterminacy of the) cultural action generally. Whereas the indeterminacy of the cultural action of modernity—whether religious, political, or poetic—can be described *subjectively*, that of the medieval cultural action can most aptly be described *religiously* and *imperially*.[15] Religion and empire in the Middle Ages and modern subjectivity correspondingly frame how the action in a given cultural domain—such as politics—may be relevant for or transferrable to that in others—poetry, philosophy, the arts, and so on. In order to keep the focus on the open-endedness of the cultural action, indeterminacy according to these parameters will be understood and described in this study in terms of *potential*.[16] Potential is the possibility for moves to be made and, by extension, for moves made in any one cultural domain to

---

15. Based on the assumption of a connection between the (indeterminate) constitution of the individual self and its (similarly indeterminate) cultural and social situation or *position* (a connection that is also implicit in the cited passage from Habermas), I make reference in this study to *the medieval self* and *the modern self*, to be sure, as cultural players whose actions have to be described as accurately as possible.

16. I use the term *potential* to describe the room, leeway, or indeterminacy in a society for moves to be made. *Freedom* can be understood as a related term designating individuals' capacity to employ or take advantage of such potential according to the resources available to them. Correspondingly, I am as interested in the ways that new social arrangements open up new possibilities for people as I am in the ways new social arrangements may limit, restrain, or fix the positions of people (especially when the arrangements are viewed retrospectively). I understand *freedom* (and by extension *potential*) *relationally* in a manner consistent with the view of Zygmunt Bauman: "For *one* to be free there must be *two*. Freedom signifies a social relation, an asymmetry of social conditions; essentially it implies social difference—it presumes and implies the presence of social division. Some can only be free in so far as there is a form of dependence they can aspire to escape" (*Freedom*, 9). Accordingly, as we observe in this study, Christianity liberates from the temporal and spatial constraints of pagan religious practices (as will be seen in this chapter); adventure and love will involve an emancipation of people

be relevant for and reiterated in others throughout the cultural action, *independent of their original specific (i.e., religious, political, or poetic) intention or purpose.*[17]

Cultural indeterminacy is not specific to modernity, as inclined as one might be to see indeterminacy and modernity as two sides of the same coin. Modern Europeans move and compete in faster and more complex ways than their medieval predecessors, and *subjectivity* is a designation one could give to this greater velocity and variability in the action. However rapidly the cultural action changes in modernity, the differences between modern subjectivity and the—also indeterminate, as we shall see—medieval parameters of religion and empire should not obscure the continuities connecting medieval individuals with modern ones.[18] Arguably the most pronounced of these continuities in the literary sources examined in this study is the quest for one's own advantage and the advantage of one's own achieved via competitive performances.[19] Attention to this continuity enables the appreciation of a novel medieval disposition of self and cultural resources that is this study's principal point of focus. *In the medieval cultural action of the twelfth and thirteenth centuries, we observe new moves at European courts, by means of which courtiers wager*

---

from the exclusivity of the absolute orientation of self toward the heavenly afterlife (as we shall see in later chapters).

17. The absolute investment of self in an*other* is the principal such move to be scrutinized in this study.

18. This seems an appropriate point to reference Ulrich Beck's *Risk Society* (originally published in German in 1986). This book was very much shaped by the nuclear disaster at Chernobyl, and the urgency of Beck's case is doubtless strengthened by the recent nuclear disaster at Fukushima, as well as by the ever-increasing evidence of manmade global warming and its destructive consequences. Beck reserves the designation "Risk Society" for the latest, postindustrial stage of cultural history, although he concedes risks are not an "invention of modernity": "Risks are not an invention of modernity. Anyone who set out to discover new countries and continents—like Columbus—certainly accepted 'risks.' But these were *personal* risks, not global dangers like those that arise for all of humanity from nuclear fission or the storage of nuclear waste. In that earlier period, the word 'risk' had a note of bravery and adventure, not the threat of self-destruction of all life on Earth" (21). Without disputing Beck's contention that the modern globalized and individualized cultural action has possibly reached a critical point and that disasters of global dimensions have become possible if not probable today, one must question Beck's somewhat dismissive view of the role played by risk in the medieval and early modern periods. The association of medieval and early modern risk with a "note of bravery and adventure" is simplistic and smacks of a romanticizing view of the days of yore. On a different front, Beck indirectly draws attention to the crucial question of the *sustainability* of the cultural action that I am endeavoring to describe in the present book.

19. As a concrete example of continuities between the Middle Ages and modernity, see the essays in Linda Gregerson and Susan Juster's edited collection, *Empires of God*, which stress the ongoing importance of religion and empire in Europe's self-understanding into the early modern period, when religion and empire serve as forces driving Europe's colonization of the New World.

or invest themselves absolutely in the interest of a particular, specific worldly end, a "perishable good." The increasing prevalence of this innovative cultural move—which in romance poetry is invariably rendered as the crucial moment of a contest or game—marks the transition from a society based on sacrifice to the medieval risk-reward society. In the next chapter, my focus will be on the development of religion and empire in late antiquity as (indeterminate) parameters of cultural action, according to and by means of which medieval courtiers will endeavor to obtain advantages and realize their potential. In the remainder of this chapter, I seek further to illustrate and exemplify cultural action as I have outlined it above, and to indicate how (monotheistic) religion and empire emerged in the ancient world as parameters of cultural action, by means of an overview of the competitions occurring at and among four ancient cities.[20]

A RACE OF FOUR CITIES: TROY, JERICHO, ROME, AND JERUSALEM

The historical kernel of the action at Troy would have been in the late Bronze Age, in the latter part of the second millennium BCE. The poetic rendering of the action, as preserved in Homer's epic poem, was composed around the seventh century BCE. As frequently happens later, the cultural action occurs as the siege of a city.[21] Troy is only the latest and greatest prize the Achaeans seek, and the most formidable one in view of the continuing strong resistance of the city's inhabitants that is not yet over when Homer's song ends. The ostensible aim of the Achaeans is the recovery of Helen, the abducted wife of Menelaus, but the action is also manifestly about acquiring the city's *resources:* the women of Troy, the lives of the heroic warriors of Troy, horses with chariots, basins with handles, tripods, cauldrons, gold, and bronze. In the previous successful sieges of other cities referenced in Homer's poem, the Achaeans have already earned many prizes, and it is a dispute over one of these that provides Homer's narrative focus. It is evident from the start of Homer's poem that the struggle between Achilles and Agamemnon over Briseis is also about which of them is *best*—the applicable term is ἄριϛτος, the etymological

---

20. Three of these four cities are in Asia. "Like much else that is defining of European culture, the walled, largely self-governing urban space had originated in Asia" (Pagden, *Peoples and Empires*, xviii).

21. Sieges of cities are, of course, also a conspicuous constituent element of the medieval courtly romances, which seems to be suggestive of a broader cultural pattern.

ancestor of *aristocracy*.[22] Both men lay claim to this status, the former on the basis of divine parentage, ferocity, and victories in battle—the latter on the basis of his kingship.

The value of individuals in the *Iliad* is tangible and, with rare exceptions, immediately evident. Before the initial conflict below the walls of Troy, when the Trojan king Priam surveys the enemies arrayed against him, he *immediately* recognizes the best among the Achaeans: Agamemnon, Odysseus, Ajax (in descending hierarchical order)—by this time, Achilles is angrily waiting by his ships. The concern about who is best arises and is maintained, even as there seems to be no overarching standard according to which a definitive comparative evaluation might be made. Barring fate alone, the principal gods and goddesses are the greatest powers, and they exercise the greatest control over things (and hence over the values things can have), but each deity's sway remains closely connected to a particular, discrete cultural domain.[23] Each deity is sovereign in some area—for example, Zeus in the broad political view and administration of things, Hera in fidelity and matrimonial matters, Ares in war, Aphrodite in love—but the various sovereignties are not articulated, constituent components of any identifiable broader design, such as providence or empire. The relations among the deities are characterized by unpredictability and volatility.[24] Zeus has power over other deities, but it is far from the absolute sovereignty claimed by the God of Abraham over rival gods and his Israelites that we shall observe below. The authority of the sky god is limited by fate and also by concern about how he will be seen if he undertakes something against the will and pleasure of the other deities. Zeus is thus constrained, though only unpredictably so, by the views and feelings of the other deities, and he sometimes even seems moved by mortals when they successfully appeal to him with their prayers and sacrifices.

Similarly, there seems to be no overarching organizational principle for sorting out the relative worth of mortals in the action around Troy, beyond the kind of immediate assessment made by Priam when he first beholds the

---

22. On Homer's depiction of society in the Iliad, M. S. Silk, in his *Homer: The Iliad*, observes: "Above all, there is the individualist ethic to which the aristocratic heroes subscribe; their concern for personal honour [...] and their competitive ambition 'always to be best' (VI.208)" (25).

23. "The Iliad makes it clear that over a wide area of behaviour and experience, the gods are to be thought of as sources of permanent human faculties and—especially—momentary human impulses" (Ibid., 71).

24. "In paganism, it was the behaviour of the gods that counted and the gods were nothing if not volatile" (Lewis, *Ritual Sacrifice*, 49).

Achaean host before his city's walls.[25] As with the gods, the value of mortals is attached to discrete, immediately evident characteristics and capacities. One can receive advantages from the start by being born of a god and a mortal (as Achilles, Aeneas, and Sarpedon), one can be of great age and experience (as Nestor), one can be clever and resourceful (as Odysseus), one can wield great political power (as Agamemnon), one can be a lover and not a fighter (as Paris), one can be swift of foot (Ajax minor). The value of these different attributes and capacities fluctuates according to the exigencies of the moment, but it is difficult to see them as systematically articulated. The status of Aphrodite and Paris, for example, is greatest in the domain of erotic love. Their limitations become quite evident, and they are chided when they engage themselves militarily and their efforts fall short (Paris failing before Menelaus, Aphrodite before the mortal Diomedes). Capacities in one cultural domain cannot readily be translated into those of another. There seems to be no common cultural *currency* throughout the action. Accordingly, it seems difficult to see mortals in the *Iliad* as endowed with abiding personal qualities—such as character, courage, or cowardice—to the degree that events and the roles mortals play in them are determined in a manner that is continuously immediate, rather than based on any longer term considerations such as abiding characteristics of self. Athena leads Diomedes, and Apollo leads Hector to victory at different moments in the conflict before Troy. In the latter case, even a seasoned veteran such as the major Ajax—whom no one considers a *coward*—flees for his life.

Outcomes in the cultural action around Troy are largely fixed according to the various discrete capacities attached to gods, mortals, and events, which are not systematically articulated among each other beyond the immediate assessment of them as better or worse.[26] This is the case in the military conflict before the walls of the city, and this is the case as well in the athletic competitions among the Achaeans that are arranged as part of the funeral rites for Patroclus near the end of Homer's poem. The dynamics of the funeral games

---

25. Correspondingly, the narrative frequently proceeds from one event to the next without evidence of a broader organizational principle, particularly in the lengthy battle scenes on which Silk observes: "Particular heroes have their particular hours of glory, the tide of battle ebbs and flows for both armies, various gods intervene at various moments—all with the result that, while some events follow earlier events 'by probability or necessity' (as Aristotle puts it), many others merely 'come next,' as unpredictably as, indeed, the actual events of an inconclusive war might strike an eye-witness at the time" (*Homer*, 33).

26. Silk's introduction to the Iliad stresses *immediacy* as a central aspect of this epic poem, both generally, "Despite its pervasive stylization, the poem has an extraordinary immediacy all its own" (54), and more specifically in its characterizations, "Like so much else in the *Iliad*, its human figures are strikingly immediate and alive" (72).

are similar to those of warfare (correspondingly, the terms Ἆθλος, Ἆθλον, and ἀθλητής, the etymological ancestors of "athletics" and "athlete," mean "champion, master of a given thing," "a contest in war or sport," and "prize, reward, recompense," respectively).[27] The only manner for mortals to access and endeavor to influence the higher Olympian level, at which outcomes are being decided, is by means of prayers and sacrifices at the scattered temples of the different deities in their various discrete domains. The logic of self-investment as sacrifice in the Trojan cultural action is immediate, domain-specific, and quid-pro-quo, much like a bribe.[28] Typically turning to the deity in charge of the pertinent cultural domain, according to the exigencies of the moment, mortals try to achieve specific aims with their prayers, burnt animal offerings, and libations: the release of a captured relative, survival in a pending battle, hitting one's target with an arrowshot, winning a footrace. The lack of an overarching standard of evaluation might be related to the dubious efficacy of these sacrifices to shape outcomes in a consistent way. Prayers accompanying sacrifices may be heard but not heeded, heard and heeded only in part, or not heeded at all by whimsical deities in their various separate domains, who are themselves engaged in unpredictable contests with one another. The doubtful efficacy of sacrifices is one of the things that makes the lot of mortals in the Trojan action seem very difficult. The risk-reward ratio is bleak even for the very *best*, as we see in Achilles's lament to Priam near the end of Homer's epic, when the Trojan king tearfully begs him for the body of his son Hector:

So the immortals spun our lives that we, we wretched men,
Live on to bear such torments—the gods live free of sorrows.[29]

The consolations of heroism are meager, as M. S. Silk has observed: "Achilles, the supreme achiever, sums up his experience of life, not in terms of glory and hope, but through the image of the urns of Zeus. That image promises

---

27. *Liddell and Scott's Greek-English Lexicon*, 16. All translations of the ancient Greek terms are from this text.

28. Lewis addresses what I am calling the "quid-pro-quo" nature of pagan sacrificial practices in this way: "Sacrifices could serve as means of winning divine favour for specific purposes—to ensure a good hunt or harvest, to grant fertility or success in war, to ensure protection for the family of community, to preserve good health and strength and generally acquire what was most meaningful and necessary in life" (*Ritual Sacrifice*, 3). In her characterization of pagan Roman religious practices, Valerie Warrior uses the term *do ut des* rather than quid-pro-quo, though the basic principle is same: "Thus, traditional Roman religion was essentially pragmatic, a contractual relationship based on the so-called principle of *do ut des* (I give so that you may give). The gods were asked, and the hope was that they would respond favorably" (*Roman Religion*, 6).

29. Homer, *Iliad*, 605.

blessings as well as afflictions, but afflictions predominate and, in particular, nothing is said of any permanent consolation."[30] Overall at Troy, the experience of joy is sparse and fleeting in a cultural action organized hierarchically and immediately according to one's greater or lesser share in a given cultural resource at a given moment. Gods tend to succeed over demigods and heroes, and demigods and heroes over rank and file mortals by virtue of their relatively greater incipient share in military prowess, political sovereignty, cleverness, beauty and seductiveness, and so on. Evaluations are made according to the interests and capacities of the most immediately pertinent cultural domain (war, love, wisdom, etc.), and the incipient superiority of some over others results in a cultural action that is highly determinate, especially for the mortals in it who dispose of fewer resources.[31]

The action at Jericho as recounted in the book of Joshua, a near contemporary of the action at Troy and also structured as the siege of a city, looks quite different.[32] This action is articulated with the history of the tribes of Israel extending back to Abraham. For many generations, the Israelites have been unified or integrated as the "seed of Abraham" under a single leader or paterfamilias and their single God. Those who assault the walls of Jericho are likely made more effective than the frequently divided Achaeans by an administrative structure instituted by Moses on the advice of his father-in-law Jethro, not long after the exodus from Egypt began. Holy men, handpicked by and answerable to Moses, supervise thousands, hundreds, fifties, and tens (Ex 18:18–26).[33] This administrative and legal apparatus ensures that the Israelites follow the many laws handed down from on high, so as to enable Moses as head of the whole people to dedicate himself more completely to his role as principal mediator between his people and the Lord. The thoroughgoing integration of the tribes of Israel, achieved by means of laws and an administrative structure, underpins their status as the single chosen people of their single God. Burnt animal offerings are made, as they are in the Trojan action, but not at the scattered temples of various deities in charge of discrete cultural domains and not mainly on a quid-pro-quo basis to achieve immediate ends.

30. Silk, *Homer*, 85.

31. Reith would say that such a culture leaves no room for chance: "Nowhere in ancient or *primitive* cosmology do we find systematic consideration of chance as a phenomenon in its own right. Instead, its occurrence was consistently conflated with notions of destiny and the will of the gods" (*Age of Chance*, 17).

32. In his study, *The Iliad: Structure, Myth, and Meaning*, Bruce Louden questions why the numerous potentially productive parallels between Greek and Israelite culture have not been more closely examined (8).

33. Here and elsewhere in this study, unless otherwise specified, I cite the online *Biblia Sacra Vulgata*. English translations are from *The Holy Bible: Authorized King James Version*.

The single Lord God, set beyond all other gods, has set His people apart from all others in the interest of a collective reward that requires the deferment of immediate gratification and a *longer-term* posture.

Long before Jericho, there are indications in the cultural action of the Israelites that obeying and fearing the Lord and following His commandments—that is, an abiding inner attitude, orientation, or *character*—can be as good as making sacrifices and has potentially begun to replace them. The Israelites make their sacrifices on altars not to be fashioned of hewed stone, corresponding to a more mobile, fluid kind of piety. This piety is not fixed to the particular holy sites of discrete cultural domains, but rather borne by the flesh via circumcision, by stone tablets with the laws inscribed in them, by the arc constructed to house these tablets, and by an abiding internal attitude of fearful reverence and obedience to the single Lord God, He who possesses an integrated sovereignty in all cultural domains. The mobility of the religion of the Israelites will be reinforced during a later period, when portable canonical literature is produced. As repositories of religion, holy scriptures help further to disengage religion from the sacrificial logics of discrete cultural domains and put it into circulation. Scriptures set forth new dualist parameters of risk and reward that pertain no longer immediately and directly to the characteristics of sacrificial rites in discrete cultural domains, but rather to the integration and mobilization of the various capacities of self for the sake of a single way of believing and living. Via the holy scriptures of the Israelites—and later those of the Christians—the loci of risk and reward shift from the more immediate characteristics of particular offerings at particular times and places to the organization of *all* the resources of self, and to whether these resources are sufficiently integrated and focused so as to measure up to the dictates of that absolutely *other* One.

The action of the Israelites at Jericho seems thoroughly articulated. The Will of the Lord as conveyed to patresfamilias such as Abraham and Joshua provides the overarching standard that seems absent in the action at Troy. The Israelites are an integrated and mobile force, uniformly obedient to the Lord's instructions and thereby seemingly made all the more effective. Recently circumcised and bearing the arc before them as they circle the city's wall for six consecutive days, they effect with a collective shout on the seventh day what the Achaeans take some ten years to accomplish. The walls of Jericho come tumbling down and the Israelites take possession of their prize. As in the cultural action elsewhere, this prize includes precious metals—gold and silver—but here it is a collective reward that is supposed to come into the Lord's treasury and not be distributed to individuals (thus seeming to forestall the kind of disintegrative strife that comes about between Agamemnon and Achilles).

In the broader integrated history of the Israelites, the fall of Jericho marks the point at which they begin to take possession of the reward promised by the Lord to Abraham, the same "land flowing with milk and honey" (Ex 33:3) promised to Abraham's seed. Jericho is a short-term outcome in a longer-term cultural action, in which the Promised Land as a collective reward is supposed to be conferred upon the chosen people for living justly and obeying the Will of its single God. The Israelites engage themselves in the action, as the events at Jericho and elsewhere in their history show, in competitions with other peoples—Canaanites, Jebusites, Hittites, Philistines. Correspondingly, the "monolatry" of the ancient Israelites, as which it has been termed by Nili Fox, involves a God who has gained ascendency over other deities and idols (without yet having done away with them completely).[34]

Outcomes in the competitive cultural action of the Israelites at Jericho and elsewhere are shaped by the possibility of a universal evaluation of cultural resources for which I use the descriptive term *dualist*. In this study, this term describes a kind of cultural action in which a single God (or idea) presents an absolutely *other* perspective according to which all cultural resources—all those discrete domains we saw in the action at Troy—are to be seen as uniformly articulated or integrated. Though the Lord of the Israelites sometimes acts in ways that are reminiscent of the immediate and volatile approach to things characteristic of the multiple deities at Troy, His action seems relatively fixed by the covenant with His chosen people and by His laws. In this mortal world, the Israelites are supposed to be both liberated and constrained by the Lord's *master plan*, but events recorded in Exodus, when the Israelites create their golden calf and temporarily revert to idolatry in Moses's absence, show the obligation to fear and obey the Lord to be a new locus of indeterminacy in the cultural action. The Israelites are supposed to fear and obey the Lord, collectively and individually, *but they might not*. The dualist evaluation of cultural resources does not necessarily replace the logics of religious

---

34. On the religiosity of the ancient Israelites, Fox observes "a diverse society, exhibiting variant religious expressions [...] What has been labeled diffused monotheism or monolatry coexisted with polytheistic cults, at least among certain groups in certain periods. Radical monolatry at best was an ideal promoted by prophets and other reformers who in their own minds may actually have perceived YHWH in monotheistic terms. What percentage of the general population fit into each group is unknown, though our sources suggest that a sizable portion of Israelites recognized YHWH as the Supreme National God and worshipped him, if not exclusively, then in concert with other divinities who seem to qualify as members of his host" ("Concepts of God," 344–45). The emergence of Judaism as a scriptural monotheistic religion begins in the sixth and fifth centuries BCE and continues into the early centuries of the Common Era, alongside the emergence of Christianity as a scriptural monotheism. See also the introduction in Philip R. Davies, *On the Origins of Judaism*, 1–5.

practices associated with discrete cultural domains, but rather becomes an*other* option—to be sure, the one the Israelites are *supposed* to choose—situated alongside or superimposed upon them. Overall, the availability of a new dualist evaluation of cultural resources, which encompasses and articulates older domain-specific ones, increases the indeterminacy of the cultural action in a way that makes the attitudes and actions of individual mortals matter more. The articulation of cultural resources according to the dualist *master plan* of the Israelites disengages them from the scattered, fixed, discrete pagan temples of the multiple deities and renders the relationships among them more fluid and indeterminate. Selves and things receive a new value, supposedly their highest one, by virtue of their successful participation in the dualist longer-term grand design, even as the possibility of (lapses into) more immediate, short-term, domain-specific cultural evaluations remains. A striking aspect of this increased indeterminacy is that an entirely new possibility manifests itself. According to circumstances, the very same thing can be highest or lowest, best or meanest. Abraham is created in God's divine image and, as paterfamilias of the Israelites, ranks highest, and he is also merely *pulvis et cinis*—"ashes and dust" (Gen 18:27).

As important as Troy and Jericho will be for the European cultural action, the Middle Ages are much more directly affected by events at two later ancient cities that grow out of and compete with the earlier ones. The Troy of Homer is connected to the history of Rome in the first century BCE in the *Aeneid* of Publius Vergilius Naro. In Virgil's epic poem, Aeneas and his group of Trojan refugees flee from their burning city and embark on an odyssey that spans more than seven years. They are brought eventually to Italy where they lay the foundations of Rome and the Roman empire in military struggles with the Latins and their military leader Turnus, Aeneas's principal rival for the hand of the Latin princess Lavinia. The prevalent disposition of cultural resources in the action around Virgil's Rome-to-be remains much as it was at Homer's Troy. The various gods and goddesses continue to hold sway in their different, discrete cultural domains. In the cultural action recorded by Virgil, as at Homer's Troy, "love of honor and appetite for glory," according to Gransden,[35] characterize the competitive approach both to warfare and athletic competitions in the interest of tripods, green palms, armor, gold, and silver. In the competitions, the various gods still play the main role in fixing outcomes on a moment-by-moment basis. Aeneas's ongoing difficulties in reaching his own *promised land* that has been prophesied to him, and in realizing the destiny

---

35. "A thirst for individual glory is thus the prime motivation of many of the heroes of the *Aeneid* no less than in the *Iliad*" (Gransden, *Virgil,* 89).

which Jupiter announces for him early in the epic—that his descendants will be "Lords of the world, the toga-bearing Romans"[36]—are mainly due to the continuing enmity of Juno (the reiteration and elaboration of Homer's vengeful Hera). In Italy as at Troy, the most important outcome is determined by fate and the gods. In the final verses of Virgil's poem, Aeneas kills Turnus in single combat, and nothing stands in the way of the prophesied marriage of Aeneas and Lavinia and the cultural joining of the Trojans and Latins that later results in the Romans. Though fixed from the mortal perspective, this positive outcome for Aeneas and the Trojans has to be sorted out in an ongoing competition between Jupiter and Juno, with the former acting as the custodian of Aeneas's fated ascendancy in Italy and the latter employing every device at her disposal to avert or postpone it. These gods contend with each other over the course of Virgil's poem, according to the exigencies of the immediate circumstances, until a breakthrough is achieved. Recognizing that Juno can and will continue to complicate and postpone things indefinitely, Jupiter makes a deal with her. Aeneas will kill Turnus and the Trojans will win the battle, but effectively lose the war. Trojan language, dress, and customs will be submerged by Latin ones, and Italian valor will be the strength of the later Rome. Jupiter acquiesces to Juno's demand: "Once and for all, Troy falls, and with her name let her lie fallen."[37]

The pagan sacrificial logic of discrete cultural domains is not undone or overcome in Virgil's poem, even as an idea gradually comes to interconnect them. Though her position is contrary to fate and the supreme sky-god's own inclinations, Juno's vested interests have to be taken into consideration. In the final outcome, the diminishment of the importance of Aeneas's Trojan heritage is balanced by Virgil against his project to underscore Rome as Troy reborn. The founder of the Roman empire, Julius Caesar, will be the descendent of "Iulus"—that is, Ascanius, Aeneas's son by his deceased Trojan wife. The longer-term history resulting in the "Trojan Caesar" foretold by Jupiter at the outset of Virgil's poem is not prevented by the arrangement made with Juno near the end. Without transforming the basic organization of the cultural action according to discrete domains with their respective patron deities, which was also characteristic of Homer's Troy, Virgil nevertheless shows the cultural action at his Rome-to-be as occurring in a way that is consistent with a *global* principle. The grand design into which Virgil's poetic action merges, for better or worse, is the poet's own imperial Rome and that of his contemporary

---

36. Virgil, *Aeneid*, 13.
37. Ibid., 398.

Augustus Caesar, son of the deified Caesar.[38] The indeterminacy of the action as rendered by Virgil paves the way to Rome's universal imperial mission in the latter first century BCE—and in later times, to the medieval Christian reiteration of the Roman empire as the *Holy* Roman Empire. The medieval people on whom this study focuses will consider that the cultural action depicted by Virgil merges with their own. Ladies and knights at medieval courts and in medieval romances will be the cultural heirs of Dido, Lavinia, Aeneas, and Ascanius, as well as their latest rivals.

The action at Jerusalem, the last of our four cities, reveals some of the most important moves medieval people will later use to make the imperial Rome of Aeneas and Virgil their own. The figurative moves employed by the Apostle Paul, who writes about a century after Virgil in the early first century CE, make it possible to speak of a *military* action occurring at this city as the site of Jesus Christ's Crucifixion and Resurrection. With *succincti lumbros vestros in veritate*—"loins girt with truth," *loricam iustitiae*—the "breastplate of righteousness," *scutum fidei*—the "shield of faith," *galeam salutis*—the "helmet of salvation," and bearing *gladium spiritus (quod est verbum Dei)*—"the sword of the spirit that is the Word of God," Christian soldiers take possession of Jerusalem, *stare adversus insidias diaboli*—by "standing against the wiles of the devil." The Jerusalem of which Christian soldiers are supposed to take possession, as set forth here in military terms by Paul (Eph 6:11–17), is not the literal, historical city, "which now is, and is in bondage with her children," but rather the free allegorical Jerusalem, "mother of us all" (Gal 4:25–26). In contrast to the approach of the Israelites at Jericho, who followed the dictates of the law and precise instructions given to them by the angel of the Lord, Christian soldiers are supposed to occupy their heavenly Jerusalem by means of faith (and in his Epistle to the Hebrews 11:30, Paul retrospectively asserts that the success of the Israelites at Jericho was *really* due to *their* faith).

Paul's Christian view of the cultural action at Jerusalem grows out of a lengthy and complex history. It is a reiteration and extension of the cultural action of the Israelites, but with some definitive elaborations that seek to set it beyond its monotheistic predecessor and contemporary. Christians form a unified community like the Israelites, but they are integrated and universal in

---

38. The words "for better or worse" in this sentence allude to the different ways Virgil's Rome-to-be has been seen by scholars as connected to Augustan Rome via the battle between Aeneas and Turnus and the brutal slaying of the latter by the former: is the poem Augustan or anti-Augustan? See Andreola Rossi's treatment of this scholarly discussion in her *Contexts of War*, 150–52. Gransden states more generally that "Virgil's vision of Roman history forms the central organizing principle of the *Aeneid*" (*Virgil*, 44).

an unprecedented way that Paul puts like this: "There is neither Jew nor Greek, there is neither bond nor free, there is neither male nor female, for ye are all one in Christ Jesus" (Gal 3:28). The Christian community for Paul potentially includes *all* of humanity (hence my use of the term *global* to characterize it) and, despite its many different parts, is fluidly articulated, with Christ as its head,

> Ex quo totum corpus compactum et connexum per omnem juncturam subministrationis, secundum operationem in mensuram uniuscujusque membri, augmentum corporis facit in aedificationem sui in caritate.

> From whom the whole body fitly joined together and compacted by that which every joint supplieth, according to the effectual working in the measure of every part, maketh increase of the body unto the edifying of itself in love. (Eph 4:16)

The most important move that enables the constitution of this fluidly articulated, potentially universal community is the disengagement of Christians by means of faith from the laws of the Israelites. Observing it is possible for Jews to be unjust knowing the law, and for Gentiles to be just *not* knowing it, Paul reasons that what is truly important is an abiding inner posture or attitude of belief rather than the law (somewhat as Abraham and Isaac had once discovered the advantages of an inner posture of abiding obedience over those of concrete sacrifices). With his figurative moves, the Apostle seems to reject the law and take it a step further at the same time, aligning circumcision and the stone tablets borne by the arc at Jericho with the fallen "outward," fleshly man and sin, while on another level regarding the gospel of faith as written "in the fleshly tables of the heart" (2 Cor 3:3).

The Christian disengagement of self from the law via faith (see Gal 2:19), and the global extension of the fluidly articulated Christian community enabled by it,[39] reiterates, varies, and extends the dualist evaluation of cultural resources that we observed in more limited and exclusive dimensions in the action of the Israelites at Jericho. Selves and things are good (righteous) or bad (sinful) *across the board,* depending on whether they are based on faith or the law, on spirit or the flesh. In Christianity, this universal dualist disposition is brought about by sin, which, even as it renders selves in terms of their sameness, effectively incapacitates them:

---

39. Consistent with the idea of Christianity being fashioned by Paul into what I term a *global religion* is the heading of the first chapter of Hans Küng's *Great Christian Thinkers*: "Paul: Christianity Becomes a World Religion" (5).

Scio enim quia non habitat in me, hoc est in carne mea, bonum. Nam velle, adjacet mihi: perficere autem bonum, non invenio.

I know that in me (that is, in my flesh,) dwelleth no good thing: for to will is present with me; but how to perform that which is good I find not. (Rom 7:18)

The burden of *sin*—a term that encompasses all the difficulties and troubles associated with the mutability of the flesh and other physical-material cultural resources as universally harnessed in Christianity—far surpasses anything humans can do to offset it. Only a sacrifice of the same universal dimensions—the self-sacrifice of divinity occurring in the Crucifixion—can ensure a favorable outcome. By means of faith in this Sacrifice, the immense weight of the burden of sin is removed from Christians. They are effectively released by means of faith from the immediate need to tend to the demands of various discrete cultural domains. They no longer have to endeavor to control the mutability of things and achieve positive outcomes by means of discrete quid-pro-quo sacrifices to the numerous fickle deities in charge, as people continued to do in the pagan Greco-Roman cultural action—and would continue to do in the cultural action of pagan Celtic and Germanic peoples long into the Middle Ages.[40]

More important for Paul, Christians are released from the laws that structure(d) the cultural action of their own monotheistic predecessors and guide(d) them in the direction of their own "promised land" as their reward. All Christians have to do in order to take possession of their heavenly Jerusalem is believe that the debt they owe has been paid in full for them by Christ's sacrifice, and in so doing, die to the world and the flesh in emulation of Him. Outside of faith and the love of one's neighbor that faith brings with it, according to Paul's *streamlining* of the multiple laws of the Israelites, Christians are not constrained in their lives in any way, a condition the Apostle puts this way in Romans 13:7:

---

40. "Utter devotion to many deities is difficult for any human being, but monotheism supplies the kind of focus that makes a more fervent devotion possible, and the intensity of the personal relationship between divine and human is given its fullest expression" (Fowler, *Perspectives of Reality*, 21). Though her study is devoted to Hinduism, Fowler offers observations that are relevant to this study, for example, in seeing dualism as a definitive characteristic of monotheism, generally: "Monotheism is a dualistic principle, one that separates the divine from the world and from humanity [. . .] the monotheism of Judaism, Christianity and Islam considers the nature of the divine to be separate from creation in order to maintain divine transcendence and omnipotence" (20).

> Reddite omnibus debita: cui tribulatum, tributum: cui vectigal, vectigal: cui timorem, timorem: cui honorem, honorem.
>
> Render therefore to all their dues: tribute to whom tribute is due; custom to whom custom; fear to whom fear; honour to whom honour.

These various imperatives are *licenses* rather than obligations. Leaving no aspect or cultural domain of a believer's life untouched, Paul's Christianity pervades and articulates them spiritually, while at the same time, leaving concrete political, social, and economic relations largely intact. The fluidly articulated, potentially universal Christian community as constituted in Paul's Epistles establishes new parameters that will shape the cultural action of medieval Europe and, by extension, that of European modernity. Christian selves and things are both absolutely the *same* in sin and absolutely *other* by virtue of grace, and an unprecedented degree of indeterminacy is thereby achieved. As long as a given thing—for example, tribute, custom, fear, honor—is conveyed in Paul's fluid Christian sense, nothing prevents it from being exchanged or transferred freely throughout the cultural action.

Shown the way by Paul, Christians reiterate and radicalize the risks and rewards of the Israelites' dualist arrangement of cultural resources. In the Christians' global dualism, the permanent joyful bliss of the heavenly Jerusalem associated with the Resurrection is the counterpart to the painful burden of sin associated with the Crucifixion. Because one is bound in this mortal life to the flesh and mutable things, the joy experienced by Christian soldiers as they take possession of their heavenly city via faith in Christ's Crucifixion and Resurrection is only a minute anticipatory measure of the full draught of bliss to be possessed in the heavenly afterlife. In the Christian cultural action, the reward enabled by faith is no longer a temporal promised land to be conferred upon one's people in this life and this world, as it was with the Israelites at Jericho, but rather a heavenly kingdom not to be experienced in this life at all. In Christians as understood by Paul, the inner attitude of fearful obedience and reverence is reiterated and varied in the speculative posture of faith. Faith, *fides*—the lynchpin in the evaluation of selves and things both as what they are *all alike* (sinful/indebted) *and* as absolutely *other* (redeemed)—is *sperandarum substantia rerum, argumentum non parentium*—the substance of things hoped for, the evidence of things not seen (Heb 11:1).

For the speculative effort involved in achieving the reward of the heavenly city, Paul alternately employs a figurative move that puts athletic events to Christian use and bears directly on my view of cultural action as competitive performances:

Nescitis quod ii qui in stadio currunt, omnes quidem currunt, sed unus accipit bravium? Sic currite ut comprehendatis.

Know ye not that they which run in a race run all, but one receiveth the prize? So run, that ye may obtain. (1 Cor 9:24)

The prize for which Paul here admonishes the athletes of Corinth and by extension all Christian competitors to run is the *coronam incorruptam,* the "incorruptible crown" of the heavenly kingdom (1 Cor 9:25). One has only to imagine this crown as crafted of heavenly gold, silver, and gemstones in order to see the Christian correspondents in the cultural action to the rewards we have seen at Troy, Jericho, and Rome.

In the cultural action at these four ancient cities, individuals and groups invest themselves and the resources available to them in the interest of reward. The action occurs as competitive performances in wars and games, the distinction of which hinges on the specific rules of engagement or play. What are the available strategies and moves? What are the implications of non-engagement or standing pat? How much aggression may be employed and with what means? What are the rewards in the case of victory and the penalties in the case of defeat? What are tolerable levels of pain and shame?[41] As competitions in wars and games, the cultural action at the four cities is constantly being viewed, assessed, or "witnessed," as Taylor puts it,[42] from different perspectives, as it will also be in the Middle Ages. At each of the surveyed cities, the

---

41. Richard Rorty offers a view of pain/shame as a common denominator of human experience that goes in the direction of a potential *global ethics* of cultural action: "The view I am offering says that there is such a thing as moral progress, and that this progress is indeed in the direction of greater human solidarity. But that solidarity is not thought of as a recognition of a core self, the human essence, in all human beings. Rather, it is thought of as the ability to see more and more traditional differences (of tribe, religion, race, customs, and the like) as unimportant when compared with similarities with respect to pain and humiliation—the ability to think of people wildly different from ourselves as included in the range of 'us'" (*Contingency,* 192). Coming from a different direction, Hans Küng's ecumenical vision of a global ethic advocates a commitment to a culture (1) of non-violence and respect for life, (2) of solidarity and a just economic order, (3) of tolerance and a life of truthfulness, and (4) of equal rights and partnership between men and women (*Yes to a Global Ethic,* 17–25).

42. In her book *Fictions of Evidence,* Jamie Taylor focuses on the importance of "witnessing" for cultural production in the past, as well as for our own access to that production: "By paying close attention to the forms and practices of witnessing, as well as to the implicit claims of authenticity and truth witnessing assumes, we can read across the past and the present to conceptualize what it means to produce and to analyze the 'evidence' of a life. Indeed, we can ask ourselves by what means we produce and analyze the Middle Ages itself. If we, as scholars of the Middle Ages, are witnesses to it, then we must take care to recognize our own role as *narratores* of the past" (198).

most crucial events take place before critical onlookers and judges. One of the *most watched* events in the ancient world would have been Achilles's pursuit of Hector around the walls of Troy, a *race* in which the competitors, the stakes, and the action and its critical assessment are succinctly and effectively transmitted in one of the highlights of epic poetry:

> They raced, one escaping and one in pursuit
> and the one who fled was great but the one pursuing
> greater, even greater—their pace mounting in speed
> since both men strove, not for a sacrificial beast
> or oxhide trophy, prizes runners fight for, no,
> they raced for the life of Hector breaker of horses.
> Like powerful stallions sweeping round the post for trophies,
> galloping full stretch with some fine prize at stake,
> a tripod, say, or woman offered up at funeral games
> for some brave hero fallen—so the two of them
> whirled three times around the city of Priam,
> sprinting at top speed while the gods gazed down.[43]

Other such crucial events in the cultural action lack the descriptive language of athletic events, which is used in this passage contrastively to highlight the high stakes of the competition, but they still possess a transparently athletic or physical dimension, along with the critical assessment of invested spectators. The cultural action of the Israelites begins when God changes Abram's name to Abraham and makes his covenant with him:

> And when Abram was ninety years old and nine, the LORD appeared to Abram, and said unto him, I am the Almighty God; walk before me, and be thou perfect. (Gen 17:1)

Henceforth, Abraham's *gait* and that of his progeny will be viewed and assessed by their God according to the most rigorous standard of perfection. In contrast to this global view of the cultural action of the Israelites in Genesis, the Roman poet Virgil zooms in on a moment preceding the hunt undertaken by Aeneas's Trojans and Dido's Carthaginians. The manner in which the poet establishes Aeneas's ascendency, as he leads the Trojans' procession into view, suggests that significant outcomes can be momentary and hinge on

---

43. Homer, *Iliad*, 546–47. Rossi observes the "dynamic connection" between athletic contests and war in Achilles's pursuit of Hector (*Contexts of War*, 98–100).

intangibles such as physical beauty, superior aloofness, contagious confidence, well-coiffed hair:

> Resplendent above the rest, Aeneas walked to meet her,
> To join his retinue with hers. He seemed—
> Think of the lord Apollo in the spring
> When he leaves wintering in Lycia
> By Xanthus torrent, for his mother's isle
> Of Delos, to renew the festival;
> Around his altars Cretans, Dryopës,
> And painted Agathyrsans raise a shout,
> But the god walks the Cynthian ridge alone
> And smooths his hair, binds it in fronded laurel,
> Braids it in gold; and shafts ring on his shoulders.
> So elated and swift, Aeneas walked
> With sunlit grace upon him.[44]

Whether of global or momentary situational dimensions, assessed competitions characterize the cultural action we have observed at the four cities, and they also characterize the relationships *among* the earlier and later ones. Virgil's Rome-to-be, as we have seen, finds additional value in the cultural resources attached to Aeneas and his band of Trojan refugees by connecting them with the flourishing imperial Rome of the poet's own time. While the disposition and evaluation of cultural resources remains largely immediate and domain specific, as it had been in the *Iliad*, a greater indeterminacy in the action is achieved by opening up the epic action onto the poet's imperial present. According to the arrangement made by Jupiter and Juno near the poem's end, Troy is finished, once and for all. That Troy nevertheless lives on in Rome is perhaps the clearest indication of the indeterminacy of the new arrangement, whereby whatever residual glory claimed by the once great city of Priam now accrues to Rome. According to the competitive dynamics of cultural expropriation as rendered by Virgil, all the positive resources associated with Troy are to be harnessed for the Rome of the Caesars, while all its negative aspects are to be left behind. Correspondingly, the cultural action becomes indeterminate in a way that leaves room for the transfer of cultural resources from Troy to Rome to occur without the vested interests of important parties, such as Juno, being unduly harmed. When Aeneas is wounded by an arrow at a crucial moment in the fighting near the end of Virgil's epic,

---

44. Virgil, *Aeneid*, 100–101.

we have an exceedingly rare moment in the ancient epic action when a figure of such great stature is wounded inexplicably, in a way that heightens suspense and suggests that the final outcome—despite all the prophecies—is still up in the air:

> A winging shaft—look!—whizzed and struck the man,
> Sped by who knows what hand, what spinning gust
> What stroke of luck, what god won this distinction
> For the Rutulians. Glory for the shot
> Went afterward suppressed; no claims were made
> By anyone of having hit Aeneas.[45]

In view of her ongoing enmity and continuing interventions against the Trojans, Juno or one of her divine or mortal proxies would have to be regarded as the prime suspect behind this shot. But the same indeterminacy that makes it impossible to establish the identity of the marksman also makes room for the agreement between Juno and Jupiter and, beyond this, for an imperial Rome with Trojan roots that will rely on the benevolent favor of *all* the gods, including Juno, as it pursues its universal mission.[46] The forces that have led to the undoing of Troy, even at the moment of Aeneas's military victory, themselves have to be undone, mitigated, and made indeterminate, and distancing the highly suspicious Juno from the wounding of Aeneas helps to achieve this end. An indeterminacy consistent with universal ambitions constructively subsumes local vested interests, as the imperial promise of Virgil's Rome-to-be is set above the fated doom of Homer's Troy.

In the action at Virgil's Rome-to-be, Troy finally falls and Rome is henceforth in ascendency. We have seen that Pauline Christianity is also structured internally by a competitive relationship with its Judaic origins. Though it is the inheritor of much of Judaism, Christianity seemingly must outdo its predecessor, and in his Epistles Paul highlights this outdoing with the terminology of athletic performances. For Paul, the children of the Israelites fall short of righteousness, "Because they sought it not by faith, but as it were by the works of the law. For they stumbled at that stumbling stone" (Rom 9:32). By contrast, the path to be traversed by the Christian runners is clearly marked out, and these are exhorted by Paul to beware of all entangling obstacles as they put themselves into play before the watching crowds:

---

45. Ibid., 125.
46. Jupiter's final words in the poem, Gransden notes, "promise Juno a secure and honoured place in the Roman pantheon [. . .] This reconciliation of opposites is the true resolution of the poem" (*Virgil*, 87).

Ideoque et nos tantam habentes impositam nubem testium, deponentes omne pondus, et circumstans nos peccatum, per patientiam curramus ad propositum nobis certamen.

Therefore, since we are surrounded by such a great cloud of witnesses, let us throw off everything that hinders and the sin that so easily entangles, and let us run with perseverance the race marked out for us. (Heb 12:1)

Here as further above, Paul disengages the language of athletic performance from the domains of sports and warfare, and adapts it to the Christian engagement in the cultural action generally. In Paul's view, Christians can and will outrace the "stumbling" children of the Israelites, as they can and will also outrun all the pagan peoples of the ancient world, Romans and Barbarians alike, who—from the Christian perspective—will be slowed by the various "stumbling stones" associated with the organization and evaluation of cultural resources in discrete domains with their different respective deities in charge.

Paul's efforts are largely devoted to staking out parameters of cultural action that demonstrate Christians' ascendency over their Israelite predecessors and rivals. The relationship between Christian competitors and pagan Greco-Roman ones will be most compellingly and universally articulated some four centuries later. The ensuing chapter will further elaborate and exemplify some of the characteristics of (the indeterminacy of) the cultural action as surveyed in the latter part of this chapter, with a consideration of the action as organized in and around a text of seminal importance for the self-understanding of medieval Europeans who remain under the prevailing cultural influence of Rome: Augustine's *Civitas dei contra paganos—The City of God against the Pagans*, arguably the most capacious articulation of the Christian-imperial parameters of cultural action in the European Middle Ages.[47]

---

47. For Küng, Augustine is the "father of all western Latin theology" (*Great Christian Thinkers*, 6).

CHAPTER 2

The Medieval Self as Bankroll

THE CITY OF GOD: OTHERNESS AS A GLOBAL PARAMETER OF ACTION

In the previous chapter, I considered—and began to question—the notion that the European Middle Ages can be viewed as static in comparison to the progressive dynamism of modernity. The stasis one frequently finds associated with medieval culture is connected to institutionalized communal rituals and the authority of foundational writings by authors such as St. Augustine of Hippo, which set the most important longer-term parameters for experience and action. By contrast, in modernity one seems to be set loose. The modern self as subject, freed from the authority of institutional religion as it is freed from "historical obligations" generally—to reiterate the words of Habermas,[1] begins to posit the parameters of its own experience and action by the time of the Reformation. Based on the conventional division of European cultural history into three epochs—antiquity, the Middle Ages, and modernity— modernity is also associated with a return to or rebirth of antiquity, and the intervening millennium is assessed as if it were of minimal value for, if not a

---

1. Habermas, *Philosophical Discourse*, 13.

detriment to, cultural growth. Ernst Robert Curtius once characterized the Latin Middle Ages as "the crumbling Roman road from the antique to the modern world."[2] In this chapter, I share Curtius's general notion of conveyance, but view the road as not so dilapidated and the traction for modernity as not so tenuous. In keeping with my consideration of culture as *action*, I employ a correspondingly dynamic metaphor in the title of this chapter: "bankroll"—the gambler's store of resources that is suggestive of the cultural growth that will occur in the High Middle Ages. The present chapter picks up where the last one left off and further elucidates how this later crucial point in the European cultural action is reached.

In the action associated with Jerusalem in the previous chapter, we saw that a point was reached when people could be both absolutely the *same* in sin and absolutely *other* by means of faith—*fides*, which Paul sometimes cast as a competitive *exertion* of self, analogous to competition in an athletic event. We further observed that this dynamic coincidence of sameness and otherness, added to and in combination with the continuing, domain-specific evaluations of pagan sacrificial practices and the laws of the Israelites as alternative possibilities, leads to an unprecedented degree of indeterminacy and complexity in the cultural action. In the writings of St. Augustine of Hippo (354–430 CE), particularly in his *Civitas Dei contra paganos—City of God against the Pagans* (completed in 426 CE) the dynamic coincidence of sameness and otherness first set forth by Paul is maintained and expanded in ways that largely shape the parameters of cultural action in the Middle Ages. This authoritative patristic work, rather than constraining the potential of self for growth, actually increases and widens this potential by elaborating the Pauline speculative posture or exertion of faith and giving it patently imperial Roman dimensions.

The reasons that Augustine gives for the composition of his *City of God* show him to be in competition with the pagan sacrificial culture that we observed at Homer's Troy and Virgil's Rome-to-be in the previous chapter. His immediate purpose in writing concerns the endangered integrity of the Roman empire. Augustine and his fellow Christians stand accused of having undermined the political integrity of imperial Rome with their uniquely Christian refusal to pay tribute to the multiple gods and make sacrifices to these gods in their various discrete domains of sovereignty. Augustine's text allows us to hear the Christians' detractors arguing that imperial Rome has hitherto successfully incorporated all the various gods of the peoples and territories it conquered. Before the advent of Christianity—and so the detractors—the

---

2. Curtius, *European Literature*, 19.

multiple gods had been appeased and Rome had fared well. With the increase in numbers and influence of Christians, according to the pagans, a decline set in, and the Visigoths' sack of Rome in 410 CE is the result of this decline. Augustine is sensitive, even defensive in the face of this accusation—for example, in his rejoinder that the Christian God's benevolence became manifest during the sack when Christians seeking refuge in their churches were left unharmed by the rampaging Visigoths. Beyond such more immediate purposes, one of Augustine's broader aims is to counter accusations in a comprehensive theological and philosophical way by setting forth the ascendancy of Christianity over the sacrificial rites associated with the pagan gods. With sarcastic reference to his detractors as "wise men," Augustine characterizes the pagan culture of sacrifice in a manner that, however exaggerated it may seem, is consistent with our observations in the previous chapter:

> Verum quia terrena ciuitas habuit quosdam suos sapientes, quos diuina improbat disciplina, qui uel suspicati uel decepti a daemonibus crederent multos deos conciliandos esse rebus humanis atque ad eorum diuersa quodam modo officia diuersa subdita pertinere, ad alium corpus, ad alium animum, inque ipso corpore ad alium caput, ad alium ceruicem et cetera singula ad singulos; similiter in animo ad alium ingenium, ad alium doctrinam, ad alium iram, ad alium concupiscentiam; inque ipsis rebus uitae adiacentibus ad alium pecus, ad alium triticum, ad alium uinum, ad alium oleum, ad alium siluas, ad alium nummos, ad alium nauigationem, ad alium bella atque uictorias, ad alium coniugia, ad alium partum ac fecunditatem et ad alios alia cetera.[3]

Either out of their own daydreaming or out of demonic deception these wise men came to believe that a multiplicity of divinities were allied with human life, with different duties, in some strange arrangement, and with different assignments: this one over the body, that one over the spirit; in the body itself, one over the head, another over the neck, still others, one for each bodily part; in the mind, one over the intelligence, another over learning, another over temper, another over desire; in the realities, related to life, that lie about us, one over flocks and one over wheat, one over wine, one over oil, and another over forests, one over currency, another over navigation, and

---

3. The Latin text of Augustine's *Civitas Dei contra paganos* (abbreviated below as *CD*) is from *Avrelii Avgvstini Opera, De Civitate Dei Libri I–X* (vol. 47) and *De Civitate Dei Libri XI–XXII* (vol. 48). Book, chapter, and page numbers are referenced in the notes. Here *CD*, XIX.17.684.

still another over warfare and victory, one over marriage, a different one over fecundity and childbirth, so on and so on.⁴

Augustine counters the accusations of such "wise men" with the dualist architecture of his city, in which the multiple allegiances and sacrifices to the many gods correspond to a city of sin and the flesh, and the Christian belief in a single One corresponds to a city of the spirit: *Vna quippe est hominum secundum carnem, altera secundum spiritum*⁵—"One city is that of men who live according to the flesh. The other is of men who live according to the spirit."⁶ Oppositional and leveling dualist terms are clear in passages such as this, in which we see Augustine's systematic alignment of the pagan culture of sacrifices with man (rather than God), sin (rather than just living), and the flesh (rather than the spirit): *Quod itaque diximus, hinc extitisse duas ciuitates diuersas inter se atque contrarias, quod alii secundum carnem, alii secundum spiritum uiuerent: potest etiam isto modo dici quod alii secundum hominem, alii secundum Deum uiuant*⁷—"When, therefore, we said that two contrary and opposing cities arose because some men live according to the flesh and others according to the spirit, we could equally well have said that they arose because some live according to man and others according to God."⁸ The Christian God's city involves what could be considered a *streamlining* of religious practices in the direction of a single-minded investment of self: *Caelestis autem ciuitas <cum> unum Deum solum colendum nosset eique tantum modo seruiendum*⁹—"The heavenly City, on the contrary, knows and by religious faith, believes that it must adore one God alone."¹⁰ Against the multiple dispersed sacrifices of pagan antiquity, Augustine opposes a very different conception of sacrifice that is, nevertheless, quite visibly an extension and variation of the same basic sacrificial principle:

> Proinde uerum sacrificium est omne opus, quo agitur, ut sancta societate inhaereamus Deo, relatum scilicet ad illum finem boni, quo ueraciter beati esse possimus. Vnde et ipsa misericordia, qua homini subuenitur, si non propter Deum fit, non est sacrificium. Etsi enim ab homine fit uel offertur, tamen sacrificium res diuina est, ita ut hoc quoque uocabulo id Latini

---

4. Augustine, *City of God, Books XVII–XXII*, 227.
5. Idem, *CD*, XIV.1.414.
6. Idem, *City of God, Books VIII–XVI*, 347.
7. Idem, *CD*, XIV.4.418.
8. Idem, *City of God, Books VIII–XVI*, 354.
9. Idem, *CD*, XIX.17.684–85.
10. Idem, *City of God, Books XVII–XXII*, 227.

ueteres appellauerint. Vnde ipse homo Dei nomine consecratus et Deo uotus, in quantum mundo moritur ut Deo uiuat, sacrificium est.[11]

> There is, then, a true sacrifice in every work which unites us in holy communion with God, that is, in every work that is aimed at that final Good in which alone we can be truly blessed. That is why even mercy shown to our fellow men is not a sacrifice unless it is done for God. A sacrifice, even though it is done or offered by man, is something divine—which is what the ancient Latins meant by the word *sacrificium*. For this reason, a man himself who is consecrated in the name of God and vowed to God is a sacrifice, in as much as he dies to the world that he may live for God.[12]

Augustine reiterates and varies the ancient pagan logic of "sacrifice" in this dualist and universal Christian sense. Collectively (insofar as they are conceived as a city) and individually (though the individual remains in a secondary position), Christians make themselves a sacrifice by "dying to the world" in order to live for God. In the heavenly city, Christians collectively become "God's Temple": *Huic nos seruititem, quae* λατρεία *Graece dicitur, siue in quibusque sacramentis siue in nobis ipsis debemus. Huius enim templum simul omnes et singuli templa sumus, quia et omnium concordiam et singulos inhabitare dignatur*[13]—"Both in outward signs and inner devotion, we owe to Him that service which the Greeks call *latreía*. Indeed, all of us together, and each one in particular, constitute his Temple because He deigns to take for a dwelling both the community of all and the person of each individual."[14] The uniquely Christian form of sacrifice becomes a continual kind of dedication or service to God, which undoes the spiritual and material infrastructure of dispersed pagan altars in discrete cultural domains and articulates or integrates them into the whole community of believers, collectively and singly. The scattered, fixed temples of the multiple deities are replaced in Augustine's postulations by the single, universal, and highly mobile Christian community—the mobility of which is further enhanced by this community's adoption of the *codex* as the format for its holy scriptures.[15]

---

11. Idem, *CD*, X.6.278.
12. Idem, *City of God, Books VIII–XVI*, 125–26.
13. Idem, *CD*, X.3.275.
14. Idem, *City of God, Books VIII–XVI*, 120; Augustine's employment of the Greek term *latreía*—"worship" or "service to the Gods" (*Liddel and Scott's*)—presents another Christian extension and elaboration of an originally pagan move.
15. Christianity is mobile in the way the religion of the Israelites, as discussed in the previous chapter, was mobile. It is disengaged from the scattered sites of pagan sacrifices and goes

Augustine's theology rests largely on this dualist Christian conception of self-sacrifice, which involves the opposition of an evil, sinful, worldly realm given up to vices of the body (immorality, licentiousness, drunkenness, carousing[16]) and to vices of the soul (including idolatry, another allusion to the culture of sacrifice he is rejecting[17]), to a good, just, spiritual realm of Christians, who in this temporal life are in a state of exile and who are oriented toward the heavenly kingdom as their true home. This religious move has everlasting implications but it is also a competitive move made at a particular crucial moment in the history of late imperial Rome. It is abundantly clear, in view of the Visigoths' sack of Rome, that this world is a turbulent, chaotic place. Peace, justice, and order become with Augustine, "rewards which the soul is to enjoy in the blessedness which is to follow the present life,"[18] which are described in detail in their proper place near the end of the *Civitas Dei* and rendered in terms of peace and eternal life, with the stress in both falling on the idea of permanence.[19] It is not difficult to understand why (Christian) people in imperial Rome, in the years following the sack of the city in 410 CE, would have placed a high value on things everlasting. The more immediate concerns of the moment serve to reinforce the dualist elements in Augustine's text and to advance *otherness* as an imperial, *global* parameter of action.

THE CITY OF GOD: SAMENESS AS A GLOBAL PARAMETER OF ACTION

Augustine's dualism plays a paramount role in the religious design of his *City of God,* but elsewhere we observe a different evaluative tendency that stresses the sameness rather than the otherness of the heavenly and worldly cities. One of the ways in which the complexity of Augustine's *urban design* becomes evident is in his evaluation of perishable worldly goods—those things corresponding to *man* and *the flesh*—as not *intrinsically* evil. The Christian self,

---

wherever Christians go. An important aspect of this mobility, also mentioned in the previous chapter, was the development of holy scriptures as repositories of religion which, due to their portability, reinforce the *fluidity* of the religious action. This is especially the case with the early Christians, who were, according to Ian F. McNeely and Lisa Wolverton, "among the first to adopt a new physical format for the book, the very one we use today: the codex" (*Reinventing Knowledge,* 45–46). The new format—which needs also to be regarded as a technology—was *faster,* enabling more rapid access to passages than scrolls.

16. Augustine, *CD,* XIV.2.349.
17. See idem, *City of God, Books VIII–XVI,* book XIV, chapter 2.
18. Idem, *City of God, Books XVII–XXII,* 489.
19. Ibid., 505–6.

misusing its free will, can become entangled in these goods and find itself unwilling or unable to make its way back to God. But in a crucial passage, Augustine states that the failure to move in the direction of God's heavenly reward has to do with the *action of turning away itself*, rather than with the lower objects or goods toward which the movement is directed: *Cum enim se uoluntas relicto superiore ad inferiora convertit, efficitur mala, non quia malum est, quo se conuertit, sed quia peruersa est ipsa conuersio*[20]—"When the will, abandoning what is above it, turns itself to something lower, it becomes evil because *the very turning itself—ipsa conuersio—*and not the thing to which it turns is evil."[21] Hence, to the degree perishable worldly goods as God's creations are not seen as intrinsically evil, an evaluative logic of sameness—which has been connected in the critical literature to the influence of Plotinus and Neoplatonism[22]—rather than an evaluative logic of otherness manifests itself. To the degree perishable goods are evaluated as obstacles inhibiting or preventing one from achieving one's heavenly reward (i.e., as *temptations*), they are to be mistrusted, if not rejected, according to a leveling evaluative approach that opposes them as evil to the absolutely *other* good.

In the previous chapter, we saw Jerusalem dualistically structured as a sinful worldly city and as a divine heavenly city in the Epistles of Paul. Augustine reiterates Paul's move and structures his imperial city in *Civitas Dei* similarly.[23] Both Jerusalem and Augustine's *civitas*-modeled-on-imperial-Rome are bipartite. Each contains within it a sinful physical-material (i.e., fleshly) and a divine spiritual-intellectual part. While the two parts within Paul's Jerusalem and within Augustine's City of God are dualistically opposed or juxtaposed, *Jerusalem* and *Rome*, respectively, are nevertheless, at the same time, constructions that subsume and articulate the two parts comprising them. This is to say, the worldly and heavenly "cities" or parts are absolutely different within Jerusalem and within Rome, but they also nevertheless overlap to the point of being virtually indistinguishable. In the newly indeterminate, global cultural action of Christianity as conceived by Augustine, the dualist architecture discussed above is accompanied by a kind of universal *demographics* according to

---

20. Idem, *CD*, XII.6.361.
21. Idem, *City of God, Books XVII–XXII*, 255; italics and Latin text added.
22. See Bowery, "Plotinus," 654–57. Moves of a more overtly monist evaluative tendency provide Augustine with the means to mitigate the kind of leveling that can occur in a stark dualist arrangement of things, such as Manichaeism, which leaves no room, for example, for individual free will. For a detailed study of Augustine's relationship to Manichaeism, see BeDuhn, *Augustine's Manichaean Dilemma*.
23. Augustine connects his allegorical understanding of Jerusalem to his own bipartite imperial city. See particularly his *City of God, Books XVII–XXII*, book XVII, 20–21.

which *all* inhabitants can be seen in like terms. Augustine sets a universal tone for all the inhabitants of his bipartite city: "The simple truth is that the bond of a common nature makes all human beings one."[24] He puts forth the idea that the two opposed parts of the city are inextricably intertwined in history: *Perplexae quippe sunt istae duae ciuitates in hoc saeculo inuicemque permixtae, donec ultimo iudicio dirimantur*[25]—"linked and fused together, only to be separated at the Last Judgment."[26] With respect to the heavenly city, Augustine writes:

> Dum apud terrenam ciuitatem uelut captiuam uitam suae peregrinationis agit, iam promissione redemptionis et dono spiritali tamquam pignore accepto legibus terrenae ciuitatis, quibus haec administrantur, quae sustentandae mortali uitae adcommodata sunt, obtemperare non dubitat, ut, quoniam communis est ipsa mortalitas, seruetur in rebus ad eam pertinentibus inter ciuitatem utramque concordia.[27]

> As long as her life in the earthly city is that of a captive and an alien (although she has the promise of ultimate delivery and the gift of the Spirit as a pledge), she has no hesitation about keeping in step with the civil law which governs matters pertaining to our existence here below. For, as mortal life is the same for all, there ought to be common cause between the two cities in what concerns our purely human living.[28]

The coincidence of the interests of worldly and heavenly cities visible here is made more inextricable by the Christians' permitted use of all cultural resources throughout society, as long as this use occurs in a manner consistent with peaceful order and the worship of their single God:

> Haec ergo caelestis ciuitas dum peregrinatur in terra, ex omnibus gentibus ciues euocat atque in omnibus linguis peregrinam colligit societatem, non curans quidquid in moribus legibus institutisque diuersum est, quibus pax terrena uel conquiritur uel tenetur, nihil eorum rescindens uel destruens, immo etiam seruans ac sequens, quod licet diuersum in diuersis nationibus,

---

24. Ibid., 84.
25. Idem, *CD*, I.35.34.
26. Idem, *City of God, Books I–VII*, 72.
27. Idem, *CD*, XIX.17.684.
28. Idem, *City of God, Books XVII–XXII*, 227.

ad unum tamen eundemque finem terrenae pacis intenditur, si religionem, qua unus summus et uerus Deus colendus docetur, non impedit.²⁹

So long, then, as the heavenly City is wayfaring on earth, she invites citizens from all nations and all tongues, and unites them into a single pilgrim band. She takes no issue with that diversity of customs, laws, and traditions whereby human peace is sought and maintained. Instead of nullifying or tearing down, she preserves and appropriates whatever in the diversities of divers races is aimed at one and the same objective of human peace, provided only that they do not stand in the way of the faith and worship of the one supreme and true god.³⁰

Augustine grants ample leeway to Christians to make use of *all* cultural resources, in what seems a pacifistic Christian reiteration of pagan Rome's century-long incorporation of diverse peoples, realms, languages, and traditions into its empire.³¹ Similar thoughts are articulated elsewhere in Augustine's writings, notably in the fourth book of his *Doctrina Christiana* (books 1–3 from 396/397 CE and book 4 in 426 CE), in which he urges Christians to use the pagan Greco-Roman educational system for their own purposes, particularly the study of languages, science, history, and the liberal arts—and of the latter, particularly the art of rhetoric. Christians should learn to speak persuasively and ornately, because they have much at stake in effectively presenting their gospel and should not be at a disadvantage vis-à-vis rhetorically accomplished opponents of their faith. In the *Doctrina,* one sees Augustine harnessing everything in Greco-Roman antiquity that might be of use to Christians. As long as it involves "no offense against divine law," Augustine does not see increased knowledge in *any* field as necessarily antagonistic or contrary to Christianity, in contrast to recurring repressive religious tendencies in medieval and modern times.

The integrative logic of sameness, according to which the culture of multiple, dispersed, fixed sacrifices is transformed into a unified, mobile, and global Christian culture of the Single Sacrifice, thus seems to have an inexorable impetus that carries over to the relationship between the heavenly and

---

29. Idem, *CD,* XIX.17.685.
30. Idem, *City of God, Books XVII–XXII,* 228.
31. "The City of God does not care in the least what kind of dress or social manners a man of faith affects, so long as these involve no offense against the divine law. For it is faith and not fashions that bring us to God. Hence, when philosophers become Christians, the Church does not force them to give up their distinctive attire or mode of life which are no obstacle to religion, but only their erroneous teachings" (Ibid., book XIX, chapter 19, 229–30).

worldly cities within Rome. The overlap or articulation of the two cities is so thoroughgoing that it is impossible even for the holy Augustine himself to disentangle them, as the Bishop confesses:

> Quae cum ita sint, non tribuamus dandi regni atque imperii potestatem nisi Deo uero, qui dat felicitatem in regno caelorum solis piis; regnum uero terrenum et piis et impiis, sicut ei placet, cui nihil iniuste placet. Quamuis enim aliquid dixerimus, quod apertum nobis esse uoluit: tamen multum est ad nos et ualde superat uires nostras hominum occulta discutere et liquido examine merita diiudicare regnorum.[32]

> The power to give people a kingdom or empire belongs only to the same true God who gives the Kingdom of Heaven with its happiness only to those who believe in Him, while He gives the earthly city to both believers and unbelievers alike according to His Will which can never be unjust. This much of what I have said so far God wanted to be clear to us. However, it would be too much for me and beyond my powers to discuss men's hidden merits and to measure in an open balance those which have been rewarded by the establishment of kingdoms.[33]

Augustine's incapacity here is bound to his own fallibility and mortality, the human condition shared by just and unjust alike. Overall, the cultural action seems to have become more difficult to assess. In this life, during which the two cities comingle, those who are manifestly evil can experience good fortune while those who are good can be visited with all manner of calamities and grief. Augustine's mortal incapacity to evaluate cultural goods, to comprehend the sometimes seemingly unjust fluctuations in this temporal life, seems to follow from the subordination of the dispersed pagan sacrifices in discrete cultural domains to the culture of the single, universal Christian sacrifice. The latter achieves uniformity and mobility in the disposition of cultural resources, but seemingly at the cost of the immediacy of the dispersed individual points of contact with the otherworld that was seen in pagan sacrificial culture to guarantee the efficacy of sacrifices (however doubtful this was in its own right) and thereby to shape the values of things. For Christians, the status or value of cultural resources cannot and will not be known directly and certainly until things are sorted out in a definitive way when final outcomes are revealed on Judgment Day, which Augustine sees as occurring in this way:

---

32. Idem, *CD*, V.21.157.
33. Idem, *City of God, Books I–VII*, 291.

Cum uero ad illud Dei iudicium uenerimus, cuius tempus iam proprie dies iudicii et aliquando dies Domini nuncupatur: non solum quaecumque tunc iudicabuntur, uerum etiam quaecumque ab initio iudicata et quaecumque usque ad illud tempus adhuc iudicanda sunt, apparebunt esse iustissima. Vbi hoc quoque manifestabitur, quam iusto iudicio Dei fiat, ut nunc tam multa ac paene omnia iusta iudicia Dei lateant sensus mentesque mortalium, cum tamen in hac re piorum fidem non lateat, iustum esse quod latet.[34]

When we come to that judgment of God the proper name of which is "judgment day" or "the day of the Lord," we shall see that all His judgments are perfectly just: those reserved for that occasion, all those that He had made from the beginning, and those, too, He is to make between now and then. Then, too, it will be shown plainly how just is that divine decree which makes practically all of God's judgments lie beyond the present understanding of men's minds, even though devout men may know by faith that God's hidden judgments are most surely just."[35]

The timeless certitude of Judgment Day, whereby the otherness of the Christian elect is confirmed and the providential master plan behind history revealed, is set off from the indeterminate sameness of the mortal, temporal cultural action leading up to it. In this life, it remains impossible to know—except indirectly or *virtually* via *faith*—who will be rewarded in the afterlife for their various wagers and investments. In Augustine's *City of God,* the virtual status of the Christian self—considering itself via faith to be in possession of something it does not yet have and might not in the end receive—is reiterated *throughout a Christian cultural action of imperial Roman dimensions.* In view of the tendency of a certain disposition of self to underlie the disposition of cultural resources generally, referenced in the previous chapter,[36] the status of things not destined for eternal life corresponds to the unfinished, *virtual* condition of the Christian self:

Naturae igitur omnes, quoniam sunt et ideo habent modum suum, speciem suam et quandam secum pacem suam, profecto bonae sunt; et cum ibi sunt, ubi esse per naturae ordinem debent, quantum acceperunt, suum esse custodiunt; et quae semper esse non acceperunt, pro usu motuque rerum, quibus

---

34. Idem, *CD,* XX.2.701.
35. Idem, *City of God, Books XVII–XXII,* 253.
36. Again, see Habermas, *Philosophical Discourse,* 20, and my related discussion in the previous chapter.

Creatoris lege subduntur, in melius deteriusue mutantur, in eum diuina prouidentia tendentes exitum, quem ratio gubernandae uniuersitatis includit; ita ut nec tanta corruptio, quanta usque ad interitum naturas mutabiles mortalesque perducit, sic faciat non esse quod erat, ut non inde fiat consequenter quod esse debebat.[37]

All natures are good simply because they exist and, therefore, have each its own measure of being, its own beauty, even, in a way, its own peace. And when each is in the place assigned by the order of nature, it best preserves the full measure of being that was given to it. Beings not made for eternal life, changing for better or for worse according as they promote the good and improvement of things to which, by the Law of the Creator, they serve as means, follow the direction of Divine Providence and tend toward the particular end which forms a part of the general plan for governing the universe. This means that the dissolution which brings mutable and mortal things to their death is not so much a process of annihilation as a progress toward something they were designed to become.[38]

Cultural goods for Augustine can only be comprehended as things in flux that are headed towards their providential end. From God to humanity, animals, plants, and inanimate objects, all cultural resources are related by their common participation in God's overarching master plan. People dispose freely of themselves, others, and all things as they proceed toward their final status or true *value,* which remains yet to be conclusively determined.

Final outcomes will hinge on whether a given self or thing is oriented toward the creator or creation. But since there is no way to know things *conclusively* before Judgment Day, a wide range of dispositions of self and cultural resources is enabled within the parameters of otherness and sameness laid out by Augustine. The most important development for the purposes of this study is a Christian self that disposes freely of resources in all cultural domains: an integrated, mobilized self with single-minded purpose that is *supposed* to give itself up absolutely as a sacrifice, or *die to the world* in the interest of the heavenly afterlife. However, as we already know, *it might not.* Liberated from the immediate demands of pagan sacrificial practices as well as from the laws of the Israelites, the Christian has greater potential to try out new moves with cultural resources, the values of which are now also in flux according to the dynamic Christian conception of things. St. Augustine's imperial Christian

---

37. Augustine, *CD*, XII.5.359.
38. Idem, *City of God, Books XVII–XXII*, 252–53.

parameters of otherness and sameness, themselves speculative, will invite further speculations. Christians are pointed in the direction of the *other*, absolutely *other* ventures that we shall observe in later chapters.

LOSS, REITERATION, GROWTH

By means of the division of his identifiably imperial Roman City of God into two opposed yet thoroughly intertwined cities, Augustine counters pagan critics and puts Christianity and Christians beyond reproach in the time following the Visigoths' sack of the city in 410 CE. Of longer-term cultural consequence is that Augustine's bipartite *civitas*-modeled-on-imperial-Rome fashions the historical city of his time into a new, *real* Rome, the spiritual and intellectual characteristics of which allow for the disengagement of the city from its perishable physical-material infrastructure and suit it to continuity during the turbulent centuries to come. The expression *dark ages* aptly describes the overall energy level of the cultural action of the early Middle Ages. Curtius's above-referenced designation of the Middle Ages as a "crumbling road" is justified by the rapid fall away from the standards of the physical-material infrastructure of imperial Rome in the centuries after Augustine. In stark contrast to the continuing quality and intensity of cultural developments in Byzantium and the eastern Mediterranean, the maintenance of the imperial infrastructure throughout much of the former Western Roman empire is largely discontinued. As time passes, it becomes increasingly difficult to find people who know how to maintain the physical-material infrastructure or make necessary repairs to it. The cultural *light* becomes discontinuous and dim at best. The action slows and becomes more localized. During long periods in large areas, the imperial Roman parameters of action are limited to those of the "spiritual city" cultivated in bishoprics and the narrow confines of scattered cloisters, which remain intermittently under siege by various different enemies of the faith. Perhaps not surprisingly, medieval people begin to make their own new cultural marks at those points where they understand themselves to rise again to a level of action that they regard as in some way comparable to that of imperial Christian Rome.

Where such marks are made, we observe the lasting influence of Augustine's writings. The rule of the Carolingian Charlemagne (742–814 CE), traditional originator of the *holy* Roman empire, aligned conquest and Christianity in the forced conversion of pagan peoples, but he also cultivated pacifistic Roman religious, intellectual, and artistic pursuits at the ruler's court in Aachen and at monasteries (which soon began to be reorganized along Benedictine lines throughout the Carolingian realm[39]). On Charlemagne's favored reading material, his biographer Einhard notes, "The subjects of the readings were the stories and deeds of olden time: he was fond, too, of St. Augustine's books, and especially of the one entitled *The City of God.*"[40] Charlemagne's military action establishes a domain in Europe that begins again to approach the Western European dimensions of the ancient Roman empire, but he and his contemporaries are unable to reiterate an administrative and physical-material infrastructure of sufficient effectiveness and dimensions that could begin to provide the Carolingian Roman empire with comparable longevity. Cultural action according to identifiably Augustinian parameters is again visible during the reign of the Saxon emperors, notably Otto I (912–73 CE), whose employment of his court as an educational institution for the training of imperial bishops accompanies and reinforces the ascendency he achieves by means of military victories.[41] Bishops-in-training at Otto's court later become heads of imperial archbishoprics with their distinctively medieval combination of religious and worldly authority, a medieval iteration of the Augustinian overlap of heavenly and worldly cities that we observed above. Besides being beholden to Otto and acquiring needed administrative skills, these bishops-in-training have the opportunity to familiarize themselves more generally with the literary culture of antiquity, which begins to hone some of the intellectual skills that will be needed for the scope and intensity of the cultural action at European courts in the twelfth and thirteenth centuries.

In the midst of the twelfth-century cultural action is the Bishop of Freising Otto, half-brother of Emperor Konrad III, uncle of Konrad's successor Frederick I ("Barbarossa"), and trusted advisor of both. Around the middle of this century, Otto authors two chronicles (the latter together with his continuator Rahewin) that are already highly regarded in his own lifetime, the *Chronicle of Two Cities* (*Chronica de duabus civitatibus*) and the *Deeds of Emperor Frederick* (*Gesta Friderici Imperatoris*), of which the former especially merits discussion in this context because of its manifest indebtedness to Augustine's *City of God.* This chronicle is a universal history beginning with Adam and Eve and ending in his own time, but in the prologues of the eight books comprising

---

39. See Lawrence, *Medieval Monasticism*, 66–82.

40. "Einhard tells of Charlemagne's great admiration for the writings of St. Augustine, above all for his *City of God.* That Charlemagne could have conceived of a higher role than that of a mere earthly king is not at all improbable. He may have seen himself as God's directly appointed agent, with a delegated authority that transcended that of every other Christian, pope included, but an authority he must use to fulfill God's purpose" (Dahmus, *Seven Medieval Kings*, 113).

41. See Jaeger, *Origins of Courtliness*, passim and 121.

his chronicle, Otto puts forth his view of history and the bipartite status of cultural resources in a way that shows his book to be a specifically medieval iteration of the Augustinian cultural parameters that we observed earlier in this chapter. Otto first sets forth a view of worldly and heavenly cities which, like that of Augustine, is starkly dualist. Otto—*de rerum temporalium motu ancipitique statu*—pondering the "changes and vicissitudes of temporal affairs," concludes based on the guidance of his reason, *Proinde quia temporum mutabilitas stare non potest, ab ea migrare, ut dixi, sapientem ad stantem et permanentem eternitatis civitatem debere quis sani capitis negabit?*[42]—"Since things are changeable and can never be at rest, what man in his right mind will deny that the wise man ought, as I have said, to depart from them to that city which stays at rest and abides to all eternity?"[43] The two cities posited by Otto here at the beginning of his chronicle, *una temporalis, alia eterna, una mundialis, alia caelestis, una diaboli, alia Christi*—"the one of time, the other of eternity; the one of the earth, earthly, the other of heaven, heavenly; the one of the devil, the other of Christ," are rendered according to the dualist, global, cultural parameter of otherness that is familiar to us from Augustine. Elsewhere, though, Otto is inclined to reiterate the opposing evaluative tendency of Augustine in underscoring the thoroughgoing interconnectedness of the two cities in this temporal life. In the prologue to the third book, for example, Otto's dualist discourse gives way to the idea of the single, all-encompassing imperial *civitas* of Rome:

> Hic iam, quod supra distuli, solvendum puto, quare unius urbis imperio totum orbem subici, unius urbis legibus totum orbem informari Dominus orbis voluerit. Primo, ut dixi, ut ad maiora intelligenda promptiores ac capatiores essent mentes hominum. Secundo, ut his modis unitis unitas commendaretur fidei, quatinus unius urbis terrore ad unum hominem colendum homines universi constricti unam quoque fidem tenendam caelestemque in ea non hominem tantum, sed auctorem omnium colendum ac adorandum Deum addiscerent.[44]

> I think I ought to answer the question why the Lord of the universe wished the whole world to be subject to the dominion of one city, the whole world to be moulded by the laws of one city. In the first place He wished it, as I have said, that the minds of men might be more ready to understand, more

---

42. Otto, *Ottonis Episcopi*, 6.
43. Idem, *Two Cities*, 93.
44. Idem, *Ottonis Episcopi*, 133.

capable of understanding great matters. Secondly, He wished it that unity of faith might be recommended to them after they had been united in this way, in order that all men, being constrained by their fear of a single city to revere one man, might also learn that they ought to hold to one faith, and through that faith might learn that God must be revered and adored not merely as a celestial being but as the Creator of all.[45]

Otto here addresses the importance of the emergence of the Roman empire, of which he views the medieval imperial house of the Hohenstaufen to which he belongs as the contemporary continuation.

Otto's views on the constitution of imperial Rome manifest his understanding and continuation of Augustine's merging of heavenly and worldly cities. Nothing may be outside of or lost to Christianity in its imperial Roman form: *all* cultural resources not at cross-purposes with faith have to form a meaningful, positive part of it. In the prologue of his fourth book of *Two Cities,* Otto further seems to mitigate if not overturn his initial dualist evaluation of cultural resources in addressing the propriety of churchmen such as himself holding worldly authority, or *hanc gloriam honoremque temporem*[46]—"temporal glory and honor,"[47] as he puts it. Otto first concedes the validity of the dualist argument that could be made on the basis of holy scriptures for strictly differentiating the *sacerdotalis et regalis*[48]—"the priestly and the kingly,"[49] along with the various cultural domains with which they are associated. But he then points out that historical practice has diverged from such a strict dualist differentiation and that there is a divine purpose in this divergence:

> Preterea probatae sanctitatis viri inveniuntur, qui haec habuisse, qui cum his regnum Dei acquisisse creduntur. His ergo aliisque modis, quos longum est exequi, probatur et Constantium ecclesiae iuste regalia contulisse et ecclesiam licite suscepisse. Dum enim ab eis querimus, quo iure reges id habeant, respondere solent: ex ordinatione Dei et electione populi. Si ergo Deus ordinando, quod regibus predictus honor impenderetur, iniuste non fecit, quanto magis et id ordinando, ut ab illa persona ad ecclesiasticam traduceretur, iniustus dicendus non est?[50]

---

45. Idem, *Two Cities*, 220–21.
46. Idem, *Ottonis Episcopi*, 180.
47. Idem, *Two Cities*, 272.
48. Idem, *Ottonis Episcopi*, 181.
49. Idem, *Two Cities*, 272.
50. Idem, *Ottonis Episcopi*, 182.

Men of established sanctity are found who are believed to have had kingly honors, to have won the kingdom of God in addition to those kingly honors. By these arguments, therefore, and by others which it would take too long to recount, it is shown that Constantine properly bestowed royal powers upon the Church, and that the Church legitimately accepted them. For when we inquire of kings by what sanction they have their powers, they are accustomed to reply, "By the ordination of God and election by the people." If, therefore, God did not act unrighteously in ordaining that the aforesaid honor should be conferred upon kings, how much more surely is He not to be called unrighteous for ordaining this also, that the honor should be transferred from that role to the ecclesiastical authority?[51]

Otto's strategic employment of the possibilities afforded by the indeterminately juxtaposed parameters of otherness and sameness in Augustine's bipartite *civitas* here serves the interests of imperial archbishops and bishops as *principes imperii,* or *Reichsfürsten,* in whose authority temporal and heavenly cultural resources overlap. After centuries of decline and (only intermittently successful) reiterations of the Roman imperial idea, we find ourselves with Otto in the midst of the period of cultural growth upon which this study focuses in subsequent chapters.

The next chapter will examine in greater detail the medieval cultural action as it occurs among some of Europe's most *resourceful* political players (i.e., princes), aspects of which these passages from Otto's *The Two Cities* already provide some glimpses.

THE NEW MEDIEVAL MOVE EXEMPLIFIED

In the remainder of this chapter, I illustrate what I mean by the term "bankroll," in order to exemplify *the new medieval move* introduced in the previous chapter and to demonstrate how the speculative posture of faith as we have observed it above—as a dynamic relation of otherness and sameness—is extended and varied in romance poetry of the High Middle Ages. I turn for this purpose to two significant episodes in courtly romances from the first decades of the thirteenth century, Wolfram von Eschenbach's *Parzival* and Gottfried von Strassburg's *Tristan.*

Near the end of Wolfram's romance, Parzival has already won the grail and has been accompanied to the grail kingdom by his pagan half-brother Feirefiz,

---

51. Idem, *Two Cities,* 273.

who shares Parzival's European father, but was born of an African mother. Feirefiz consequently has a black-and-white speckled complexion and, according to Wolfram's universal conception of chivalric culture, he is, along with his brother Parzival, one of the world's best knights. His life is dedicated to chivalric adventuring in the interest of earning love's reward. Upon arriving at the grail court, Feirefiz observes a procession in which the grail is carried before him by Parzival's beautiful maternal aunt, Repanse de Schoie. Feirefiz is unable to see the grail because he is not a Christian, but he is stricken by the sight of Repanse de Schoie and falls immediately in love with her, forgetting the love of the pagan woman Sekundille that he had previously sought to win. We observe all the characteristic symptoms of love's exertions, though as a consequence of Feirefiz's unique complexion in Wolfram's poetic idiom, only the lighter parts of the African knight's complexion pale. Feirefiz wants to gain possession of his beloved and his desire has a patently erotic aspect. When told by Parzival that he must be a Christian and baptized in order to marry and possess his new beloved, Feirefiz declares himself to be willing:

> Parzivâl zuo sîm bruoder dô
> sprach "wiltu die muomen mîn
> haben, al die gote dîn
> muostu durch si versprechen
> unt immer gerne rechen
> den widersaz des hôhsten gotes
> und mit triuwen schônen sîns gebotes."
> "*Swâ von ich sol die maget hân,*"
> sprach der heiden, "daz wirt gar getân,
> und mit triuwen an mir erzeiget."[52]
> (816.24–817.3)

"If you want my aunt," Parzival told his brother, "you must forswear all your gods for her sake and be always ready to fight the Adversary of God on high, and faithfully observe God's Commandments." "*Whatever will assure me of winning that maiden* shall be done, fully and faithfully," answered the Infidel.[53]

Parzival frames the baptism in starkly dualist terms as the acceptance of a single deity that has superseded all other deities and stands opposed to a

---

52. Wolfram von Eschenbach, *Parzival* (Lachmann); italics added. Numbers of Middle High German verses here and elsewhere are cited paranthetically in text.
53. Wolfram von Eschenbach, *Parzival* (Hatto) 405; italics added.

single diabolical adversary, and Feirefiz agreeably responds with his equally stark investment of self in the perishable, fleshly love of a woman. As if Wolfram wanted to make sure his audience has fully understood the nature and direction of Feirefiz's self-investment in this baptism, he has Feirefiz elaborate it shortly later, when a priest joins the two brothers to carry out the baptism proper:

> Feirefiz zem priester sprach
> "ist ez mir guot vür ungemach,
> ich gloube, swes ir gebietet.
> ob mich ir minne mietet,
> sô leiste ich gerne sîn gebot.
> bruoder hât dîn muome got,
> an den geloube ich unt an sie
> (sô grôze nôt enphieng ich nie):
> al mîne gote sint verkorn."
> (818.1–9)

"If it will soothe my anguish, I shall believe all you tell me," said Feirefiz to the priest. "If her love rewards me, I shall gladly fulfill God's Commandments. Brother, if your aunt has God, I believe in Him and her—never was I in such need! All my gods are foresworn."[54]

Once baptized, Feirefiz is married to Repanse de Schoie and receives love's reward from her. Wolfram's grail romance ends with one brother (Parzival) winning the grail, and the other (Feirefiz) the woman by whom the grail is carried in procession, in a way that suggests an inextricable interrelation or congruence of divine and fleshly allegiances. The circumstances of Feirefiz's baptism, which is situated at a crucial point near the end of Wolfram's grail narrative, seem strikingly at odds with dualist aspects of the Augustinian cultural parameters, particularly the dictate that impermanent (fleshly) things have only to be used in order to make one's way back to God as the true reward and object of enjoyment. These circumstances seem to invert the dualist Augustinian terms, in making the love of Repanse de Schoie with its clearly fleshly inspirations the reason for Feirefiz's becoming a Christian. At the same time, Wolfram's text leaves no doubt that the baptism is efficacious in all senses. The Christianized Feirefiz is now able to see the grail, indicative of a

---

54. Wolfram von Eschenbach, *Parzival* (Hatto), 406.

thoroughgoing transformation of his perceptive faculties, and he is also able to take possession of Repanse de Schoie, following through with his venture for love in which the baptism plays an *instrumental* role.[55] The new cultural move occurring at high medieval courts in the imaginary action of the courtly romances, and the cultural *growth* in which these moves can result, is concretely and succinctly stated in the above-cited words with which Feirefiz invests himself: "I believe in him *and her*" (italics added).

A comparable exemplary case of the medieval self as a "bankroll" occurs in the *Tristan* of Wolfram's principal poetic rival, Gottfried von Strassburg. The episode in question involves the ordeal of the glowing hot iron undergone by Isolt.[56] Again charged with maintaining an adulterous relationship with the King's nephew Tristan, Queen Isolt is pressured to submit to the ordeal. She must take the glowing iron in her hand without burning herself in order to prove her innocence. At the appointed time and place, Isolt arrives in a boat on the bank of the Thames, where the Archbishop of Canterbury awaits to oversee the proceedings. Tristan, supposed by all to be in exile, has already been in contact with Isolt, and they have together devised another of their joint deceptive maneuvers. He now awaits Isolt on the river bank, disguised as a pilgrim in rags. Declaring with feigned sarcasm that if she allows any man of rank to carry her to shore, tongues will again begin to wag and accuse her of untoward activity, Isolt requests that the poor pilgrim—whom nobody suspects is Tristan—bear her through the shallow water from the boat onto the bank. The selection of the humble pilgrim for this purpose seems to be safe to the unsuspecting assembly, and there is general consent. While carrying Isolt onto the bank, the pilgrim—on a secret signal from Isolt—stumbles, falls, and lands with the lady lying in his arms. A brief tumult ensues, the pilgrim is rebuked for his carelessness and allowed to go on his way, and the trial by ordeal continues. Isolt is now in a position to propose the wording of the oath that she will swear to her husband Marke and the assembled clergy and nobility in this way, manifesting remarkable poise under pressure and presence of mind as she does so:

---

55. As striking as it is, the final episode involving Feirefiz goes unmentioned in many critical studies. Henry Kratz addresses the episode in this way, in his comprehensive study *Wolfram von Eschenbach's "Parzival"*: "Feirefiz [. . .] takes on the complexion of a comical character in this last book, the demon lover who is so obsessed with his love that he has thoughts for nothing else, and will do anything to obtain his gratification" (410). However "comical" this episode may be, it nonetheless remains remarkable that Wolfram can craft an imaginary world in which a "demon lover" can get what he wants via baptism.

56. For a more detailed consideration of Isolt's ordeal in the broader context of ordeals in history and literature, see Ziegler, *Trial by Fire*, 123–32.

vernemet, wie ich iu sweren wil:
daz mînes lîbes nie kein man
dekeine künde nie gewan
noch mir ze keinen zîten
weder ze arme noch ze sîten
ane iuch nie lebende man gelac
wan der, vür den ich niene mac
gebieten eit noch lougen,
den ir mit iuwern ougen
mir sâhet an dem arme,
der wallaere der arme.
sô gehelfe mir mîn trehtîn
und al die heiligen, die der sîn,
ze saeden und ze heile
an disem urteile![57]
(15706–20)

Hear the oath which I mean to swear: "That no man in the world had carnal knowledge of me or lay in my arms or beside me but you, always excepting the poor pilgrim whom, with your own eyes, you saw lying in my arms." I can offer no purgation concerning him. So help me God and all the Saints that be, to a happy and auspicious outcome to this judgment.[58]

Isolt and Tristan have thus far relied on their own strategic ingenuity in the various ploys with which they have prevented their illicit love from being exposed, with occasional recourse to only two confidants, the maidservant Brangaene and Tristan's servant Curvenal. This time the lovers' actions involve the speculation that *God* will also be complicit and become an instrument whereby their adulterous love might be preserved and continued.

The speculative stratagem pays off. Isolt swears according to the wording she has proposed, grasps the glowing iron, and does not burn herself, proving the *truth* of her oath. Gottfried explains how such a thing could happen, thereby seeming to extend the Augustinian cultural parameter of *sameness* to utmost lengths:

dâ wart wol g'offenbaeret
und al der werlt bewaeret,

---

57. Gottfried von Strassburg, *Tristan* (Ranke).
58. Gottfried von Strassburg, *Tristan* (Hatto), 247.

daz der vil tugenthafte Crist
wintschaffen alse ein ermel ist.
er vüeget unde suochet an,
dâ man'z an in gesuochen kan,
alse gevuoge und alse wol,
als er von allem rehte sol.
erst allen herzen bereit,
ze durnehte und ze trügeheit.
ist ez ernest, ist es spil,
er ist ie, swie sô man wil.
daz wart wol offenbâre schîn
an der gevüegen künigîn.
die generte ir trügeheit
und ir gelüppeter eit,
der hin ze gote gelâzen was,
daz s'an ir êren genas.
(15733–50)

Thus it was made manifest and confirmed to all the world that Christ in His great virtue is pliant as a windblown sleeve. He falls into place and clings, whichever way you try Him, closely and smoothly, as He is bound to do. He is at the beck of every heart for honest deeds or fraud. Be it deadly earnest or a game, He is just as you would have Him. This was amply revealed in the facile Queen. She was saved by her guile and by the doctored oath that went flying up to God, with the result that she redeemed her honour.[59]

In a most striking way, Christ is *put into play* here by the poet Gottfried, via his character Isolt, in the interest of doctored oaths, fraud, and games.[60] The outcome of the trial-by-ordeal involves both veracity and guile, and by rewarding both, it suggests that *truth* has shifted in the direction of the efficacy of the lovers' strategic moves and shown itself as something *made* by enterprising individuals in their own interest, rather than as something *other,* preexisting, unchanging, or essential in the scheme of things—such as a dualistic truth at odds with the lovers' machinations.

In different ways, but directed toward love as the same perishable end, Wolfram and Gottfried operate according to the indeterminate cultural

---

59. Gottfried von Strassburg, *Tristan* (Hatto), 248.
60. Nigel Harris offers a perceptive consideration of religion in Gottfried's romance in his "God, Religion, and Ambiguity."

parameters that we observed with Augustine earlier in this chapter. Religious and worldly resources are strictly separated and hierarchically arranged according to a dualist logic. The God that helps Feirefiz see the grail and receive his reward of love from the grail bearer is the One who must be recognized and accepted as superior and opposed to the many gods of polytheism. The God to whom Isolt swears her oath hands down His unquestioned Judgment from on high in the form of the lady's unburned flesh. At the same time, heavenly and worldly resources are so thoroughly interconnected as to be indistinguishable. Christian divinity pervades *all* cultural resources in these two episodes—as it is "bound to do"—sanctifying a fleshly (and, in the case of Isolt and Tristan, *adulterous*) love, making it holy. Judging by these two cases in the imaginary action of the courtly romances, a point in the cultural action seems to have been reached where the Christian self, having sufficiently integrated and concentrated its various capacities, is willing and able to put itself into play *again,* tapping in new and different ways into the dynamic potential of sameness and otherness that is in the speculative posture of faith. As Feirefiz and Isolt show us, striking new moves at court involve the speculation that Christians will experience growth and joy by investing themselves absolutely in the perishable cultural resources of this world. These investments of self might seem to us somewhat like Augustine's view of the evil will as a "turn" away from God to lower things, but the *players* at courts of nobility in the High Middle Ages seem to be confident that they will be agile enough to avoid stumbling and keep themselves on course—and that their new moves will pay off in the end.

CHAPTER 3

Rules of the House

COURTLY REPRESENTATION AS ARISTOCRATIC COMPETITION

The medieval risk-reward society is situated at the courts of competing households of nobility, where the action unfolds according to the global parameters elucidated in the previous chapters and where the tone is set at the highest political levels for new cultural moves. In the consideration of medieval courtly culture presented in this chapter, I align my view of culture as competitive action with Jürgen Habermas's understanding of the public domain in the Middle Ages as one of representation—a *repräsentative Öffentlichkeit* or "representational public"—to which no private domain is as yet juxtaposed.[1] I assume there is no domain or aspect of courtly culture—such as a private or autonomous sphere or self—that can be cordoned off from the representational cultural action of courtliness,[2] because this action needs to be

---

1. See Habermas, *Strukturwandel der Öffentlichkeit*, 17–25. One of the principal characteristics of medieval representation, distinguishing it for Habermas from both antiquity and modernity, is the lack of a rigorous distinction between public and private spheres.

2. Also belonging to this action is the material infrastructure of the unfolding of imperial representation: cathedrals, great halls, etc. See, for example, Niehr, "Herrscherliche Architektur."

understood in an imperial Christian sense, *and as competition*. I differ from a tendency in the critical literature on courtly culture to place emphasis on something apart from, outside of, or opposed to the court as constituted via representation.³ In my view, nothing is exempt from the *all-inclusive "public"* in which courtly representation unfolds *as action* and in which things become real and receive their true values for medieval courtiers. Representation is the definitive game at medieval courts, and it affects cultural trends generally, even for those excluded from direct access to it.⁴ What I call the "Rules of the House" become manifest as the best cultural *players—best* in the sense of the Greek αριϛτος (best) and the Latin *princeps* (first)⁵—set the tone for the cultural action by establishing and maintaining their ascendency *competitively*. Events of different kinds at court—for example, coronations, weddings, festivals, tournaments, and literary performances, as well as effective military leadership—involve standards that princely competitors need to be seen to achieve or surpass. By successfully embodying an absolute, divine authority in the competitive action of representation, princes demonstrate and reinforce

---

3. An example of this critical tendency, to which I also turn in other contexts, is Bumke's *Courtly Culture*. Bumke considers that the brutality of everyday medieval life, particularly that of incessant feuds and warfare, shows the cultural action associated with festivals, tournaments, and literary performances at court to be unrealistic and, in the latter case, fictional in the sense of unreal or untrue. For Bumke, *reality itself* is at odds with courtly culture. Though my view of them is different, I am grateful to Bumke for the wealth of primary sources his *Courtly Culture* makes available. Horst Wenzel, in his *Höfische Repräsentation*, considers courtly culture to be qualified if not criticized by secret, quasiprivate, more strictly individual moments, subsumed by the Middle High German term *heinliche*, which seem to go in the direction of a kind of privacy, if not private sphere.

4. Though the results of courtly representation may be of consequence throughout society, the direct participation of non-nobles in it is generally precluded. The courtly sources show that non-noble people endeavoring to engage in the courtly chivalric action typically appear ridiculous and tend to end badly (in the "summer songs" of the poet Neidhart, peasant-like characters make a rare appearance in court literature, but in a way that can be read as a satire of the courtly love tradition; by contrast, *der guote Gêrhart* of the poet Rudolf von Ems is the story of a merchant who seems to have the wherewithal to fare well in courtly surroundings). See also Bumke, who observes that courts exclude "villains" (*Courtly Culture*, 58). The "Rules of the House" tend to exclude peasants and burghers from the action at court, though the latter to a somewhat lesser degree according to their relatively greater command of cultural resources. With few exceptions, courtly representation is mostly a *closed game of nobility*, because of the resources required to participate at this level of the cultural action. Contests in and among courts thus involve a narrow spectrum of *elite* cultural players of nobility.

5. *Principes* is a group that becomes ever larger in the Middle Ages. In antiquity the title *princeps* was exclusively reserved for Augustus and subsequent Roman emperors, while in the Middle Ages, it becomes more broadly available. See Ehlers, "Die Reichsfürsten," 199–209; especially 199.

their own power and joyfully benefit and enrich all those with a stake in it.[6] I focus below on some of the principal features of medieval courtliness as the dynamic, competitive unfolding of the representational culture of noble households. In the final part of this chapter, a brief diachronic view is offered of the political action of medieval popes, emperors, and rival princes, particularly of the increasingly intense and complex competitions from the late eleventh to the early thirteenth century, in which my focus will be on innovative new cultural moves with global implications.

A sacrosanct status adheres to medieval emperors, kings, and princes.[7] As the foremost of a select group of rival peers of nobility, emperors are positioned to achieve via representation the best possible embodiment of divine authority that can be achieved in this temporal, mutable world. It is as if emperors were most perfectly aligned with the *otherness* of the heavenly kingdom that we observed in the previous chapter.[8] Augustine points the way for rulers when he writes in his *City of God* that those emperors are truly happy who successfully transfer to this temporal life the guiding principles of the heavenly kingdom:

> Sed felices eos dicimus, si iuste imperant, si inter linguas sublimiter honorantium et obsequia nimis humiliter salutantium non extolluntur, et se homines esse meminerunt; si suam potestatem ad Dei cultum maxime dilatandum maiestati eius famulam faciunt; si Deum timent diligunt colunt;

---

6. The early thirteenth-century advice Thomasin von Zirclaria gives to *herren* (which can be rendered as "lords" or as "noblemen") provides contemporary corroboration for the quasi-divine ascendancy of which I speak: *Nu wil ich râtn den herren allen / daz siz lieht nien lâzen vallen, / wan si suln uns liuhten vor, / uns si uns bringent vür daz tor / dâ immer sunne schîn: / si mugen gern dâ inne sîn* (*Der Welsche Gast*, [Rückert], vv.8241–46)—"Now I propose to advise all the noblemen not to drop the lantern, for they should show the way ahead for us until they bring us to the gate where is always sunshine. They would very much like to be inside" (Thomasin von Zirclaria, *Der Welsche Gast [The Italian Guest]* [Gibbs and McConnell], 152).

7. See Friedrich Heer's observations on sacral kingship in the context of his discussion of Charlemagne, which seem relevant here: "In Europe, as in all ages whenever sacral royal power has developed [...], monarchy has its roots in archaic, magical depths. At bottom, the king is a magus (the kings of ancient Egypt wear an imitation lion's tail, like the master magicians in prehistoric cliff and cave drawings). He is a 'god' on earth, high priest (like Melchizedek). He bears the power and attributes of divinity, of priests, of magicians" (*Holy Roman Empire*, 15).

8. Benjamin Arnold puts things in these terms: "Ideologically, the empire was the terrestrial manifestation of a lordly hierarchy encompassing heaven and earth, from the Holy Trinity which was its protector, and in whose name the imperial letters were therefore issued from the chancery, through the saints who were the patrons and legal owners of the cathedral and monastic churches and their lands, to the emperor and pope as temporal and spiritual heads of the Christian Church and the Roman Empire" (*German Knighthood*, 9–10).

si plus amant illud regnum, ubi non timent habere consortes; si tardius uindicant, facile ignoscunt; si eandem uindictam pro necessitate regendae tuendaeque rei publicae, non pro saturandis inimicitiarum odiis exerunt; si eandem ueniam non ad impunitatem iniquitatis, sed ad spem correctionis indulgent; si, quod aspere coguntur plerumque decernere, misericordiae lenitate et beneficiorum largitate compensant.[9]

We call those Christian emperors happy who govern with justice, who are not puffed up by the tongues of flatterers or the services of sycophants, but remember that they are men. We call them happy when they think of sovereignty as a ministry of God and use it for the spread of true religion; when they fear and love and worship God; when they are in love with the kingdom in which they need fear no fellow sharers; when they are slow to punish, quick to forgive; when they punish, not out of private revenge, but only when forced by the order and security of the republic, and when they pardon, not to encourage impunity, but with the hope of reform; when they temper with mercy and generosity the inevitable harshness of their decrees.[10]

We see here that the Christian emperor's high political authority is to be an anticipation of God's authority in the heavenly kingdom, scaled to the virtual status of selves and things in this world. Accordingly, Augustine continues the passage above as follows: *Tales Christianos imperatores dicimus esse felices interim spe, postea re ipsa futuros, cum id quod expectamus aduenerit*—"We say of such Christian emperors that they are, in this life, happy in their hope, but destined to be happy in reality when that day shall come for which we live in hope." Implicit in this final line from Augustine is that emperors, kings, and princes, however divine their associations and inspirations may be, also are mortal like everybody else. They are also subject to the indeterminate mutability and perishability of things in this temporal life. Kings form part of a hierarchical structure according to which court society and medieval society seem to be organized somewhat as pagan societies of antiquity had been, as the latter were observed in the first chapter of this study. One's position and *value* hinge on the greater or lesser resources at one's disposal. However, weighing against the hierarchical manner of appraising things and immediately evaluating *more as better*—which is perhaps nowhere more tangible than in the sacrosanct status of emperors and kings—is the *sinful sameness* of the

---

9. Augustine, *Avrelii Avgvstini Opera, De Civitate Dei Libri I–X*. Book, chapter, and page numbers are referenced in the notes; here, Book 24, chapter V, 160.
10. Idem, *City of God, Books I–VIII*, 296–97.

human condition, which results in a more indeterminate cultural action. The approach to things at courts of nobility tends to be *bullish* overall with regard to the value invested in perishable resources, as we shall see exemplified below in the sources, but the availability of dualist, leveling moves *in* the representational culture of courts—visible as poetic elaborations of Ecclesiastes 1:2, *Vanitas vanitatum omnia vanitas*, "Vanity of vanities, all is vanity"—enables courtiers at all levels to *hedge their bets*.[11]

Medieval emperors and princes actively *perform* courtly culture in representational events that reveal competition among imperial rivals, its critical assessment, and—"with the nod of a God who exchanges kingdoms"[12]—the outcomes that structure the cultural action among the highest potentates. One such event in which lords of noble households may be seen to excel is the festive procession, an example of which is provided by King Philip of Swabia and his wife, the Byzantine Princess Irene. The King and Queen engage themselves on Christmas Day 1199 in Magdeburg, and the action of the momentous occasion—which underscores the above-discussed sacrosanct status of the imperial dignity—is recorded by the poet Walther von der Vogelweide in this way, step by imperial step:

> Ez gienc eines tages als unser hêrre wart geborn
> von einer maget dier im ze muoter hât erkorn
> ze megdeburc der künic philippes schône
> dâ gienc eins keisers bruoder und eins keisers kint
> in einer wât swie doch die namen drîge sint
> er truoc des rîches zepter. und die krône
> Er trat vil lîse im was niht gâch
> im sleich ein hôh geborniu küneginne nâch
> rôse âne dorn ein tûbe sunder gallen
> diu zuht was niener anderswâ
> die düringe und die sahsen dienten alsô dâ
> daz ez den wîsen müeste wol gevallen.

> There went forth once—it was the day our Lord was born / of a maid, the mother whom his choice alighted on—/ at Magdeburg, Philip the King in

---

11. The strongest criticisms of worldly elements and aspects of courtliness and courtly representation tend, not surprisingly, to come from more or less starkly dualist monastic, clerical, or ecclesiastical perspectives; see Bumke, *Courtly Culture*, 415–23; and Jaeger, *Origins of Courtliness*, 176–94. It is important to recognize that such criticisms of worldliness do not stand outside courtly representation, but represent alternative possibilities within it.

12. Otto, *Two Cities*, 370.

lordly splendor. / There walked a Kaiser's brother and a Kaiser's son / in one raiment, though the names are three upon this one. / He bore the Empire's crown and the Empire's scepter. / He strode in gentle cadence, he knew no haste; / and after him a high-born Queen serenely paced, / rose without thorn, dove without gall, in stately leisure. / Ceremony, grace, decorum never were elsewhere. / The Saxons and Thuringians wrought such service there, / it must have brought the wise ones all deep pleasure.[13]

Walther's gnomic poetry provides invaluable insights into the cultural action of the highest households of the imperial nobility in the late twelfth and early thirteenth century. This poem shows the procession of Philip and Irene, and the celebratory occasion of which it is a part, to be a closely scrutinized performance with a clearly physical, even quasi-athletic dimension. The emphasis placed on the pace and grace of movement renders the procession akin to a choreographed performance. The imperial insignia of crown and scepter borne by Philip manifest the political dimension of his authority, not only symbolically or abstractly but concretely and visibly in the solemn yet elegant bearing of them. The connection between political and religious authority is clear in the initial verses, in which Philip—as brother of an emperor, son of an emperor, and himself—is cast as a religious-political enactor of the Trinity. Queen Irene performs effectively in tandem with her husband with her serene and stately pace, also joining the political and the religious, and inspiring Walther's descriptive use of Marian tropes ("rose without thorn," "dove without gall"). Walther's poetic likening of Philip to the Trinity and of Irene to the Virgin reveals the fluid interconnection of political, religious, and poetic dimensions of medieval emperorship within the dynamic, *physical* accomplishment of emperorship as a representational performance.

In the final verse of this passage, Walther brings his poetic perspective into alignment with the assessment of the *wîsen*—"wise," which is connected to the immediately preceding verses extolling the high standard of service provided by the Thuringian and Saxon hosts. The procession is the key part of a broader festive occasion, the preparation of which is also subject to scrutiny and judgment. All those present, from the Emperor to servants and guests, make possible and participate in this representational action in their own way. If the transitional verse, *Diu zuht was niener anderswa*—"Ceremony, grace, decorum never were elsewhere," can be regarded structurally as an *apo koinu* connecting and applying both to the preceding verses and the following ones,

---

13. Walther von der Vogelweide, *Single-Stanza Lyrics*, 148–49. This edition includes Walther's lyrics and English translations on facing pages.

then Walther's status as a spokesperson for the wise judges is associated with the procession proper. Wise judges—Walther seems to be saying in solidarity with them—conclude that all aspects of this representational performance are of an appropriately high level, exceeding those of any such event elsewhere.

Critically comparing the different processions of potentates on different occasions, the judges mentioned by Walther effectively determine which ones most successfully manage to bring the mutable, variable things of this temporal life into their most joyful imperial Christian alignment. The manifest joy of a representational event such as this is the best indication of the optimal political management of the risky and potentially painful mutability of things. In the cited verses by Walther, one of the variant manuscripts has the word *vreude*—"joy," instead of *zuht*—"courtliness."[14] Either term aptly illustrates an important outcome of such an event, but the former more directly exemplifies what can be regarded as one of the main "Rules of the House." One can and should expect *joy* to mark the outcome of a successful, well-accomplished representational event. A Latin chronicle of the same procession judged by Walther confirms his positive assessment and underscores joy as the marker of this particular successful outcome:

> Omnesque qui aderant, quorum inconprehensibilis exstitit numerus, corde gaudentes, animis exultantes, manibus applaudentes, vocibus perstrepentes, opera vigilantes huic sollemnitati uniformiter arriserunt, ipsam per omnia debite devotionis tripudio peragentes.
>
> All those who were there in inconceivably large numbers, were joyous in their hearts and exulted in their souls, they applauded, cheered loudly, and were incessantly active; all found great pleasure in this celebration, which they attended to the end with devoted exultation.[15]

Joy is supposed to accompany effective political leadership in representational events, such as this procession. It helps to make religious and political authority in this mutable life real and tangible to medieval courtiers. While this temporal joy is an infinitesimal measure of the bliss God will bestow upon his elect in the afterlife, it seems to be sufficiently substantial to serve as a point of reference around which the representational cultural action of courts can be organized.

---

14. Ibid., 148.

15. By the author of the *Halberstädter Bischofschronik*, Latin text and English translation cited from Bumke, *Courtly Culture*, 611.

Elsewhere in Walther von der Vogelweide's gnomic poetry, we observe another of the important ways in which imperial performers need to ensure that their political engagements bring about what amounts to a joyous congruence of heavenly and worldly concerns. Emperors and princes are supposed to be bounteous, as God will be in the hereafter with his elect.[16] Largesse is viewed by contemporary judges as one of the expected features of effective leadership. Two poems directed by Walther to the same Philip of Swabia show the gifts of a ruler also to be an *investment* occurring in an imperial contest among rulers past and present, in which standards have been set and continue to be set. The following passage from the first of these poems shows that a shrewd emperor does well to emulate the approach of Alexander the Great, who was renowned in the Middle Ages for his gift-giving generosity. The ancient emperor's legendary largesse is viewed by Walther, and needs to be seen by Philip according to the following verses, as an investment that will yield an immense return, seemingly heavenly in its dimensions:

> nû hâst dû guot und êre.
> *daz ist* wol zweier künige hort
> die gib der milte beide
> Diu milte lônet sam diu sât
> diu wünneklîche wider gât
> dar nâch man si geworfen hât.
> wirf von dir milteklîche
> swelh künig der milte geben kann
> si gît im daz er nie gewan
> wie alexander sich versan
> der gap und gap *und* gap sim elliu rîche.

In your keeping now are wealth and honors, / treasure ample for two kings. / Give both to Generosity. / Her wage is like the seed cast down / that rises up in glory again / in what measure it was sown. / Then cast away with generous freedom! / To the king who gives her all he can / Generosity gives what he never won. / That Alexander, how wise that man! / He gave, and gave, and she gave him every kingdom.[17]

---

16. Richard Kaeuper sees largesse as an aspect of the "social dominance of knights," and as one of the means whereby knights endeavored to maintain a difference between themselves and the increasingly prosperous merchant classes as of the twelfth century (*Chivalry and Violence*, 193–98). Kaeuper's view of largesse in terms of competitions with a rival class is generally consistent with my approach to cultural action in terms of competitions.

17. Walther von der Vogelweide, *Single-Stanza Lyrics*, 152–53.

In a manner consistent with the triune description of him at the procession at Magdeburg, the emperor may be expected to be bounteous and shower his courtly elect with the blessings of his largesse. On the earthly, temporal plane, an important tone is being set for the medieval risk-reward society: the emperor may expect that resources thus bestowed are a *material* investment that will yield future returns far in excess of the initial outlay. In the second poem, the economics of largesse are phrased with more contemporary references:

> Philippes künic die nâhe spehenden zîhent dich
> dun sîst nicht dankes milte des bedunket mich
> wie dû dâ mite verliesest michels mêre
> dû möhtest gerner dankes geben tûsent pfunt
> danne drîzec tûsent âne danc dir ist niht kunt
> wie man mit gâbe erwirbet prîs und êre
> Denke an den milten salatîn
> der jach daz küniges hende dürkel solten sîn
> sô wurden si erforht und ouch geminnet
> gedenke an den künig von engellant
> wie tiure man den lôste dur sîne milten hant
> ein schade ist guot der zwêne frumen gewinnet.

> King Philip, close observers all complain of you: / it seems you do not gladly give; and I think, too, / you lose far more by acting in that manner. / Give a thousand pounds with pleasure: better so / than *thirty* thousand grudgingly. You do not know / how one, by giving, gains renown and honor. / Think of Saladin, poised to give. / It was he who said, the hands of a king should be a sieve: / then men would fear that hand, and men would love it. / Think of *him,* late of England, / ransomed—and at what cost—for his great, free-giving hand. / It is a handsome loss that brings a double profit.[18]

As in the previous passage, but this time employing models from recent history, Walther here shows that a certain standard has been set by princes—such as the famous Sultan Saladin and King Richard I of England ("Lionheart")—that Philip needs to try to match if not exceed. Walther's advice to Philip regarding largesse in the above-cited cases amounts to courtly *investment counseling.* It shows that the efficacy of an emperor's gifts qua investments is assessed competitively in relation to the level of performance of one's aristocratic peers, past and present.

---

18. Ibid., 150–51.

The maximum representational investment of medieval emperors, kings, and princes, outside of warfare and ransoms (such as that paid for Richard I of England, referenced above), is made to underwrite court festivals, in view of the lavish manner in which these are depicted. Festivals are seminal in courtly representation as they provide the most conspicuous stage for displays of largesse and often subsume other representational events of smaller dimensions (e.g., processions, tournaments, literary performances, etc.). The joy associated with court festivals is significant enough to make it a structural marker in the Arthurian romances, as we see in Chrétien de Troyes's detailed description of the festival in celebration of Erec and Enide's marriage, which marks the successful outcome of the first part of this romance:

> Quant la corz fu tote asanblee,
> N'ot menestrel an la contree
> Qui rien seüst de nul deduit
> Qui a la cort ne fussent tuit.
> An la sale mout grant joie ot.
> Chascuns servi de ce qu'il sot:
> Cil saut, cil tunbe, cil anchante,
> Li uns sifle, li autres chante,
> Cil flaüte, cil chalemele,
> Cil gigue, li autres vïele
> . . . .
> Li rois Artus ne fu pas chiches:
> Bien comanda as penetiers
> Et as queuz et aus botelliers
> Qu'il livrassent a grant planté,
> Chascun selonc sa volanté,
> Et pain et vin et veneison.
> Nus ne demanda livreison
> De rien nule, que que ce fust,
> Qu'a sa volanté ne l'eüst.
> Mout fu granz la joie el palés.[19]
> (1997–2029)

---

19. Chrétien de Troyes, *Érec et Énide* (Poiron). Poirion's edition includes both Old French editions and modern French translations of all of Chrétien's romances. Interestingly, in view of the parameters of my study, this edition endeavors to grasp the poet's narrative art, "dans son évolution et sa globalité" (lv). Numbers of Old French and Middle High German verses from the romances here and elsewhere are cited parenthetically in text.

When all the court was assembled, every minstrel in the land who knew any kind of entertainment was present. In the hall there was great merriment; each contributed what he could: one jumped, another tumbled, another performed magic, one told stories, another sang, one whistled, another played, this one the harp, that one the rote, this one the flute, that one the reed pipe, the fiddle or the Vielle [. . .] King Arthur was not parsimonious; he ordered the bakers, cooks, and wine-stewards to serve bread, wine, and game in great quantity to each person—as much as he wished. No one requested anything, whatever it might be, without receiving all he wanted. There was great joy in the palace.[20]

This passage and others like it in the later romances show court festivals to be investments in joy.[21] These verses also suggest the degree to which, in court festivals of the twelfth century, politics, poetry, and performance arts intermingle. The French poet's King Arthur, "not at all niggardly," achieves the standard of generosity that Walther von der Vogelweide admonishes Philip of Swabia to strive for. A couple of generations later, in the early years of the thirteenth century, the German poet Hartmann von Aue bases himself on the romances of Chrétien at the beginning of his own *Iwein* (ca. 1210) with a similar depiction of a festival at King Arthur's court. There has never been one like it before or since, Hartmann tells us in his prologue.[22] Never before or since has there ever been so many exemplary ladies and knights as there. Hartmann concludes his description of the Arthurian festival with the lament that the level of joy experienced by Arthur and his courtiers at that festive event can no longer be achieved in his own time. Hartmann here reiterates descriptions of court festivals that would have been familiar to knowledgeable members of his audiences from Chrétien's romances, but his performance of *Iwein* also occurs about a generation after another great festival that marks a singular moment in the cultural action of the twelfth century that would have been just as familiar.

On Pentecost of the year 1184, Emperor Frederick I ("Barbarossa") staged a three-day festival in Mainz to mark the occasion of the knighting of his two sons, the future Henry VI and Frederick, Duke of Swabia.[23] Contemporary

---

20. Chrétien de Troyes, *Erec and Enide* (Carroll), 62.
21. On the connection between joy and historical festivals, Bumke notes that the chronicler Rolandinus Patavinus characterizes a festival held in Treviso, north of Venice, as "a court feast of pleasure and joy" (*Courtly Culture,* 220).
22. Hartmann von Aue, *Iwein* (Benecke and Lachmann), vv. 1–58.
23. A detailed description of this three-day festival is provided by Bumke, *Courtly Culture,* 203–7; see also the essay of Josef Fleckenstein, "Friedrich Barbarossa."

witnesses record the number of guests from different countries and speaking different tongues to be in the tens of thousands and to include as many as seventy imperial princes. Accommodations, food, and gifts were distributed lavishly by Frederick, his sons, and other high princes. A *gyrus,* or war game, was played in which as many as twenty-thousand participate,[24] including Barbarossa himself, and the festival also included entertainment that would have resembled that described by Chrétien in the passage above. The festival as rendered poetically by Chrétien in the previously cited passage seems to be brought to life by Barbarossa in the political action at Mainz, as if the historical emperor has resolved he will not be outdone by the fictional King Arthur and his imaginary knights and ladies.[25] Taking part in the culturally productive convergence of politics and poetry in court festivals, the poet Heinrich von Veldeke—who was himself present at Barbarossa's festival and writes about midway between Chrétien and Hartmann—makes use of this historic festival in his description of the wedding festivities at the end of his Aeneid-romance (the *Eneit*), one of the medieval vernacular reiterations of Virgil's epic poem:

> ich enuernam uon hohzeiten
> in allen weilen maere,
> div als groz waere,
> alsam do het Eneas,
> wan div ze Meginze da was,
> die wir selbe sahen,
> dez manige ueriahen,
> daz si waere vnmaezleich,
> da der chaiser Fridereich
> gap zwein seinen sunen swert,
> da manich tausint marche wert
> verzeret wart vnd uergeben
> . . . .
> dem cheiser Fridereiche
> geschach so manich ere,
> daz man immer mere
> wunder da uon sagen mach
> vncz an den iungisten tach
> an lugene fur war.

---

24. Bumke, *Courtly Culture*, 205.

25. "Those who hosted the great feasts were often driven by the desire to outdo all previous feats through the most extravagant lavishness" (Ibid., 4).

es wirt noch uber hundert iar
von im gesaget vnd geschriben.[26]
(347.14–348.3)

I never knew of a celebration anywhere else that was as large as that held by Aeneas except the one at Mainz where Emperor Frederick knighted his sons. We don't need to ask about that for we saw it ourselves. It was matchless: goods worth many thousand marks were consumed or given away [. . .] It brought Emperor Frederick such honor that one could indeed keep saying more wondrous things about it until doomsday, without lying. Over a century from now they will still be telling and writing accounts of it.[27]

Heinrich appends this reference to Barbarossa's court festival to Aeneas's moment of ascendency in Italy, when the Trojan exile weds Lavinia after defeating his rival Turnus, which confers upon the imaginary event some of the residual joy that occurred at the Pentecost festival in Mainz. When Hartmann composes his *Iwein* decades later, the fame of Barbarossa's festival would long have formed part of the cultural associations and expectations connected to festivals as representational events. By the time Hartmann renders his imaginary Arthurian festival in the early thirteenth century, the levels achieved in the past by Chrétien's King Arthur in poetry and by Frederick I in politics are well-known standards that buttress Hartmann's lament about the diminished quality of the courtly culture in his own time but that also serve to inspire him and his audience to rise to a higher level.[28]

Frederick's court festival at Mainz shows this emperor to be an exemplary investor in joy more than a generation before Walther's advice to Philip of Swabia regarding standards of largesse. Contemporary judgments about the related action in political and poetic domains show us that it is incumbent on high medieval imperial performers to commit their considerable resources in a way that courtly joy will be achieved and political authority consolidated, if not expanded. We observe that the cultural action is continually about rising to or surpassing standards set by illustrious emperors, kings, and other rulers

---

26. Heinrich von Veldeke, *Eneasroman*.
27. Idem, *Eneit*, 150.
28. While Walter Haug's consideration of Hartmann's *Iwein*-prologue stresses the idea of the development of fiction as an "autonomus medium," which remains difficult to the degree that the idea of "autonomy" seems to disengage poetry from its courtly setting and thereby to be culturally premature, I agree with Haug's idea that Hartmann is interested in romance poetry as something dynamic and *in the present,* or what Haug elsewhere calls a "literary and intellectual process" (see *Vernacular Literary Theory,* 118–31, and especially 126).

of the distant or recent past, as well as of the present. To be sure, courtiers are quite aware that the joy realized by exemplary performances in representational events cannot be fixed and lasting in this mutable world. Criticisms of the efficacy of representational efforts at court, especially reiterations of monastic-dualist perspectives, are numerous and form part of courts' self-representation, for example in the well-worn phrase, *Liep âne leit mac niht gesîn*—"There can be no love without pain." The murder of Walther von der Vogelweide's imperial patron Philip of Swabia in 1208 is one of the many vicissitudes seemingly at odds with the joy achieved in representational events. But the availability and use of the monastic *contemptus mundi* theme by courtly poets indicates room is made *within* the representational action at court for a dualist evaluation of physical-material cultural resources as worthless, if not as a great liability. The alternative grace/sin provides a more appropriate criterion for the evaluation of events in medieval courtly culture than the (modern looking) alternative ideal/reality.[29] The allegorical figure of Dame World, a beautiful lady in front and maggot-infested carcass behind, strikingly brings home the dualist leveling evaluation of physical-material cultural resources. Medieval courtiers know well that the value of things can vary significantly from that accomplished and joyfully experienced in the conspicuous, pompous events of courtly representation, such as processions and festivals.

A broad view of courtly representation—which considers this not only as discrete representational events at court, but more generally as the successful incorporation, cultivation, and exhibition of imperial authority—needs to include potentates' very *public* engagements in the warfare and feuding that is endemic to medieval society. The joyful ordered harmony visible in festive representational events at court is not undone or disproven by military action, but rather is contingent on it. My final example of representational courtly culture, which provides a transition to the intermittently bellicose cultural action discussed in the next section of this chapter, is military commandership.[30] In the prologue of his *Deeds of Emperor Frederick I—Gesta Friderici imperatoris*—Otto of Freising views the ability to wage war as a necessary characteristic of imperial leadership and arranges this ability alongside the four Socratic virtues as a divinely inspired personal characteristic that sets Barbarossa apart from Roman emperors of the past:

---

29. Bumke builds the murder of Philip by Otto von Wittelsbach into his introductory oppositional juxtaposition of the romantic image of the Middle Ages, which developed in the nineteenth century, to what Bumke calls "medieval reality" (see *Courtly Culture*, 1–3).

30. With regard to the activities of emperors, Arnold writes: "Military commandership was their original business, and this did not change throughout the Middle Ages" (*German Knighthood*, 6).

Inter omnes enim Romanorum principes tibi pene soli hoc reservatum est privilegium, ut, quamvis a prima adolescentia bellicis desudasse cognoscaris officiis, obscenum tibi nondum vultum fortuna verterit. Sic etiam temperans in prosperis, fortis in adversis, iustus in iudiciis, prudens et acutus in causis esse cognosceris, ut non solum ex convictu haec tecum coaluisse, sed tamquam divinitus inspirata et a Deo tibi ob universale totius orbis emolumentum concessa fuisse videantur.[31]

Because for you almost alone, of all the princes of the Romans, has this privilege been reserved that, although you are known to have exerted yourself since early youth in the duties of war, not yet has Fortune turned upon you her malign aspect. You are known to be temperate in prosperity, brave in adversity, just in judgment, and prudent and shrewd in courts of law, not merely from daily habit but as though divinely inspired and granted you by God for the general advantage of the whole world.[32]

Otto's assessment of Barbarossa's successes in his various endeavors draws attention to the variety of skills involved in the superlative representation of imperial authority. This passage suggests that success in one endeavor is likely to be connected with success in others, that the prince who prevails in military contests on the battlefield will successfully embody authority in representational events at court (such as Barbarossa's involvement in the court festivals of Mainz that we observed above), and vice versa.[33]

In its medieval manifestation, the Roman empire continues to be a domain in which peace and order have to be maintained by the successful implementation of military force—and presumably *will* be a "divinely inspired ruler" (*tamquam divinitus inspirata*). The medieval Roman empire follows the one of antiquity with respect to the basically military status and function of the imperial office as generalship. The most illustrious early medieval emperors, Charlemagne and Otto I, respectively responsible for the revival of the Roman empire under the Franks in the ninth and tenth centuries and its more specifically German-Italian continuation under the Saxon emperors in the tenth

---

31. Otto, *Gesta Friderici Imperatoris*, page 11, lines 29–30.
32. Idem, *Deeds of Frederick Barbarossa*, 27.
33. In a letter to Otto written by Frederick in 1157, the emperor himself arranges his warlike activity alongside the pleasures of religious edification that he receives from reading in his uncle's *Chronicle of the Two Cities:* "After the sweat of war we ardently desire from time to time to delight ourselves therein and to be instructed in the virtues by the magnificent achievement of the emperors" (*Deeds of Frederick Barbarossa*, 17). Though the latter (religious edification) represents a welcome respite from the former (warfare), there is no reason to oppose the two activities. They need rather to be regarded as complementary.

and eleventh centuries, set the tone for the later medieval imperial action in important respects. Einhard's biography of Charlemagne shows this emperor's military engagements to have consisted largely of campaigns against rival peoples, many of them pagan: Bretons, Hungarians, Lombards, Saxons, and others. Widukind, chronicler of the Saxons in the eleventh century, connects military success with the imperial dignity more directly in reporting that Otto I's army proclaimed him, *pater patriae, rerum dominus imperatorque*—"father of the fatherland, lord of the world and emperor"—after a victory over the pagan Hungarians in 933.[34]

In these earlier medieval cases, political and religious efforts coincide in the military performances of emperors. This also remains the case later on, though the cultural action of *principes* becomes more complicated from the late eleventh century onward, as the increasingly intense ideological and military competitions among emperors and popes overlap with the emperors' ongoing military struggles for ascendancy over noble rivals.[35] During this entire period, the ability of emperors and princes to wage war as no one else tends to place them in the most advantageous positions with respect to the overall disposition of cultural resources. The successes of Henry IV against Gregory VII in the late eleventh century and those of Frederick I against his various papal adversaries in the twelfth century are largely based on emperors' possession and implementation of military resources that their papal and lay rivals do not possess—part of the same general store of resources that is also invested in festivals, tournaments, and literary performances. In the following section, I focus more closely on the increasingly complex religious-political contests occurring at the highest political levels among popes and emperors, with particular focus on innovative global moves made from the late eleventh to the early thirteenth century.

INVESTITURES: A DIACHRONIC VIEW OF THE POLITICAL ACTION

In this section, I understand the term *investiture* not just in the narrower medieval sense as the ceremonial investment of another imperial official such as a bishop with the insignia of office but also in a broader sense as *investments* of authority in the highest imperial Christian officers in the Holy Roman Empire by the holders of those offices themselves and their supporters.

---

34. See Schieffer, "Konzepte des Kaisertums," 49.
35. See also the historical overview presented by Michael Frasetto, "History of Emperors."

During the time of Charlemagne and the Carolingian revival of the Roman empire, the stage is first set for the relative status of heavenly and worldly cultural resources, and the concomitant investitures of authority over these resources, to become a contentious issue in later centuries. When Pope Leo III takes his initiative and places a crown on Charlemagne's head on Christmas day in Rome in 800, investing him with imperial authority as *Imperator Romanorum*—"Emperor of the Romans"—he makes a move that introduces a new consideration into politics at the highest level: from whom other than the pope might an emperor henceforth expect to receive his status as such? Whatever Leo's precise intentions may have been, the possibility that popes make emperors becomes tangible, with all its attendant implications regarding the status and alignment of cultural resources in the empire.[36] For many centuries, until about the mid-eleventh century, the papacy shows little inclination or capacity to take advantage of Leo's initiative in order to shape outcomes in the religious-political arena. Emperors tend to dominate in their interactions with popes, and by virtue of the imperial dignity they are also set above their aristocratic peers and competitors.

The ascendancy of emperors eventually begins to depend on *investitures* in the narrower and better-known sense of the word, that is, on emperors' ability to elect imperial bishops and invest them with the insignia of their office. As the imperial church takes shape in the tenth and eleventh centuries, bishops are the supreme spiritual shepherds of their flocks, sovereign lords over archbishoprics as temporal political domains, and invariably beholden in a personal way to the emperor who selected them. In the previous chapter, we saw that Otto, Bishop of Freising, specifically addresses and justifies this overlap of spiritual and temporal authorities in his *Chronica de duabis civitatibus—Chronicle of Two Cities*—which was patently modeled on Augustine's *City of God*. By means of their selection of imperial bishops, emperors effectively put on display the high religious-temporal authority of their office that empowers them to make such investitures. Also, by means of the loyal imperial bishops, emperors place themselves in an advantageous position vis-à-vis their rival noble peers who, though nominally subservient according to the official electoral rules of the imperial power game, show themselves continually as competitors interested in maintaining and expanding the resources of their own households and occasionally in making plays for the imperial dignity itself. The competitions begin to become especially keen and complex in the latter eleventh century, during which time popes begin to question the ascendancy

---

36. Some of the possible reasons behind Leo's coronation of Charlemagne are addressed in Joseph Dahmus, *Seven Medieval Kings*, 112–13.

of emperors that had long been in place and insist on their own very different assessment of the status of cultural goods in the Holy Roman Empire.

Among the more competitive and influential popes in the High Middle Ages are Gregory VII in the latter eleventh and Innocent III in the early thirteenth centuries. In competition with his main imperial rival, Henry IV, Gregory reiterates, varies, and expands the move of his papal predecessor Leo III centuries earlier in claiming for the papacy the right to invest the imperial dignity in kings and also the right to depose kings and release their vassals from their vows of fealty in the event a king is deemed not "suitable." I. S. Robinson writes: "The king must be 'suitable' (*idoneus*) for the duties prescribed by the Church. He must be 'obedient, humbly devoted and useful to holy Church'; he must serve the pope as his feudal lord."[37] Somewhat paradoxically, the way to this ambitious papal move has also been prepared by the efforts of earlier emperors such as Henry III and his predecessors to reform the Church by rooting out abuses pertaining to simony and celibacy.[38] These earlier reformer-emperors contributed to a reformed, spiritualized, and energized Church that now in turn begins to censure the involvement even of emperors in religious matters. The reform of the Church carried out by Gregorius that comes to bear his name includes, but eventually goes far beyond, his assertion that clerical offices cannot be conferred by a layperson, which results in the famous "contest" concerning the emperor's investiture of imperial archbishops. A full appreciation of the implications of the reforms initiated by Gregory and carried out intermittently by his papal successors involves understanding *ecclesia* in a universal, religious-political sense, consistent with the bipartite global parameters of imperial Christianity as articulated by Augustine. However, we observe with Gregory that the tables have been turned on the emperors, and the papacy is now supposed to be playing the leading role.[39] In a letter to Henry dated September 8, 1075, Gregory admonishes the king to "recognize the empire of Christ above you" and informs him that the imperial coronation will take place only if Henry promises to obey the apostolic see.[40] The Gregorian reform movement thus arranges the medieval equivalents of Augustine's religious city of the Christian *ecclesia*—"elect"—and the fallen temporal city of the flesh *hierarchically* so that the popes—as recognized sovereigns over the

---

37. Robinson, *Papacy*, 441.
38. See Frasetto, *History of Emperors*, 10–11.
39. "Gregory's vision of politics—the king of the Germans as the vassal of the pope—would continue (albeit intermittently) to influence the curia's view of the relations of empire and papacy throughout the Middle Ages" (Robinson, *Papacy*, 411).
40. Ibid., 402. Gregory made the imperial coronation contingent on Henry making this concession.

superior, religious domain—possess supreme power. In effect, a pope's dualist postulation of the inherent superiority of the spiritual *otherness,* of which he claims to be the chief representative, is pitted against the emperor, though the pope is clearly making a play for cultural resources *across the board.* Henry is threatened by Gregory's move with a vast diminishment, including the imperial and royal dignities themselves, the loyalty of the noble vassals above whom he is placed by virtue of these dignities, and the cultural resources of which emperors traditionally disposed by way of their designation and investment of archbishops.[41]

Henry counters by insisting emperors are made directly by God and by endeavoring to depose Gregory and *invest* in a more cooperative antipope, employing to his advantage the military resources available to him. Rivals of Henry observe the ongoing contest closely, formulate strategies to better their own positions, and put forward antikings to advance their interests. Loosened from their oaths of fealty to Henry after his excommunication by Gregory, the rival princes plan a diet in Augsburg in early 1077 to discuss deposing Henry. Gregory is on his way to preside over this diet on the invitation of the princes when he is intercepted by Henry at Canossa in late January 1077. Standing in a hair coat and barefoot in the snow outside the castle, in the posture of the penitent, Henry makes a political play that resonates through the centuries and results in the popular German expression "Gang nach Canossa."[42] Foregoing for a while the military approach he has used earlier and will use later in his contests with the papacy, Henry forces Gregory's hand in a different way, effectively using the rules of the *ecclesia* against his papal rival. Henry's conspicuous act of penitence compels Gregory—as it evidently must—to *forgive* him his sins and restore him to communion and the community of God's elect. The emperor's room for action is thereby temporarily increased, though the competition remains ongoing and he will eventually be excommunicated again. Henry's tactical victory at Canossa preempts the move of rival princes against him, but it might be regarded as a strategic mistake over the longer term, for his penance signals acquiescence to the Gregory's postulation of papal supremacy.[43]

---

41. Disengaging the princes from their obligation to be loyal to the king was an original cultural play on the part of Gregory. Robinson notes, "It was unprecedented for a pope to use the power of binding and loosing to depose a king and absolve his vassals from their fealty to him" (Ibid., 403).

42. The expression "Gang nach Canossa" can be still be applied today as a description of *any* endeavor to acquire forgiveness that is experienced as uncomfortable and humbling.

43. See Robinson, *Papacy,* 407.

Gregory VII and Henry IV open up new possibilities in the ongoing contests between emperors, popes, and princes that continue into the twelfth and thirteenth centuries. For a long time, the competition is less keen, owing largely to the strong starting position of the Hohenstaufen emperor Frederick I ("Barbarossa"), and to the papacy's willingness to back away from the "hierocratic" Gregorian position of papal ascendancy. Popes instead begin to adopt a "Gelasian" position according to which religious and worldly domains and their corresponding cultural resources are to be assessed as "separate, but equal."[44] The plays for power made by Gregory nevertheless remain available and are employed again in the early thirteenth century by Innocent III, following the sudden death of Barbarossa's son Henry VI. During the minority of Henry's son Frederick (the future Frederick II), Innocent exploits the imperial power vacuum and reasserts for the papacy and himself the role of kingmaker in the rivalry between Philip of Swabia—the prince advised by Walther von der Vogelweide in the passages cited earlier in this chapter—and Otto of Brunswick.[45] As a poetic performer in different imperial households at different times, it is perhaps not surprising Walther considers that God alone makes kings.[46] In the verses below, Walther bitterly renders Innocent's endeavor to play kingmaker in imperial affairs—based on the hierocratic postulation of the superiority of the religious over the worldly domain—as a *power play*, pure and simple:

> Ahî wie kristenlîche nû der bâbest lachet
> swanne er sînen walhen seit ich hanz alsô gemachet
> daz er dâ seit des solt er niemer hân gedâht
> er gihet ich hân zwêne allamân under eine krône brâht
> Daz siz riche stoeren *unde brennen* unde wasten
> ie dar under *w*üelen in ir kasten
> ich hân si an mînen stok gemennet, ir guot ist allez mîn
> ir tiuschez silber vert in mînen *w*elschen schrîn
> ir pfaffen ezzent hüenr und trinkent wîn
> und lânt die tiutschen vasten.

---

44. See Ibid., 480–82. The Concordat of Worms in 1122—a compromise between imperial and Gregorian positions regarding the investiture of bishops and abbots—also had a temporarily calming effect.

45. In 1198, there is a situation that favors a comeback of the Gregorian idea: Henry VI dies suddenly, and Frederick II, as a minor, becomes ward of the pope as his feudal lord: "Now at last it was practicable to speak of the pope's 'investing' the emperor with the empire; to attribute to the pope the right to depose a monarch and to choose his successor according to the principle of suitability' (*idoneitas*)" (Robinson, *Papacy*, 522).

46. Walther begins one of his gnomes with the pronouncement, *Got gît ze künige swen er wil*—"God gives to whom He will the kingdom of men" (*Single-Stanza Lyrics*, 166–67).

Oh how the Pope laughs now, so like a Christian, / as he tells his Italians, "I've got it all arranged, Listen!" / The things he says down there he never even should have thought. / "Two tedeschi beneath one crown," he says: "that's what I have wrought. / Let them lay waste the Empire, burn it, bring it under—/ we rummage in their chests while all that's going on there. / I've goaded them to my big pole there, all their goods are mine, / their German silver emigrates to my Italian shrine. / Eat chicken, churchmen—all you priests, drink wine, / and let the Germans fast up yonder."[47]

With their German resentment toward Rome, these verses regarding the "waste" of imperial resources caused by the pope anticipate moves Martin Luther will make centuries later.[48] However, the resource-saving disengagement of Christians as individuals from the (wasteful) imperial Church is not yet available as a move in the cultural action, as it will have become by Luther's time. According to the prevailing cultural parameters, Innocent's move for cultural resources, here excoriated by Walther, is a necessarily imperial and religious one with global implications.[49] No imperial competitor in the early thirteenth century action is in a position to match Innocent's resources, and the papacy nears the apogee of its ascendancy. But it does so by putting into play a new scenario, as Hauck observes: "The highest bishop of the church was the absolute ruler in secular affairs. But, at the same time, the transformation of the papacy to a primarily secular power was accomplished."[50]

What goes around comes around. The papacy will have only intermittent success as a secular player in the cultural action over the longer term. The worldly resources to which Innocent lays claim for his imperial *ecclesia* will seldom provide the papacy with adequate military means to compete effectively with emperors and kings. Eventually, these resources will be considered—for example, from the Lutheran perspective centuries later—to have thoroughly sullied and corrupted the papacy and Rome. The moves of Luther and others, which later will effectively *invest* the (subjective) individual with an absolute religious authority and disengage it from the imperial Christianity of the Middle Ages, are not yet available in the time of Walther, but popes such as Gregory VII and Innocent III are preparing the way for them.

---

47. Ibid., 174–75.
48. I will look at some of these moves in the final chapter of this study.
49. Albert Hauck observes in his pointedly titled article, "Innocent III Desired to Rule the World," "To Innocent, the essence of papal power was in the union of the priestly and the imperial dignity. In conformity with its origins and purpose, the imperial power belonged to the pope" (16).
50. Ibid., 16–17.

In making their *global* move for ascendancy by arguing for the contiguous alignment of spiritual-intellectual and physical-material cultural resources, with the former above the latter, these popes strengthen the tendency to assess cultural resources as universally integrated or articulated. As a consequence, *potentially,* the global play made for worldly resources by representatives of the spiritual ones (on the basis of the supposed superiority of the latter) might be reiterated, varied, and employed for different purposes. At culturally bullish courts, poets might be seen to vary the global plays of popes and emperors when they sanctify physical-material resources by investing them with absolute value.[51] Innocent III and other imperial performers in the High Middle Ages jointly shape a dynamic stage of the European cultural action in which new global plays manifestly made in the interest of perishable goods become increasingly prominent and consequential.[52] The poetic action on which I focus in the next chapter contributes in its own conspicuous ways to this cultural trend that will have longer-term consequences. Much later, when the individual Christian self is definitively set loose from the imperial Christian church in the early Reformation, this will occur as a *global move par excellence* by means of which the individual becomes a *kingdom* unto itself.

---

51. This may happen most pointedly in Gottfried von Strassburg's romance of Tristan and Isolt, with its rendering of an adulterous love of the flesh as a quasireligious *summum bonum.*

52. Also contributing to the mentioned dynamism of the European cultural action during this time is the reception and processing of hitherto unknown works by Aristotle and the gradual rise of universities, which impart their own distinctively intellectual momentum to the assessment of perishable goods. See, for example, Richard E. Rubenstein's *Aristotle's Children.*

CHAPTER 4

The Poetic Action

WARS, TOURNAMENTS, VERSES: THE PLACE OF POETRY AT COURT

Manuscript illuminations such as those preserved in the Codex Manesse suggest poetry needs to be viewed as analogous to other kinds of competitive cultural action in and among noble households, and not as the discrete or *autonomous* object of investigation as it is treated by some scholars.[1] The illumination of the poet-performer Gottfried von Strassburg renders him in action in the midst of spectators who observe him with indications of joyful interest that shine through the medieval conventions of pictorial representation.[2] Gottfried's effort is arrayed in the codex alongside illuminations of other

---

1. For example, see Haug, *Vernacular Literary Theory*, which discusses court poetry in terms of literary autonomy.
2. The Library of the University of Heidelberg has made the Manesse Codex illuminations available online at http://digi.ub.uni-heidelberg.de/diglit/cpg848?&ui_lang=eng (accessed July 1, 2015). The illumination of Gottfried von Strassburg is 364r. Gottfried holds a diptych, likely a reference to his learned status (*Codex Manesse*, 246). While it is difficult to know if the performance depicted in the illumination is a poetic one—the visual organization of the male figures in this illustration also suggests an academic disputation—it is situated among many other illuminations depicting representational events at court, including the composition and

79

kinds of performances that are of value for courts, such as tournaments and warfare. The action depicted in the codex illuminations frequently includes onlookers, whose close attention to the various performances suggests the importance of their ongoing assessment. The view of poets' performances as analogous to competitive performances in tournaments and on the battlefield is more than a product of the imagination of patrician burghers in Zurich, who produced the Codex Manesse around 1300 and are looking back to the flourishing of courtly culture in the late twelfth and early thirteenth centuries. The Manesse illuminations, as well as historical and poetic sources such as those documenting the court festival of Frederick I in Mainz in 1184,[3] suggest that the courtly poets' performances need to be viewed not only according to their own specific poetic characteristics—as these become particularly evident in prologues, narrative excurses, and epilogues[4]—but also according to characteristics they share with other kinds of competitive performances that are involved in the representational culture of medieval courts.

In the poetic action to be examined in this chapter, we observe medieval poet-performers with an increasing diversity of characteristics, interests, and strategies, engaging themselves competitively with pagan and Christian writers of antiquity. The medieval performers show themselves to be aware that the poetic action has been shaped by illustrious great poets of the past but also that they can and should be expected to hold their own. They are cognizant that their own efforts will be closely scrutinized and that they will have to show themselves up to the task. The manner of their engagements tends to combine respect for the luminaries of the past with a very tangible sense of the need to rise at least to a comparable level. The competitive dynamics visible diachronically in the engagement of medieval poets with those of antiquity and the earlier Middle Ages also characterizes contests among medieval poets synchronically. Here, too, one finds poet-performers lauding great contemporaries, even as they engage in the poetic action in ways that suggest they will try to do as well or better.

The poetic competitions occur in ways that are consistent with the global parameters of cultural action as elaborated in the writings of St. Augustine.

---

performance of poetry (Ibid., xviii). The context provided by the Codex, which contains lyric poetry besides the many illuminations of the poets themselves, seems to invite a reading of the illustration of Gottfried in particular as a representational performance, even if this is rendered with visual conventions drawing attention to learnedness. Interestingly, a similar visual organization of figures is employed in the illumination of Klingsor von Ungarland (219v), which depicts the competition of singers at the Wartburg castle and therefore much more clearly references a poetic performance (Ibid., 246).

3. See Fleckenstein, "Friedrich Barbarossa."
4. See Haug's introductory remarks, *Vernacular Literary Theory*, 1–6.

FIGURE 1. The poet Gottfried in Action—Cod. Pal. germ. 848, Große Heidelberger Liederhandschrift (Codex Manesse), 364r. Used with permission of the Universitätsbibliothek Heidelberg.

We have seen that Augustine places many of the educational structures, as well as much of the poetic and literary action associated with pagan Rome, in the service of Christianity. This occurs as an outgrowth or elaboration of Augustine's global conception of Christianity in terms of *sameness* that endeavors to account for everything possible as serving a higher, heavenly purpose, as belonging in some sense to God's providential master plan.[5] Augustine consequently makes room in his bipartite conception of the Christian life for pagan things with an originally non-Christian function to assume a Christian value, thereby culturally clearing the way for refitting *lower* things with *higher* purposes.[6] In the medieval poetic action, the indeterminate relationship between high and low things as shaped by Augustine leaves room for the articulation of literary, Latin-based narrative traditions and the *high* things associated with them, with orally transmitted, vernacular, performance-based modes of poetic presentation and their correspondingly *lower* concerns. Isolated endeavors to involve vernacular (oral) narrative traditions in the literary poetic action occur already in Carolingian times, as we shall see, but their continuous involvement in the literary poetic action of Europe begins first with the flourishing of vernacular poetry in the twelfth century.

At noble courts in the High Middle Ages, with their basically military orientation and interests, the involvement of the vernacular languages in the literary poetic action enables the literary emergence of Celtic and Germanic heroic narrative materials, such as those about Arthur, Siegfried, Brunhilt, and the Nibelungs, that had originally relied for their transmission on oral preservation and presentation. As the *lower*—because originally non-Christian, vernacular, and orally transmitted narrative materials come into play in the literary poetic action at the courts of noble households, the indeterminacy of the action and concomitant potential for innovative moves increases. For example, the pagan Roman heroic narrative material preserved in the Latin-based culture of Christianity—such as Virgil's *Aeneid*—can appear alongside the literary newcomers in new ways. Virgil's epic poem, which gives tribute to the greatness of Rome in the time of the "divine" Augustus becomes, in Heinrich von Veldeke's vernacular romance reiteration of it, a vehicle for the praise of the medieval Rome of emperor as well as *divus* Frederick Barbarossa and his imperial

---

5. In the latter part of the second book of his *On Christian Doctrine*, Augustine surveys much of pagan Roman culture and undertakes what might be regarded as a kind of *salvaging operation*, declaring many things to be consistent with Christian belief and rejecting other things as evil (53–78).

6. An important example of such refitting is Augustine's Christian appropriation of the art of rhetoric in the fourth book of *On Christian Doctrine* (117–69).

chivalric host,[7] whom medieval audiences would have been as likely to associate with (the originally vernacular and orally transmitted accounts of) King Arthur and his courtiers as with anything *Roman* in the stricter sense. Perhaps the most significant new move in the poetic action at courts is romance narrative with its principal concerns of adventure and love, which manifest new global dispositions of self that we will observe in detail in the subsequent chapters. In the twelfth century, with epics, romances, and songs of love, court poets emerge as competitors in the literary poetic action alongside the authors and scribes of monasteries and cathedral schools. Their commandeering of vernacular languages and narrative traditions in the literary poetic action deserves to be regarded as a cultural *game changer,* which sets a new course for literary and cultural developments in Europe in the coming centuries.[8]

Thus, the competitive engagements of court poets and audiences' assessments of these engagements are dynamically situated at medieval courts of nobility between *high* and *low* things; Latin and the vernacular languages; literary and oral modes of presentation and reception; the grace bestowed by God from on high and the honor won by courtiers for their chivalric efforts in the world; divine love and the fleshly love of a lady or knight. The poetic action at courts unfolds, as well, between the timeless, unchanging truth of an "epic past" (i.e., the biblical one) and the mutability of the open-ended present.[9] The valuation of things in poetry becomes correspondingly more fluid

---

7. I discussed Heinrich's homage to Frederick Barbarossa's court festival in Mainz in the previous chapter. In the introduction of his translation of *The Deeds of Frederick Barbarossa,* Mierow notes that the term *divus,* the ancient designation for the divinity of the original Caesars, is used in references to Frederick both by his biographer Rahewin and by the emperor himself, and Mierow explains his translation of this term: "There is some question regarding the meaning of *divus* as used by a writer of the twelfth century. But it has been rendered, quite literally, 'divine' in the thought that this best reflects the growing sense of the sacrosanct character of the person of the emperor" (13).

8. See also the remarks with which Sarah Kay begins her study *Courtly Contradictions*: "The apparently irresistible advance of courtly literature [. . .] is an elite movement, firmly invested in the social and moral gulf defining the refined (*courtois*) from their antithesis (the *vilain*); but the lure of exclusivity seems to have ensured that the class of the self-styled *courtois* would ineluctably expand, so that courtliness spilled out further and further from the small local courts that first fostered it and eventually merged with the broad stream of Western culture" (1).

9. See Bakhtin, "Epic and Novel." It seems valid to suggest that the moments of Resurrection and Crucifixion seem, to some degree, to constitute an "absolute past" or a "valorized temporal category" for the Middle Ages that would be consistent with Bakhtin's understanding of the term "epic past" as used in the cited chapter (15 and passim). Romance poetry would move things in the direction of what Bakhtin calls the "inconclusive present" (27), which the novel as modern artistic form will apprehend most capably. In this study, I suggest that Christianity, for all the *absoluteness* of its past, nevertheless *also* pervades time in a way that provides an avenue for eventually experiencing the present as something "inconclusive."

and has to be sorted out in the ongoing competitive action within these widened and increasingly indeterminate parameters. The German poet Wolfram von Eschenbach tells us something along these lines with the verses of his *Parzival*-prologue,[10] which apply as well to the increasingly indeterminate parameters of the poetic action generally as they do to the proper assessment of this particular romance:

> ouch erkante ich nie sô wîsen man,
> ern möhte gerne künde hân,
> welher stiure disiu maere gernt
> und waz sî guoter lêre wernt.
> dar an si nimmer des verzagent,
> beidiu si vliehent unde jagent,
> si entwîchent unde kêrent,
> si lasternt unde êrent.
> swer mit disen schanzen allen kan,
> an dem hât witze wol getân,
> der sich niht versitzet noch vergêt
> und sich anders wôl verstêt.[11]
> (2.5–16)

> I have yet to meet a man so wise that he would not gladly know what guidance this story requires, what edification it brings. The tale never loses heart, but flees and pursues, turns tail and wheels to the attack and doles out blame and praise. The man who follows all these vicissitudes and neither sits too long nor goes astray and otherwise knows where he stands has been well served by mother wit.[12]

As one of the premier poet-performers of his time, Wolfram conveys here a general impression of the dynamics of the poetic action at courts in the early thirteenth century. The correct assessment of the value of poetic performances is increasingly showing itself to involve a *lêre*—"edification"—that is not a static truth, but rather a nimble mastery of *schanzen*—"vicissitudes." More than anything else, we observe that the poetic action at courts in the twelfth

---

10. Kathryn Starkey's study, *Reading the Medieval Book*, endeavors to negotiate the aforementioned fluid cultural parameters in the case of Wolfram von Eschenbach's other significant romance, *Willehalm*.

11. Wolfram von Eschenbach, *Parzival* (Lachmann). Numbers of Middle High German and Old French verses from the romances here and elsewhere are cited parenthetically in text.

12. Wolfram von Eschenbach, *Parzival* (Hatto), 15.

and thirteenth centuries is a collective endeavor made by poets and audiences to arrive at new assessments of mutable, perishable goods, such as honor and love, the interest in which necessarily involves "vicissitudes" and the ability to "follow" them. The next two chapters examine the specific characteristics of adventure and love, respectively, as absolute investments in finite, perishable goods, as such investments occur in the imaginary action of the romances. In the poetic action of composing and performing poets to be examined in this chapter, my focus will be on the parameters of poetry as competition, the various resources different poets put into play (especially including the vernacular and its narrative traditions), and a few of the more striking moves employed by some of the poetic luminaries.

BENCHMARKS OF PERFORMANCE

An especially appropriate passage for exemplifying the parameters of the poetic action at courts in the High Middle Ages is a lengthy excursus in the *Tristan* romance of Gottfried von Strassburg (composed ca. 1215), which is inserted into the poem at the moment Tristan is about to be made a knight.[13] The imaginary occasion Gottfried is about to depict is correspondingly festive, evocative of the festival in Mainz in 1184 at which Barbarossa's sons were knighted. The splendor of the festive event that Gottfried needs to describe for his audience is such that he fears his talent may not be equal to the task, or at least so he says. The rhetorical profession of incapacity is well-worn. In actuality, audiences and rivals do well to be skeptical toward poetic professions of incapacity and to assume these may merely be the prelude to a high-quality effort, which turns out to be the case here. Gottfried prefaces his critical review of the poetic action by stating that other great poets have already set a standard so high that, even if he had twelve times his own capacity to think and speak, he would still not be able to rise to a comparable level.[14] Gottfried's reference to past great poetic efforts, the level of which he fears his own effort will not reach, opens the door to laying out past performances and assessing them in terms that are familiar to us:

jâ ritterlîchiu zierheit
diu ist sô manege wîs beschriben

---

13. For alternative interpretations of this passage, see Mark Chinca, *Gottfried von Strassburg: Tristan*, 58–69; and Christoph Huber, *Gottfried von Strassburg: Tristan and Isolde*, 53–65.
14. See Gottfried von Strassburg, *Tristan* (Ranke), vv. 4589–620.

> und ist mit rede alsô zetriben,
> daz ich niht kan gereden dar abe,
> da von kein herze vröude habe.[15]
> (4616–20)

> Knightly pomp, I declare, has been so variously portrayed and has been so overdone that I can say nothing about it that would give pleasure to anyone.[16]

We saw in the previous chapter that the measure of success for events in the political action at court is the experience of pleasure or joy, and Gottfried here indicates—though feigning the posture of someone too discouraged to exert himself—that the realization of *vröude,* pleasure, joy—would also be the way to assess whether a poetic performance has risen to the necessary level.

Gottfried's profession of incapacity is a rhetorical ploy, and the perceptive audience member perceives it as such. It provides the prelude to a lengthy excursus that involves the assessment of other vernacular poet-performers and subsequently an invocation of Apollo and his muses. In this excursus, Gottfried clearly accomplishes what he claims in the beginning to have no hope of accomplishing. While he continues to profess that he is unequal to the challenge and daunted by the competition, Gottfried parades his detailed knowledge of the vernacular poetic action and his familiarity with the sources of poetic inspiration in Greco-Roman antiquity. As he does this, he shows indirectly but quite tangibly that he is, after all, putting forth an extraordinary effort—perhaps indeed harnessing many times his normal narrative powers—in the interest of joy.

Gottfried's review begins with his predecessor in the performance of romance poetry, Hartmann von Aue. Gottfried lavishes praise upon Hartmann, above all on account of that poet's *cristallînen wortelîn* (v. 4629)—"crystal words"[17]—a stylistic feature the verses of Gottfried not surprisingly share. Hartmann capably adorns his tale with well-crafted, transparent verses, which Gottfried considers will inevitably have a pleasing effect on knowledgeable observers and thus lead to joy: *Si koment den man mit siten an, / si tuont sich nâhen zuo dem man / und liebent rehtem muote* (vv. 4631–33)—"Gently they approach and fawn on a man, and captivate right minds."[18] Subsequently,

---

15. Gottfried's Middle High German verses are cited from *Tristan* (Ranke).
16. Gottfried von Strassburg, *Tristan* (Hatto), 105.
17. Ibid.
18. Ibid.

Gottfried disparages his principal rival and competitor, Wolfram von Eschenbach, whose stylistic inclinations—from Gottfried's perspective—go too far in the direction of the unpredictability of the "vicissitudes" Wolfram is interested in following. Gottfried does not deign to mention his rival by name, but the substandard performer he has in mind is quite clearly Wolfram. Gottfried considers that the poet in question *jumps around too much* with his story and does so to such a degree that courtiers are left in the dark.[19] The verses of the unnamed poet-performer, according to Gottfried, fall short of fulfilling the principal purpose of the poetic action at court: *Ob man der wârheit jehen sol, / dâne gât niht guotes muotes van, / dâne lît niht herzelustes an* (vv. 4678–80)— "To speak the truth, no pleasurable emotion come from it, there is nothing in it to delight the heart."[20] Even if not named, Wolfram is of such stature that people will know whom Gottfried is criticizing here, whether they agree with his criticism or not. Gottfried reckons with this and may well hope that leaving his famous rival unnamed will be perceived as a snub to Wolfram, rather than as an indirect way of drawing attention to his fame.

Gottfried's review of romance performers also goes on to include positive assessments of other romance poets such as Bligger von Steinach and Heinrich von Veldeke, but the winner of the contest is clear to Gottfried from the beginning, despite any claims Wolfram might want to make.[21] There is no competitor at Hartmann's level, so Gottfried confers the prize for romance poetry to him, with the complicity of the wise ones among his audience[22]:

swer guote rede ze guote
und ouch ze rehte kan verstân,
der muoz dem Ouwaere lân
sîn schapel und sîn lôrzwî.
(4634–37)

Those who esteem fine language with due sympathy and judgment will allow the man of Aue his garland and his laurels.[23]

---

19. See Gottfried von Strassburg, *Tristan* (Ranke), vv. 4638–90.
20. Gottfried von Strassburg, *Tristan* (Hatto), 105.
21. See, in particular, Ibid., vv. 4642–44.
22. The "wise ones" were involved in a similar way in the political action discussed in the previous chapter, in particular that involving the imperial procession at Magdeburg recorded poetically by Walther von der Vogelweide.
23. Gottfried von Strassburg, *Tristan* (Hatto), 105.

In regarding Hartmann as the rightful winner of the laurels, Gottfried renders the poetic action in the competitive manner appropriate to it. As has happened since Greco-Roman times, the laurel wreath goes to the winner of a *contest*. Laureates include athletes, poets, conquering generals, and—in more recent European history—scientists and peacemakers. In his review of other poetic performances artfully integrated into his own, Gottfried awards the laurel wreath to his predecessor Hartmann, even as he himself assumes the role of supreme poetic arbiter and lays out for his audiences and for us a view of the poetic action *as competition*.[24]

Gottfried's review provides benchmarks for the assessment of poetic performances at court. It shows these performances to share important basic features, some of which are already familiar to us from our survey of the political action in the previous chapter. The poetic performances, as the political ones, are supposed to realize joy for those involved in them. The realization of joy as an outcome for the court depends, as Gottfried's review shows, on the ability of individual poet-performers to harness the resources available to them and put them effectively on display for their audiences. In my further consideration of the poetic action in this chapter, I endeavor to see things according to the competitive benchmarks employed by Gottfried in his review, and I focus particularly on developments associated with increases in the value of poetry in the vernacular languages. We shall observe that success in the poet-performers' competitive endeavors at court has particularly to do with their ability to articulate the *higher* and *lower* cultural resources mentioned above, and—as we shall see below—with their ability to discover things of value among the latter. In order to see the poetic action in its broader literary-cultural context, we shall first consider a few noteworthy initial achievements involving vernacular poetry in the centuries leading up to its great flourishing at French- and German-speaking courts in the twelfth and thirteenth centuries. We focus then on some significant moments in the performances of some of the premier poets in this flourishing: Marie de France, Chrétien de Troyes, Hartmann von Aue, Wolfram von Eschenbach, and our self-styled arbiter, Gottfried von Strassburg.

---

24. Gottfried's review also includes the performers of love lyrics, or the *nahtegalen* (v. 4751)—"nightingales," as he calls them. According to the specific musical and metric characteristics of their art, the performers of the love lyrics also pursue joy, the same goal as that of the performers of romance poetry (vv. 4759–69). In the pursuit of joy via the love lyrics, a certain poet from "Hagenouwe," whom we know to be called Reinmar, was once supreme among the German poet-performers and "carried their banner," as Gottfried puts it; but since the death of Reinmar, the leader among the singers of love has been Walther von der Vogelweide (vv. 4802–12), the same one whose gnomic poetry provided insights into the political action that we observed in the previous chapter.

THE VERNACULAR AS POETIC RESOURCE

Consideration of poetic action involving vernacular languages and the narrative traditions associated with them takes us back to the Carolingian revival of the Roman empire in the early ninth century, when a monk named Otfried von Weissenburg—the first poet working in the German vernacular whose name is known to us—composes a harmonization of the Gospels in Old High German verses and presents it to his probable lord Liutbert, the Archbishop of Mainz, with a prefatory letter in Latin asking him to appraise the style of it. The letter to Liutbert lays out Otfried's purpose in composing his *Evangielienharmonie* and enables an understanding of the monk's literary activity as a competitive effort in at least two ways.

First, concerning himself with matters of style, Otfried begins his letter with the rhetorical profession of inability to accomplish the poetic task that is already familiar to us and then predictably rises to the occasion. Corresponding to the Carolingian ambition to align itself with the glory of Rome and be enduring competitors of renown in the ongoing *imperial* action, there is a need to compete in the *literary poetic* action. This means the Franks must *engage* the poets of antiquity, and Otfried shows us the elite company to which he thinks his Germanic brethren must aspire:

> Virgilius, Lucanus, Ovidius caeterique quam plurimi suorum facta decorarent lingua nativa, quorum jam voluminum dictis fluctuare cognoscimus mundum, nostrae etiam sectae probatissimorum virorum facta laudabant, Juvenci, Aratoris, Prudentii ceterorumque multorum, qui sua lingua dicta et miracula Christi decenter ornabant; Nos vero, quamvis eadem fide eademque gratia instructi, divinorum verborum splendorem clarissimum proferre propria lingua, dicebant pigrescere.[25]

> Virgil, Lucan, Ovid and many others, embellished their deeds in their native language—with the sayings of whose works we know the world to be now awash and that they even praised the deeds of the most-tried men of our religion—of Juvencus, Arator, Prudentius and many others, who embellished the sayings and miracles of Christ properly in their own tongue; whereas we, although instructed by grace in that same faith, were, they said, lazy in putting forth the most brilliant splendor of the divine words in our own language.[26]

---

25. Otfried von Weissenburg, *Otfrids Evangelienbuch*, 4.
26. Citing James Marchand's online translation of Otfried von Weissenburg, "Ohtfrid's Letter to Liudbert."

Otfried here invokes the high poetic level of antiquity in order to show how far short of it the Franks are languishing. The problem has not been the lack of knowledge, ability, or skill, but rather the lack of *effort*, and Otfried sets forth to remedy this. With his Old High German vernacular rendering of the Gospels in verses, Otfried proceeds with a vigor that belies his initial profession of incapacity. Thanks in part to Augustine's harnessing of imperial Rome's educational and literary resources for Christian purposes, pagan poets such as Virgil, Lucan, and Ovid serve as inspirations for Otfried, even if their importance for his Christian purposes pertains primarily to the high standard of stylistic excellence they have established. Otfried is aware of the high level of competition into which he is entering on behalf of the Franks, just as he is aware that there is no longer any alternative to competition other than the shame of inaction, the fault of "laziness." The stakes are also high in view of Otfried's petition to have his own stylistic effort judged at the highest episcopal level in Mainz. In view of subsequent literary history, the outcome in this case is success. Otfried's harmonization of the gospels will come to be regarded as an important early moment in the literary history of the European vernacular languages, suggesting that the assessment of Luitbert—and probably also those of the "worthy brothers and the reverend lady Judith" who inspired him to write (discussed below)—were positive.

The second manner in which Otfried's poetic efforts need to be appreciated as competitive concerns content rather than style. With his biblical poetry, Otfried also involves himself in a cultural competition that fully deserves the designation *rivalry*. In his letter to the archbishop, this rivalry constitutes the first and foremost reason for undertaking his effort:

> Dum rerum quondam sonus inutilium pulsaret aures quorundam probatissimorum virorum eorumque sanctitatem laicorum cantus inquietaret obscenus, a quibusdam memoriae dignis fratribus rogatus, maximeque cujusdam venerandae matronae verbis nimium flagitantis, nomine Judith, partem evangeliorum eis Theotisce conscriberem, ut aliquantulum hujus cantus lectionis ludum saecularium vocum deleret; et in evangeliorum propria lingua occupati dulcedine, sonum inutilium rerum noverint declinare.[27]

> Wherefore, since at times the sound of useless things have beat on the ears of some men of highest quality, and the obscene song of laymen disturbed their sanctity, I was asked by certain brothers worthy of memory—and especially

---

27. Otfried von Weissenburg, *Otfrids Evangelienbuch*, 4.

through the words of a certain reverend lady named Judith who strongly urged me on—to write for them in German part of the Gospels, so that a small amount of the reading of this song might cancel out the play of worldly voices; and, occupied with the sweetness of the Gospels in their own language, they would be able to forego the sound of useless things.[28]

The poet's literary effort is being made to counter the deleterious effect of *sonus inutilium*—"useless sounds," in particular, *cantus obscenus*—"obscene songs." Much about the parameters of this rivalry remains unclear, but some things can be surmised. The *probatissimorum virorum*—"men of highest quality" are presumably of the highest political and social rank, and these men, to Otfried's dismay, occupy themselves with an "obscene" poetry that is beneath their dignity.[29] Though the attempt to identify Otfried's "obscene" poetic rival for the attention of such men remains speculative, the rival's general characteristics are consistent with orally transmitted poetry in the vernacular. The unspecified songs are presumably "obscene" in dealing with something other than divine Christian truths, indeed in dealing with anything at all—such as events heroic, amorous, or erotic—that might be deemed erroneous, distasteful, or disgusting from a Christian perspective. Whatever the exact parameters of this competition may have been, it seems Otfried's literary effort is largely motivated by the perceived need to occupy the minds of "men of highest quality" with vernacular poetic words of the highest quality, both in style and content. Otfried has no doubt that the sweet vernacular sound of the Gospels—*evangeliorum propria lingua dulcedine sonum*—will prevail in the competition for the attention of these important men and strengthen them in their sanctity, thus countering the effect of "obscene songs."

If Otfried is aware of any risk involved in his engagement in the poetic action—besides not rising to the necessary poetic level—he shows no sign of it in his letter to Liutbert. Looking forward to the High Middle Ages, uses of the vernacular languages will range far beyond the Carolingian verse reiterations of Holy Scriptures. The *vulgar* languages will be available as a literary resource throughout the poetic action at courts, and it is instructive to consider the role Otfried's early efforts may already be playing in this. Otfried's initial and relatively modest (i.e., in view of what is to come) extension of the Christian

---

28. Marchand, "Ohtfrid's Letter to Liudbert."

29. Haug considers that Otfried's intended audience is monastic (*Vernacular Literary Theory*, 31), but there is no way to know with certainty, based on the letter alone, whether the poet's use of the superlative "probatissimorum virorum" referred to "tested men" among an exclusively monastic audience. His *global* ambition on behalf of the Franks suggests the possibility that his poetic efforts might refer to monastic, clerical, and lay communities alike.

and Latin-based cultural apparatus of books and book-learning to include the vernacular languages as a literary resource extends the cultural reach of God's word, but something else is simultaneously achieved: God's word and "obscene songs" become associates and competitors on the same cultural *playing field*. As the holy words of God are fashioned in the vernacular in order to contend with competitors, the means are also made available for the originally "obscene" verses to become literary. As this occurs, the "obscene" verses seem to acquire a different value or status. Their literary inscription preserves them and the deeds they celebrate—even if in the context of a cultural apparatus originally foreign to them—from the oblivion into which they might fall if the oral transmission of them through the generations weakens and ultimately lapses. The involvement of "obscene" verses in the literary poetic action *lifts* them into a cultural sphere heretofore occupied by holy scriptures, patristic writings, and the poetry of pagan antiquity as refitted to Christian purposes. As *high*, literary Latin poetry engages *low*, originally oral, vernacular narrative traditions, the poetic action will necessarily become less determinate and more varied. The relative values of things—such as that of Latin vis-à-vis the vernacular languages with their various associated concerns—will come increasingly into flux.

There are already indications of new valuations of cultural resources in the time of Otfried von Weissenburg. In Einhard's biography of Charlemagne, we learn that the emperor had a collection of songs set down in writing for posterity about the deeds and wars of ancient kings. With the exception of a single Germanic heroic lay (the *Hildebrandslied*), accidentally preserved on the front and back inside covers of a religious manuscript, no such songs in the German vernacular have survived. Some of the cultural resources associated with the "useless sounds" against which Otfried competes are nevertheless making headway in the literary poetic action and thereby inevitably achieving a different value. The other significant harmonization of the Gospels composed in the ninth century in the German vernacular, in roughly the same cultural (i.e., monastic) situation in which Otfried worked, is the Old Saxon *Heliand*. The *Heliand* gives Holy Scriptures a Germanic-heroic form and content, in a manner one suspects would have made Otfried, his holy brothers, and the reverend lady Judith *cringe* if they ever chanced to read or hear it. The anonymous author of the *Heliand* tells the story of Christ in the alliterative long-lines of heroic epics such as Beowulf. Correspondingly, Christ is depicted, as Francis Gentry observes, using the "typical Germanic terminology for chiefs like *drohtin* (lord), *uualand* (ruler), *uualdandes barn* (child of the ruler), *thiodo drohtin* (lord of the peoples), and *mildi mundboro* (generous protector), and the Apostles with the exception of Judas, are characterized as excellent thanes." Gentry draws attention specifically to the *Heliand*'s Germanic-heroic iteration of Matthew 5:6:

> "Blessed are they which do hunger and thirst after righteousness: for they shall be filled." This is rendered as: "Those too are fortunate who desired to do good things here, those fighting men who wanted to judge fairly. With good things they themselves will be filled to satisfaction in the Chieftain's kingdom for their wise actions; they will attain good things, those fighting men who judged fairly here."[30]

The heroic rendering of the story of Christ tailors the Word of God to a specific strategic purpose. In the ninth century, the continental Saxons are among the last of the pagan peoples long settled in northern Europe. Charlemagne has endeavored to overcome them in a series of long and bloody wars and to convert them to Christianity from their polytheistic pagan beliefs. The *Heliand* is generally consistent with this Carolingian effort, but instead of proceeding with military force—the method for which Charlemagne is perhaps best known—its aim is to proselytize with words rather than at the point of a sword. This poem competes in its own way for the minds "of most proven men" (*probatissimorum virorum*), as Otfried puts it, but the *minds* in question belong to Saxons who seemingly do not yet possess the requisite spiritual-intellectual capacity for the apprehension of the basic tenets of Christianity, even if these were rendered in a Germanic vernacular as Otfried does.[31] Instead, Christ's life is cast in terms with which a Germanic warrior culture can identify to some degree. As this occurs, some of the "useless sounds" against which Otfried is competing seemingly make inroads into the literary cultural action, to be sure, not in the form of "old rude songs," but rather in a very heroic-looking vernacular rendering of the Gospels. The poetic action is visibly widened as it involves low (potentially "obscene") cultural resources in high Christian ways, which in turn seemingly affects the values of things generally. In the introduction to his translation of the *Heliand*, Ronald Murphy writes that its author, "created a unique synthesis between Christianity and Germanic warrior-society—a synthesis that would

---

30. Gentry, "German Literature to 1160," 72.
31. In the introduction of his edition of *Hêliand*, John E. Cathey offers a concrete example: "The Germanic ethic required behavior that with Christian sensibility was understood as *superbia*. To the traditional Germanic, and thus Saxon, mind-set the egocentric goal of achieving fame in this world as an individual (and proper status for one's family) was all that would live on after one's death. Tales told of dead heroes constituted the only transcendent realm in a world defined merely by what is here and now" (13).

ultimately lead to the culture of knighthood and become the foundation of medieval Europe."[32] We have observed such a "synthesis" occurring by means of the literary involvement of new poetic competitors and the concomitant availability of new cultural resources associated with the vernacular languages. Over time, vernacular sounds and the things associated with them will increase in literary and cultural value, especially during the widening and intensification of the poetic action that occurs in the High Middle Ages.

In the centuries after the period of cultural growth under the Carolingians, there is little evidence of sustained literary action in the vernacular languages. In the tenth and eleventh centuries, available cultural resources seem to be invested in other ways—for example, in defending and preserving Christendom against pagan aggressors such as Vikings and Magyars—and literature reverts almost exclusively to Latin as the holy language of Augustine's heavenly *City of God*. During this time, the literary action seems scarcely shaped by vernacular narrative traditions. In the exceptional case of the *Waltharius* epic (ca. 920), Germanic-heroic material negotiates the transition to literary Latin culture according to circumstances that are now difficult to reconstruct.[33] When the vernacular languages again begin to be employed as literary resources in the High Middle Ages, we observe interesting new developments. Sometime during the first decades of the twelfth century, Frau Ava, the first woman poet writing in the German vernacular who is known to us by name—the female counterpart to Otfried von Weissenburg in this regard—composes four works of biblical poetry based on the redemptive value of Christ's life. Ava's literary engagements suggest the parameters of the poetic action in the coming century will be different and more varied than those in which Otfried and the anonymous Saxon author of the *Heliand* were engaged. Gentry observes that Ava's efforts forego rhetorical moves, such as the professions of incapacity we have seen elsewhere, and engage holy scriptures in a direct, personal way.[34] The earliest vernacular poetry in the High Middle Ages is a continuation of the biblical poetry that we saw during the Carolingian period, but the efforts of poets such as Frau Ava indicate that the poetic action to come will involve a broader spectrum of voices, concerns, and approaches.

---

32. See the commentary of G. Ronald Murphy in his edition of *Heliand*, xiii.

33. See Kratz, "Waltharius."

34. "Her work is a song of praise by a pious Christian of Christ's act of Redemption. She does not take the rhetorical approach of lamenting the modest poetic gifts she, as a woman, possesses; the humility formulas that one frequently encounters in the writings of other medieval poets are not found in Ava's writings. She considers her poetic activity a natural outcome of her beliefs, and this view was no doubt shared by the audience that she addresses as 'lieben mîne herren' (my dear lords)" (Gentry, "German Literature to 1160," 112).

STARS IN COMPETITION

The culturally most significant performances in the vernacular poetic action of the High Middle Ages are the courtly romances.[35] The poetic action associated with the romances arguably reaches its greatest complexity and widest cultural range, drawing upon and articulating *high* and *low* cultural resources in the interest of joy. Writing sometime in the second decade of the thirteenth century, Gottfried von Strassburg looks back over a couple of generations of romance poetry in the German vernacular in his literary review and judges outcomes based largely on an aesthetic and stylistic standard of elegant clarity. The descriptive survey of the poetic action to be offered below extends the review to include the French beginnings of romance poetry, and seeks also to draw attention to the diverse cultural resources involved in the poetry, as well as to some of the noteworthy characteristics of the poetic action as competition. As we saw in Gottfried's review, and will see in greater detail below, the parameters of the poetic action at court become most tangible in prologues, epilogues, and excursuses, in which the best poet-performers—the *stars* of the twelfth and thirteenth centuries—step forward to provide their medieval audiences and us with perspectives of the poetic action and of the standards according to which the action needs to be assessed.

The performances of the French poet named Marie provide instructive views of the narrative action at noble courts in the latter half of the twelfth century, around the same time Chrétien de Troyes begins to undertake his own innovative performances.[36] Marie's *lais* share some of the characteristics of longer courtly romances, in particular their rhymed octosyllabic couplets, their investment in love, and their apparent provenance from orally

---

35. I understand *performance* as a *process* that includes both the composition of romance poetry as well as its presentation to a courtly audience (the latter understood either as spectators or readers). Though little is known about the specifics of individual performances, it is commonly accepted that the courtly poets performed their works *live* before courtly audiences (which does not exclude the possibility that individual reading might also already have been making some inroads). Evelyn Birge Vitz explores the connections between oral performance and the early development of the French verse romances in her *Orality and Performance in Early French Romance*.

36. In the foreword of their translation of Marie's *Lais*, Robert Hanning and Joan Ferrante write: "Marie de France was perhaps the greatest woman author of the Middle Ages and certainly the creator of the finest medieval short fiction before Boccaccio and Chaucer" (1). More recently, R. Howard Bloch describes Marie as "a writer more deeply embedded in surrounding culture, both learned and popular, than heretofore acknowledged and as a complex figure that is just the opposite of the simple, natural, spontaneous, and moderate image that has flourished since the eighteenth century" (*Anonymous Marie de France*, 315).

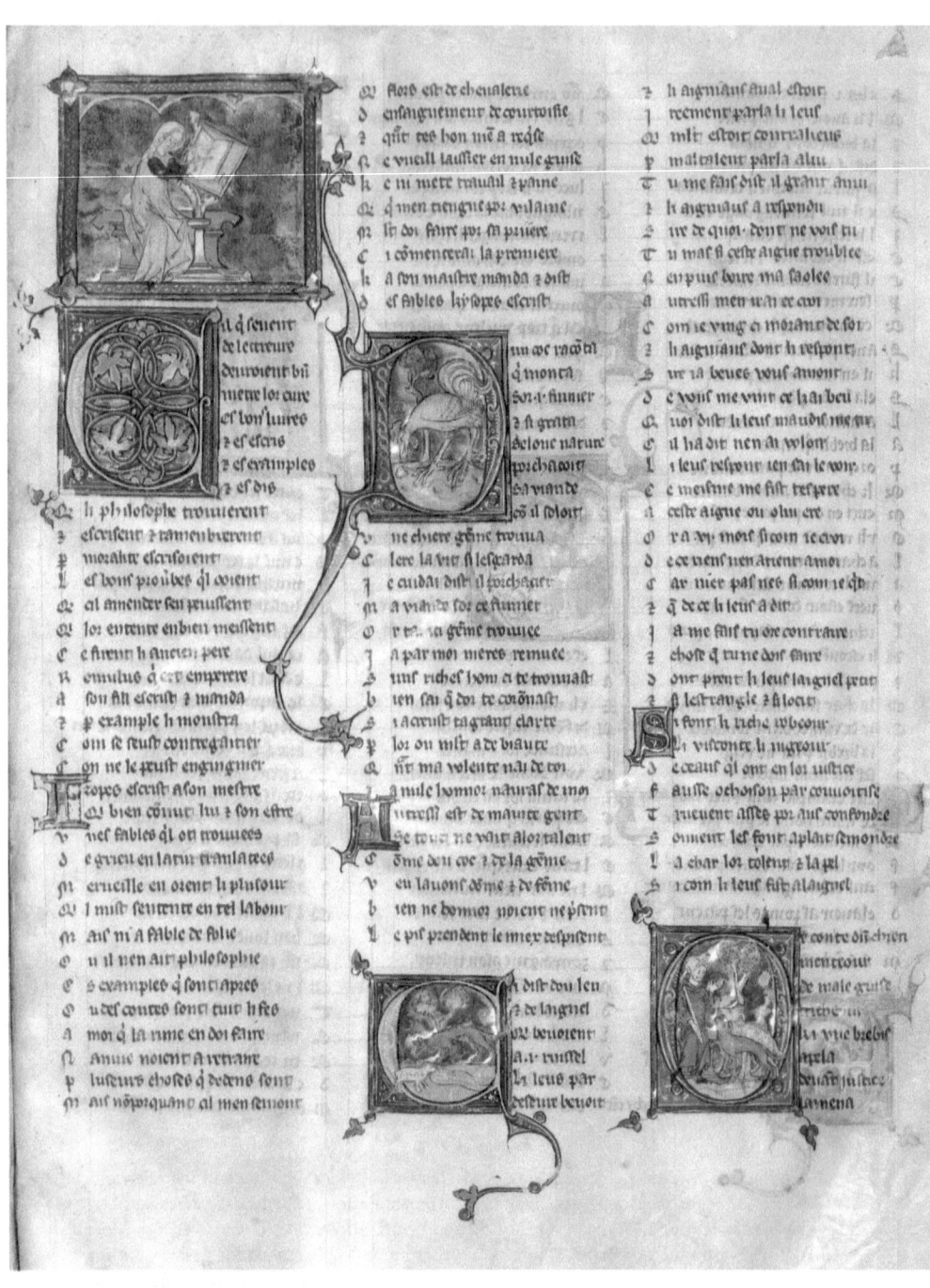

FIGURE 2. Marie de France writing Fables. MS 3142 Folio 256. Bibliotheque Nationale de France (BnF). © BnF, Dist. RMN-Grand Palais/Art Resource, NY.

transmitted (i.e., vernacular) narrative traditions.³⁷ Also, we observe signs in the prologue with which she prefaces her *lais*—though subtle ones—that she conceives of the poetic action as competition:

> Ki Deus ad duné escïence
> E de parler bon eloquence
> Ne s'en deit taisir ne celer,
> Ainz se deit volunters mustrer.
> Quant uns granz biens est mult oïz,
> Dunc a primes est il fluriz,
> E quant loëz est de plusurs,
> Dunc ad espandues ses flurs.
> Custume fu as ancïens,
> Ceo testimone Precïens,
> Es livres ke jadis feseient,
> Assez oscurement diseient
> Pur ceus ki a venir esteient
> E ki aprendre les deveient,
> K'i peüssent gloser la lettre
> E de lur sen le surplus mettre.³⁸
> (1–16)

Anyone who has received from God the gift of knowledge and true eloquence has a duty not to remain silent: rather should one be happy to reveal such talents. When a truly beneficial thing is heard by so many people, it then enjoys its first blossom, but if it is widely praised its flowers are in full bloom. It was customary for the ancients, in the books which they wrote (Priscian testifies to this), to express themselves very obscurely so that those in later generations, who had to learn them, could provide a gloss for the text and put the *finishing touches* to their meaning.³⁹

Marie begins this passage with a reiteration of a conviction we have seen elsewhere in the cultural action, such as with Otfried von Weissenburg above. If one possesses the necessary resources to engage oneself poetically, one

---

37. Romance proper is, of course, a longer narrative form than the *lai*. But the two poetic forms are close enough that Hanning and Ferrante refer to them as a "collection of short romances and tales" (Marie de France, *Lais*, 1).

38. Old French verses are cited here from Marie de France, *Lais de Marie de France* (Micha).

39. Marie de France, *Lais* (Burgess and Busby), 41; italics added.

should do so. The floral analogy, to which the involvement of capable poet-performers in the poetic action is linked in the ensuing verses, underscores the necessity of engagement at the same time as it suggests parameters for assessing Marie's efforts. Successful engagement in the action for Marie is analogous to the full blossoming of *granz biens*—"a truly beneficial thing." Such a full blossoming is associated with the pleasing visual and olfactory sensations of a naturally unfolding process, and it is also contingent on consensus. It takes the praise of many people, and consequently a process of evaluation, for the full blossoming of a truly beneficial thing to occur. With her ensuing reference to the ancients and their books, Marie provides additional details regarding the criteria according to which the evaluations leading to praise are made. Marie views the previous poetic action as something *unfinished*. The ancients with their books have left something obscure that is still in need of completion. Medieval poet-performers possessing the necessary resources have the obligation to familiarize themselves thoroughly with the ancient books, to hone their own skills with their help, and to involve themselves directly in the poetic action in order to *finish* something that has been left incomplete. The move of which Marie avails herself as a medieval poet-performer with her reference to the books of the ancients—to "put the finishing touches to their meaning"—can be seen as corresponding to the "full bloom" of "a truly beneficial thing" that is referenced in her likening of the poetic action to the blooming of flowers. In its association with the floral imagery, the medieval completion of something left incomplete in the books of the ancients amounts to the flourishing of whatever good things those ancient books contained before the engagements of medieval poet-performers. In contrast to Otfried, Marie articulates the medieval relationship to antiquity in less overtly competitive terms, underscoring instead its collaborative aspect. But the twelfth-century courtier, like the ninth-century monk, views the ancients both as a model to be studied and emulated, and as a standard to which one must endeavor to rise. Marie's use of the word *surplus*—"finishing touches"—also casts the ancients' standard as something unfinished that is in need of completion, possibly hinting—however subtly—that medieval poet-performers may in some sense surpass it if they proceed knowledgably and skillfully enough.[40]

---

40. Logan Whalen, in *Marie de France and the Poetics of Memory*, includes among the implications of these verses "the justification for taking preexisting material and adapting it to the concerns at hand" (41). Here Whalen also surveys the extensive critical literature seeking an explanation of these verses by pursuing Marie's reference to Priscian. Bloch approaches Marie's *surplus* somewhat differently, connecting it by way of *gloser* and *sens* to a joy with patently erotic characteristics (*Anonymous Marie de France*, 47).

In the remainder of her prologue, Marie provides further important information about her vernacular verses. Her own poetic engagement will not be about finishing an incomplete ancient book or even about rendering an ancient Latin book in the vernacular, adding her "surplus" as she does so, but rather about certain *lais*:

> Des lais pensai, k'oïz aveie.
> Ne dutai pas, bien le saveie,
> Ke pur remambrance les firent
> Des aventures k'il oïrent
> Cil ki primes les comencierent
> E ki avant les enveierent.
> Plusurs en ai oï conter,
> Nes voil laisser ne oblier.
> Rimé en ai e fait ditié,
> Soventes fiez en ai veillié.
> (33–42)

I thought of the lays which I had heard and did not doubt, for I knew it full well, that they were composed, by those who first began them and put them into circulation, to perpetuate the memory of adventures they had heard. I myself have heard a number of them, and do not wish to overlook or neglect them. I have put them into verse, made poems from them, and worked on them late into the night.[41]

The *lais* Marie is crafting form part of the so-called *matière de Bretagne* that seems to be conveyed by the same storytellers to whom we see Chrétien de Troyes making reference below.[42] A reason why it would be important to preserve the *lais*, as Marie is doing, is because they belong to orally transmitted poetry that could be forgotten and lost if not set down in writing. This view is supported by the repetition in the cited verses of the verb "to hear," and the stated interest in not wanting the *aventures*—"adventures"—to be forgotten. Marie's vernacular verse rendering of possibly oral narrative material for her courtly audiences seems to bring us far from her introductory views of the poetic action as the consensus-or-praise-contingent flowering of a "truly

---

41. Marie de France, *Lais* (Burgess and Busby), 32.
42. On similarities in the approaches of Marie and Chrétien to the poetic action, especially regarding the status of the Celtic *matière de Bretagne*, see K. Sarah-Jane Murray, *From Plato to Lancelot*, xvii–xviii.

beneficial thing," or as placing the "finishing touches" on the Latin books of the ancients. Yet a possibility Marie seems to leave open is that the vernacular *lais* amount to a specifically medieval and vernacular "fruition" or "completion" of the poetic action of the ancients. While this possibility remains speculative, one more immediate goal is clear. At the end of her prologue, Marie reveals her principal reason for engaging in the poetic action in the ways we have observed thus far. She hopes her involvement with the *lais* might please the king, *a ki tute joie s'encline*—"to whom all joys pay homage." If this happens, it will in turn bring great joy to Marie herself: *Si vos les plaist a receveir, / Mult me ferez grant joie aveir* (vv. 51–52)—"If it pleased you to accept them, you would bring me great joy." Marie's prologue ends by underscoring a joy that is both an individual one of the poet and a general courtly one vouchsafed by the king to whom the *lais* are dedicated. The full blossoming of poetry and its "completion," joyfully realized, are the aim of Marie's poetic investment of self and the reason behind those late nights working on her *lais*.[43]

In what counts as the first of the Arthurian romances,[44] Chrétien de Troyes's *Érec et Énide*, we observe in the prologue many of the moves we see with Marie, even if Chrétien shapes the action more sharply in aligning himself more squarely with the ancients and in placing emphasis on the competition with contemporary poet-performers. Each part of this memorable inauguration of the Arthurian romance tradition is significant with respect to the parameters of action that we have been considering, so the prologue is cited here in its entirety:

> Li vilains dit an son respit
> Que tel chose a l'an an despit
> Qui mout valt mialz que l'an ne cuide.
> Por ce fet bien qui son estuide
> Atorne a bien quel que il l'ait;
> Car qui son estuide antrelait,
> Tost i puet tel chose teisir
> Qui mout vandroit puis a pleisir.
> Por ce dist Crestiens de Troies
> Que reisons est que totevoies
> Doit chascuns panser et antandre

---

43. This is another rhetorical commonplace, but one which can of course also be true in fact.

44. A *claim to fame* that continues to be underscored in the critical literature, for example in the article by Donald Maddox and Sara Sturm Maddox, "*Érec et Énide:* The First Arthurian Romance."

A bien dire et a bien aprandre;
Et tret d'un conte d'avanture
Une mout bele conjointure
Par qu'an puet prover et savoir
Que cil ne fet mie savoir
Que s'escience n'abandone
Tant con Dex la grasce l'an done.
D'Erec, le fil Lac, est li contes,
Que devant rois et devant contes
Depecier et corronpre suelent
Cil qui de conter vivre vuelent.
Des or comancerai l'estoire
Qui toz jorz mes iert an mimoire
Tant con durra crestiantez:
De ce s'est Crestiens vantez.[45]
(1–26)

The peasant in his proverb says that one might find oneself holding in contempt something that is worth much more than one believes; therefore a man does well to make good use of his learning according to whatever understanding he has, for he who neglects his learning may easily keep silent something that would later give much pleasure. And so Chrétien de Troyes says that it is reasonable for everyone to think and strive in every way to speak well and to teach well, and from a tale of adventure he draws a beautifully ordered composition that clearly proves that a man does not act intelligently if he does not give free reign to his knowledge for as long as God gives him the grace to do so. This is the tale of Erec, son of Lac, which those who try to live by storytelling customarily mangle and corrupt before kings and counts. Now I shall begin the story that will be in memory for evermore, as long as Christendom lasts—of this does Chrétien boast.[46]

Chrétien's performance is about finding value in something that one might initially be inclined to hold in contempt, thereby making the most of what Marie would call a "truly beneficial thing." As with Marie, finding such value involves the engagement of performers in command of the requisite resources. Chrétien's reference to the skills associated with the art of rhetoric—*A bien dire et a bien aprandre*—brings the Latin books of the ancients and a familiarity

---

45. Chrétien de Troyes, *Érec et Énide* (Dembowski).
46. Idem, *Erec and Enide* (Carroll).

with them into play as resources in his own performance. In contrast to the more subtle and varied approach taken by Marie, Chrétien considers that it is the literary resources of antiquity that will bring out the full potential of the contemporary storytellers' tales (in the form of his *mout bele conjointure*),[47] rather than vice versa. As with Marie, Chrétien's performance envisions a joy or *pleisir*—"pleasure"—that will be a general, courtly one, and Chrétien also clearly puts his own qualifications and efforts on display as he discusses these matters. But the more pointed way in which his effort is made, and the markers whereby he aligns himself with the books and learning of the ancients and against the crudeness of the vernacular narrative material as previously handled, distinguishes his performance markedly from hers. In contrast to Marie's relatively humble reference to her working late into the night, Chrétien ends his *Érec et Énide* prologue with the boast that his work will be remembered *tant con durra crestiantez*—"as long as Christianity endures." This boast, besides its self-referential worth, has the effect of aligning the value of Chrétien's learned treatment of the subject matter with the high political and social status of "kings and counts," before whom the story has been "mangled and corrupted" by inferior performers until now.

Chrétien's speculation on the romances and the value of his *mout bele conjointure*—"beautifully ordered composition"—lives up to his claim and turns out to be an immensely successful poetic move.[48] The joy that courtiers and later populations will find in this new kind of poetic action and its later permutations continues to the present day, but in our context, it is important to appreciate the initial parameters of this immensely successful and fruitful poetic speculation. Chrétien is engaged in a rivalry with or competition against "those who wish to make their living by storytelling in the presence of counts and kings." To a much greater degree than Marie, Chrétien emphasizes the possibly *low*, and hence suspect, value of the vernacular tales of adventure as performed by poets who, it would seem, lack the necessary resources to realize their full value. The tales are justifiably held "in contempt," regarded as "useless" to use the term of Otfried, or as in need of "finishing" to use that of

---

47. Murray's above-cited preface to Chrétien de Troyes understands *conjointure* according to its Old French significance: "to unite, to assemble" (*From Plato to Lancelot*, 183). The term thus serves well to illustrate the conjoining of ancient and medieval Celtic poetic traditions that is occurring in the poetry of Chrétien, by virtue of his rhetorical accomplishment.

48. Matilda Bruckner writes on the medieval reception of Chrétien: "His most successful stories and heroes, *Lancelot* and *Perceval*, supply the kernels for enormous romance cycles in prose, where they are completely absorbed and rewritten for readers whose voracious appetite for more leads to compilations like the Vulgate cycle, combining Arthurian and Grail history" ("Chrétien de Troyes," 93–94).

Marie, as long as they are not *leveraged* by the cultural resources a performer such as Chrétien can bring to bear.[49]

The romance action of the twelfth and early thirteenth centuries largely occurs according to the dynamic parameters set forth by Marie and Chrétien in their prologues. From the start, we observe an indeterminacy—an "unfinished" condition—that enables and calls for moves and variations by subsequent poet-performers. These moves are most conspicuously preserved in prologues and in increasingly lengthy and complex excursuses, in which the poets competitively place their own efforts and the criteria for the adequate assessment thereof on display. A noteworthy example from the romance action in German is provided by Hartmann von Aue, the same poet to whom Gottfried conferred the laurel wreath for romance poetry in his literary review at the beginning of this chapter. Basing himself on Chrétien's *Érec et Énide*, Hartmann composes and performs his *Erec* about a generation later (ca. 1180), and he takes the occasion of the description of Enite's second horse—the one given to her after her happy reconciliation with her husband near the end of the romance—to highlight his own poetic engagement and to unveil interesting new poetic moves.[50] Hartmann's description of the horse, saddle, and saddle cloth, which occupies some five hundred verses, in comparison to the fifty or so lines in Chrétien's text upon which it is based, would today most aptly be considered *creative fiction*. Hartmann's competitive elaborations take their cue from those of Chrétien, and he indirectly claims to base himself on the French author, but Hartmann himself is the source of the elaborations, as a closer look at the specific moves he makes reveals.

Chrétien already recognized the importance of the narrative moment in which Enide receives the second of two horses given to her as gifts. Following her steadfast loyalty to her husband in the many difficult adventures they have faced together, Enide is now reconciled with him, jointly with him in command of her world again, and she must be given an appropriately grandiose horse to ride. Chrétien gives her a palfrey with marvelous characteristics befitting the occasion. One side of the palfrey's head is white, the other black, and the two sides are separated by a green line running down the middle. In addition, the bridle, breast strap, and saddle with which the horse is fitted are *boene et bele* (v. 5330)—"fine and beautiful."[51] The breast strap is studded with emeralds, the saddle is covered with precious cloth, and episodes from

---

49. See Lawrence Harf-Lancer's essay, "Chrétien's Literary Background."
50. For a more detailed consideration of Enite's second horse and its gear as a literary-theoretical reflection, see my article "Theorizing German Romance."
51. Chrétien de Troyes, *Erec and Enide* (Carroll), 102.

the story of Aeneas are carved on the ivory saddlebows. Chrétien assures us that the craftsmanship of the Breton sculptor was *soutix*—"delicate"—his carvings *bien tailliee*—"fine" and *tote a fin or apareilliee*—"all embellished with gold"—and that he dedicated seven years of labor exclusively to this work.

Hartmann varies and significantly extends Chrétien's description of these things, beginning with the horse, which he renders as entirely black on one side and white on the other. The German poet also provides a brief account of the horse's provenance, stating that its strange characteristics can be explained by the fact it was not bred in any real geographical place, but rather in an imaginary landscape of adventure in which the dwarf-like king Guivreiz— the host of Erec and Enite at this point in the romance—took it away from a savage dwarf in front of a mountain cave. Hartmann's description of the horse and its trappings elaborates and distinguishes itself from that of Chrétien by underscoring the value of these things in its own singular way, according to what might be called a *gold standard*. The dispossessed dwarf calls after Guivreiz and offers him three thousand marks of gold for returning the horse, which the latter refuses, suggesting the imaginary animal's even greater worth. The same gold standard is visible in Hartmann's rendering of the saddle which, beyond the gold embellishments, precious stones, and ivory mentioned by Chrétien, would be worth more than its own weight of the precious metal. Hartmann spins out Chrétien's rendering of the physical-material characteristics of the horse and its gear, and of their value, and he does the same with the literary-artistic work of the French poet's unnamed Breton sculptor, for whom the German poet invents the name "Umbriz." Hartmann's Umbriz renders things on a grander scale than Chrétien's unnamed craftsman. His carvings of *daz lange liet von Troiâ* (v. 7546)—"the long song of Troy"[52]—for example, in contrast to the French version, linger on the siege and destruction of the city (overlapping some events in Homer's *Illiad*). As in the French version, Aeneas's subsequent journeys are etched in images on the saddle (i.e., those events corresponding to Virgil's poem), but Hartmann includes a saddlecloth on which are depicted the four elements and the diverse beasts inhabiting them, as well as Jupiter and Juno enthroned in the heavens. The saddlecloth is also decorated, in the fine work of Umbriz, with images of the story of Thisbe and Pyramus, reinforcing the images of the story of Dido from the *Aeneid* and driving home the point that Enite is rising above the problems associated with the kind of love that leads to ruin rather than joy, the kind of love Enite and Erec themselves have managed to overcome. Hartmann's many

---

52. Middle High German verses are cited from Hartmann von Aue, *Erec* (Cramer). English translations are from Hartmann von Aue, *Erec* (Vivian); here 136.

elaborations, only the most significant of which have been mentioned here, place his knowledge of the books of the ancients very much on display. As the divergence from his story proper becomes ever wider and more elaborate, it becomes more difficult to ignore that the creative digressions are as much about Hartmann's literary qualifications as they are about the characteristics of the imaginary horse he is describing.

The manner in which Hartmann displays his literary qualifications includes the effort to provide parameters for critically assessing these qualifications. In a striking poetic move, Hartmann fashions an imaginary rival, one who resembles a know-it-all show-off among the members of his audience, who presumes to take over the poetic performance at the moment Hartmann is discussing how challenging an adequate and competent description of the saddle will be:

"nû swîc, lieber Hartman:
ob ich ez errâte?"
ich tuon: nû sprechet drâte.
"ich muoz gedenken ê dar nâch."
nû vil drâte: mir ist gâch.
"dunke ich dich danne ein wîser man?"
jâ ir. durch got, nû saget an.
(7493–99)

"Now keep quiet, dear Hartmann, and see if I can guess." "I shall, but speak quickly." "I have to think about it first." "Then very quickly. I'm in a hurry." "Do you think I'm a smart man?" "Certainly, but tell me now, for God's sake."[53]

As the ensuing exchange occurs, we may need to imagine Hartmann facing in one direction as himself, and in the opposite direction as his upstart rival, in his live performance of this *confrontation* before his courtly audience. In the ensuing back-and-forth between Hartmann and his imaginary rival, the latter advances, point by point, a plausible description of a real saddle, but his approach is plodding and tentative at best, likely based on practical experience with saddles, and it lacks the kind of polish and flair that would need to come from book learning and a full appreciation of the role *this* saddle has to play in Hartmann's narrative. The attempts on the part of the rival to describe the saddle are met, point by point, with skepticism and ridicule by Hartmann.

---

53. Hartmann von Aue, *Erec* (Vivian), 136.

When the rival finally asks if he got the description right, Hartmann responds and resumes control over his story in this way:

"sô hân ichz doch errâten?"
jâ, dâ si dâ trâten.
"ich hân lîhte etewaz verdaget?"
jâ enwizzet ir hiute, waz ir saget.
"enhân ich danne niht wâr?"
niht als grôz als umbe ein hâr.
"hân ich danne gar gelogen?"
niht, iuch hât sus betrogen
iuwer kintlîcher wân.
ir sult michz iu sagen lân.
(7516–25)

"So I did guess then?" "Yes, you hit it right on the head." "Have I perhaps forgotten something?" "Right now you don't know what you're saying." "So I'm not right?" "Not by a mile." "Did I lie then?" "No, your childish fancy betrayed you. You should let me tell you."[54]

The imaginary rival put into play by Hartmann in this staged stichomythia falls woefully short of the mark and is silenced in the end, not without a bit of "contempt" on the part of Hartmann (citing the term used by Chrétien). With this poetic move, Hartmann finds another way to place his performance on a higher level, corresponding to the high value of the events and things as he has been describing them. The engagement with his imaginary rival demonstrates that the value of the story as rendered by Hartmann has little to do with a standard of empirical probability, as a plodding "childish fancy" might have us believe. It has much to do with the capable and expeditious realization of narrative potential in the context of performance, staying poised and graceful under pressure, putting the "finishing touches" on parts of the story that can be made better. This is what Hartmann endeavors to do with his extensive original elaborations of the description of the horse as one finds it with Chrétien. Relying heavily on the Latin books of the ancients and the systematic learning associated with them, the same cultural resources into which Marie and Chrétien were tapping, Hartmann gives Enite a mount truly worthy of the occasion, and he gives his audience an artistic tour-de-force that magnifies the joy of the moment of Enite's ascendancy after her many troubles.

---

54. Ibid.

Hartmann von Aue's competitive relationship to Chrétien leaves the latter unquestioned as the originator of the story, even as the German author's creative additions extend, diverge from, and "finish" his French predecessor's work, as the example of the description of Enite's second horse shows. Wolfram von Eschenbach, the poet-performer disparaged in Gottfried's literary review, proceeds quite differently as he works in the first decade of the thirteenth century, in ways that sharpen the poetic competition significantly. Wolfram differs from poets such as Marie, Chrétien, and Hartmann, especially in the ways he underscores his performance as an unlettered and chivalric poet, rather than as a learned and clerical one.[55] Wolfram's chivalric orientation is underscored in a famous excursus that scholars have called the *Selbstverteidigung*—"self-defense"—in which the poet aggressively holds his own against the anger of unnamed ladies, whose ire he seems to have incurred by accusing one among their number of infidelity. The excursus is situated between the rendering of the birth of Parzival and his mother Herzeloyde's departure with her infant son into the wilderness. In the story proper at this point, as in the "self-defense," the main theme is fidelity—a quality Herzeloyde possesses in overabundance, but which is contrastively lacking in the lady Wolfram has chastised here. Wolfram pointedly states that his anger is directed at one woman alone, but that if ladies choose to attack him collectively, they can expect to encounter strong resistance: *Doch sulen si sich vergâhen niht / mit hurte an mîn hâmît: / si vindent werlîchen strît* (vv. 114.26–28)—"They should not gallop ahead of themselves and charge at my palisade, they will meet stiff opposition there!"[56] In the following verses, Wolfram highlights the resistance aggressors against him will encounter by presenting his chivalric qualifications:

> Schildes ambet ist mîn art:
> swâ mîn ellen sî gespart,
> swelhiu mich minnet umbe sanc,
> sô dunket mich ir witze cranc.
> ob ich guotes wîbes minne ger,
> mag ich mit schilde und ouch mit sper
> verdienen niht ir minne solt,
> al dar nâch sî si mir holt.
> vil hôhes topels er doch spilt,
> der an ritterschaft nâch minnen zilt.
> (115.11–20)

---

55. Wolfram's unlettered chivalric approach is very much at odds with the great amount of book learning in his romance; see Arthur Groos, *Romancing the Grail*.
56. Wolfram von Eschenbach, *Parzival* (Hatto), 68.

> My hereditary Office is the Shield! I should think any lady weak of understanding who loved me for mere songs unbacked by manly deeds. If I desire a good woman's love and fail to win love's reward from her with shield and lance, let her favour me accordingly. A man who aims at love through chivalric exploits *rolls the dice* for high stakes.[57]

The final verses of the cited passage establish an important connection between the performance of the poet Wolfram and those of the imaginary knights and ladies in his story. Adventure, understood both as a narrative performance (i.e., a *story* of adventures) and as the chivalric pursuit of honor and love in the imaginary action of the romances, is a high-risk game of chance in which one wagers oneself. The reference here to the chivalric profession and deeds-in-arms underscores the basic orientation of Wolfram's poetic engagements. It gradually becomes clear that the poet in his "self-defense" is not only critically juxtaposing the infidelity of the lady he has chastised to the great fidelity Herzeloyde manifests in the imaginary action of his romance, but he is also warning the unnamed ladies whose wrath he has incurred that they should not underestimate his fortitude. He is also positioning himself vis-à-vis rivals in the poetic action. Common to the poet's investment of himself on these different fronts—on behalf of the imaginary knights and ladies in his romance, against the ladies who are angry at him, vis-à-vis his poetic rivals—is that he is a knight, and a tested and confident one judging by his swagger. The chivalric resources he can commit to any one of these purposes can also be brought to bear for the others. Apparently, Wolfram's audiences, unnamed ladies nursing a grudge, and poetic rivals would do well to respect his accomplishments as a chivalric performer, be this in battle, tournaments, or poetry.[58]

Wolfram profiles himself as a knight in a manner that distinguishes him markedly from his German predecessor Hartmann von Aue, who also called himself a knight in two of his narrative works but aligned his chivalric status with a clerical position of literacy and indebtedness to the books of the ancients.[59] Wolfram contrastively elaborates the characteristics of his own chivalric profile in an unprecedented way in the final verses of his "self-defense":

---

57. Ibid. The Middle High German *topels* refers specifically to dice, so I have slightly modified Hatto's rendering "gambles" with the italicized words.

58. In the forward of his *Parzival*-translation, Hatto offers remarks on Wolfram's chivalric posture in these verses that are consistent with my observations here: "In his Apology, inserted between the second and third chapters, Wolfram takes his stand not as a poet but as a knight, and in such bold and definite terms that he would have been howled down by the roughnecks of Thuringia had he not been a crack-jouster" (10).

59. For example, in the prologues of his religious narrative *Der arme Heinrich* and of his Arthurian romance *Iwein*, Hartmann presents himself as a *learned* knight.

hetens wîp niht vür ein smeichen,
ich solte iu vürbaz reichen
an disem maere unkundiu wort,
ich spraeche iu die âventiure vort.
swer des von mir geruoche,
der enzel si ze keinem buoche.
ichne kan deheinen buochstap.
dâ nement genuoge ir urhap:
disiu âventiure
vert âne der buoche stiure.
(115.21–30)

Unless the ladies thought it flattery, I should go on offering you things as yet unheard of in this story, I would continue this tale of adventure for you. But let whoever wishes me to do so, not take it as a book. I haven't a letter to my name! No few poets make their start from them: but this story goes its way without the guidance of books.[60]

Wolfram's not knowing a single letter of the alphabet is consistent with the lack of explicit references in his poetry to ancient books, which the poetry of Marie, Chrétien, Hartmann, and Gottfried contains. It is *not* consistent with his extensive depictions of medical procedures, the properties of gems and other stones, and astronomical bodies and occurrences—to mention only some of the many things in Wolfram's romance that indicate his familiarity with the contents of ancient books or medieval versions of them.[61] It seems improbable if not impossible that Wolfram was illiterate, but this is the way he proudly engages himself in the poetic action.[62] By diverging from other recent poet-performers and their habitual affiliation with the Latin books of ancient authors, Wolfram possibly appeals to the unlearned among "the most proven men and women" among his audience (elaborating the phrase of Otfried von Weissenburg), and perhaps also to the learned among them who might be amused and entertained by the unlearned pose of a performer whom they are

---

60. Wolfram von Eschenbach, *Parzival* (Hatto), 68–69.
61. G. Ronald Murphy's *Gemstone of Paradise* explores the connections between the (gem) stones that are so pervasive in Wolfram's romance and the poet's conception of the Holy Grail. Wolfram's extensive knowledge of science, medicine, and other cultural domains is also treated by Arthur Groos.
62. The term *literacy* of course involves a variety of different capacities that may be present in different degrees in a single individual poet-performer; see Groos's comments pertaining to literacy in the High Middle Ages (*Romancing the Grail,* passim and especially 33–35).

in a position to know is not so. The latter, with some suspension of disbelief, might also find value in the unlettered chivalric posture for its intrinsic characteristics, which more closely approximate the core military functions of the chivalric profession and noble courts than book learning and the polish and flourishes of rhetorical schooling (which some knights might regard as frills).

In Hartmann's depiction of Enite's wonderful horse, we saw him flush out the corresponding passage in Chrétien's *Érec et Énide* significantly. One of the creative elaborations of this description was the name "Umbriz," which Hartmann gave to the craftsman, who can therefore be regarded as the imaginary creator of Hartmann's many additions to the description of the saddle and saddle blanket. We also saw with Hartmann that the value of the narrative additions he makes depends not on anything factual or probable, but rather on "finishing" the potential of the story—such as that of the moment when Enite rides forth in appropriate style toward a happy ending with her husband. Hartmann's efforts in this particular description exemplify his engagement in the poetic action more generally, helping us to understand the relationship between his *Erec* (and *Iwein*) and the French poet's *Érec et Énide* (and *Yvain*) in terms of an ongoing competition in which the attempt is always being made by the best poet-performers to realize more fully and completely the potential of a given story. Similarly, in the performance of his grail romance, Wolfram surveys the previous poetic action and engages it, with Chrétien de Troyes and Hartmann von Aue serving both as resources and rivals.[63] Wolfram's pointedly chivalric approach to the action, as visible in his "self-defense," places him much more at odds with his illustrious, learned, clerically trained predecessors, not to mention with his consummately learned contemporary Gottfried von Strassburg, than they are from each other as a consequence of their common foregrounding of that training. Two more examples from Wolfram's *Parzival* underscore this point.

One of Wolfram's striking moves involves pointedly addressing poetic rivals in the interest of his characters. An important moment in Wolfram's story occurs when the uncouth Parzival first arrives from his mother's wilderness at Arthur's court to become a knight. Wild, unlettered, full of energy and potential, and completely forthright (though still inexperienced and naïve), Parzival is here cast much as Wolfram has cast himself in his "self-defense"—someone whom one suspects the poet-performer would happily take under his wing. At this important juncture, comparable in significance to the moment in

---

63. Basing himself on concepts elaborated by Bakhtin, Groos sees Chrétien de Troyes and Hartmann von Aue as representative of a "monologic" clerical variety of narrative, while Wolfram's narrative manifests a "heterogenic pluralism" that is "highly unusual for a medieval narrative around 1200" (Ibid., 25).

which Enite receives her horse with Hartmann's clerically trained flourishes, Wolfram steps out of his story into a brief excursus in which he engages poetic rivals on behalf of his hero:

> mîn hêr Hartman von Ouwe,
> vrou Ginovêr iuwer vrouwe
> und iuwer hêrre der künc Artûs,
> den kumt ein mîn gast ze hûs.
> bitet hüeten sîn vor spotte.
> ern ist gîge noch diu rotte:
> si sulen ein ander gampel nemen:
> des lâzen sich durch zuht gezemen,
> anders iuwer vrouwe Enîde
> unt ir muoter Karsnafîde
> werdent durch die mül gezücket
> unde ir lop gebrücket.
> sol ich den munt mit spotte zern,
> ich wil mînen vriunt mit spotte wern.
> (143.21–144.4)

Sir Hartmann of Aue, I am sending a stranger to the palace to visit your lord and lady, King Arthur and Queen Ginover. Kindly shield him from mockery. He is no fiddle or rote. In the name of all that is seemly let people find something else to strum on!–otherwise your Lady Enite and her mother Karsnafite will be dragged through the mill and their reputations lowered! If I am to twist my mouth to jibes, with jibes I will defend my friend![64]

Only a few verses later, Wolfram seeks to defend his hero on a different front. To those who might be inclined to find fault with the young and inexperienced Parzival because they compare him negatively with the fine courtly bearing of Gottfried's Tristan when the latter first arrives at Marke's court, Wolfram has this to say:

> in zôch dehein Curvenâl:
> er kunde curtôsîe niht,
> als ungevarnem man geschiht.
> (144.20–22)

---

64. Wolfram von Eschenbach, *Parzival* (Hatto), 83.

> No Kurvenal had reared him, he knew nothing of fine manners as is often the case with a stay-at-home.[65]

The peasants' proverb cited by Chrétien in his *Érec and Énide*-prologue seems pertinent at this moment: "What you scorn may be worth much more than you think." Wolfram's aggressively defensive posture toward poetic rivals suggests indirectly that Parzival's worth may be much more than it may seem to be at this moment, that the derision he soon receives at Arthur's court from Keie will be more than sufficient. Poetic rivals should not take advantage of Parzival's inexperienced condition at this vulnerable moment, Wolfram seems to say, and thereby add insult to injury. In this brief excursus, Wolfram articulates the competitive action among poet-performers with the imaginary performances of the knights and ladies in their stories. The former can become advocates, allies, and supporters of the latter, and motivating the alliance in this case is a standard of chivalric excellence that Parzival has not yet achieved (though he will), rather than anything associated with "fine manners."

The move with which Wolfram perhaps most pointedly distinguishes himself from poetic rivals involves his posture toward his predecessor and source, Chrétien de Troyes. By means of additions such as his challenge to Hartmann (and also implicitly to Gottfried, with his Curveval-reference), Wolfram increases the dimensions of the grail story significantly beyond that of Chrétien's unfinished *Perceval*. The similarities of *Parzival* to *Perceval* show that the latter was a source for the former, but Wolfram brashly brushes Chrétien off as his source and claims instead to base himself on the story of a mysterious and otherwise unknown Provençal "master," whom he calls "Kyot."[66] Somewhat like Hartmann's "Umbriz," but in a much more encompassing way, Kyot stands in for a later poet-performer's creative elaborations of an earlier one.[67] As an

---

65. Wolfram von Eschenbach, *Parzival* (Hatto), 83.

66. "Kyot" possibly points in the direction of a historical *Guiot*, but no scholarly consensus has ever coalesced in this regard, which still leaves us with an *imaginary* Kyot as the most likely explanation for Wolfram's extensive elaborations.

67. "Kyot" provides a possible way of understanding the enigmatic lines that follow Wolfram's claim that his story proceeds without the guidance of books: *ê man si hete vür ein buoch, / ich waere ê nacket âne touch, / sô ich in dem bade saeze, / ob ich des questen niht vergaeze* (vv. 116, 1–4)—"Rather than that it be taken as a book, I should prefer to sit naked in my tub without a towel—provided I had my scrubber!" (Wolfram von Eschenbach, *Parzival* [Hatto], 69). Remembering that Wolfram is performing in front of a live audience, he might well be saying he would rather be standing stark naked in front of his audience than have his tale understood as book based, as long as he has a little bush (*questen*) to cover up his *nakedness* (i.e., the fact that the story is his own creation). In a certain sense, Wolfram *is* naked: what the audience is hearing and seeing is *him* and *his* story. The "Kyot" that he will later introduce as his source would seem to function well as such a *questen*—"scrubber," by means of which the

important element in his own chivalric *finishing* of the story, Wolfram crowds Chrétien out of the picture and claims to share credit only with the unknown and probably invented Provençal. In his prologue, Wolfram had already indicated the lengths to which he would have to be able and willing to go in his performance:

nu lât mîn eines wesen drî,
der ieslîcher sunder pflege
daz mîner künste widerwege:
dar zuo gehôrte wilder vunt,
ob si iu gerne taeten kunt
daz ich iu eine künden will.
(4.2-7)

Grant there were three of me, each with skill to match mine: there would still be need of unbridled inspiration to tell you what, single-handed, I have a mind to tell![68]

The inspiration will not be lacking. Wolfram follows through with his initial boast and successfully brings his principal heroes Parzival and Gawan to the joyful ends of their respective adventures. The rich transmission of Wolfram's grail romance, and the esteem in which he was held by later poet-performers, suggests his speculation regarding the value of a strongly chivalric "finishing" of Chrétien's unfinished grail story was a quite successful one.[69]

Near the beginning of this chapter, we considered Gottfried von Strassburg's "literary review," and we turn now to the performance from which this review was taken, the romance *Tristan*, which predictably adds more superlative poetic moves to the ones we have already seen. We observed above that Gottfried thinks little of Wolfram's pointedly unlettered chivalric approach, and that he prefers instead a clerical, rhetorical standard of stylistic clarity and formal elegance, which he sees most joyfully realized by Hartmann von Aue, the winner of his laurel wreath for narrative poetry. Gottfried takes a bookish

---

poet-performer covers this nakedness, though people still clearly see and know who is standing in front of them.
68. Wolfram von Eschenbach, *Parzival* (Hatto), 16.
69. Unfinished, both in the way that any and every previous work is unfinished and in need of completion by later poets, but also unfinished in the conventional sense: Chrétien's story breaks off in the middle of Gauvain's adventures following Perceval's stay with the hermit. On Wolfram's extraordinary impact in the subsequent poetic action in the German vernacular, see Bumke, *Wolfram von Eschenbach*, 29–32; and Dallapiazza, *Wolfram von Eschenbach*, 28–29.

approach to questions of narrative style, organization, and adornment, but this approach is no less strikingly novel in its own way than that of Wolfram, perhaps necessarily so in view of the subject matter. How can the maximum possible courtly joy be gained from a story about an adulterous love affair in which a king is cuckolded by his wife and nephew? What good to the court is the love between the bravest, handsomest, and most effective knight and the most beautiful and resourceful lady, when the lady is married to another? The answers to these questions, as suggested by Gottfried in his prologue, amount to an unprecedented speculation on the value of a love that can only be *fully* appreciated by a smaller population of courtiers with very special characteristics, to which the poet addresses himself here more specifically:

> ein ander werlt die meine ich,
> diu samet in eime herzen treit
> ir süeze sûr, ir liebez leit,
> ir herzeliep, ir senede nôt,
> ir liebez leben, ir leiden tôt,
> ir lieben tôt, ir leidez leben.
> dem leben sî mîn leben ergeben,
> der werlt wil ich gewerldet wesen,
> mit ir verderben oder genesen.
> (58–66)

> I have another world in mind which together in one heart bears its bittersweet, its dear sorrow, its heart's joy, its love's pain, its dear life, its sorrowful death, its dear death, its sorrowful life. To this life let my life be given, of this world let me be part, to be damned or saved with it.[70]

Later in this study, we shall see that investments in love in the High Middle Ages have primarily imperial or universal rather than individual parameters. Even as an individual experience, love is supposed to be joyful for the court as a whole, that is, for the noble households of *principes*. Love serves as a resource and a reward on account of the universal value it has beyond individuals and couples. The individual experiences love as something universal without yet being positioned to harness, contain, or otherwise lay claim to it as something purely or strictly individual. Gottfried nevertheless seems to take steps in the direction of a love of more differentiated, possibly *individualized* dimensions (i.e., at least in terms of different individual *communities* at court). The good

---

70. Gottfried von Strassburg, *Tristan* (Hatto), 42.

and the joy in the love of Tristan and Isolt is not for *everybody* at court, he tells us in the cited passage, but for a more limited and specific group, the *edele herzen*—"noble hearts." This poetic move intends not to exclude anyone at court, but rather to identify, cultivate, and extol a more limited population that is capable of accomplishing something of value *for everyone*. The noble hearts are capable of realizing a special, higher joy in love, because they are prepared to accept the pain that always goes along with it, which makes love all the more joyful and sweet:

> diz leit ist liebes alse vol,
> daz übel daz tuot sô herzewol,
> daz ez kein edele herze enbirt,
> sît ez hie von geherzet wirt.
> (115–18)

This sorrow is so full of joy, this ill is so inspiriting that, having once been heartened by it, no noble heart will forego it!⁷¹

Gottfried invests in a *higher* love—a love that only a *specialist* courtly population of noble hearts is able to appreciate—and thereby gives *high* a new and very different sense (vis-à-vis the Christian parameters of love). But he also hedges his bets by conceding *vröuden*—"courtly joys," though doubtless less refined and valuable ones than those to which the noble hearts have access, to the "world of the many" (see vv. 45–53). The two populations with their different levels of joy in love remain connected by virtue of a consequential poetic move that Gottfried makes in the very first verses of his romance:

> Gedaehte mans ze guote niht
> von dem der werlde guot geschiht,
> sô waere ez allez alse niht,
> swaz guotes in der werlde geschiht.
> (1–4)

If we failed in our esteem of those who confer benefits on us, the good that is done among us would be as nothing."⁷²

---

71. Ibid.
72. Ibid., 41; I will return to this passage from Gottfried's prologue in chapter six, where the focus falls more squarely on the proper appraisal of the efforts of the lovers Tristan and Isolt in the imaginary action.

In these beginning verses, before the more specific terms of Gottfried's poetic performance (i.e., the story of adulterous love) have become clear, the court as a whole is being addressed and asked to accept a general *accounting*. *Everything* done for the good of the court needs to be valued, presumably even a good that some or even many might not be in a position to understand or recognize as such. Gottfried thereby establishes at the outset parameters that he regards as appropriate for the accurate assessment of the value of Tristan and Isolt's love—and for the assessment of his own poetic performance of it.[73]

The balance Gottfried strikes in his poetic performance between the capacities and preferences of the noble hearts and those of the "world of the many," in order to realize the greatest possible value in love for the court, seems to be precarious. The medieval continuators of Gottfried's unfinished romance will heap praise on him for the rhetorical, stylistic standard of his verses, without endeavoring to reiterate, critically engage, or elaborate the moves whereby Gottfried preserves the absoluteness of (adulterous) love and confers the task of competently evaluating and experiencing it to specialists at court best equipped to accomplish this. The continuators of Gottfried's unfinished romance seem to speculate that their own audiences are not likely to have *edele herzen* among them who will respond joyously to such moves, or they perhaps doubt that their own ability to adorn such a challenging subject matter beautifully and pleasingly will be up to the task.[74] The value of love for later medieval poet-performers and audiences is thereby set accordingly. The assessments of modern poets, artists, and audiences will be individualized and varied. Negative appraisals include that of the famous philologist and editor Karl Lachmann in the early nineteenth century, who considered that *Tristan* contains little more than *Üppigkeit oder Gotteslästerung*—"voluptuousness or blasphemy."[75] Richard Wagner, quite differently, finds in the absolute love of Gottfried's performance an artistic move worth reiterating for his individualized modern audiences (just as he also finds value in Wolfram's *Parzival*). We observe that the standard set by Gottfried's poetic moves in the second decade of the thirteenth century is not again reached in the Middle Ages and remains a challenge and inspiration to modern audiences. One might therefore be tempted to maintain that Gottfried earns the role of supreme arbiter that he plays in the poetic *review* with which we began this chapter.

---

73. Compare Haug, who, based on a detailed analysis of Gottfried's prologue, states the poet is developing what amounts to an "ethics of love" (*Vernacular Literary Theory*, 196–227).

74. Monika Schausten's *Erzählwelten* presents detailed considerations of the medieval continuations of Gottfried's unfinished poem by Ulrich von Türheim (201–50) and Heinrich von Freiberg (251–86).

75. Lachmann, *Kleinere Schriften zur Philologie*, 159. The English rendering is mine.

We must of course bear in mind that Gottfried's review includes only the principal German poets (i.e., the French poets were *first,* and the German poets have the disadvantages and advantages associated with their retrospective positions vis-à-vis their predecessors) and that his assessment of Wolfram—in view of the latter's lasting record of success—is harsh and indicative of the intensity of the competition between these two luminaries of very different poetic inclinations.

We have seen in this chapter that poet-performers at noble courts in the High Middle Ages regard the poetic action as something that can and must be made better, or *finished,* and poets do so with varying degrees of capacity and flair. Poet-performers engage each other with reference to standards that have been set, which they hope at least to equal if not surpass with their own innovative moves. The joy of the court seems largely to depend on the competitive efforts of the poet-performers, so those with any poetic talent should engage themselves—work late into the night, as Marie tells us she did—to maintain or improve their own position and to help insure that the action at court is moving in a fruitful and gratifying direction. We have also observed, in the competitive give-and-take among the medieval poet-performers, that new standards are continually being set by tapping into the potential of the vernacular languages and their associated narrative traditions. The poetic action at medieval courts is largely about achieving an optimal, joyful convergence of the *high* cultural resources associated with the language of God since Roman antiquity and the *lower* ones associated with the emerging vernacular languages of European peoples in the Middle Ages. In the next two chapters, we turn to the imaginary action of the romances and to its principal speculative concerns: adventure as a play for the regard in which one is held by one's courtly peers and love as the investment of oneself in another.

CHAPTER 5

Adventure as a Cultural Wager

DYNAMICS OF ADVENTURE

Rendered in the verse romances by the Old French *âventure* and its Middle High German derivative *âventiure,* the term *adventure* designates both the narrative performances of poet-performers such as Marie de France, Chrétien de Troyes, Hartmann von Aue, and Wolfram von Eschenbach, as well as the efforts of figures such as Erec, Enide, and Parzival in the imaginary action of the romances. The poets in their performances of the romances before courtly audiences as well as the imaginary characters with their chivalric deeds before the eyes of their own courtly peers *in* the romances are jointly engaged in adventure as a competitive move. As we saw in the previous chapter, top romance performers compete with each other at the courts of noble households, mustering the resources available to them in order to rise to the highest level. In the imaginary action of the romances, adventure as a cultural move occurs as the questing self engages another mutable self or thing in this temporal world in a newly indeterminate way in the interest of growth. We shall observe in this chapter that this move happens *competitively* as a speculative wagering of self.

The imaginary adventuring of knights and ladies in the romances has dynamics that are specific to it and others—such as the interest in joy as outcome and the understanding that one has to engage oneself if one possesses the necessary resources—that it shares with competitive performances in other cultural domains. Since the adventuring of the knights and ladies in the romances is *imaginary*—a specific kind of action occurring as mental simulations and their accompanying physiological sensations—it seems to be at the farthest remove from any kind of embodied, *real* cultural practice.[1] *Imagining* something seems to be different, possibly categorically different, from actually *doing* something. Hence, the *pretend* or *make believe* status of adventures in romance poetry tends to be what is definitive of them in some scholarly views.[2] The times and places at court in which people occupy themselves with imaginary adventures—such as the moment when the live performer Wolfram defends his Parzival when the latter first arrives at Arthur's court[3]—might also be considered *pretend* in the same way as the imaginary action in the romances. However, as the understanding of *adventure* as something *unreal* is widened to include the embodied poetic action of live performers and audiences at real historical courts, it is on a slippery slope. When and where do *pretend* events stop and *real* ones begin? If the actual live performances of rival poets at courts were to be understood in some way as unreal, would the same not be true of chivalric tournaments (as pretend warfare along the lines of chivalric contests in the romances), or perhaps also of courtly festivals such as Barbarossa's in Mainz in 1184 (as a staged show of imperial unity under the banner of chivalry that seems in many ways to bring the action of the romances to life)?[4]

Close scrutiny of the dynamics of the *physical-material infrastructure of imaginary action* makes it more difficult for us to fix or isolate this action as something *unreal*. Research using functional magnetic resonance imaging (fMRI) into brain activity that occurs when people read fictional narratives

---

1. All courtiers have an interest in adventure, and ladies frequently share with knights the direct involvement in the vicissitudes of adventuring, as in the cases of Antikonie and Enide to be examined in this chapter.

2. I again cite as an example Bumke, who writes: "The courtly poets constructed an image of society that lacked everything that made life difficult and oppressive" (*Courtly Culture*, 4). Alternately, Rüdiger Schnell has argued for a "free space" within which court poetry needs to be see as operating ("Kirche, Hof, und Liebe").

3. Wolfram von Eschenbach, *Parzival* (Lachmann), here vv. 143.21–144.4; this passage was discussed in the previous chapter.

4. Bumke aligns court festivals with court poetry, conceding some *reality* to them, but maintaining that the festival, just as poetry, lacks "the gloomy aspects of daily life" (*Courtly Culture*, 4). The discrepancy between a more or less explicitly *unrealistic* poetry and festive context, on the one hand, and the "gloomy" reality of medieval life, on the other, shapes Bumke's conception of courtly culture in general. On the relationship of Barbarossa's festival in Mainz and the ideals of knighthood, see Fleckenstein, "Friedrich Barbarossa."

suggests that *all* imaginary action is physiologically *embodied*.[5] The mental simulation of events involved in the apprehension of fictional narratives produces measurable activity in the brain and hence is *real* in this respect. Regions of the brain involved in the understanding of imaginary actions in stories and those involved in actually carrying out such actions largely overlap, suggesting that the apprehension of language more generally is grounded in visual and motor simulations. Reading the words *run* or *kick,* for example, involves mental simulations in the same regions of the brain that are involved in running and kicking. Extending the insights of this modern scientific research to past times, it seems to follow that medieval people who watch and listen to a poet-performer relating an account of chivalric action would neurologically simulate the hoofbeats of a galloping horse and the impact of swords on shields in their comprehension of a story about chivalric deeds-in-arms as it progresses. In modern readers of a medieval romance, these actions also are simulated, though presumably with less vividness and accuracy, corresponding to the lack of a live performer and their relatively diminished experience in the life domains to which the narrative events corresponded in medieval culture.[6]

Research suggests that neural simulations of imagined actions go beyond discrete simple events like running, kicking, or galloping. An fMRI-based study by Speer, Reynolds, Swallow, and Zacks of brain activity during reading shows that the apprehension of far more complex fictional narratives—involving imaginary interactions with characters and objects, the spatial and temporal layouts of situations, and goals and intentions—activates the same regions of the brain that are active when such matters are negotiated in embodied, real-world action:

> Readers dynamically activate specific visual, motor, and conceptual features of activities while reading about analogous changes in activities in the context of a narrative: regions involved in processing goal-directed human activity, navigating spatial environments, and manually manipulating objects in the real world increased in activation at points when those specific aspects of the narrated situation were changing. For example, when readers processed changes in a character's interactions with an object, precentral and parietal areas associated with grasping hand movements increased in activation.[7]

---

5. See Yarkoni, et al., "Pictures of a Thousand Words"; and Speer, et al., "Reading Stories."

6. See Mar and Oatley, "Function of Fiction": "Personal experience plays an important role in how transported or immersed in a piece of narrative fiction a reader becomes" (here 178).

7. Speer, et al., "Reading Stories," 995–96.

Narrative action involving purposeful, goal-directed movement and the manipulation of objects is thus neurologically embodied, whether such action involves a person walking through a room and pausing to pick up a shiny object from a table along the way, the Pauline-Augustine self moving through the world toward its heavenly reward without letting itself be distracted by the attractive people and things beckoning to it, or a knight fighting his way through a wasteland in search of the Holy Grail. One of the conclusions of the cited study is that "the use of sensory and motor representations during story comprehension may reflect a more general neural mechanism for grounding cognition in real-world experience."[8] Scientific evidence supports the idea that imaginary actions associated with chivalric adventuring in the romances is grounded in neurological processes in regions of the brain that are involved in observing or carrying out the same actions in one's life experience, such as encountering opposition in the pursuit of one's goals, dealing with the death in combat of a loved one, and balancing supremely important life priorities. Another study has suggested that fictional narratives, understood as simulative models, provide a manner of rehearsing what I have been calling different *dispositions of self*:

> Story engagement is the structured recreation of an abstracted social interaction. This supplies advantages beyond spontaneous imagination. When reading, we are also recipients of a narrator's or protagonist's construal of the situation and its solution, and such a contribution may provide us with new perspectives and possibly new solutions. Narratives allow us to try out solutions to emotional and social difficulties through the simulation of these experiences, as we try to comprehend the actions of protagonists and ponder how our own responses may compare were we presented with the same situation.[9]

It seems to follow that medieval courtiers, having elsewhere imaginatively rehearsed a certain disposition of self by reading or hearing treatises by St. Augustine or stories of eremitic saints, would find their brains similarly *exercised* by the simulations generated by the chivalric romances—for example, the visual and motor simulations of the violent struggles of knights against chivalric opponents, giants, or dragons, which would overlap somewhat with those of saints against demons. But different activations would need to occur in the simulation of the dynamics and purposes of adventure, that

---

8. Ibid., 998.
9. Mar and Oatley, "Function of Fiction," 183–84.

is, those involving the orientation of self toward mutable things as opposed to the otherworldly reward of the saints' striving. By way of their involvement in the imaginary action of the romances, courtiers would become accustomed to and practiced in the spatial and temporal *twists and turns* of things that are involved in *new* kinds of absolute investments of self. If narratives such as the saints' lives or Augustine's *City of God against the pagans* can be assumed to activate regions of peoples' brains and bodies in ways that help them live holy lives and turn away from the temptations of temporal cultural goods, then the chivalric romances might be expected to help people in the complex engagements with mutable selves and things that are involved in adventuring and loving. The simulative models involved in imaginary adventuring prepare, rehearse, reinforce, and otherwise enable adventurous (and amorous) action, understood here as the competitive endeavor to derive optimal enjoyment from the temporal, perishable resources of this world.[10]

Imaginary adventuring is construed in this chapter—as it is construed generally in this study—as a cultural move, a disposition of self that remains available throughout the cultural action. In this chapter, the dynamics of imaginary adventuring will be illustrated in two related ways, with the help of verses from significant courtly chivalric romances produced in the late twelfth and early thirteenth centuries. First, the focus in the continuation of this section below will be on the dynamics of adventure as a cultural wager. Adventure is set forth in the romances as a new disposition of the Pauline-Augustine self, in which spiritual-intellectual and physical-material resources

---

10. A passage from the didactic work of Thomasin von Zirclaria, *Der Welsche Gast* [Rückert], from the second decade of the thirteenth century, provides medieval corroboration of the broader applicability of the imaginary action of the romances: *Wâ ist Êrec und Gâwân / Parzivâl und Îwân? / ich weiz si ninder. Daz geschiht / dâ von daz wir haben niht / Artûs inder imme lant. / lebt er, wir vunden sâ zehant / in der werlde rîter gnuoc / die sô vrum sint und gevuoc / daz mans möht heizen Îwæn, / als mich dunkt und als ich wæn. / vür wâr ich ez iu sagen wil, / man vunde noch der rîter vil, / daz si an der tugende wec / uns möhten wol erstaten Êrec* (vv. 6325-38)—"Where are Erec and Gawain, where are Parzival and Iwein? I don't know that they are anywhere, and this has come about because we do not have Arthur in this country. If he were alive, we could immediately find plenty of knights in the world who were so decent and just that people could call them Iwein or so it seems to me or so I believe. Indeed, I want to say to you that many knights could still be found who through their virtues could easily take the place of Erec" (*Der Welsche Gast [The Italian Guest]* [Gibbs and McConnell], 130). In their commentary on this passage, the translators Gibbs and McConnell arrive at an observation similar to mine: "Thomasin highlights his despondence at the apparent absence of virtuous people by this lament for the central heroes of Arthurian romance and for King Arthur himself. The message would be very clear to an audience conversant with the tales of Chrétien de Troyes, and, in German, of Hartmann von Aue and Wolfram von Eschenbach. Yet his final comment here shows that, for him, these are the representatives of courtly values, which could still be revived by others" (239).

have been articulated by means of faith. Beyond its Christian disposition in the interest of the heavenly reward, the medieval self in adventure is opened up to and absolutely invested in another, temporal, worldly good—*honor,* the regard in which one is held by one's courtly chivalric peers. Pending circumstances and outcomes, this novel disposition of self leads to joy and growth in the event of success, to pain and decline in the event of failure.[11] Characteristic of the adventurous disposition of self are the indeterminate movements of selves and things through time and space, which occur in a manner akin to the movements of rolling dice or knights in a melee. Not coincidentally, where adventures are being depicted in the first significant verse romances by poet-performers such as Chrétien de Troyes, Hartmann von Aue, and Wolfram von Eschenbach, the descriptive language of choice is that of games and particularly games of chance.

After considering the dynamics of adventure as a cultural wager based on individual examples from different romances, I look more closely at two of the most illustrious verse romances, Chrétien's *Érec et Énide* and Wolfram von Eschenbach's *Parzival.* My main focus will be on *highlights* from these romances that show the adventurous wagering of self to be the principal concern. I also look at the role played by an important narrative design of the early verse romances, the "mout bele conjointure" of Chrétien de Troyes, as a poetic arrangement of adventures in Chrétien's *Érec et Énide,* and—though significantly varied and extended—in Wolfram von Eschenbach's *Parzival.* This narrative design presents itself as a poetic move whereby adventures in the imaginary world of the knights and ladies of King Arthur's court are conveyed to medieval courtly audiences in an optimally joyful way. In the bipartite arrangement of adventures begun by Chrétien (and reiterated and varied by later poet-performers such as Wolfram), as in adventures as single efforts, we continue to observe that the action occurs competitively. The manner in which adventures are arranged in series creates imaginary worlds that are in competition with one another—as well as with monastic views of the world of a more sharply dualistic bent. These competing imaginary worlds of adventure have ideological values and implications (i.e., monastic, clerical, courtly chivalric), as a consideration of the contrasting evaluations of adventuring by Chrétien, Wolfram—and of the famous Cistercian monastic writer Bernard of Clairvaux—will show.

·

---

11. For a wide-ranging study of pain in the works of the poet Hartmann von Aue, see Scott Pincikowski, *Bodies of Pain.*

The orientation of self in adventure is succinctly stated by the knight Kalogreant at the beginning of Hartmann von Aue's *Iwein* (ca. 1205). Having left the court of Arthur in search of adventure, Kalogreant finds himself in the wilds of the forest Breziljân, where the going is arduous. The wild space of Kalogreant's purposeful adventurous movement resembles a chivalric reiteration of the departure into the desert of eremitic saints. The chivalric forest and the eremitic desert are remote from the comforts of the world and characterized by difficulty of movement and the value attached to engagements with the spirits, people, and objects inhabiting them. Compared to the heavenly purpose of the eremite, for whom the wilderness is usually a one-way route leading irrevocably away from the things of the world, the aim of Kalogreant's staking of self is very different. When the knight comes to a clearing, he finds a wild man to whom he explains that he is seeking adventure. When the wild man fails to understand and asks him what adventure is—*âventiure? waz ist daz?*—Kalogreant replies:

> ich heize ein riter und hân den sin
> daz ich suochende rîte
> einen man der mit mir strîte,
> der gewâfent sî als ich.
> daz prîset in, und sleht er mich:
> gesige aber ich im an,
> sô hât man mich vür einen man,
> und wirde werder danne ich sî.[12]
> (530–37)

I am called a knight, and my purpose is to ride in search of a man who is armed like me and will fight with me. He will gain fame by defeating me, while if I win the victory, I shall be thought a valiant warrior and esteemed more highly.[13]

What is at stake in adventure as defined here by Kalogreant is the value of the courtly chivalric self.[14] The principal term for the growth of self in question is

---

12. Hartmann von Aue, *Iwein* (Benecke and Lachmann). Numbers of Middle High German and Old French verses from the romances here and elsewhere are cited parenthetically in text.

13. While I cite Richard Lawson's more recent translation of Hartmann's *Iwein* elsewhere, in this case I prefer the more literal rendering of J. W. Thomas, 61.

14. I differ from those scholarly appraisals that have viewed Kalogreant's definition of adventure as an indication of his shortcomings or of a flawed approach. See, for example,

honor (Old French *enor,* Middle High German *êre*), understood as the regard in which one is held by one's courtly peers. The fluctuating value of self that is evident in Kalogreant's definition contrasts with the determinate value of self that we observed in the first chapter of this study. In the cultural action at Troy, the status of figures such as Achilles and Hector was relatively fixed and not subject to the variability associated by Kalogreant with the outcomes of the most proximate individual contests. The warrior (Achilles) wins all the battles, the lover (Paris) loves the most beautiful woman, the trickster (Odysseus) outwits his adversaries, the sage (Nestor) has the best overview of the action based on its history. In the cultural action at a place like Troy, the outcomes of individual contests are largely fixed from the start by the status of the contestants engaged in them and by the decisions of *higher-ups.* In the high medieval chivalric action as rendered by Kalogreant in his definition of adventure, the value of self is relatively indeterminate, variable, and dependent on the most recent outcomes and the immediately upcoming ones.

The variability of the value of self in adventuring corresponds to an increasingly indeterminate, fluid cultural action based on adventurous elaborations of the Pauline-Augustine bipartite self. This Christian self, as we observed in earlier chapters, is already indeterminate or *virtual* because of the different orientations of the cultural resources articulated in and by it. Resources such as spirit and intellect tend toward the immutable heavenly kingdom as the highest and greatest principle of integrity, while resources such as flesh and matter tend toward the often painful disorder associated with mutability and disintegration (= *evil,* from a leveling, dualist perspective). These contrasting orientations are joined together in a self that is *racing,* like Paul's Christian athlete in 1 Corinthians 9:24, for the heavenly prize of the afterlife. The final outcome of the race is not yet decided, but it is clear that the outcome will be based on the articulation of these resources and, particularly, on how individuals dispose of the physical-material ones. Since the definitive criteria for deciding winners and losers are unknowable in this life and will not be completely clear until Judgment Day, there is wide latitude for the Christian self to try out different cultural moves such as adventure. Adventure increases the indeterminacy of the Christian's involvement in the cultural action by adding to the uncertainty of the race for the heavenly prize another level of indeterminacy connected to placing oneself at risk in the interest of a mutable worldly good such as honor, as we see in the case of Kalogreant. If the status of

---

Jaeger, *Origins of Courtliness,* 245. However flawed Kalogreant himself might be, the idea that his approach is flawed is not supported by the chivalric action as Hartmann renders it, or as it tends to be rendered in the verse romances generally.

the Pauline-Augustine Christian *athlete* racing for the otherworldly prize was already indeterminate, corresponding to God's outstanding final judgments concerning ultimate winners and losers, the adventurous turn toward and investment in mutable things adds additional major *hurdles* to the race.

Kalogreant's definition of adventure underlies what is generally called *knight errantry*. A knight risks what he is and has by putting himself in motion and riding from the comforts of the court into a forest full of challenges. He knows that other knights are doing so, for which reason he may not remain idle (as we shall see in *Érec et Énide* below), and he knows that opportunities to engage one or another of these knights will come. The possibility of increasing the value of self, referenced above by Kalogreant, is always accompanied by the inverse possibility of a decreased value of self in the case of defeat. Kalogreant does not mention the latter eventuality, but he soon experiences and later reports it in the continuation of Hartmann's narrative. Exposing oneself to risk in adventure is not limited to chivalric contests, because there are numerous other opponents against whom adventuring knights have to contend, such as beasts, giants, and demons. But the status accruing to adventuring knights based on successful engagements with such creatures is negligible compared to the honor to be gained from prevailing against a qualified knight. This honor is usually directly proportional to the regard in which the opponent is held upon entering a given contest. In this respect, the dynamics of knight errantry somewhat resemble those of a zero-sum game (an idea to which I return below). Knights engage in this *game* as contestants for honor as a cultural resource that tends to be regarded as limited. The honor of knights in this ongoing chivalric action is variable and continually in flux. Some knights have more of it than others, and the relative positions of knights are continually contingent on the most proximate outcomes, recent and upcoming. The *ongoing* importance of the most proximate outcomes makes knight errantry look like an extended venture. Whatever one's status might be at a given moment, there is always the possibility of growth if one can figure out how to engage oneself successfully, or of the inverse if one fails to do so.

The twists and turns of knight errantry—experienced physiologically by audiences of the romances, as we saw at the outset of this chapter—vary significantly from the action of eremitic saints, despite some similarities between romance poetry and hagiographical literature. The saints occasionally vie with each other in holiness, but their principal purpose is to overcome the temptations of the world as embodied by the devils and demons against which they frequently contend. There is no evident limit to the grace bestowed upon the saints as they move toward their heavenly reward, so the endeavors in which they are involved cannot be regarded as zero-sum—based on the assumption that there is an infinite supply of grace. Similarly, single *one-off* outcomes along the way—Antony's victory over a particular demon or beast, for example—do not seem to be as definitive of the saintly action as victories in combat are in the chivalric action. The saints' struggles with demonic adversaries and their occasional *holier than thou* engagements among themselves always seem to have more to do with who they are from the start than with how they perform at specific times and places. Saints are all winners and can be so because the resource they strive to possess is seemingly limitless and timeless. The adventurous pursuit of honor, in contrast to the saintly pursuit of grace, structures the temporal world in a different and more complicated way, which is shaped by the supposition that the coveted reward is available only in a limited supply. In the imaginary action of the romances, we see ladies and knights endeavoring to master their world in a way that maintains their interest in the heavenly reward at the same time as they strive for limited and variable resources such as honor and love. As they open themselves up to and engage the twists and turns of mutable worldly things as opportunities for growth, something new and different is happening: ladies and knights are becoming *players* and thereby setting a new cultural trend.

The romances show the dynamics of adventure as defined and undertaken by Kalogreant, and as I have descriptively elaborated these dynamics above in connection to knight errantry, to underlie other chivalric contests for honor among knights. These include chivalric action in tournaments and trials-by-combat at court. We saw in our survey of the poetic action in the previous chapter that the poet-performer Wolfram von Eschenbach likened chivalric exploits in pursuit of love to a high-stakes game of dice. In the imaginary action of Chrétien de Troyes's *Lancelot*, we find the same gaming analogy used by the knight Gauvain when Meleagant has appeared at Arthur's court for a trial-by-combat with Lancelot. As often occurs in the chivalric action under certain circumstances, one knight can stand in for another, and Gauvain volunteers to do this for the absent Lancelot with these words:

> Bien me cuit a vos aquiter;
> Mes se vient a plus poinz giter
> Et g'en giet plus que ne façoiz,
> Si m'aist Dex et sainte Foiz,
> Quan qu'avra el geu tot an tasche
> Prendrai, ja n'en avrai relasche.[15]
> (6759–65)

---

15. Chrétien de Troyes, *Lancelot ou le Chevalier.*

> I am confident that I will acquit myself well. It is like casting dice; and with God and Saint Foy on my side, I shall cast more points than you, and before it's over I shall pocket all the wagers.[16]

Gauvain's likening of his intended chivalric action to a throw of the dice underscores the indeterminacy of outcomes in chivalric combat. Despite his confidence and hope that God and Saint Foy will stand by him, there is no way to know what the final result will be. Based on Meleagant's homicidal *track record* to this point, combat with him—were it to occur—might well result in death, so Gauvain's play must be regarded as an *absolute* wagering of self.[17]

In Wolfram's own grail romance, *Parzival*, chivalric engagement is depicted with a variety of playful imagery to underscore the indeterminacy of adventuring. The below-cited passage describes a moment when the knight Gawan and the lady Antikonie jointly contend against the inhabitants of the castle of Bearosche.[18] Antikonie and Gawan are attacked because they have been caught in a moment of physical intimacy. Gawan's actions are considered a violation of the trust of his host, King Vergulaht (Antikonie's brother), and his actions are presumed to have dishonored Antikonie, though Wolfram stresses in his depiction of the amorous activity that the lady is a willing participant, and the poet continues to express the view that nothing dishonorable has occurred. In the ensuing engagement with the angry castle residents, Gawan and Antikonie retreat into a tower of the castle, which they use as a defensive position. Antikonie initially takes charge of the joint defense and gives Gawan a heavy chess board to use as a shield to defend himself. The lady then proceeds to make use of the chess pieces in this way:

> ez waere künec oder roch,
> daz warf si gein den vîenden doch:
> ez was grôz und swaere.
> man sagt von ir diu maere,
> swen dâ erreichte ir wurfes swanc,
> der strûchte âne sînen danc.
> diu küneginne rîche
> streit dâ ritterlîche,

---

16. Idem, *Knight of the Cart*, 290.

17. Gauvain's speculative engagement of himself in this episode is all the more significant if, as Emmanuèle Baumgartner maintains, this knight can be regarded as a "role model for new knights" at this stage of the history of romance poetry ("Chrétien's Medieval Influence," 217).

18. Wolfram here relates an adventure based on a similar one in Chrétien's *Perceval*, but he elaborates it extensively.

bî Gâwân si werlîche schein,
daz diu koufwîp ze Tolenstein
an der vasnaht nie baz gestriten:
wan si tuontz von gampelsiten
unde müent ân nôt ir lîp.
swâ harnaschrâmec wirt ein wîp,
diu hât ir rehtes vergezzen,
sol man ir kiusche mezzen,
sine tuonz dan durch ir triuwe.
(408.29–409.15)

The pieces were large and heavy. Yet king or rook, she hurled them at the enemy. And it is narrated that whoever was hit by her throws was toppled, despite himself. The puissant Princess acquitted herself there like a true knight, she was seen fighting at Gawan's side with such spirit that the huck-stresses at Dollenstein never fought better of a Shrovetide, except that they do it at a frolic and exert themselves without cause. If one were asked to judge of their modesty, women who begrime themselves with armour forget their nature, unless loyal affection inspires them.[19]

Gawan and Antikonie—with Wolfram backing them up—have established that they have much to gain from each other in love, and they had begun to invest themselves in this when they were first assaulted by the castle residents. They now defend the honorability of their intentions with this spirited resistance. The contest of Antikonie and Gawan against the inhabitants of the castle precedes the scheduled single contest against Kingrimursal, whom Gawan had come to Vergulaht's land to find for the purpose of settling a dispute. As a prelude to the chivalric contest that is supposed to ensue, the action of Antikonie and Gawan against their adversaries resembles *chivalry*—which Wolfram explicitly, though clearly also quite playfully, states in the cited passage—and this action endeavors to preserve their honor intact.[20] In the case of Gawan, his honor has already been impugned by the accusation made much earlier in the romance that his father slew Kingrimursal's father in a cowardly way.[21] Gawan's honor

---

19. Wolfram von Eschenbach, *Parzival* (Hatto), 210.
20. Compare Michael Dallapiazza, who considers that Antikonie (among other female figures crafted by Wolfram) conducts herself in a way that is remarkably self-conscious and self-determining, despite the patriarchal structures in which the figure is imbedded (*Wolfram von Eschenbach*, 112).
21. See Wolfram von Eschenbach, *Parzival* (Hatto), 212. This accusation is later revealed not to be true.

is now further impugned by the accusation that he has dishonored Vergulaht's sister. Overall, Gawan and Antikonie stand to decline in status if the various accusations against them can be made to stand. Wolfram's unconventional chess-based variation of adventure involves a diverse array of performers in the action, ranging from the lady and knight themselves to the "huckstresses" of the German village of Dollenstein—apparently a reference to a local custom in which the village women playfully mimic chivalric contests as part of a Shrovetide procession.[22] With this reference, Wolfram playfully extends the corresponding episode in Chrétien's earlier grail romance in the direction of Shrovetide merrymaking, though the joyful antics of the "huckstresses" also serve as a point of contrast. Antikonie's spirited defense of Gawan and herself, in contrast to the action in Dollenstein, has more serious implications.

The complex indeterminacy of this multifaceted, imaginary chivalric action is oriented toward the serious consideration articulated in the final four verses of the cited passage. Wolfram first pronounces a general rule according to which a woman immodest enough to wear armor has forgotten her "nature," only to overturn it in the case of women such as Antikonie who are motivated by loyalty. Antikonie is hereby aligned with other significant female characters in Wolfram's romance, most notably Parzival's mother Herzeloyde and cousin Sigune.[23] The association of Antikonie with Herzeloyde and Sigune as exemplars of great loyalty, which is suggested by Wolfram's use of the term *triuwe*—"loyal affection"—lends a more serious tone to this otherwise playful adventure and provides a view of Antikonie's "chivalric" engagement with chess pieces as something more *real* and consequential in its own imaginary way than the Shrovetide playacting of the village women. The joint adventure of Antikonie and Gawan brings together the finest qualities and utmost exertions of a woman and a man who both engage themselves in the valorous manner of knights, a cross section of medieval life ranging from castles to villages, and a chivalric contest that mixes together unconventional chess moves and the tumultuous gyrations of Shrovetide play-acting—all in the important interest of framing and underscoring the great loyalty of the "puissant princess."

In another noteworthy and influential case of the dynamics of adventure, we observe another of the ways in which Chrétien de Troyes—the reputed inventor of Arthurian romance—is a trendsetter. The giving and receiving of blows with lance and sword is like rolling dice and chess pieces in motion,

---

22. See Bumke, *Wolfram von Eschenbach*, 84.
23. My view of Antikonie is consistent with that of Marions Gibbs in her article, "Ideals of Flesh and Blood," 24–25.

but it is also like speculative lending and borrowing with a view to making a profit. We see this in the poet's depiction of the battle between Cligès and the Duke of the Saxons:

> Molt sont andui li vasal large
> De cos doner a grant planté,
> S'a chascuns boene volanté
> De tost randre ce qu'il acroit,
> Ne cil ne cist ne s'an recroit,
> Que tot sanz conte et sanz mesure
> Ne rande chetel et ousure
> Li uns a l'autre sanz respite.[24]
> (4064–71)

> Both knights were generous in giving blows aplenty, and each was quite willing to return what he was given. Neither of them grew weary of repaying, without accounting and without measure, both capital and interest to his enemy unceasingly.[25]

Doubtless informed and inspired by earlier passages such as this one, the German poet Hartmann von Aue elaborates chivalric adventuring as speculative moneylending with greater differentiation and detail in his description of the trial-by-combat between the knight with the lion (Iwein incognito) and Gawein near the end of his *Iwein*.[26] The initial verses of Hartmann's depiction of the combat between these two knights reiterates the basic terms of Kalogreant's definition of adventure near the beginning of this same romance, but with a manifestly entrepreneurial gist:

> Wer gerne lebet nâch êren,
> der sol vil starke kêren
> alle sine sinne
> nâch etelîchem gewinne,
> dâ mit er sich wol bejage
> und ouch vertrîbe die tage.
> also heten sî getân:

---

24. Chrétien de Troyes, *Cligès* (Dembowski).
25. Idem, *Cligès* (Kibler), 172.
26. W. H. Jackson offers a perceptive analysis of this episode in his *Chivalry in Twelfth-Century Germany*, 267–70.

> ir leben was niht verlân
> an dehein müezekheit.
> in was beiden vil leit
> swenne ir tage giengen hin
> daz sî deheinen gewin
> an ir koufe envunden,
> des sî sich underwunden.
> (7175–88)

> He who likes to acquire honor has to direct all his thoughts to some type of livelihood, so that he can achieve something and pass the time acceptably. They had done so. They had not spent their lives in idleness. Both were unhappy when days passed without their finding any profit in the trade to which they had devoted themselves.[27]

The adventurous desire to increase the value of self that we saw with Kalogreant is here rendered as a prescriptive orientation to life. In the pursuit of greater worth, or *êren*—"honor"—knights have to engage themselves in a speculative cultural action analogous to the profit-seeking give-and-take of moneylenders and investors. As chivalric competitors *at the top of their game*, Iwein and Gawein best exemplify that one has to engage oneself if one has the resources to do so. There is a chivalric imperative to be *entrepreneurial* and the realization of this imperative is here appropriately depicted with the terminology and imagery of investment and profit seeking, which Hartmann develops further in the ensuing verses:

> sî wâren zwêne maere
> karge wehselaere
> und entlihen ûz ir varende guot
> ûf einen seltsaenen muot.
> sî nâmen wuocher dar an
> sam zwêne werbende man.
> (7189–94)

> The two, well known as clever moneylenders, made loans from their stock in trade in a strange way. They made a profit from it, like two entrepreneurs.[28]

---

27. Hartmann von Aue, *Iwein* (Lawson), 311.
28. Ibid. According to James Aho in his *Confession and Bookkeeping*, the Christian merchant first becomes visible based on business records preserved from the early fourteenth century. This episode in Hartmann's romance documents the existence of the Christian merchant—or at

The action of knights resembles that of moneylenders both in the logic of exchange and in the quest for gain. The knights' *investments* are "strange," however, because of the deadly extremes to which they are willing to go in pursuit of their reward. What is being *lent* and *borrowed* here are the potentially lethal blows of lances and swords. It seems likely that Hartmann bases himself here on the cited depiction of the battle between Cligès and the Duke of the Saxons in Chrétien's *Cligès,* or a similar depiction elsewhere, and transfers the speculative economics of that contest to this one. The longer and more detailed rendering of Hartmann, from which the above-cited passages are taken, corresponds to the inherent descriptive potential for chivalric purposes of the terminology of speculative moneylending, which the German poet finds worthy of extensive elaboration. It corresponds as well to the great significance of the narrative moment in which the combat between Iwein and Gawein occurs.

Acting in a manner consistent with Kalogreant's definition of adventure, which he heard with his own ears at the beginning of this romance, Iwein has set forth in pursuit of honor and has experienced many vicissitudes along the way before this moment. By putting himself in the position to engage Gawein, Iwein now stands to earn a huge reward, but the great prowess of the combatants prevents either knight from being able to overcome the other. The quality of their actions is deemed so high that an outcome in favor of one or the other would be unjust, and when their identities are finally revealed, the combat is halted because the combatants are friends. The inheritance dispute is resolved by King Arthur in a separate legalistic maneuver, and the combat between Iwein and Gawein remains undecided in a way that demonstrates and confirms the great chivalric worth of *both* contestants.[29] This adventure nevertheless continues to manifest a zero-sum logic, because neither knight is able to expropriate any honor from the other, that is, the conflict is resolved in a manner that does not involve one knight overcoming or yielding to the other. We thus observe, under certain circumstances, that competitive chivalric exchanges perceived to be of a sufficiently high level or quality—as one tends to find them in close proximity to Arthur's court, where the overall quality of

---

least a "strange" (= *seltsaene*) chivalric permutation thereof—somewhat earlier (by implication, the more conventional merchant upon which the chivalric permutation was based must also have been around). If profit-seeking is stigmatized in Christian religious contexts, as Aho maintains, this does not always seem to be the case in the courtly chivalric context of romance poetry.

29. Compare the reading of Christoph Cormeau and Wilhem Störmer in *Hartmann von Aue,* which states that the outcome of the day-long battle is the absolute equality of the combatants (216).

knights improves—occasionally end in such a way that the value of both contestants is maintained, if not enhanced. In his successful chivalric *transactions* with Gawein as the exemplar of Arthurian chivalry, Iwein demonstrates in a conspicuous way before the eyes of Arthur's assembled court that his initial speculative pursuit of honor has paid off in the end, despite the many vicissitudes he has had to manage.

The final exemplary individual case of the dynamics of adventure that I would like to present is noteworthy in placing the chivalric wagering of self in a clear relationship to its broader social purpose. *Joie de la Curt*—"Joy of the Court"—is the name given to the last adventure in Hartmann von Aue's *Erec*-romance, which occurs after the happy culmination of the joint adventures of Erec and Enite.[30] In this adventure, Erec engages the knight Mabonagrin, who on account of a vow made to his lady lives with her in isolation from the court. Because he is the best knight in the realm, Mabonagrin's self-imposed isolation is experienced by the court and by the knight himself as detrimental and painful. This situation is somewhat analogous to Erec's earlier loss of courtly chivalric status and the associated loss of courtly joy as a consequence of his self-imposed isolation in the intimate company of Enite earlier in the romance. Mabonagrin's isolation from the court accompanies an extraordinary kind of chivalry, in which this knight has been able to maintain the highest reputation even while engaged in uncommonly brutal practices, such as beheading his defeated opponents and placing them on stakes surrounding the secluded garden where he resides with his beloved. The "Joy of the Court" will be restored by the knight who is able to overcome Mabonagrin in combat. The latter will be freed by defeat from his vow to live in isolation (and thus presumably also freed from the brutal kind of fighting he employs during this isolation) and allowed to rejoin the court; the court in turn will rejoice again in being able to count their greatest knight among their number.

When the "Joy of the Court"-adventure first presents itself, Erec pursues it relentlessly, as if to demonstrate that he has grasped in his own joint adventures with Enite that one can never rest on one's laurels or close oneself off to an opportunity to increase one's worth, however difficult the chance may be. In response to the last of many attempts to dissuade him from an adventure that nearly everyone assumes will result in his death, Erec persists in his resolve to risk himself and articulates his resolve with the characteristic terminology of a wager:

---

30. See Jackson's observations on this episode (*Chivalry in Twelfth-Century Germany*, 126–27). The episode is also at the end of Chrétien's *Érec et Énide*, but Hartmann lengthens and elaborates the speculative imagery that is of special interest to us.

dô sprach der künec Êrec:
"ich weste wol, der Saelden wec
gienge in der werlde *eteswâ,*
rehte enweste ich aber *wâ,*
wan daz ich suochende reit
in grôzer ungewîsheit,
unz daz ich *nû* vunden hân.
got hât wol ze mir getân
daz er mich hât gewîset *her,*
dâ ich nâch mines herzens ger
vinde gar ein wunschspil,
dâ ich lützel wider vil
mit einem wurfe wâgen mac.
ich suochtez *unz an disen tac:*
gote lob, *nû* hân ichz vunden
dâ ich wider tûsent phunden
wâge einen phenninc.
diz sint genaedeclîchiu dinc,
daz ich *hie* vinde solh spil."[31]
(8520–39)

Then King Erec replied, "I knew well that the road to Salvation passed *somewhere* in the world, but I did not know *exactly where*, so in great uncertainty I rode out seeking until I found it here *now*. God has treated me well by directing me *here, where* I may find, according to my heart's desire, the ideal game *where* with one throw I can wager a little to win a lot. *Until today* I have been seeking it. Praise God, *now* I have found it, *where* I can wager a penny against a thousand pounds. It is a fortunate thing to find such a game *here*."[32]

The significance of the Middle High German term *Saelde*—"Salvation"—as well as of the related term *genaedeclîchiu*—"fortunate"—is here indeterminately positioned between Christian salvation and the more *chancy* good fortune of Lady Luck. Erec's postulation that the path of *Saelde* leads *eteswâ*—"somewhere"—through this temporal world is generally consistent with observed aspects of Augustinian thinking (in particular the global parameter of sameness that we observed in chapter two of this study) in assuming that heavenly

---

31. Hartmann von Aue, *Erec* (Cramer). I have added italics in the Middle High German verses and in the English translation to underscore the spatial and temporal *specificity and uniqueness* of Erec's wagering of self.

32. Hartmann von Aue, *Erec* (Vivian), 146–47; italics added.

and worldly spheres overlap. Erec's questing posture is also consistent with the disposition of the Christian cultural *athlete* coursing toward his otherworldly prize, a movement that is the dynamic manifestation of the indeterminacy of the overlap of heavenly and worldly cities, of the spirit and the flesh, which are bound together dynamically (i.e., indeterminately)—in this case as *motion*—as long as final outcomes remain undecided.[33] Erec engages any eventuality along the way as a dynamic, integrated Christian self, as he indicates in saying that God has guided him to this auspicious time and place. Yet Erec's disposition of self in the "Joy of the Court"-adventure clearly directs him toward an outcome and reward that is very different from the otherworldly Christian one. Erec's adventurous orientation is that of Kalogreant (note particularly the common use of the adverb *suochende*—"seeking"—in their respective statements) and he has arrived at a unique place and time (the singularity of which is underscored in the above-cited verses by the temporal and spatial modifiers placed in italics), in which it is possible to wager himself utterly in the interest of a worldly reward that approaches *heavenly* dimensions (i.e., the thousand pound payoff on the penny wager).

The most appropriate way for Erec to describe his competitive engagement of self for the "Joy of the Court" is with the terminology and dynamics of high-risk gambling. In the ensuing lengthy passage (vv. 8540–75), in which this speculative imagery is further elaborated, Erec continues to liken his engagement in this adventure to participation in a game of chance, and it becomes clear that his investment of self—just as that of Kalogreant—is in something worldly, temporal, and hence evanescent, though it remains an absolute investment nonetheless. In this zero-sum action for high stakes, the competitors put their honor as the *currency* of adventure at stake and then contend for it, winner take all, whereby their lives as well as their honor are also at risk. The outcome of the coming contest determines whether Erec achieves "great fame" and is praised universally and fully—*daz ich vol ze lobe stê* (v. 8558)—or whether his honor and thus his chivalric self will be "entirely" lost—*oder daz si gar zegê* (v. 8559). In either case, despite the invocation of God (v. 8560)—which serves again to remind us that he enters the fray both as a Christian and as a chivalric competitor—the outcome will be the result of Erec's individual engagement at this particular time and place. It will be the result of a unique, singular application of strength, skill, and experience,

---

33. A more religious view of Erec's speculative action in this adventure is suggested by W. H. Jackson, with reference to crusading propaganda: "Erec's view of the combat as wager, in which he has little to lose and much to gain, invites comparison with the crusading metaphor of the battle against the heathens as an easy purchase of salvation, which any 'prudent merchant' (i.e., any wise knight) should grasp" (*Chivalry in the Twelfth-Century Germany,* 131–32).

and of *intangibles* ranging from God's favor to the luck of a winning throw of the dice.[34]

We have observed that adventure adds to the indeterminacy already associated with God's inscrutable plan another layer of indeterminacy connected to the wagering of self for some other mutable self or good. In their adventurous moves, knights and ladies in the imaginary action of romance poetry seem to be exploring how much there may be to gain between the good use and the sinful enjoyment of temporal goods—here adapting terms developed by Augustine in his *De Doctrina Christiana*.[35] As they do so, the absolute posture of faith seems to be reoriented speculatively in a different direction and to a different end. In the early twelfth century, the influential Cistercian abbot and author Bernard of Clairvaux provides a view of worldly knighthood in his *De laude novae militiae*—"In Praise of the New Knighthood" addressed to the Knights Templar, which provides a competing monastic view of the risks and rewards involved in worldly knighthood, and hence of those involved in the imaginary adventuring of the romances:

> Quis ergo, o milites, hic tam stupendus error, quis furor hic tam non ferendus, tantis sumptibus ac laboribus militare, stipendiis vero nullis, nisi aut mortis, aut criminis? Operitis equos sericis, et pendulos nescio quos panniculos loricis superinduitis; depingitis hastas, clypeos et sellas; frena et calcaria auro et argento gemmisque circumornatis, et cum tanta pompa pudendo furore et impudenti stupore ad mortem properatis [. . .] Super haec omnia est, quod armati conscientiam magis terret, causa illa nimirum satis levis ac frivola, qua videlicet talis praesumitur et tam periculosa militia. Non sane aliud inter vos bella movet litesque suscitat, nisi aut irrationabilis iracundiae motus, aut inanis gloriae appetitus, aut terrenae qualiscumque possessionis cupiditas. Talibus certe ex causis neque occidere, neque occumbere tutum est.[36]

> O knights, what is this error so stupendous, what is this madness so unacceptable, to fight at such great cost and effort, with no rewards other than those of death or crime? You cover your horses in silks and put over your

---

34. See Cormeau and Störmer's analysis of the *Joie de la curt*-episode (*Hartmann von Aue*, 189–90), which stresses, as other scholars have done, that this episode has a special status in Hartmann's romance by virtue of standing out in a conspicuous way after the apparent end of the difficult challenges Erec and Enite have faced. They also posit a change on the part of Erec—he is not the same knight as the one at Karnant—with which I concur, even if Cormeau and Störmer give little emphasis to the *wager* that is being made.

35. See particularly the first book in Augustine's *On Christian Doctrine*, where the proper uses and enjoyment of things is laid out in detail.

36. Bernard of Clairvaux, "Liber ad Milites Templi," 216.

coats of mail I know not what sort of cloth hangings; you paint your spears, shields and saddles; you decorate your bridles and spurs with gold, silver and jewels, and you hurry to your deaths with such great pomp, with shameful madness and shameless rashness [. . .] Over and beyond these points, if the cause for which such a dangerous service is undertaken is really quite frivolous and lacks seriousness, then this has the effect of bringing fear to a soldier's conscience. The only things that cause conflicts and start wars are feelings of irrational anger, the pursuit of vain glory, or the desire for some piece of land. It is certainly not safe to kill or be killed for such causes.[37]

For Bernard, the basic orientation of worldly knights is evil and foolish because the *entire* Christian self—body and soul—is being risked for no good reason. Worldly knights fight on account of "frivolous" things that are no more substantial than "vain glory" (= "honor," in the romances) and land, and when knights kill or are killed on account of such things they lose themselves utterly in crime and death. The path to the otherworldly prize is thus closed off completely from worldly knights, according to Bernard's view. In this view, there is no room for a courtly God who might smile upon the skillful efforts of knights and ladies in action, or for a God who might be inclined to open the doors of paradise to a knight who has been killed in a joust for reputation, land, or love. Bernard's monastic view forms part of an ongoing competition between monastic and courtly chivalric cultural players in the twelfth and thirteenth centuries, in which there are rival conceptions of the risks and rewards involved in worldly chivalric action. An important point on which Bernard and courtly chivalric players seem to agree is that worldly knighthood places the Christian self *absolutely and utterly at risk*. Beyond this jointly held assumption concerning the absolute *initial* investment risked in chivalric action, monastic and courtly chivalric views diverge sharply with respect to possible outcomes. In the monastic view, no good can come from worldly chivalry. In the courtly chivalric view advanced in the romances, as we have seen, chivalry in the form of adventure is an opportunity to increase one's individual honor and contribute as well to the general "Joy of the Court." In adventuring, knights seem to consider—in pointed contrast to the view of Bernard—that they will be able to *enjoy* some other temporal, mutable self or thing utterly and completely without giving up their position in the Christian race toward the otherworldly prize—which Bernard would deny them as soon as the twists and turns of adventure begin. Correspondingly, the courtly poet-performers pointedly differ from Bernard by finding great value in things

---

37. Idem, "In Praise of the New Knighthood," 218–19.

associated with worldly knighthood that are repugnant to the monk: horses covered in silks, coats of mail covered with cloth hangings, painted spears, shields and saddles, bridles and spurs decorated with gold, silver and jewels, long hair, delicate hands, long flowing robes with voluminous sleeves—the very *stuff* of romance poetry.[38] Bearing Bernhard's monastic and starkly dualistic assessment of the value of worldly chivalry in mind as a point of contrast and comparison, I turn now to a consideration of conspicuous features or *highlights* in two of the most illustrious verse romances, with particular focus on the manner in which individual adventures in them are arranged.

HIGHLIGHTS FROM CHRÉTIEN DE TROYES'S *ÉREC ET ÉNIDE*

The first courtly chivalric verse romances order individual adventures according to different narrative designs. One of the more influential of these is the *mout bele conjointure*—the "beautifully ordered composition"—accomplished by Chrétien de Troyes in what is considered to be the first Arthurian romance, *Érec et Énide*.[39] This pleasing narrative design is reiterated by Chrétien in his *Yvain,* and it serves as a model that is employed, adapted, and elaborated by later poet-performers such as Hartmann von Aue and Wolfram von Eschenbach, whose *Parzival* we shall examine below. As a "beautiful" narrative arrangement designed to be "pleasing" to courtly audiences, Chrétien's *conjointure* is the poetic equivalent of the silks, paints, jewels, and other frivolous aesthetic things condemned by Bernard of Clairvaux, who associates such things with the sinful orientation of worldly knights. Bernard never mentions courtly poetry or romances in the cited treatise (the latter predates the former by about a half-century), but it seems safe to assume Bernard would have disapproved just as strongly of romance performances designed to be "beautiful" and "pleasing" to their audiences for aesthetic rather than spiritual-religious reasons. Further, it would be consistent with Bernard's position to condemn romance performances because of the basic orientation of the individual adventures within them toward some mutable self or thing. From a dualist monastic perspective, individual adventures would have to be considered evil in their orientation, and romance as a "beautifully ordered composition" of individual adventures would necessarily take matters from bad to worse. From the courtly

---

38. These things are all referenced in the broader context from which the above-cited passage is excerpted.

39. Chrétien de Troyes, *Érec et Énide* (Dembowski); the *mout bele conjointure* is in v. 14.

chivalric perspective, the posture of self that is visible in adventure corresponds to a new openness toward and involvement in the mutability of worldly things, and romances as broader narrative arrangements of individual adventures competitively endeavor to maximize courtly joy with specifically poetic means.

Scrutiny of the *mout bele conjointure* of Chrétien's *Érec et Énide* shows that the features we observed in individual adventures—the speculative self-investment, painful effort, and joy involved in adventure as a successful competitive engagement of self—also serve as structural markers of longer narrative segments. The action of Chrétien's romance begins at the court of Arthur where the King calls for renewing the tradition of the hunt for the white stag. The ensuing discussion between Arthur and his nephew Gauvain shows this hunt to be a competition in two different ways. The knight who succeeds in bringing down the white stag will have conducted himself with the greatest fortitude and expertise in the highly prized and definitively aristocratic cultural action of the hunt, engagement in which is meritorious in its own right. Besides this, the winner gains the right to bestow a kiss on the lady of his choice, who will henceforth be regarded as the most beautiful of all. The parameters of the hunt as a contest of the knights' skill and of their ladies' beauty become clear as Gauvain questions the advisability of such a competition. More than five hundred ladies are served by knights at Arthur's court, Gauvain points out. Each will regard his own beloved lady as most beautiful. When the knight who wins the contest by bringing down the stag exercises his right to bestow the kiss on his own beloved (which Gauvain seems to regard as inevitable), all the other knights and ladies will be unhappy. The possibility of discord or conflict is not raised explicitly, but Gauvain seems to be concerned that the court will be an unhappier place at the end of the hunt than it is at the beginning. Having already determined that the hunt will go forward, Arthur carries through with his intention despite Gauvain's reservations. The first narrative segment of Chrétien's romance is marked by the action of the hunt and by the differing speculations of Arthur and Gauvain concerning its value for the court. Arthur's position is consistent with the consideration that the skill, strength, speed, and luck manifested by the winner of the hunt, combined with the revelation of the beauty inspiring such a high level of performance, must be brought to the fore and cultivated as the resources upon which Arthur's courtly order is based. By contrast, Gauvain's approach is *bearish*. No vicissitude in the hunt-less future preferred by Gauvain is likely to affect the court as negatively as he believes the outcome of the hunt itself will do, so he argues—though without success—that one should *stand pat*.

The action involving Erec is arranged alongside that of Arthur's hunt and involves some of the hunt's difficult issues, in particular the risk of conflict in competitions involving the courage, skill, and luck of knights and the associated beauty of their ladies.[40] The manner in which Erec engages himself has the effect of separating these difficulties from Arthur's courtly entourage until the successful conclusion of Erec's adventures and Arthur's hunt. As the hunt is beginning elsewhere and the sounds of it are still within earshot, we behold Erec galloping along on a charger to join Queen Guenievre and one of her maids. Though their common destination remains unstated, the movement of this party alongside the action of the hunt suggests that they have been set in motion by King Arthur's resolution and intend to join the hunting party. Erec's initial status as described by Chrétien at this point corresponds to the regard in which he is held at court:

> De la Table Reonde estoit,
> An la cort mout grant los avoit.
> De tant com il i ot esté,
> N'i ot chevalier si loé,
> Et fu tant biax qu'an nule terre
> N'estovoit plus bel de lui querre.
> (83–88)

> He was of the Round Table and had received great honor at court: as long as he had been there no knight had been so highly praised.[41]

A knight distinguished by such praise always needs to be in play for more, as we have been able to observe, even if Erec is not at this moment among those involved in the hunt. Instead of engaging the hazards of the hunt, the queen, her maidservant, and Erec come unexpectedly upon a trio of travelers. The ensuing interactions with the unknown knight, his lady, and their dwarf, turn out to be hazardous in a way that causes Erec's path to diverge from that of the other knights of Arthur's court. First, the efforts of the queen to discover the identities of the strangers results in an affront when the dwarf lashes her inquiring maidservant with his whip. Sent by the queen to succeed where the maidservant failed, Erec receives the same shameful treatment. Since Erec wears no armor and is armed only with his sword, he resists responding aggressively to the lashing that he receives from the dwarf. He fears the dwarf's master, the fully armed unknown knight, will kill him if he retaliates. In this

---

40. Donald Maddox and Sara Sturm Maddox, in their "*Érec et Énide*" also draw attention to the ways in which Erec's adventures and the Arthurian hunt for the white stag are intertwined.
41. Chrétien de Troyes, *Erec and Enide* (Carroll), 38.

first encounter, the honor with which Erec entered the action has thereby been diminished. Under the circumstances (i.e., lacking the arms he needs in order to fight), Erec must regard what has occurred as merely the first exchange in an ongoing contest, a chivalric *repeated game,* and he informs the queen that he resolves to pursue the unknown knight, lady, and dwarf with a view to winning back the honor he has lost: *Itant bien prometre vos vueil / Que, se ge puis, je vangerai / Ma hontë, ou la crestrai!* (vv. 244–47)—"But I want to promise you that, if I can, I will either avenge my shame or increase it!"[42]

Erec's strategy is consistent with the variable status of the courtly chivalric self that we observed in the first part of this chapter. The enterprising, speculative posture Erec adopts in pursuit of honor is that of other adventuring knights and ladies.[43] The extended adventurous action in which Erec's disposition of self results is now arranged alongside the hunt in the foreground of the first structural segment of Chrétien's romance. The possibility of a painful diminishment of self, but also of joyful growth, is central in both narrative strands. It remains latent in the hunt as the ominous possibility of discord about which Gauvain was concerned, and it is much more tangible and overt in the extended competitive action in which Erec is involved. The ladies in whose company Erec initially appears are painfully slighted by the actions of the unknown knight's party. Later on, in the contest for the sparrow hawk, the unknown knight slights other ladies and knights when he endeavors to claim the prize for his own companion. By this time, Erec's speculative approach has put him in a position to contest the unknown knight's claim. He has acquired the armor he needs for battle without losing his opponent from view, and in Enide and her great beauty, he has acquired the means to contest the knight's perennial claim to the sparrow hawk. When the knight claims the prize on the day of the contest, it is already abundantly clear to the assembled spectators that Enide is the most beautiful lady by far and that Erec has the looks of a knight of the highest category. The rival knight's claim to the sparrow hawk is therefore a tangible slight to Erec and Enide, and on the occasion of this confrontation, as opposed to the earlier one, Erec has the means to respond. He does so successfully in the ensuing fierce battle, the outcome of which is rendered in this way by Chrétien after Erec's victory:

---

42. Ibid., 41.

43. In his analysis of this romance, Jean-Paul Allard underscores the quest for honor in a manner consistent with my understanding of the Kalogreant episode earlier in this chapter, as well as what Allard calls a "Noblesse de la force et force de la noblesse" (*L' initiation royale,* 98). Allard further considers that Erec's adventures and the honor they bring him serve to demonstrate his worthiness to be king.

> Onques, ce cuit, tel joie n'ot
> La ou Tristanz le fier Morhot
> An l'isle Saint Sanson vainqui,
> Con l'an feisoit d'Erec iqui.
> Mout feisoient de lui grant los
> Petit, et grant, et gresle, et gros.
> Tuit prisent sa chevalerie,
> N'i a chevalier qui ne die:
> "Dex, quel vasal, soz ciel n'a tel."
> (1245–53)

> I don't believe there was such joy on the isle of Saint Sanson, where Tristan defeated the savage Morholt as there was around Erec. He was greatly praised and honored by short and tall, by thin and fat; everyone esteemed his knightly prowess. There wasn't a knight there who did not say: "God, what a vassal! He has no equal under the heavens."[44]

This is the first strong indication that the first part of Chrétien's romance, in which the action at the outset seemed *dicey,* will have a joyful culmination. In the cited passage, Chrétien captures the joy of the moment of Erec and Enide's ascendancy, and he preserves this until their arrival at Arthur's court, where the couple's joy leads to and becomes part of a general courtly joy.

By the time of their arrival at Arthur's court, the hunt has long since been completed, Arthur himself has brought down the white stag, and everyone has agreed to wait for the bestowal of the kiss until Erec's return. The defeated knight, whose name turns out to be Yder, has by this time already arrived at Arthur's court and carried out his promise to Erec to convey his apologies to the queen and her maidservant. When Arthur finally bestows the kiss upon the most beautiful lady at court, the discord or conflict about which Gauvain was initially concerned now seems inconceivable. The lady in question is Enide, who is universally acclaimed as the most beautiful. The kiss is bestowed with unanimous consent, and the hunt is joyfully concluded on the basis of Erec's engagements, which have recovered his lost honor and then some at the expense of Yder, and acquired the person of Enide—whose full value is only beginning to become clear at the moment of the kiss. Arthur's resolution to undertake the hunt for the white stag shows itself, in the end, to have been a highly successful speculation for one and all.

---

44. Chrétien de Troyes, *Erec and Enide* (Carroll), 53.

When Arthur has bestowed the kiss upon Enide, Chrétien tells us the first part of his romance is finished—*Ici fenist li premiers vers* (v. 1808)—"Here ends the first movement."[45] His "beautifully ordered composition" now continues with a second, longer narrative segment that reiterates the basic parameters of the first, though beginning at the higher level of honor won by Erec in the first segment, which is described in this way at the culmination of the tournament following his marriage with Enide:

> Or fu Erec de tel renon
> Qu'an ne parloit se de lui non:
> Nus hom n'avoit si boene grace
> Qu'il sanbloit Ausalon de face
> Et de la lengue Salemon,
> Et de fierté sanbla lyon,
> Et de doner et de despandre
> Refu il parauz Alixandre.
> (2223–30)

Now such was Erec's renown that people talked of no one else; no man had such exceptional qualities, for he had the face of Absalom and resembled Solomon in his speech. For ferocity he was like a lion, and in giving and spending he was like Alexander.[46]

In the second part of the romance, Erec is unable to maintain this high status for long. After returning to his homeland from Arthur's court, he invests himself so completely in Enide's intimate company that he neglects everything else. Erec falls away from his position of high honor without realizing it, until he overhears a sigh of lament from Enide. When Erec compels her to tell him the reason for her sigh, she reveals his lapse in these stark terms:

> Vostre pris est mout abessiez:
> Tuit soloient dire l'autre an
> Qu'an tot le mont ne savoit l'an
> Meillor chevalier ne plus preu;

---

45. Ibid., 60. Glyn Burgess writes about the occasion of this verse: "Enide has just received the Kiss of the White Stag. The Arthurian court is becalmed after threats of disorder and dissension. The various threads of the lengthy introduction to the romance have been brought together satisfactorily" (*Chrétien de Troyes*, 15).

46. Chrétien de Troyes, *Erec and Enide* (Carroll), 65.

Vostres parauz n'estoit nul leu.
Or se vont tuit de vos gabant,
Jeusne et chenu, petit et grant;
Recreant vos apelent tuit.
(2560–67)

Your renown has greatly declined. Previously everyone used to say that there was no better or more valiant knight known in all the world: your equal was nowhere to be found. Now everyone holds you up to ridicule, young and old, high and low; all call you a recreant.[47]

Enide's words remind us that honor is never lasting but has continually to be maintained. The only way to do this is to engage oneself again, which Erec immediately proceeds to do, this time in the company of his wife: *Erec s'an va, sa fame an moinne, / Ne set ou, mes en avanture* (vv. 2778–79)—"Erec rode off leading his wife, knowing not where but open to adventure."[48]

Erec and Enide begin their joint adventures that make up the second part of Chrétien's romance in a condition of estrangement from one another.[49] Though traveling together and engaging challenges jointly, they do not journey as man and wife. Erec maintains a distance from Enide and commands her not to speak, no matter what she sees. As they make their way through all these difficult adventures, Erec repeatedly manifests the prowess for which he has previously been praised, and Enide—besides her resourcefulness, which enables the couple to elude numerous mortal dangers—demonstrates her loyal love for Erec, despite his neglectful and abusive treatment of her, by warning

---

47. Ibid., 68.
48. Ibid., 71.
49. The second part of the Chrétien romance consists of two distinct series of adventures, which I recapitulate here in the interest of furnishing a complete view of the *structure* of this romance. In the first series, the couple contends with (1) robber knights (whom Erec kills or disperses); (2) a first count, who endeavors to take Enide from Erec (whom Enide outwits); and (3) the chivalric adversary King Guivret (whom Erec defeats and makes his vassal after suffering grievous wounds). In the second series of adventures, the couple engages (4) two giants (both killed by Erec, though the fighting causes his wounds to open); (5) a second count, who endeavors to take Enide from Erec (who is held off by Enide and later killed by the temporarily revived Erec); and (6) Guivret, a second time (who has come to help the couple, fights unknowingly against Erec, and then helps the couple once he has recognized them). The two series of adventures are divided by an interlude in the company of Arthur's knights and ladies. This interlude, to which the narrative design gives special emphasis, is characterized above all by Erec's reluctance to accept any comfort and his eagerness to put himself back into action as soon as possible, despite his injuries.

him repeatedly of impending dangers and thereby risking his anger by breaking his command not to speak.⁵⁰ In their joint adventures, each finds the way to the other, and they are reconciled not long before Erec's second fight against Guivret. The reward they give and receive shortly thereafter, during their stay in Guivret's castle, is the first marker of the joyful culmination of the second narrative segment of Chrétien's romance:

> Or ot sa joie et son delit.
> Ansanble jurent an un lit,
> Et li uns l'autre acole et beise:
> Riens nule n'est qui tant lor pleise.
> Tant ont eü mal et enui,
> Il por li et ele por lui,
> C'or ont feite lor penitance.
> Li uns ancontre l'autre tance
> Comant il lui puise pleisir:
> Del sorplus me doi bien teisir.
> (5245–54)

> Now she was embraced and kissed; now she had everything she wished; now she had her joy and her delight. They lay together in one bed, and embraced and kissed each other; nothing else pleased them as much. They had endured much pain and trouble, he for her and her for him, that now they had done their penance. They vied in finding ways of pleasing each other; about the rest I must keep silent.⁵¹

Chrétien here characterizes the adventurous engagements of Enide and Erec in the second part of his romance as a "penance," but the manner in which its conclusion is marked seems only very precariously Christian. The joy of the couple's conjugal love is manifestly physical to a degree that causes the narrator to desist from further detailed description. As such, the love achieved again by the couple hardly seems distinguishable in its intensity from the one in which Erec earlier lost himself and his reputation. The crucial difference here is that Erec will not linger long and exclusively with the reward of love, but returns in a timely way to chivalric action. By the end of the romance, after Erec's victory in the "Joy of the Court"-adventure (Hartmann von Aue's

---

50. Per Nykrog considers, with good reason, that the "qualités exquises d'Enide"—"the exquisite qualities of Enide"—which include clear-headedness, good judgment, courage, and patience, are what save Erec in the end (*Chrétien de Troyes*, 79).

51. Chrétien de Troyes, *Erec and Enide* (Carroll), 101.

version of which we observed above), the couple again possesses honor in plenitude to match the joy of love they find in the above-cited verses. The ongoing adventurous engagements of Enide and Erec enable them to optimize their status while simultaneously expanding courtly joy to places in need of it. The ensuing coronation of the couple at Arthur's court in Nantes gives appropriate political dimensions to the joy with which the adventurous action of this romance concludes.[52]

It is important to recognize that the love in which Enide and Erec invest themselves at the end of the second structural segment—and had invested themselves before at Carnant—is absolute in the same way that Erec's engagement in the "Joy of the Court"-adventure will be. Erec and Enide do not hold any part of themselves back from their engagement in chivalric action in the interest of honor, or from their engagement in love. They indicate, however, by the end of the romance that they are managing these *different absolute concerns* more capably.[53] The most visible indication of this increased capacity is their awareness of the necessity to keep themselves in action. Honor and love can bring joy to knights and ladies, but only as long as they continue to be engaged and successful. As soon as they close themselves off from the opportunity of gain, their status painfully decreases, as we saw earlier with Erec.

The need to keep oneself in play for the sake of growth and joy is articulated by the structural characteristics of Chrétien's narrative design, that is, by the poet's arrangement of individual adventures. The bipartite structure of Chrétien's romance, consisting of the two longer narrative segments (with the second one itself divided into two corresponding parts), has been regarded as similar to the typological relationship of the Old to the New Testament.[54] Analogous

---

52. Similarly to Allard, Donald Maddox places emphasis on the coronation of Erec, in which the romance culminates, and sees this narrative in terms of a "process" that leads in this direction: "The principle of nobility as 'an aptitude and a process' would admirably describe the adventures of Erec and Enide, whose beauty both individually and as a couple repeatedly indicates their moral and spiritual qualities. Likewise, the above principle applies equally well to the idea of monarchy as the product, not of accidental circumstances of birth, wealth, prestige, or election, but rather of the process by which one demonstrates a particular aptitude to reign" (*Structure and Sacring*, 176). The idea of kingship as something that has to be *performed* is consistent with my view of the political cultural action as developed in the third chapter of this study.

53. Compare the summation of Donald Maddox and Sara Sturm Maddox, who write that Chrétien's overriding concern in this romance "has been with intimately relating, in increasingly nuanced and profound ways, the story of the eponymous couple and the socio-political issues that were adumbrated in the initial segment" (*Érec et Énide*, 116).

54. Hugo Kuhn drew attention to this bipartite structure in his seminal article "Erec" (133–50). My own observations are indebted to those of Kuhn, especially the following: "It is not the advent of a new 'worldliness' or 'immanence' of a 'courtly classicism,' or a direct unification of service to the world and service to God, in which the new courtly ideal of living that becomes

to the way that the New Testament both fulfills and supersedes the Old Testament according to a Christian allegorical understanding of the Bible, the status achieved by Erec and Enide by the end of the romance's second part might be seen as fulfilling and superseding the status they achieved in the first. The presence in this romance of the bipartite structure of biblical typology as an organizing narrative principle would amount to a new and original artistic reiteration of an older cultural move. The bipartite relational logic of prefiguration and fulfillment found in the Christian typological understanding of the bible possibly becomes for Chrétien a structural design according to which adventures can be arranged in a beautiful and pleasing way. Assuming the bipartite design of this romance reiterates the typological relationship between Old and New Testament as a poetic move in the interest of courtly joy, the significance of the bipartite structure in its poetic, courtly chivalric reiteration would become newly indeterminate. For example, in the poetic reiteration of the religious typological structure, it becomes more difficult to say exactly how the Erec and Enide of the second part of the romance have fulfilled and superseded the Erec and Enide of the first part, even if something presumably remains of the religious relational logic. More important than any sort of religious lesson for Chrétien, for later poets reiterating the bipartite design, and for their courtly audiences, would likely have been the tested potential of the typological structure—assuming this indeed underlies Chrétien's *mout bele conjointure*—to maximize the experience of joy. In any case, the *content* of the bipartite structure in Chrétien's poetic iteration of it is the courtly chivalric content of adventure, and the first of Arthurian romances is manifestly about a joy that is courtly chivalric.

Chrétien's bipartite narrative arrangement of adventures in his *Érec et Énide* is as innovative as it is beautiful and pleasing on account of its balanced

---

visible here is grounded, but rather a connection of both by means of the same inner structure that is present both here and there: an *analogia entis* in the truest sense of the word" (150; my English rendering of Kuhn's German). Kuhn's recognition of this bipartite structure has continued to occupy an important position in the scholarly understanding of romance structure, according to D. H. Green, even as attention has been increasingly drawn to other structural devices that suggest what Green calls the "double cycle" was one narrative possibility—albeit an important one—among many (*Beginnings of Medieval Romance*, 131–32). Implicated in the possible religious typological underpinnings of romance design is the question of *change*, which Carolyn Walker Bynum considers in her book, *Metamorphosis and Identity*. Bynum regards change, first, in terms of radical change (i.e., the replacement of one thing by another that is completely different) and, second, in terms of the evolution of a given self or thing that remains largely identical. Interestingly for the purposes of this study, the romances are composed at a time in the late twelfth century when a new understanding of change is occurring, according to Bynum: "In a quite stunning shift of intellectual paradigms, people were increasingly fascinated by change of the first sort I sketched above—radical change, where an entity is replaced by something completely different" (25).

bipartite proportions and correspondences. In what is presumed to be his final romance, the unfinished *Perceval,* the French poet continues his innovations by including a second chivalric protagonist (Gauvain) alongside his principal one, in a narrative arrangement that is also pleasingly proportioned and identifiably bipartite as far as the unfinished narrative goes. In the first decade of the thirteenth century, the German poet Wolfram von Eschenbach engages the grail romance of his illustrious French predecessor in his composition and performance of *Parzival,* which adopts the two-protagonist model and continues the preexisting tendency toward narrative innovation and the bipartite organization of the imaginary action.[55] The imaginary action of Chrétien in *Érec et Énide* shows us that knights and ladies have much to gain in honor and love, whereas Bernard of Clairvaux—as we saw earlier in this chapter—considers they can only be diminished if not completely *bankrupted* in such pursuits. From the monk's perspective, adventuring inevitably and irrevocably leads to a reduction or loss of self, whereas for Chrétien and his courtly audiences, it holds forth the promise of adding immeasurably to it in a manner that is both individually and collectively beneficial and joyful. The competition between the former approach to things and the latter, which can be inferred on the basis of the monk's treatise "In Praise of the New Knighthood" and the French poet's first romance, becomes much more tangible with the grail romance of Wolfram, who raises the stakes considerably on previous and contemporary monastic and courtly chivalric rivals.

HIGHLIGHTS FROM WOLFRAM VON ESCHENBACH'S *PARZIVAL*

Many of the narrative moves Wolfram makes reiterate earlier ones by Chrétien, but the German poet is clearly intent on outdoing his predecessor wherever he can.[56] *Outdoing* takes the form of creative recasting and embellishing, which the German poet takes so far that he even playfully asserts that his romance is not based on that of Chrétien at all, but rather on the writings of

---

55. Bumke's *Wolfram von Eschenbach* presents a comprehensive overview (in German) of the scholarship on Wolfram's *Parzival* and his other poetic works. With respect to Wolfram's adaptation of the two-hero model, see Marianne Wynn, "Parzival and Gâwân: Hero and Counterpart."

56. On Wolfram's elaborations of Chrétien more generally, see Hatto's "Introduction to a Second Reading" in his translation of Wolfram's *Parzival* (412–38). Dallapiazza provides a synopsis of Wolfram's romance that also includes considerations of how it differs from the grail romance of Chrétien (*Wolfram von Eschenbach,* 31–82).

a certain mysterious "Kyot," as we observed in the previous chapter. One of the noteworthy consequences of Wolfram's many creative elaborations of the tale as he found it with Chrétien is that his narrative arrangement, although still identifiably bipartite, cannot in the same way be regarded as pleasingly proportional. Wolfram's famously dark, sprawling style corresponds to the complex indeterminacy of the imaginary action he renders, the tone of which is established in the first verses of his romance:

> Ist zwîvel herzen nâchgebûr,
> daz muoz der sêle werden sûr.
> gesmaehet unde gezieret
> ist, swâ sich parrieret
> unverzaget mannes muot,
> als aglestern varwe tuot.
> der mac dennoch wesen geil:
> wande an im sint beidiu teil,
> des himels und der helle.
> der unstaete geselle
> hât die swarzen varwe gar,
> und wirt ouch nâch der vinster var:
> sô habet sich an die blanken
> der mit staeten gedanken.
> (1.1–14)

> If vacillation dwell with the heart the soul will rue it. Shame and honour clash where the courage of a steadfast man is motley like the magpie. But such a man may yet make merry, for Heaven and Hell have equal part in him. Infidelity's friend is black all over and takes on a murky hue, while the man of loyal temper holds to the white.[57]

From the outset, the German poet frames the imaginary action in the broadest possible, *global* terms. The terms *zwîvel, sêle, himel,* and *helle*—"vacillation," "soul," "heaven," and "hell," respectively—introduce a patently religious dimension that is indeterminately juxtaposed to a more general one of central importance in Wolfram's romance: *unverzaget mannes muot*—"the courage of a steadfast man," which is as descriptive of the ideal posture of enterprising knights and ladies as it is of the Christian soul persevering in the face of the mutability of things. In the face of such mutability in the world and within, one

---

57. Wolfram von Eschenbach, *Parzival* (Hatto), 15.

must not waver. Wolfram's initial statements seem to be that one must forge ahead despite all the variability and resistance one will inevitably encounter. The initial verses of Wolfram's prologue urge upon courtly chivalric audiences a posture of unbending resolution. Whereas the monk Bernard of Clairvaux, as we have seen, urges people to turn away from investing themselves in mutable things, Wolfram conversely urges them to move boldly forward with "loyal temper." Looking forward to the content of his story, Wolfram's prepares his audience to reckon with the possibility that the temporal joys one achieves in honor and love, if one proceeds steadfastly, will be favorably regarded by the Almighty when final rewards are distributed. Wolfram adopts the chivalric posture that we saw in the *Érec et Énide* of Chrétien and intensifies it as an unwavering adventurous approach to the world. At the same time, he widens the scope of the imaginary action in which this newly focused adventurous approach is tested to an unprecedented degree. The indeterminate juxtaposition of religious and worldly things and the unwavering approach to them mentioned in the romance's first verses are manifested in the adventures of the two principal protagonists, which are structured according to Wolfram's elaboration of Chrétien's bipartite structural design.[58]

The first narrative segment of Wolfram's romance is devoted to the adventures of Parzival and leads in the direction of an exemplary standard of knighthood.[59] The second structural segment of Wolfram's grail romance is

---

58. My previous observations on the possible novel employment of the typological structure for courtly chivalric purposes in the case of the French poet would apply as well to Wolfram's romance.

59. As with the romance of Chrétien above, I render these adventures here schematically in order to furnish a structural overview. Following Wolfram's vastly longer and quite different version of the story of Parzival's mother Herzeloyde and father Gahmuret (in relation to the corresponding part of Chrétien's grail romance), Parzival has resolved that he wants to become a knight and has departed from the wilderness settlement of his mother in search of Arthur's court. Unbeknownst to him, his departure causes his mother Herzeloyde to perish of grief. His subsequent moves bring him to (1) the duchess Jeschute, from whom he forcefully takes kisses and tokens of "love" (as he naively and mechanically follows the advice his mother has given him), which later causes the duchess's husband Orilus to believe she has entertained a lover and to inflict a severe punishment upon her; (2) his cousin Sigune, with her recently slain lover, Schionatulander, in her lap, from whom he discovers his name; (3) Arthur's court, where Parzival becomes a knight, at least in name and appearance, by slaying the "Red Knight" Ither with a javelin, stripping his body of the armor, and donning it himself (at which point Parzival himself becomes known as the "Red Knight"); (4) the castle of the sage knight Gurnemanz, who provides Parzival with the courtly chivalric instruction he has been lacking on account of his upbringing in the wilderness; (5) the beautiful Condwiramurs, Queen of Brobarz, whom Parzival marries after freeing her castle from a siege and defeating a rival for the love of Condwiramurs, the knight Clamide; (6) the Grail castle, where he beholds the Grail, the marvelous procession in which it is borne before him, and the great suffering of his host, without opening up his mouth to ask the redeeming Question that would end the Grail host's suffering and turn

devoted mainly to the adventures of the knight Gawan—Parzival's Arthurian friend, supporter, and admirer—and leads in the same direction.[60] While the adventuring of Parzival clearly has a religious import, that of Gawan largely occurs in the more familiar courtly chivalric world of knights and ladies such as Erec and Enide that is the setting of the majority of the verse romances. The engagements of Gawan in the second part of the romance culminate in a grand festival in which the most important people he has engaged in his various adventures are joyously integrated into the company of Arthur by way of numerous marriages. Parzival's adventuring ends when he learns he has been called to the Grail. Parzival subsequently rides to the Grail castle with his infidel brother Feirefiz and brings joy to the long suffering company by asking the Question that heals his ailing uncle Anfortas's festering wound. Thereafter he is reunited with his wife, thoughts of whom have inspired him—at least as much as the Grail—during his many long years of adventuring.

The *global* implications of Wolfram's romance that are touched upon in the prologue come to the fore in the adventures of Parzival, who is first put into play in a way that casts him as a chivalric redeemer figure. Underscoring Parzival's future chivalric capacity, Wolfram tells us upon the boy's birth, that: *er wart mit swerten sît ein smit, / vil viures er von helmen sluoc: / sîn herze manlîch ellen truoc* (vv. 112, 28–30)—"In the course of time he grew to

---

pain to joy (because he remembers the teachings of Gurnemanz, who advised him not to ask too many questions); (7) his cousin Sigune, a second time, still with her slain lover, who condemns Parzival for having failed to ask the Question; (8) the duchess Jeschute, a second time, this time in the company of her husband, Orilus, who loses a single combat to Parzival and is compelled by the Red Knight to end his severe punishment of the duchess and restore her to his favor; and, finally, (9) the court of Arthur, a second time, where Parzival engages and defeats Sagramor and the seneschal Keie (who had insulted Parzival's honor during his first visit to Arthur's court), and is later celebrated for his many deeds of chivalric prowess when the Grail's emissary Cundrie, the "destroyer of joy," arrives and publicly rebukes Parzival for having failed to ask the Question at the Grail castle. Parzival's high repute, and that of Arthur's court by virtue of its association with him, is brought low at this moment. He must set out again, as Erec had to do in the company of his wife Enide, to regain his honor and possibly increase it.

60. Gawan's most significant accomplishments, besides the joint engagement with Antikonie discussed above, are his liberation of the "Castle of Marvels" from the magical spell placed upon it by the sorcerer Cinschor, and his acquisition of the beautiful Duchess Orgeluse during the course of a joint adventure with her in which he defeats numerous chivalric rivals, and in which she heaps verbal abuse upon him in order to test him (in a manner somewhat reminiscent of Erec's abusive treatment of Enide, albeit with the gender roles reversed). In the middle of this second segment of Wolfram's romance, the narrative focus returns to Parzival, to the circumstances under which he finds his way to his hermit uncle, Trevrizent (who happens to be the brother of the ailing grail king, Anfortas), and to the religious guidance he receives from him. The action of the second narrative segment culminates joyfully, as had that of the first (but for the continuing suffering of the Grail contingent and those held captive in the Castle of Marvels).

be a smith—with swords!—and he struck many sparks from helmets, since his heart was of manly mettle."[61] In the ensuing verses, Parzival's mother Herzeloyde demonstrates her own unwavering dedication and love by taking her newborn son to her own breast and uttering words that seem to shape Parzival's future course as much as Wolfram's chivalric qualifications of him:

> [vrou] Herzeloyde sprach mit sinne
> "diu hoehste küneginne
> Jêsus ir brüste bôt,
> der sît durch uns vil scharpfen tôt
> ame criuze mennischlîche enpfienc
> und sîne triuwe an uns begienc.
> swes lîp sîn zürnen ringet,
> des sêle unsanfte dinget."
> (113.17–24)

"The Queen of Heaven gave her breasts to Jesus," Herzeloyde said pensively, "who in the fullness of time received a bitter death on the Cross in human shape for love of us and thereby proved His devotion. Whoever makes light of His anger, his soul will fare ill at the Judgment."[62]

By extension, Herzeloyde's emulation of the posture of the Virgin is suggestive of the view of her son as a redeemer figure. The qualities of Christ as redeemer, here framed by Herzeloyde as unwavering loyalty and anger toward doubters, will also be those of Parzival, though they are merged in Wolfram's imaginary action with his status as "a smith—with swords!" The striking words and gestures of Herzeloyde, which follow immediately upon Wolfram's reference to the knightly mettle the boy will have, suggest Parzival's future engagements in the action will amount to a chivalric reiteration of the redemptive career of Christ.[63] Such a view is consistent with the unwavering and frequently angry attitude Parzival will maintain toward any and all obstacles, even those that seem divinely ordained. When Parzival becomes angry at God for outcomes he cannot fathom, he does so as a knight engaged in and following through with a redemptive mission that possesses both the courtly chivalric and the Christian parameters visible at the moment of his birth (as well as in the

---

61. Wolfram von Eschenbach, *Parzival* (Hatto), 66.
62. Ibid., 66.
63. For a consideration of the story of Parzival's parents and its importance for the romance as a whole, see Francis G. Gentry, "Gahmuret and Herzeloyde."

prologue). As Parzival progresses toward the final joyful outcome, it is as accurate to say that he unwaveringly puts things into their best possible order as it is to say that he continually manifests his shortcomings and endeavors to overcome them as part of an ongoing courtly and religious education.[64]

Parzival's unwaveringly *bullish* chivalric approach is evident from the moment he decides to become a knight. He pursues this ambition relentlessly, applying at every step all the resources available to him. Though always well-intentioned, Parzival's approach nevertheless causes significant pain and suffering to others—his mother, Jeschute, the Red Knight Ither and his many admirers, the grail contingent (all mentioned in the structural overview of narrative events referenced above).[65] Parzival occasionally expresses regret about earlier missteps, as soon as he is in a position to recognize them as such, but they never seem to slow him down or deter him. His adventurous posture is relentless, and he tends to reframe any pain caused by his chivalric approach as an adventurous challenge to be met. This is most evident in Parzival's posture and words following Cundrie's public condemnation of him before the assembled Arthurian host for his failure to ask the Question at the grail castle. When Gawan tells Parzival, as they embark on their respective adventurous paths, that he hopes God will help them with their coming challenges, the latter responds angrily to this proposition and insists on a different source of support:

> nu will ich (got) dienst widersagen:
> hât er haz, den will ich tragen.
> vriunt, an dînes kampfes zît
> dâ neme ein wîp vür dich den strît:
> diu müeze ziehen dîne hant;
> an der du kiusche hâst bekant
> unt wîplîche güete:
> ir minne dich da behüete.
> (332.1–14)

Now I will quit (God's) service! If he knows anger I will shoulder it. My friend, when your hour of combat is at hand, let a woman join issue in

---

64. A recent view of Parzival's adventures in terms of an *education* is presented by Murphy, *Gemstone of Paradise*, 207–14; especially 208.

65. The question of Parzival's guilt, or *Schuld*, has played a significant role in scholarly views of this romance; see, for example, Wolfgang Mohr, "Parzival's Knightly Guilt"; and Dallapiazza, *Wolfram von Eschenbach*, 85–86 and 90–93.

your stead, let her guide your hand! Let the love of one whom you know to be modest and given to womanly virtues watch over you there.[66]

At this crucial point in the romance, the point of transition between the first and second narrative segments, Parzival states in stark terms that he will carry forward with his unwavering chivalric approach to the action. Parzival's speculative move forward is all the more striking because he here sees the painful mutability of things that will be his next and greatest challenge as a God who finds fault with him rather than rewards him as his chivalric peers have done. At this moment, as before, Parzival moves boldly forward, angrily resolved to win the grail, if necessary without or even despite God and *banking* on the value of love. His investment in love has paid off for him in the past, and he continues to believe it will sustain him and Gawan in the future at those decisive stressful moments—with which we may assume members of Wolfram's audiences would have been viscerally familiar—when the "hour of combat is at hand."

Parzival's chivalric anger at God is addressed again in detail during his sojourn with his hermit uncle Trevrizent, which occurs near the middle of the second narrative segment of Wolfram's romance (at the moment corresponding to Erec and Enide's brief stay at Arthur's court in the second structural segment of Chrétien's romance). Trevrizent, once himself a knight, has decided to become a hermit in the mold of religious eremites after the wounding of his brother, the grail king Anfortas, and now lives in the wilderness where the exchanges between him and his still belligerent nephew occur. His assessment of Parzival's anger toward God is correspondingly monkish and critical. Parzival's conviction that he will achieve his goals with his angry approach demonstrates for Trevrizent that he is *an den witzen crank* (463.3)—"weak of understanding."[67] The contrasting positions of Parzival and Trevrizent become manifest in the following especially illustrative exchange. Parzival first articulates the courtly chivalric orientation that he believes will enable him to join the grail company, and Trevrizent responds with his conviction that his nephew is drifting precariously in the direction of *hôchvart, superbia*—"sinful pride"—and away from the attitude of humility that he thinks would be more appropriate for the grail company:

"ich streit ie swâ ich strîten vant,
sô daz mîn werlîchiu hant

---

66. Wolfram von Eschenbach, *Parzival* (Hatto), 172. I have parenthetically altered the Middle High German passage and Hatto's rendering, which are excerpted from a longer passage, in order to make clear whose service Parzival is quitting.

67. Ibid., 236.

> sich naehert dem prîse.
> ist got an strîte wîse,
> der sol mich dar benennen,
> daz si mich dâ bekennen:
> mîn hant dâ strîtes niht verbirt."
> dô sprach aber sîn kiuscher wirt
> "ir müest aldâ vor hôchvart
> mit senftem willen sîn bewart.
> iuch verleit lîht iuwer jugent
> daz ir der kiusche braechet tugent.
> hôchvart ie seic und viel."
> (472.5–17)

"I fought wherever fighting was to be had, so that my warlike hand has glory within its grasp. If God is any judge of fighting He will appoint me to that place so that the Company there know me as a knight who will never shun battle." "There of all places you would have to guard against arrogance by cultivating meekness of spirit," replied his austere host. "You could be misled by youthfulness into breaches of self-control.—Pride goes before a fall!"[68]

Pride versus humility as the appropriate attitude for the Grail kingdom continues to be at issue in the ensuing exchanges between Parzival and Trevrizent. The current grief and suffering of the Grail kingdom, Trevrizent later informs his young guest, stems from Anfortas's adventuring for the love of a lady despite the Grail's message that knights of the Grail kingdom are forbidden to fight for love. The war cry of Anfortas as he jousted for love was "Amor!," which for Trevrizent is contrary to the humility required of the Grail king: *Der ruoft ist zur dêmuot / iedoch niht volleclîchen guot* (vv. 479.1–2)— "That shout is not quite right for humility."[69] Trevrizent's quasimonastic view of Parzival's aggressive chivalric approach to the Grail as prideful and his recommendation of humility as the more appropriate attitude is joined with a correspondingly monkish rejection of fighting in the interest of love. His own chivalric background prevents Trevrizent from being as rigorous as someone like Bernard of Clairvaux in criticizing chivalric action for its investments in *frivolous* things, but the monkish posture he recommends is similar. Trevrizent would have Parzival stand down from his aggressive chivalric approach, place his trust in clergymen, and cultivate "meekness of spirit." The underlying

---

68. Ibid., 240–41.
69. Ibid., 244.

monastic orientation is directed away from all the things—the elaborate courtly pageantry, jousts for love, swordplay for honor, charging horses, colorful shields and pennants, costly pavilions, and the like—that have been the stuff of Wolfram's romance to this point.

In contrast to Chrétien's Perceval, who manifests tearful regret and readiness for penance at this juncture of the story,[70] Parzival's approach does not visibly change in the face of Trevrizent's criticisms and exhortations. His subsequent chivalric engagement after the sojourn with Trevrizent continues that which went before it, though there is a strong indication that one of the hermit's points has made a lasting impression. Close to the end of Wolfram's romance, Parzival's most difficult "hour of combat" comes: a battle against his heathen half-brother Feirefiz whose identity and relationship Parzival does not yet know. When the fighting becomes most intense, Wolfram tells us Parzival has been sustained by his trust in God since leaving Trevrizent: *der getoufte wol getrûwet gote / sît er von Trevrizende schiet* (vv. 741.26–27)— "The Christian had placed his full trust in God since leaving Trevrizent."[71] Parzival has internalized one of Trevrizent's important lessons: God will help those in need of help and prepared to receive it. Such trust doubtless prepares the way for Parzival's ascension to the Grail, but it seems just as significant that nothing else about Parzival's approach has changed. The reference to Parzival's trust in God during his battle with Feirefiz is juxtaposed to Parzival's thoughts of his wife Condwiramurs and the strength her love provides him at this crucial moment. Parzival's killing of Ither was counted by Trevrizent as a sin because the "Red Knight" was Parzival's kinsman. The present combat between Parzival and Feirefiz threatens a repetition of the same sin, and nothing in Wolfram's romance suggests Feirefiz's status as an infidel mitigates this danger. However, a catastrophic repetition of sin does not occur. As Parzival's sword strikes the top of Feirefiz's helmet in what might be a lethal blow, God causes the sword to shatter. The combat halts, the brothers engage in courteous conversation, discover their kinship, renounce their unfortunate conflict, and disaster is averted. Shortly thereafter, Parzival is summoned to the Grail by Cundrie.

Along with medieval audiences, we are left to assess this final outcome. Has Parzival adventurously forced God's hand? By trusting in God's willingness to help, Parzival has made an adjustment that has enabled a happy, rather than catastrophic and sinful outcome in this conflict between brothers—assuming

---

70. See Chrétien de Troyes, *Story of the Grail*, 458–61. Dallapiazza also observes remarkable differences between how Wolfram and Chrétien proceed in this part of the work, noting in particular that Parzival in contrast to Perceval is not transformed into a penitent (63).

71. Wolfram von Eschenbach, *Parzival* (Hatto), 369.

God's causing the sword to shatter is based on Parzival's regained trust in Him. Parzival makes room for God to help him, but he has *also* maintained his aggressive approach to chivalric adventuring in the interests of honor and love, and he has done this despite Trevrzent's admonitions to adopt an attitude of (monastic) humility. Parzival's regained trust in God cannot be mistaken for "meekness of spirit." Regained trust in God does not reduce the level or intensity of Parzival's chivalric effort, but rather becomes a constituent part of it, and it is this approach that *forces the issue*. Parzival's approach—think of the instant his sword strikes the top of Feirefiz's helmet—seems to leave no room for a solution other than the one God provides. God sides with Parzival and the sword shatters. Parzival maintains his approach until the end of Wolfram's romance. He goes on to take possession of the Grail, and when he comes across Trevrizent near the end of the romance, the hermit seems to confirm what he—and perhaps we also—may at first have been reluctant to believe:

Trevrizent ze Parzivâle sprach
"groezer wunder selten ie geschach,
sît ir aber got erzürnet hat
daz sîn endelôsiu Trinitât
iuwers willen werhaft worden ist."
(798.1–5)

Trevrizent spoke to Parzival: "A greater marvel never occurred, in that, after all, with your defiance you have rung the concession from God that His everlasting Trinity has given you your wish."[72]

According to Trevrizent's presumably sage and religiously informed perspective, Parzival has had his way.[73] His nephew has not modified his approach along the lines of a monastic dualist perspective, according to which the pain and suffering of this mortal life stem from our investment in the frivolous things of this world from which we must disengage ourselves more or less completely (the "more or less" demarcating the range of dualist positions among Bernard of Clairvaux, Chrétien's Perceval, and Trevrizent). Instead, Parzival has wagered on being able to *have it all*—honor, love, the Grail, and presumably the heavenly kingdom to come—and the wager pays off in a manner that is concretely demonstrative of *growth*. The same would seem to be true of the adventurous approach of Parzival's staunchest advocate, Wolfram von Eschenbach

---

72. Ibid., 96.
73. See also Dallapiazza, *Wolfram von Eschenbach*, 63.

himself, who puts Parzival into play as a role of the dice—*hie ist der âventiure wurf gespilt* (v. 112.9)—"With this the story has made its cast"[74]—and at the end of his romance claims success in terms that are familiar to us:

> swes leben sich sô verendet,
> daz got niht wirt gepfendet
> der sêle durch des lîbes schulde,
> und der doch der werlde hulde
> behalten kan mit werdekeit,
> daz ist ein nütziu arbeit.
> guotiu wîp, hânt die sin,
> deste werder ich ein bin,
> ob mir deheiniu guotes gan,
> sît ich diz maere volsprochen hân.
> ist daz durch ein wîp geschehen,
> diu muoz mir süezer worte jehen.
> (827.19–30)

> When a man's life ends in such a way that God is not robbed of his soul because of the body's sinning and who nevertheless succeeds in keeping his fellows' good will and respect, this is useful toil. If I have any well-wishers among good women of discernment I shall be valued the more for my having told this tale to its end. And if this was done to please one in particular, she must own I said some agreeable things.[75]

Wolfram's own poetic adventure has ended well, and he considers himself of greater worth on account of it, in a manner entirely consistent with Kalogreant's definition of adventure with which we began this chapter. The ladies who have attacked the poet-performer Wolfram, causing the poet to defend himself—as we observed in the previous chapter—would seemingly do well now to set aside their anger if not reward him for his unwavering approach to the poetic action, just as his hero Parzival has been rewarded. Moves and expected outcomes here visibly make the transition from the imaginary world of King Arthur and the grail kingdom to the poetic action of the poet-performer Wolfram in the social setting of his performance, and potentially beyond.[76]

---

74. Wolfram von Eschenbach, *Parzival* (Hatto), 66.
75. Ibid., 410–11.
76. Bumke considers that, in the end, all conflicts are resolved and a condition of beautiful harmony appears to have been established, though disruptions loom on the horizon via the

The ending verses of Wolfram's romance suggest that the successful culmination of adventuring occurs as a joyful *balance* of worldly and religious concerns.[77] Based on our consideration of Chrétien's *Érec et Énide* and Wolfram's grail romance *Parzival*, we know that such a balance is not occurring as a static harmonious closure, but rather as a dynamic and even potentially volatile juxtaposition and maintenance of *different absolute investments of self*—investments in honor, love, and one's heavenly reward.[78] The difficulty and potential volatility of this balance of absolute concerns becomes clear with the damage and pain that occurs when any one absolute investment is neglected in favor of another, as when Erec loses his interest in honor on account of his absolute self-commitment to the love of Enide at the outset of the second part of Chrétien's romance, or when Parzival causes pain to others and alienates God and his closest representatives with his total investment in chivalric honor in the first part of Wolfram's romance. Maintaining and exploiting one's investments involves, as we have seen via the cited highlights from these romances, new dispositions of self in the finite times and spaces of *this world* in which the investments are being made. New strategies and touches are needed. Seemingly, one must always be *on one's toes*, continually aware of one's position vis-à-vis the positions of others, and thinking ahead to the degree possible no matter how demanding the concerns of the moment. One must be able to give oneself over completely to worldly joys, but also know when the moment has come to take pain upon oneself in order to make the joys possible, always bearing in mind the supreme importance of winning the heavenly afterlife. The balance referenced by Wolfram in the final verses of his grail romance needs to be understood dynamically as an *expansion* of the cultural action, an enrichment that occurs as an overall increase in the joy resulting from successful religious *and* worldly investments of self. Adventure involves, as we have seen, the wagering of oneself in the interest of the regard in which one is held by other courtiers. Love involves wagering oneself for the absolute dedication for and of a single other person. We have already seen a few of the characteristics of love in this and previous chapters. In the next chapter, love as a cultural wager is in the focal point.

---

references to the Lohengrin and Prester John legends, which indicate Wolfram's narrative is open ended, and the action will be ongoing (*Wolfram von Eschenbach*, 189).

77. The idea of establishing a balance of life-concerns is by no means new. It has played a central role in scholarly appraisals of the romances. I share this idea, but add considerations that underscore and give substance to the *dynamism* of the balance.

78. If the idea of *different absolute investments* seems illogical or paradoxical, I recall here from the first two chapters of this study that the way for such an action has been prepared by and follows from the virtual constitution of the Christian self, which *already* is both what it is *and* absolutely *other*.

CHAPTER 6

Love as a Cultural Wager

DYNAMICS OF LOVE

Love as an absolute investment of self is a novel cultural move in the High Middle Ages.[1] For the first time, at European courts in the twelfth century, the Pauline-Augustinian self with its indeterminately conjoined spiritual-intellectual and physical-material resources—while still striving for its heavenly prize—invests itself *completely* in another mortal self. In so doing, the individual might seem to be acting in a manner at odds with the Christian understanding of love, as articulated for example by Augustine in his *De Doctrina Christiana*:

> Haec enim regula dilectionis diuinitus constituta est: *Diliges,* inquit, *proximum tuum tamquam te ipsum, deum* uero *ex toto corde, ex tota anima, ex tota mente,* ut omnes cogitationes tuas et omnem uitam et omnem intellectum in illum conferas, a quo habes ea ipsa, quae confers. Cum autem ait: *toto corde, tota anima, tota mente,* nullam uitae nostrae partem reliquit, quae

---

1. See Peter Dinzelbacher's article, "Über die Entdeckung." Walter Haug terms this moment "*die Geburtsstunde der modernen Liebesidee*"—"the birth hour of the modern idea of love" (*Die höfische Liebe*, 34).

161

uacare debeat et quasi locum dare, ut alia re uelit frui, sed quidquid aliud diligendum uenerit in animum, illuc rapiatur, quo totus dilectionis impetus currit. Quisquis ergo diligit proximum, hoc cum eo debet agere, ut etiam ipse toto corde, tota anima, tota mente diligat deum. Sic enim eum diligens tamquam se ipsum totam dilectionem sui et illius refert in illam dilectionem dei, quae nullum a se riuulum duci extra patitur, cuius deriuatione minuatur.[2]

This is the divinely instituted rule of love: "Thou shalt love thy neighbor as thyself," He said, and "Thou shalt love God with thy whole heart, and with thy whole soul, and with thy whole mind." Thus all your thoughts and all your life and all your understanding should be turned toward Him from whom you receive these powers. For when He said, "With thy whole heart, and with thy whole soul, and with thy whole mind," he did not leave any part of life which should be free and find itself room to desire the enjoyment of something else. But whatever else appeals to the mind as being loveable should be directed into that channel into which the whole current of love flows. Whoever, therefore, justly loves his neighbor should so act toward him that he also loves God with his whole heart, with his whole soul, and with his whole mind. Thus, loving his neighbor as himself, he refers the love of both to that love of God which suffers no stream to be led away from it by which it might be diminished.[3]

As a cultural wager at high medieval courts, love seems either to be contrary to this fundamental Christian orientation of love (consistent with the dualistic condemnation of "the enjoyment of something else"), or to be a reiteration that speculatively elaborates and reorients the global orientation in the interest of gain.[4] The court poetry examined in this chapter suggests that *both* these possibilities are in play. Of these alternative assessments of love's value vis-à-vis divine love, which appear to mark new parameters of indeterminacy in the cultural action at courts, the latter possibility will be of particular interest to us. The courtly self that is speculatively invested in love loves with "its whole heart," "its whole soul," and "its whole mind," it concentrates "all its

---

2. The Latin text is from *Avrelii Avgvstini Opera, De Doctrina Christiana*, book I, chapter 22, 17–18; italics in original. Note that the Latin variants *dilectio* and *diligo* employed here by Augustine seem to avoid the perils of *amor* while retaining the meanings of joy/pleasure and devoted attachment/love.

3. Augustine, *On Christian Doctrine*, 19.

4. Regarding the latter possibility, I recall again here, based on the first two chapters of this study, that if the idea of different absolute investments of self seems illogical or paradoxical, the way has been prepared by and follows from the virtual constitution of the Christian self, which *already* is both what it is *and* absolutely *other*.

thoughts" and "all its life and understanding."[5] If, in courtly love, the beloved toward which this concentration of all the capacities of self is oriented is not God, this does not necessarily mean that the way to God is closed, at least not for courtiers. Pauline-Augustinian cultural *athletes* are *already* engaged in the speculation that they will obtain their heavenly prize by means of a sufficiently concentrated, capable, and persistent exertion of self.[6] Ladies and knights now further speculate that the way to God might include—or might not exclude— one's absolute investment in another mortal self; that the bliss of one's heavenly reward might be anticipated by the joys of a worldly, even fleshly love; that the "current" of love referenced by Augustine might be sufficiently broad and strong to encompass and convey the interest in one's neighbor *as lover*.[7]

We have seen in earlier chapters of this study that the experience of individual enrichment in love might not always be joyful for the court as a whole. Correspondingly, one of the challenges posed by the interest in love is the optimally joyful mediation between individual and collective experiences of it. Achieving such mediation involves strategic exertions that necessitate the full use of the spiritual-intellectual and physical-material resources of lovers as courtiers.[8] In love, all the capacities of courtiers must come into play (i.e., intelligence, strength, patience, poise under pressure, well-timed open

---

5. My focus is on the *amorous orientation* of males to females and of females to males (i.e., on how love occurs in the romances). This is not to say that "amorous orientation" is the same as "sexual orientation" in the modern sense, as James Schultz reminds us in his study *Courtly Love* (xviii). We observe in this chapter that love tends to occur and be described in religious and imperial terms, consistent with the parameters observed in the initial chapters of this study. Schulz makes similar observations in his book; see, in particular, the chapter titled "Aristophilia" (79–98). For a study of a variety of other manifestations of medieval love, which finds love's "ennobling" effect to be a common characteristic, see C. Stephen Jaeger, *Ennobling Love*.

6. I base my view of the Christian *athlete* on passages such as Heb 12:1 and 1 Cor 9:24, which I cite in my first chapter.

7. Hannah Arendt makes the following observation on Augustine's conception of *caritas* in her *Love and Saint Augustine*: "what we cannot understand is how, through this love by which we deny both ourselves and the world, another person can still be considered our neighbor, that is, as someone specifically connected to us" (95). Arendt here draws attention to the indeterminacy of Augustine's conception of love in a different way than I am doing, though she arrives at a question similar to the one that I also suggest is left open: how *can* one love one's neighbor? Love as rendered in the romances may be regarded as an answer to this question.

8. In *Love and the Idea of Europe*, Luisa Passerini writes, "Love constitutes a unifying force that works in a similar way whether it is keeping a couple together or laying the foundation stones of a cohesive society" (1). On the importance of love for courtly culture, see Albrecht Classen's introduction to his edited collection of essays, *Discourses on Love*: "Courtly culture relied heavily on the theme of love in its myriad manifestations, and our modern fascination with medieval literature in turn draws from this particular phenomenon [. . .] [T]he medieval world, perhaps more than any other cultures, focused on courtly love as its most appropriate medium for self-identification" (6–7).

and covert moves). This is particularly the case because love may be at odds with the ways in which relationships in households of nobility are controlled for political purposes, most visibly by means of arranged marriages in the political interest of maintaining patrilineal bloodlines and producing legitimate heirs. The characteristics of the imaginary action involving love sometimes seem to contrast sharply with prevailing political practices, just as they may seem to contrast sharply with the characteristics of the loving posture recommended to Christians by Augustine.[9] However, given the predominantly religious-imperial rather than individual-autonomous parameters of medieval culture, as we have seen, moves made in any given cultural domain remain available for reiteration and variation throughout a cultural action of corresponding dimensions. Love occurs religiously and imperially. It is religious and imperial in its implications and reach, and remains so even when and where it seems at odds with religion and politics. With respect to the availability of love as a cultural move, it seems appropriate to reckon with an open-ended dynamic that includes moments of friction as well as moments of congruence among the interests of different cultural domains such as religion, politics, and poetry, rather than to endeavor to determine or fix this open-ended dynamic in any particular way.[10]

We considered evidence at the outset of the previous chapter that narration and its understanding involves sensory and motor simulations—physiological *action*, and the dynamics of such adventurous action as we observed them there are applicable here. In love, as in adventure, courtiers pursue new cultural interests that inform and are informed by moves being made elsewhere in the cultural action. I regard love in this chapter as a new cultural disposition of self, as an absolute *wager*, that is occurring in the imaginary competitive action of the romances. As in the previous chapter, I continue in this section below with some exemplary illustrations of love as a cultural wager that show love's absolute stakes, its global dimensions, and the tendency to render the interest in love with imagery borrowed from warfare, politics, and games.[11]

---

9. Associated with the idea of a division or tension between marriage as a political instrument and love as an individual passion is the argument of Denis de Rougemont in his *Love in the Western World*, who posits an oppositional relationship of passionate love and marriage. However, many of the examples observed in this chapter suggest there is passion (or, at least, a total commitment of the self) in marriage, and Christianity (or, at least, Christian dimensions and imagery) in passionate, adulterous love.

10. For example, in terms of some kind of *autonomy*. Haug goes in this direction when he posits for poetic treatments of love a "Freiraum" or "free space" (*Die höfische Liebe*, 34).

11. Love as art, struggle, or game is consistent with depictions of it in antiquity, such as those of Ovid. However, the absolute stakes of love at medieval courts distinguish it from love in antiquity. On this point, see de Rougemont (*Love in the Western World*, 60) and, more

In the final sections of this chapter, in order to consider how love as a cultural wager is narrated at greater length, we shall consider *highlights* from the action of two great stories of courtly love: Marie de France's tale of Lanval and his otherworldly lady, and Gottfried von Strassburg's romance of Tristan and Isolt.

•

In the previous chapter, we observed the interest in love in Wolfram von Eschenbach's *Parzival* to be aligned in the end with the quest for the grail and trust in God, and to be regarded as equally valuable. Outside of Parzival's adventuring for love and for the grail, the absolute value of love is underscored in other conspicuous ways in Wolfram's romance. For example, this is how much the love of the lady Condwiramurs is worth to the knight Clamide, who has lost any possibility of ever obtaining it by the time he utters these words:

Pilâtus von Poncîâ,
und der arme Jûdas,
der bî eime kusse was
an der triuwelôsen vart
dâ Jêsus verrâten wart,
swie daz ir schepfaer raeche,
die nôt ich niht verspraeche,
daz Brôbarzaere vrouwen lîp
mit ir hulden waer min wîp,
sô daz ich sî umbevienge,
swie ez mir dar nâch ergienge.¹²
(219.24–220.4)

Whatever the punishment their Maker has in store for Pontius Pilate and that wretched Judas who joined the traitors with a kiss when Jesus was betrayed, I would gladly accept their torment if only the lady of Brobarz were my wife by her consent, and I could hold her in my arms—come what might thereafter!¹³

---

recently, Haug, who states there is *"kaum etwas Vergleichbares"*—"scarcely anything comparable" to medieval courtly love in antiquity (*Die höfische Liebe,* 33).

12. Wolfram von Eschenbach, *Parzival* (Lachmann); Clamide offers this assessment of his love's dimensions before King Arthur and his retinue at court not long after his defeat by Parzival. Numbers of Middle High German and Old French verses from the romances here and elsewhere are cited parenthetically in text.

13. Wolfram von Eschenbach, *Parzival* (Hatto), 118.

Having fallen short in his chivalric play for the love of Condwiramurs by losing a single combat against Parzival, Clamide now contemplates the desperate company of Pontius Pilate and Judas Iscariot. The biblical proportions of Clamide's suffering serve inversely as a measure of the love that he has lost to Parzival, which seemingly would more than offset the suffering of damnation. The love Clamide forlornly continues to desire is not patently adulterous, though the stark terms he uses seem as audacious as those used to describe the love of Clamide's more famous imaginary contemporaries, Isolt and Tristan.[14] The embrace for which Clamide yearns is not elaborated in further detail, but it has a clearly fleshly component. For this love, he would be willing to place body and soul at risk. In the cited verses, there is a programmatic alignment of the rhyming phrases *umbevienge*—"hold in my arms"—and *ergienge*—"come what might." The latter phrase shows Clamide's forlorn wish to be a speculation that leaves the final outcome undecided. What *indeed* might come thereafter? Would the same punishment be given to a knight for loving a lady as that which was given to those who betrayed and condemned Christ? These words underscore Clamide's willingness to accept the suffering of Judas and Pontius Pilate in exchange for Condwiramurs, while at the same time leaving open whether this would necessarily be the case if his wish to possess the lady—to "hold her in his arms"—could somehow be fulfilled. The importance given to Clamide's statement in Wolfram's grail romance is modest, corresponding to this knight's limited role. Its primary function seems to be as an inverse marker of the value of the love of Condwiramurs that Parzival has obtained with his victory over Clamide. Yet it also serves as a demonstration of the absolute value of creaturely love, of the extremity of dimensions such creaturely love can have. The stark manner in which Clamide gives expression to what he has lost and to what he continues against all hope to aspire seems to leave little room to render the absoluteness of his investment in love in any greater terms.

Clamide's evaluation of his love for Condwiramurs explores the limits of absolute creaturely love in a manner that is consistent with Wolfram's broader poetic assessment, according to which the adventurous pursuit of love and the acquisition of God's favor weigh about equally in the scale. Elsewhere in Wolfram's romance, the possibilities of creaturely love are explored in a similarly striking way in the case of Parzival's cousin Sigune and her lover, the knight Schionatulander, who has been slain in a joust while serving for

---

14. Cundwiramurs and Parzival are married and completely devoted to one another's love, so the adulterous implications of Clamide's words—though these seem to articulate this knight's heartfelt wish—remain much more hypothetical and lack the power to provoke those around him.

her love. The scenes involving Sigune and Schionatulander render the lady holding the lifeless body of her beloved in a manner analogous to the biblical Pietà, thus seemingly appropriating the religious model for courtly chivalric use. The lady Sigune is an exemplar of fidelity, and her posture shows us creaturely love rendered in a comparably absolute way.[15] Sigune's grief over her lover's death in chivalric action is profound, but she does not take what has occurred as a warning to turn away from creaturely love, as she would doubtless be advised to do by the likes of Bernard of Clairvaux. Based on his view of worldly knighthood, surveyed in the previous chapter, the famous and influential monk would doubtless point out that Sigune's present painful state is the inevitable result of a basically sinful orientation that has invested too much value in "frivolous" things.[16] However, Sigune herself shows no signs of questioning her approach. She continues to invest herself absolutely in love, even *after* her lover's death. Wolfram tells us that her love, rather than being cut short by death, continues: *Durch minne diu an im erstarb, / daz er der vürste niht erwarb, / si minnete sînen tôten lîp* (vv. 436.1–3)—"For the sake of the love that had died with this prince without his having enjoyed her, she now loved him dead as he was."[17] Love's reward for chivalric action occurs even in this extraordinary case, as Sigune tells us in her own words:

> Mîner jaemerlîchen zîte jâr
> wil ich im minne geben vür wâr.
> der rehten minne ich bin sîn wer,
> wand er mit schilde und ouch mit sper
> dâ nâch mit ritters handen warp,
> unz er in mîme dienste erstarb.
> magetuom ich ledeclîche hân:
> er ist iedoch vor gote mîn man.
> ob gedanke wurken sulen diu werc,
> sô trage ich niender den geberc
> der underswinge mir mîn ê.
> mîme leben tet sîn sterben wê.
> der rehten ê diz vingerlîn
> vür got sol mîn geleite sîn.
> (440.1–14)

---

15. On the figure of Sigune, see Marion Gibbs, "Ideals of Flesh and Blood," 14–17.
16. See Bernard of Clairvaux's "Praise of the New Knighthood," which was also considered and cited in the previous chapter.
17. Wolfram von Eschenbach, *Parzival* (Hatto), 223.

> I shall give him love through the joyless days that remain to me. It is true love that I shall bestow on him, for he strove to win it in chivalric style with shield and lance till he died in my service. I am a virgin and unwed: yet before God he is my husband. If thoughts could produce deeds, then I have no hidden reservation that could impede my marriage. His death wounded my life. And so this ring, token of true wedlock, shall assure my safe passage to God.[18]

As inopportune as it may seem, the continuing love of Sigune upon the death of her lover is a worldly, courtly chivalric one, extended in the direction of the heavenly afterlife. She bestows it upon her lover because he has served her as knights are supposed to do, with lance and shield. Schionatulander has died in his effort to win her love, and the reward bestowed by Sigune is correspondingly varied. The spiritual and physical love and marital bond, which often mark the outcomes of successful chivalric endeavors in the romances, must be replaced here by intentions. With thoughts standing in for deeds, Sigune *gives herself* to Schionatulander as the proper reward for his chivalric investment in her, and she regards herself as his wife. Her love for Schionatulander is in this way *absolute,* as is her suffering, and by the end of Wolfram's romance, she will have perished of it. In what one might regard as Wolfram's retort to the wagging finger of Bernard of Clairvaux, the poet has Sigune express in the final verses of the above-cited passage her faithful assurance that absolute dedication to her lover and husband *in thought* will open heaven's gates for her.

With Clamide and Sigune, Wolfram finds different ways of showing what Parzival's love for Conwiramurs accomplishes in the foreground of the imaginary action of his grail romance. The pain and suffering of Sigune and Clamide and the joy of Parzival and Condwiramurs mark new ways of scaling the courtly chivalric interest in love. This interest is already absolute in a more conventionally chivalric romance such as Chrétien de Troyes's *Érec et Énide,* but the religious standards that form part of Wolfram's grail romance enable a relatively greater assessment of its depth and scope. The pain of Clamide and Sigune resulting from their absolute investment in love is an extreme version of the anguish experienced elsewhere in the romances by lovers because of love's mutability. In the interest of love, one wagers oneself for something of absolute value, but the way to the goal remains unpredictable. Receiving the reward of love hinges on many variables, foremost among them the inclinations of the other who might not be willing to bestow it, as in the case of Clamide. Even when love is mutual, it eventually ends or is transformed in a fundamental way upon the death of the beloved, as in the case of Sigune.

---

18. Ibid., 225.

In the pursuit of love's reward, the variability and mutability of things can be influenced but never be entirely fixed or controlled by one's strategic interventions. The physical disorientation and malaise associated with love is one of the most prominent and enduring manifestations of courtiers' interest in it. The turbulent dynamics of love, experienced as a physical condition (i.e., *love sickness*), also correspond to those in the give-and-take of jousting and swordplay as well as in the tumbling of dice, which Wolfram combines in his own memorable rendering of action undertaken for love: *vil hôhes topels er doch spilt, / der an ritterschaft um minne zilt* (vv. 115.19–20)—"A man who aims at love through chivalric exploits *rolls the dice* for high stakes."[19] In love, the dynamics of the Pauline-Augustinian *move* are reiterated, the self is invested absolutely in an*other* in the hope of gain, but in the reiteration—when the beloved is a lady or a knight—the move increasingly comes into view *as such,* analogous to *plays* in competitions, contests, and games. It can also be rendered as analogous to warfare, competition's most brutal form. This occurs in the case of Riwalin and Blancheflor in Gottfried von Strassburg's romance about the famous adulterous lovers Tristan and Isolt (to which I return at greater length later in this chapter). Conquest provides the appropriate imagery for describing the initial stages of the action in which Tristan's parents, Riwalin and Blancheflor, are involved in the interest of love:

er was ir in ir herze komen;
er truoc gewalteclîche
in ir herzen künicrîche.
den cepter und die crône.[20]
(726–29)

He had come into her heart, and in the kingdom of her heart wore crown and sceptre with despotic sway.[21]

When Blancheflor and Riwalin speak to each other shortly thereafter for the first time, the lady indicates love has involved injurious force, when she tells the knight that he has caused her discomfort on account of a "dear friend": *Sî sprach: "an einem vriunde mîn, / dem besten den ich ie gewan, / dâ habet ir mich beswaeret an"* (vv. 754–56)—"You have oppressed me through a friend of

---

19. Ibid., 68. The Middle High German *topels* more clearly references a game of dice. As in my fourth chapter, where I also cited these very illustrative verses, I modify Hatto's translation here, replacing "gambles" with the italicized words.

20. Gottfried's Middle High German verses are cited from *Tristan* (Ranke).

21. Ibid., 51.

mine, the best I ever had."[22] The friend, it turns out, is Blancheflor's own heart, over which Riwalin holds "despotic sway."[23] Riwalin is eventually able to perceive the possibility of love, because he has begun to wager himself for hers as she has for his, and because he applies all the intellectual resources at his disposal. In the cited verses below, the knight gives Blancheflor's demeanor and the meaning of her words close critical consideration and begins to understand the sense in which she has been "oppressed" by him. He proceeds then, in his thoughts, to take possession of what she has already made available to him for the taking:

> er trahte maneger slahte,
> waz Blanschefliure swaere
> und dirre maere waere
> ir gruoz, ir rede betrahte er gâr,
> ir sûft, ir segen, al ir gebâr
> daz marcte er al besunder
> und begunde iedoch hier under
> ir siuften unde ir süezen segen
> ûf den wec der minne wegen
>
> . . . .
>
> daz enzunte ouch sîne sinne,
> daz sî sâ wider vuoren
> und nâmen Blanschefluoren
> und vuorten sî mit in zehant
> in Riwalînes herzen lant
> und crônden sî dar inne
> im z'einer küniginne.
> (794–812)

He pondered from many sides why Blancheflor should be oppressed, and what lay behind it all. He considered her greeting, her words; he examined her sigh minutely, her farewell, her whole behavior, and so doing began to construe both her sigh and her sweet benediction as manifestations of love [...]

---

22. Ibid.
23. See also James A. Schultz's observations on the love of Blancheflor and Riwalin in his article, "Why Do Tristan and Isolde Make Love?" (73–79). Of particular importance is Schulz's observation that love (and the ensuing urge to engage in sexual activities) is internal, but not innate: "Love takes over one's heart, thereby becoming an internal force that impels the individual to engage in sexual activities. But although it is internal, it is not innate: it is always provoked by something outside the lover" (79).

This fired his spirit too, so that it returned and took Blancheflor and led her straightway into the land of his heart and crowned her there as his Queen.[24]

Here the indeterminate cultural action in which love is at stake is rendered with imagery suggestive of the painstaking reconnoitering of challenging and potentially hostile terrain, followed by assault, conquest, and the eventual coronation of a new queen in Riwalin's "kingdom of the heart." In love as in war, the self is wagered in a risky action in which possible outcomes range from the utter ruin of Clamide to the absolute joy of Parzival and Condwiramurs, from the difficulty and pain of the *paramilitary* maneuvering of Riwalin and Blancheflor to the joy they later experience for a short while in their "kingdom of love," the value of which is said to equal or surpass that of any *other* heavenly kingdom: *Sî enhaeten niht ir leben / umb kein ander himelrîche gegeben* (vv. 1371–72)—"They would not have given this life of theirs for any *other* heavenly kingdom."[25]

Decades earlier, in his romance *Cligès* (ca. 1176), Chrétien de Troyes sets forth the action undertaken by knights and ladies in the interest of love over a period of two generations. Love is a highly indeterminate and tumultuous undertaking, as indistinguishable in its effects from a bitter draught or from the pitching and turning of a boat at sea, as the sound of the Old French *l'amor* is from the words *amer*—"bitter," and *la mer*—"sea."[26] In the case of Cligès's parents, Alexander and Soredamors, we can already see the importance placed on close scrutiny, analysis, and reflection in the interest of love.[27] In contrast to the bellicose imagery employed in rendering the amorous action of Riwalin and Blancheflor, Alexander's considerations about the goal he has set for himself—the love of Soredamors—show the action for love's reward to involve both physical infirmity (i.e., love sickness) and the dynamics of a game:

Donc n'est mervoille se m'esmai
Car molt ai mal et si ne sai
Quex max ce est que me justise,
Ne sai don la dolors m'est prise.
Nel sai? Si faz. Jel cuit savoir:

---

24. Gottfried von Strassburg, *Tristan*, 52.
25. Ibid., 58–59. The Middle High German word *ander* means "other," so I have taken the liberty of inserting this word, italicized, into Hatto's English rendering here.
26. See Chrétien de Troyes, *Cligès* (Dembowski), cited below, vv. 539–57. I discuss the same play on words in Gottfried's romance later in this chapter.
27. For perceptive views of the amorous relationships of Alexandre and Soredamors, and of Cligès and Fenice, see Joan Tasker Grimbert, "*Cliges* and the Chansons," 120–36.

Cest mal me fet Amors avoir.
Comant? Set donc Amors mal faire?
Don n'est il dolz et debonaire?
Je cuidoie que il eüst.
En Amor rien qui boen ne fust,
Mes je l'ai molt felon trové.
Nel set qui ne l'a esprové,
De quex jeus Amors s'antremet.
Fos est qui devers lui se met,
Qu'il vialt toz jorz grever les suens.
Par foi, ses geus n'est mie buens;
Malvés joer se fet a lui,
Je cuit qu'il me fera enui.
Que ferai donc? Retrerai m'an?[28]
(664–77)

This malady comes from Love. How can that be? Can Love do harm? Is he not gentle and high-born? I thought that there was only good in Love, but I've found him to be a great traitor. You cannot know all of Love's games until you have tried them. One is a fool to side with him, because he is always trying to harm his own. Upon my word, his game is a bad one. It's not good to play with him, for his game will cause me grief. So what shall I do? Shall I back away?[29]

Love personified seems as violently whimsical as the capricious deities at Homer's Troy, but we continue to observe that the absolute stakes in play are specifically medieval. At the moment of these reflections, Alexander considers love's game to be rigged in such a way that he is bound to lose and experience painful diminishment. The cited verses and the episode from which they are taken show that, in the interest of love, one is simultaneously *played* and a *player*. One is *played*—in a manner reminiscent of the gods' manipulation of the lives of mortals in the action around Troy that we observed in the first chapter of this study—insofar as love is something overpowering that *happens* to people and is experienced negatively and painfully. Medieval people understand themselves in love to be like dice, jostled and moved by a force largely beyond their control.[30] The painful sense of being played by love cor-

---

28. Chrétien de Troyes, *Cligès* (Dembowski).
29. Idem, *Cligès* (Kibler), 131.
30. Along these lines, Grimbert leaves Alexander in the overpowering clutches of love ("*Cliges* and the Chansons," 127). I give greater importance to Alexander's whole-hearted

responds to the experience of being *at stake,* to being absolutely invested in something mutable and unpredictable. On the other hand, in the however difficult torments of absolute love, courtiers such as Alexander are also making love their interest and managing to find their way. If courtiers frequently come to grips with the adverse effects of being played by love, it is because they are able—*as players*—to turn things to their advantage. Like most lovers in the romances, Alexander will not "back away," as we see in the resolve with which his lengthy reflections about love conclude:

> Or face de moi tot son buen,
> Si com il doit feire del suen,
> Car je le vuel et si me plest,
> Je ne quier que cist max me lest.
> Mialz vuel qu'ainsi toz jorz ne teingne
> Que de nelui santez me veingne,
> Se de la ne vient la santez
> Dont est venue l'anfertez.
> (863-70)

Let Love do with me what he will, as he should do with his subject, for such is my wish and desire; I hope this malady will never leave me. I would rather linger on like this forever than be healed by anyone, unless it be by her from whom my illness came.[31]

Here Alexander wholeheartedly accepts that he is absolutely in play, as every true lover must eventually do, because the pain of the risk is worthwhile in view of the reward. In absolute terms, the knight here commits himself to love, *toz jorz*—"forever."

Later in this romance, Cligès along with his beloved Fenice will participate in the same difficult game. A move that Chrétien makes in rendering this love of the second generation addresses the relationship of poetry and politics that was touched upon at the beginning of this chapter. Like his father before him, Cligès resolves to journey from Greece to Arthur's court in Britain to test his chivalric mettle among the ranks of the very best knights. By the time of his departure, an exchange of hearts between the lovers has occurred—a recurring

---

acceptance of the idea that he has to be a *player,* and that, as such, he may be able to shape things to his own ends.

31. Chrétien de Troyes, *Cligès* (Kibler), 133.

convention in the poetic depiction of love in the romances.[32] Left behind in Constantinople, Fenice reflects that her own heart has left her in order to remain with her beloved Cligès, but she decides that her heart, that is, her absolute investment in Cligès, should stay where it is, with its new "master." Fenice's reflections are worth citing at length for their meticulous, critical rendering of politics at court in relation to love:

> La soit! Ja nel quier remuer,
> Einz voel qu'a son seignor remaingne,
> Tant que de lui pitiez li praingne;
> Qu'ainçois devra il la que ci
> De son sergent avoir merci,
> Por ce qu'il sont an terre estrenge.
> S'or set bien servir de losenge,
> Si com an doit servir a cort,
> Molt iert riches, einz qu'il s'an tort.
> Qui vialt de son seignor bien estre
> Et delez lui seoir a destre,
> Si com il est us et costume,
> Del chief li doit oster la plume,
> Neis quant il n'en i a point.
> Mes ici a un malvés point:
> Car il aplaigne par defors,
> Et se il a dedans le cors
> Ne malvestié ne vilenie,
> Ja n'iert tant cortois qu'il li die,
> Einz fera cuidier et antendre
> Qu'a lui ne se porroit nus prandre
> De proesce ne de savoir,
> Si cuide cil qu'il dïe voir
> . . . .
> Qui les corz et les seignors onge
> Servir le covient de mançonge.
> *Autel covient que mes cuers face,*
> *S'avoir vialt de son seignor grace;*
> *Loberres soit et losengiers.*
> Mes Cligés est tex chevaliers,

---

32. See Grimbert's discussion of Cligès and Fenice and their exchange of hearts ("*Cliges and the Chansons,*" 131–34).

Si biax, si frans et si leax
Que ja n'iert mançongiers ne fax
Vers moi, tant le sache lober,
Qu'an lui n'a riens que amander.
(4506–56; italics added)

> Let it stay where it is! I have no wish to disturb it, but let it remain with its lord until he deign to take pity on it. He is more likely to have pity on his servant there than here, since they are in a foreign land. Whoever wishes to be in his lord's good graces and sit at his right hand, as is the custom and habit of our days, must pick the feather from his head, even when there isn't one. But there is a contrary side to this: even after he has smoothed down his lord's hair the servant does not have the courtesy to tell his lord of any wickedness and evil within him, but lets him believe and understand that no one is comparable to him in valour and in knowledge, and his lord believes he speaks the truth [. . .] Anyone who frequents courts and lords must be ready to serve with lies. *My heart, too, must be ready to cajole and flatter!* But Cligès is so handsome, noble, and true a knight that no matter how it praised him, my heart could never be false or deceitful: for in him there is nothing to be improved upon.[33]

In the interest of love, a heart must be prepared to cajole, flatter, and engage in any and every kind of dissimulation with which an ambitious courtier would curry the favor of a powerful lord. Fenice's reflections here, in particular in the italicized verses, show us that in the absolute wager of self for love, one must be prepared to do and say *anything*. Politics at court provide—along with warfare, games, and physical infirmity—a manner of illustrating the lengths to which a loving heart must be prepared to go in the pursuit of its interest. While the intricacies of politics at court provide a different manner of rendering the action undertaken for love, in this case, the interest in love also inversely offers a perspective from which courtly politics can be laid open to critical scrutiny. Based on the matter-of-fact manner in which the dissimulations of courtly politics are rendered here in the reflections of Fenice, one might surmise that a lord truly deserving of all the flattery and fawning of courtiers—as deserving as Cligès is of her loving heart's ministrations—is scarce, if at all extant. In Fenice's thoughts about her heart's relationship to Cligès, love, even as it is being rendered in political terms, seems to possess a standard of excellence that is lacking in politics. Here and elsewhere, as in the narratives about love

---

33. Chrétien de Troyes, *Cligès* (Hatto), 178; italics added.

that I examine in greater detail below, love seems to establish a level of courtly accomplishment to which all lords and courtiers would do well to aspire.

HIGHLIGHTS FROM MARIE DE FRANCE'S *LANVAL*

At the beginning of Marie's lay *Lanval,* the situation of the eponymous knight seems anything but propitious in terms of the potential for growth.[34] Scots and Picts have invaded England and are laying waste to it. Arthur has sought refuge in his stronghold at Carduel, where he holds court and has distributed rich gifts, wives, and lands to his counts and barons, with the exception of Lanval. Most of Arthur's men envy Lanval's valor, generosity, beauty, and bravery, and only feign affection for him. Though he is the son of a king, the knight is far from his homeland, without resources and dependent as a member of Arthur's household on the king's generosity, which in his sole case is not forthcoming. Apparently without any recourse, Lanval is in dire straits. Resources are aplenty at Arthur's court, but despite Lanval's fine qualities—or perhaps because of envy of them—the latter experiences no enrichment. These fine qualities, possibly the source of his predicament at a court where the best is not being rewarded, nevertheless enable Lanval to take an initiative that changes everything. Despite the adverse circumstances at court in which he finds himself, Lanval engages himself in a manner that will help. Marie tells us:

> Ore est Lanval mut entrepris,
> Mut est dolent, mut est pensis!
> Seignurs, ne vus esmerveillez:
> Hum estrange descunseillez,
> Mut est dolenz en autre tere,
> Quant il ne seit u sucurs quere!
> Le chevalier dunt jeo vus di,
> Ki tant aveit le rei servi,
> Un jur munta sur sun destrer,
> Si s'est alez esbaneer.[35]
> (33–42)

---

34. *Lanval* is frequently assessed in its poetic associations with Marie's other lays, for example in the studies of R. Howard Bloch (*Anonymous Marie de France*) and Glyn S. Burgess (*Lais of Marie de France*). Its Arthurian content, amorous interests, and verse form also make this lay appropriate for the different framework in which I am considering it.

35. Marie de France, *Lais* (Micha).

Now Lanval was in difficulty, / depressed and very worried. / My lords, don't be surprised: / a strange man, without friends, / is very sad in another land, / when he doesn't know where to look for help. / The knight of whom I speak, / who had served the king so long, / one day mounted his horse / and went off to amuse himself.[36]

The term *s'esbanïer*—"amuse oneself"—is used here and elsewhere in Marie's story to designate moments when knights and ladies put themselves into play for love. Other courtiers will later "amuse themselves" at Arthur's court, but this option is apparently not available to Lanval at this point. Instead, he resolves to "amuse himself" in a landscape beyond Arthur's court, the same landscape Marie has already told us is being destroyed by Scots and Picts. Even if this were the only danger lurking in the open countryside beyond Carduel, Lanval's play for love—which his initiative progressively reveals itself to be—involves opening himself to new possibilities that also expose him to risk, as we see in the ensuing narrative. Lanval's move shows itself to be a risky enterprise that eventually enables him to overcome his difficulties and acquire the resources he needs, though the challenges he has to overcome in order to experience love's reward will be difficult and many.[37]

As he lies by a river absorbed by worries, two unknown maidens arrive to tell him he has been summoned by their lady. They lead him to their lady's pavilion, the description of which provides detailed indications of the global parameters of the cultural resources that Lanval will soon gain in love:

Treskë al tref l'unt amené,
Ki mut fu beaus e bien asis;
La reïne Semiramis,
Quant ele ot unkes plus aveir
E plus pussaunce e plus saveir,
Ne l'emperere Octovïan,
N'esligasent le destre pan.
Un aigle d'or ot desus mis;

---

36. In this chapter, I cite the verse translation of Robert Hanning and Joan Ferrante, *Lais of Marie de France*, which best brings out the features of Marie's Old French text to which I wish to draw attention in this chapter (here 105–6).

37. Bloch suggests that "Lanval's wandering off into the countryside and his encounter with the fairy lady represent a dream of possession" (*Anonymous Marie de France*, 69). In a sociopolitical direction, Bloch suggests Lanval can be seen as representative of desire for a greater share of cultural resources on the part of economically disadvantaged lower nobility and younger sons (68–71).

> De cel ne sai dire le pris,
> Ne des cordes ne des peissuns
> Ki del tref tienent les giruns:
> Suz ciel n'ad rei kis esligast
> Pur nul aver k'il i donast!
> Dedenz cel tref fu la pucele;
> Flur de lis e rose nuvele,
> Quant ele pert al tens d'esté,
> Trespassot ele de beauté.
> Ele jut sur un lit mut bel—
> Li drap valeient un chastel—
> En sa chemise senglement.
> Mut ot le cors bien fait e gent!
> (80–100)

> They led him up to the tent, / which was quite beautiful and well placed. / Queen Semiramis, / however much more wealth, / power, or knowledge she had, / or the emperor Octavian / could not have paid for one of the flaps. / There was a golden eagle on top of it, / whose value I could not tell, / nor could I judge the value of the cords or the poles / that held up the sides of the tent; / there is no king on earth who could buy it, / no matter what wealth he offered. / The girl was inside the tent: / the lily and the young rose / when they appear in the summer / are surpassed by her beauty. / She lay on a beautiful bed—/ the bedclothes were worth a castle—/ dressed only in her shift. / Her body was well shaped and elegant.[38]

The Roman Empire of Octavian/Augustus Caesar provides the best measure of the scale of the *goods* Lanval finds here. The imperial scaling of things is maintained as Marie's description moves from the tent as a whole, to the flaps whereby Lanval enters it, to the coverings of the bed, where the richness of the material surroundings merges with the body of the woman lying upon it. *Empire* comes closest to encompassing the dimensions of the resources Lanval finds here, but Marie's verses make it clear that the wealth and splendor of any temporal, historical empire falls far short of providing an adequate benchmark. The resources now within Lanval's reach seem to possess otherworldly dimensions, seemingly closer to those of the heavenly kingdom of Christianity than to those of any temporal realm. In her first words to Lanval, the

---

38. Marie de France, *Lais* (Hanning and Ferrante), 107.

lady offers her love to him, reiterating as she does so her love's *superimperial* parameters:

> Se vus estes pruz e curteis,
> Emperere ne quens ne reis
> N'ot unkes tant joie ne bien,
> Kar jo vus aim sur tute rien.
> (113–16)

> If you are brave and courtly, / No emperor or count or king / will ever have known such joy or good; / for I love you more than anything.³⁹

Lanval readily agrees to love her absolutely⁴⁰—*Jeo ferai voz comandemenz; / Pur vus guerpirai tutes genz* (vv. 127–28)—"I shall obey your command; / for you, I shall abandon everyone"⁴¹—in terms reminiscent of the allegiance Jesus required of his disciples. In exchange for his vow, he experiences a joyful expansion of self that is twofold: the lady gives herself to him physically with the promise she will continue to be with him whenever he wishes to enjoy her love, and he receives access to the kind of material resources that assuredly caught his eye when he first entered her tent:

> Un dun li ad duné aprés:
> Ja cele rien ne vudra mes
> Que il nen ait a sun talent;
> Doinst e despende largement,
> Ele li troverat asez.
> Mut est Lanval bien assenez:
> Cum plus despendra richement,
> E plus avra or e argent!
> (134–42)

> Afterward she gave him a gift: / he would never again want anything, / he would receive as he desired; / however generously he might give and

---

39. Ibid., 108.
40. Philippe Ménard stresses love as an "absolute" in Marie's poetry: "*L'amour représente le bien supreme, le vrai Bonheur, la valeur absolue*"—"Love represents the supreme good, true happiness, the absolute value" (*Les Lais de Marie*, 137).
41. Marie de France, *Lais* (Hanning and Ferrante), 108.

spend, / she would provide what he needed. / Now Lanval is well cared for. / The more lavishly he spends, the more gold and silver he will have.[42]

Out of the blue, Lanval has *struck it rich* in love. The terms for keeping his newly found wealth are straightforward. Even as the benefits of his love become provocatively clear at Arthur's court, Lanval will have to keep the source of his sudden affluence a secret. Upon conferring her various gifts to him, the lady tells him he will lose everything if he divulges the secret of their love to anyone.

Back at Arthur's court, Lanval makes generous use of all the resources newly at his disposal via love. He summons his lady when he is alone so that their love remains undiscovered, and he employs his new riches in a manner befitting an emperor or king:

> Lanval donout les riches duns,
> Lanval aquitout les prisuns,
> Lanval vesteit les jugleürs
> Lanval feseit les granz honurs.
> N'i ot estrange ne privé
> A ki Lanval n'eüst doné.
> Mut ot Lanval joie e deduit:
> U seit par jur u seit par nuit,
> S'amie peot veer sovent,
> Tut est a sun comandement.
> (209–17)

Lanval gave rich gifts, / Lanval released prisoners, / Lanval dressed jongleurs (performers), / Lanval offered great honors. / There was no stranger or friend / to whom Lanval didn't give. / Lanval's joy and pleasure were intense; / in the daytime or at night, / he could see his love often; / she was completely at his command.[43]

The same fine characteristics underscored by Marie at the beginning of the poem, which later qualified him in the eyes of his otherworldly beloved, now cause Lanval to spend his new wealth lavishly and indiscriminately, in marked contrast to King Arthur's treatment of him at the outset of this poem. Not too long after his return, the expansion of the resources of self that Lanval has

---

42. Ibid., 108–9.
43. Ibid., 110–11.

experienced in love changes the parameters of the action at Arthur's court. Previously ignored by the king and envied by courtiers, he becomes the focal point of attention after the feast of St. John, when about thirty knights *s'ierent alé esbanïer* (v. 222)—go to "amuse themselves"—in an orchard beneath a tower in which Arthur's queen is staying. Noting they have neglected to bring Lanval, *ki tant est larges e curteis / e sis peres est riches reis* (vv. 231–32)—"who is so generous and courtly, / and his father is a rich king"[44]—they return to his lodging and persuade him to join them. Standing with her ladies in a window of the tower, the queen sees the group of knights, and her gaze comes to rest on Lanval: *La maisniee le rei choisi, / Lanval conut e esgarda* (vv. 240–41)—"She saw the king's retinue, / recognized Lanval and looked at him."[45] Upon seeing him, the queen resolves to make a play for love. She surrounds herself with the court's loveliest and most refined maidens so that the number of maidens corresponds roughly to the number of knights, and *od li s'irrunt esbanïer / La u cil erent el vergier"* (vv. 245–46)—"together they went to amuse themselves / in the orchard where the others were."[46] With love in the air around him, Lanval yearns for his own beloved, but he cannot summon her before so many eyes. In his state of yearning, Lanval separates himself somewhat from the knights and maidens. When the queen sees Lanval standing alone, perhaps sensing his yearning without knowing its source, she approaches and offers him *all* her love:

Al chevaler en va tut dreit;
Lunc lui s'asist, si l'apela,
Tut sun curage li mustra:
"Lanval, mut vus ai honuré
E mut cheri e mut amé;
Tute m'amur poëz aveir.
Kar me dites vostre voleir!
Ma druërie vus otrei:
Mut devez estre lié de mei."
(260–68)

She sat beside him and spoke, / revealing her whole heart: / "Lanval, I have shown you much honor, / I have cherished you, and loved you. / You may

---

44. Ibid., 111.
45. Ibid.
46. Ibid., 111–12.

have all my love; / just tell me your desire. / I promise you my affection. / You should be very happy with me."⁴⁷

Lanval is *on a roll*. Measured by the imperial resources being made available to him, he has come a long way from his starting position. Utterly deprived of resources and affection at Arthur's court in the beginning, he has acquired the love of his otherworldly lady with her extraordinary wealth, and he has become popular among his knightly peers. Now, he is being offered the love of Arthur's queen, the highest ranking and richest woman at court.

The queen's play, coming upon the knights' decision to include Lanval among their number, marks a broader shift in the social and political dynamics at Arthur's court. The resources of love, combined with Lanval's innate and acquired characteristics, have evidently made him—from the perspective of the queen—the most desirable knight at court. Her offer of love stands to put Lanval in a position somewhat similar to that of Tristan, but in order to remain true to his love and to the exemplary characteristics he has possessed from the beginning, Lanval must recognize this moment as a challenge and handle himself adroitly. He immediately and vigorously refuses the queen's offer, at first for a reason he would give even if he had never met his own lady love:

Dame, fet il, lessez m'ester!
Jeo n'ai cure de vus amer.
Lungement ai servi le rei;
Ne li voil pas mentir ma fei.
Ja pur vus ne pur vostre amur
ne mesferai a mun seignur.
(269–74)

"My lady," he said, "let me be! / I have no desire to love you. / I have served the king a long time; / I don't want to betray my faith to him. / Never, for you or your love, / will I do anything to harm my lord."⁴⁸

Despite his own poor treatment at Arthur's hands, Lanval remains loyal to the king. Nothing in the imaginary action of this poem suggests Lanval would feign loyalty as a pretext to conceal his otherworldly love. Loyalty to the king, despite its past fruitlessness, is consistent with Lanval's exemplary courtly

---

47. Ibid., 112.
48. Ibid.

characteristics. It is because of these characteristics that he has been chosen by his otherworldly love and has been provided with the resources that he has distributed at Arthur's court so lavishly and indiscriminately. In all respects, Lanval maintains the highest courtly—and in his love, as we have seen—the highest *imperial* standard.

By contrast, the queen manifests the unenviable characteristics of the vain courtly lord imagined by Fenice earlier in this chapter, who wants to "believe and understand that no one is comparable to him." As the highest-ranking female at court on an occasion when courtiers are in play for love, the queen has difficulty believing Lanval can refuse her offer. Either because she believes it to be true according to her limited understanding, or because she wants to goad him, the queen angrily asserts that the reason for Lanval's rejection of her love is that he prefers the intimate company of males: *Vallez avez bien afeitiez / Ensemble od eus vus deduiez* (vv. 281–82)—"You have fine-looking boys / with whom you enjoy yourself."[49] It suddenly becomes difficult, after all, for Lanval to maintain the seemingly straightforward terms of his otherworldly love. In view of the queen's generally unscrupulous behavior, it seems likely some version of her fabrications will soon be circulated in the gossip at court unless Lanval puts a stop to it. Lanval must let the queen's false statement regarding his amorous allegiances stand, along with her follow-up observation that the king made a mistake in keeping a *vileins cüarz, mauveis failliz* (v. 283)—"base coward, wicked recreant"—in his household, or he must refute it. The only mistake, as suggested by Marie, that Lanval makes seems only scarcely to be a mistake: *Teu chose dist par maltalent / Dunt il se repenti sovent* (vv. 289–90)—"He said something out of spite / that he would later regret."[50] The queen seemingly pushes him into a position where he must either reveal his love or betray himself. Sensing the difficulty the queen in her vanity is having with the idea of an eligible partner refusing her advances, Lanval angrily plays his trump card:

> Jo aim e si sui amis
> Cele ki deit aver le pris
> sur tutes celes que jeo sai.
> E une chose vus dirai,
> bien le sachez a descovert:
> Une de celes ki la sert,
> Tute la plus povre meschine,

---

49. Ibid.
50. Ibid., 113.

> Vaut mieuz de vus, dame reïne,
> De cors, de vis e de beauté,
> D'enseignement e de bunté!
> (293–302)

> I love and I am loved / by one who should have the prize / over all the women I know. / And I shall tell you one thing; / you might as well know all: / any one of those who serve her, / the poorest girl of all, / is better than you, my lady queen, / in body, face, and beauty, / in breeding and in goodness.[51]

The superimperial dimensions of Lanval's otherworldly love here enable the knight to turn the tables on the queen. Not only does he, in fact, love a woman, contrary to the queen's assertion, but one whose lowliest servant is "better" than her in the most important courtly respects. Lanval thereby complicates matters for the court and for himself, not by having an adulterous affair with the queen, as Tristan does, but rather by refusing to do so. The stark terms with which he puts the queen down and confers the highest prize upon his own lady, even as they break his vow to the latter and presumably end their love and his access to further riches, do not end his struggle with the queen, but rather escalate it. Remaining true to character, the queen conveys a mendacious, distorted version of her exchange with Lanval to the king, according to which it was the knight who offered his love to *her* and, when she refused it, insulted her with boasts of his lady. The king, also continuing in character, acts on his wife's lies and proceeds against Lanval. The neglect with which he treated Lanval previously now becomes anger and malice. If Lanval cannot defend himself, the king will have him burned or hanged. By this point in the poem at the latest, it has become evident that the competition between Arthur's queen and a lady whom no one other than Lanval has ever seen has much broader implications. If Arthur's queen is not worth as much as the lowliest servant of the beloved lady whom Lanval claims for himself, how might the resources of Arthur's kingdom compare with those of Lanval's lady more generally? Beyond this, if Lanval's claim is true, then the knight has managed to make good despite the king's neglectful, if not shabby, treatment of him described at the beginning of the poem. King Arthur, according to Marie's unflattering depiction of him, might well resent that such a thing could happen without his say, or fret that such a beautiful courtly lady of great means has found the knight deserving of rich rewards when he has not.

---

51. Ibid.

Believing he has lost his lady's love, and thus the absolute investment of self he has made, Lanval pines in a way resembling the suffering of Clamide that we observed above. Clamide would accept the fate of Judas after losing his bid for love if he could receive Conwiramur's love in return, but the biblical model seems more directly applicable to Lanval, whose remorse for his betrayal is so great that the other knights fear for his life: *Mut dotouent k'il afolast!* (v. 414)—"They were afraid he'd kill himself!"⁵² As hard as things get for him, Lanval remains true to the courtly characteristics that have brought him this far. When accused by the king himself of having insulted him with his alleged insult to the queen, Lanval gives his own version of the events. He discreetly states that he made no advances to the queen and insists on the veracity of his statements regarding the beauty of his otherworldly lady:

> Lanval defent la deshonur
> E la hunte de sun seignur
> De mot en mot si cum il dist,
> Que la reïne ne requist.
> Mes de ceo dunt il ot parlé
> Reconut il la verité,
> De l'amur dunt il se vanta;
> Dolent en est, perdue l'a
> De ceo lur dit qu'il en ferat
> Quanque la curt esgarderat.
> (371–80)

> Lanval denied that he'd dishonored / or shamed his lord, / word for word, as the king spoke: / he had not made advances to the queen; / but of what he had said, / he acknowledged the truth, / about the love he had boasted of, / that now made him sad because he'd lost her. / About that he said he would do / whatever the court decided.⁵³

By sparing Arthur the public humiliation of hearing the truth about the queen's offer of love to him, Lanval remains in strict accordance with the words later stated by the Duke of Cornwall, who numbers among the barons appointed by Arthur to decide his case: *A sun seignur / Deit hum partut fairë honur* (vv. 447–48)—"A man owes his lord honor / in every circumstance."⁵⁴

---

52. Ibid., 116.
53. Ibid., 115.
54. Ibid., 117.

In spite of everything, Lanval has always conducted himself in accordance with this rule. Perhaps for this reason, there is a tangible sense that many at court—notably among them, the same Duke of Cornwall, along with Gawein and the other knights concerned about Lanval's welfare—are doubtful if not skeptical that Lanval could be guilty of a grievous crime against the king. Based on their sense of justice and propriety regarding the evidence submitted to them, the barons determine the case will be decided solely according to the veracity of Lanval's statement concerning the greater beauty of his lady.[55]

The convergences of Lanval's otherworldly love with Arthur's court have clearly stirred things up significantly. The knight's generous distribution of the wealth that he obtained in his love, during a time in which he also enjoyed his lady's private company and experienced "intense joy," has changed the knights' affection for him and put him in a position to attract the attention of the queen. The queen has turned away from her husband and offered her love to Lanval as an exemplary knight, courtier, and son of a king, who in his generous and indiscriminate disposition of resources has demonstrated that he knows how to conduct himself according to the highest imperial standard. Finally, the whole of Arthur's court has become embroiled in a legal proceeding, in which much more than the life and reputation of Lanval is at stake. As these things have occurred, the limitations of Arthur's courtly order have been exposed as it seems to undergo a painful betterment in the direction of the exemplary qualities associated with Lanval's love. Such betterment is suggested by the manner in which the trial of Lanval is decided and the poem ended. Perhaps not surprisingly, in view of Lanval's consistently exemplary courtly characteristics and conduct, and his continuing devotion to his love, his otherworldly lady has mercy on him in the end. In a transcendent moment of convergence between Arthur's court and the otherworld of Lanval's love, the lady ultimately reveals herself before the entire court. Preceded by a procession of beautiful maidens, each "more impressive than the queen had ever been,"[56] the lady appears before Arthur and his retinue in her resplendent beauty, proof of the veracity of Lanval's claim:

> La pucele entra el palais:
> Unkes si bele n'i vint mais!
> Devant le rei est descendue,
> Si que de tuz iert bien veüe.

---

55. Burgess calls justice "one of Marie's ever-present concerns," and this concern seems particularly pronounced in the Lay of Lanval (*Chrétien de Troyes*, 19–20).

56. Marie de France, *Lais* (Hanning and Ferrante), 119.

Sun mantel ad laissié cheir,
Que mieuz la peüssent veer.
Li reis, ki mut fu enseigniez,
Il s'est encuntre li dresciez,
E tuit li autre l'enurerent;
De li servir se presenterent.
(601–10)

The lady entered the palace; / no one so beautiful had ever been there. / She dismounted before the king / so that she was well seen by all. / And she let her cloak fall / so they could see her better. / The king, who was well bred, / rose and went to meet her; / all the others honored her / and offered to serve her.[57]

As in the case of the contest won by Chrétien's Enide, the level of the lady's beauty is beyond dispute, and the issue is immediately decided. Besides the unprecedented level of her beauty, the lady brings something else to Arthur's court that it did not previously possess. A new high standard of courtly excellence is conveyed by the lady's statement that the words of Lanval have been true: *De la vantance ke il fist, / Si par mei peot estre aquitez, / par voz baruns seit delivrez!* (vv. 622–24)—"And for the boast that he made / if he can be acquitted through me, / let him be set free through your barons."[58] In confirming the truth of Lanval's words, the lady also confirms the exemplary courtly characteristics and conduct the knight has manifested from the beginning of the poem. At the end of the poem, Lanval's interest in love diverges from Arthur's court. The lady and Lanval ride away together to the beautiful island of Avalon, never to be seen again—but not before King Arthur and his retinue have experienced a comeuppance that is also an enrichment. Fittingly, in view of how things have proceeded in Marie's imaginary action, Arthur is the loser in the end, but a "well bred" one capable of acknowledging the superiority of Lanval's lady, greeting her with the appropriate style, and—possibly—changing the way he deals with future exemplary knights such as Lanval at court. Marie de France probably hopes the lord to whom she has dedicated her *lais,* and the audiences before which she performs them, have been siding with Lanval from the start, and that they would agree that the high standard of excellence achieved in love is something for which political leaders and courtiers in general would do well to strive.

---

57. Ibid., 121–22.
58. Ibid., 122.

HIGHLIGHTS FROM GOTTFRIED VON STRASSBURG'S *TRISTAN*

The interests of love tend to diverge from those of the court in Marie's *Lanval*. Except for consequential moments of convergence between the otherworldly lady's domain and Arthur's court, the characteristics of the former seem absolutely *other*, as if a reiteration of the endless bounty of the heavenly kingdom. The love of Lanval and his lady exists for itself in the end, but it has nevertheless left an indelible mark on Arthur's court. In the imaginary action, we observe that the growth occurring in love does not remain without broader social and political consequences. Many aspects of the interactions between love and politics in Marie's *lai* are also present in Gottfried von Strassburg's romance of Tristan and Isolt, though in the latter, much lengthier narrative, matters are more complicated.[59] Earlier in this chapter, we looked briefly at the secret love of Tristan's parents, Riwalin and Blancheflor. Because the lady is sister of King Marke, lord over Cornwall and England, their son Tristan is born as his closest male relative. The king will consider it appropriate to designate Tristan as his heir upon discovering their familial relationship, long before there is any political or amorous interest in Isolt. The relatively greater complexity of Gottfried's love story about Tristan and Isolt is due to the resulting convergence of the interests in love and political power in this unique case. The interests of love do not diverge from the political interests of the court in Gottfried's romance, but rather have to be accommodated along with them.

The manner in which the interests of absolute love converge with the broader social and political interests of the court in Gottfried's romance has much to do with overcoming adversity.[60] The circumstances surrounding Tristan's birth set the tone in this respect for the entire romance. The love of Riwalin and Blancheflor has remained secret, and in order to maintain their secret love after Tristan is conceived, the lovers depart from Marke's kingdom and return to Riwalin's homeland. There the lovers are immediately embroiled in the ongoing military feud between Riwalin and his feudal overlord Morgan, during which Riwalin is killed in battle and Blancheflor dies in childbirth. In order to save the infant Tristan from Morgan's wrath, Riwalin's loyal servant Rual spreads word that the infant has also died. Gottfried's emotionally laden

---

59. For surveys of the great variety of modern interpretations of Gottfried's romance, see the studies of Mark Chinca (*Gottfried von Strassburg: Tristan*) and Christoph Huber (*Gottfried von Strassburg: Tristan und Isolde*).

60. In this respect, Gottfried's romance is similar to Marie's lay.

depiction of these adverse circumstances must have resonated strongly with medieval audiences familiar with the perils of feuds and warfare[61]:

> wan diz daz ist diu meiste nôt,
> die man zer werlde haben mac:
> swâ sô der man naht unde tac
> den tôtvînt vor ougen hât,
> daz ist diu nôt, diu nâhen gât,
> und ist ein lebelîcher tôt.
> in aller dirre lebenden nôt
> wart Blanscheflûr ze grabe getragen.
> michel jâmer unde clagen
> daz wart begangen ob ir grabe.
> ir muget wol wizzen, ungehabe
> der was dâ vil und alze vil.
> (1842–53)

The greatest distress in which any man can be is to see his deadly enemy before his eyes, day and night. Such peril grips at one's heart; it is a living death. Amid all this anguish of the living, Blancheflor was carried to her grave over which much observance was done with weeping and wailing. You must know that there was wild lamentation, much and overmuch.[62]

The explicit interest in love is still far in the future, but Gottfried is actually already beginning to develop his approach to it here. Love eventually shows itself as the way to overcome such adversity, to manage things in such a way that the intensity of emotion experienced negatively as hatred, anguish, and fear in the face of a mortal adversary can be experienced positively as joy. Gottfried's romance shows that court society—with love as its highest accomplishment—emerges from within strife to place people beyond it, but remains continually in danger of lapsing back into it. The vivid experience of warfare evoked by the cited verses, which is occasionally in the foreground of Gottfried's narrative, otherwise lurks in the background as the ominous

---

61. "The German aristocratic mentality took for granted violence on a considerable scale. The imperial scheme of campaigns within and beyond frontiers of the empire, and the local rivalries, which were soluble, or insoluble, only in feuds, obliged all magnates to retain substantial retinues of armed men. The political necessity itself contributed to the momentum of violence" (Arnold, *German Knighthood*, 14).

62. Gottfried von Strassburg, *Tristan* (Hatto), 65–66.

alternative to the court society of Marke as well as to the adulterous love upon which this society comes to depend.

The first significant step to address the kind of adversity visible in the above-cited verses is a wide-ranging education. Rual raises Tristan as his own son (unbeknownst to the latter and the world) and sees to it that he learns aristocratic skills such as combat and hunting. Tristan also undertakes an intensive study of languages, musical instruments, and books. The strength and agility of body and mind that Tristan acquires in his training and studies become resources upon which he will later draw in achieving outcomes that surpass those of his rivals and detractors. Tristan's preparatory engagements invariably involve coming to grips with adverse circumstances, as we observe already in the rigors of the studies to which Rual subjects him:

> daz was sîn erstiu kêre
> ûz sîner vrîheite.
> dô trat er in daz geleite
> betwungenlîcher sorgen,
> die ime dâ vor verborgen
> und vor behalten wâren
>
> . . . .
>
> und iedoch dô er began,
> dô leite er sînen sin dar an
> und sînen vlîz sô sêre,
> daz er der buoche mêre
> gelernete in sô kurzer zît
> danne ie kein kint ê oder sît.
> (2068–92)

> This was the first departure from his freedom; with it he joined company with enforced cares which had been hidden and withheld from him until then [. . .] Yet once having started on it he applied his mind and industry to it with such vigour that he had mastered more books in that short space than any child before or after him.[63]

Later in Gottfried's romance, Tristan becomes the tutor of the future queen Isolt and his future lover. Tasked by the elder Queen Isolt to instruct her, he subjects her to a similar rigorous course of study and the results are similarly successful. Having bettered themselves by means of the painful effort

---

63. Ibid., 68–69.

invested in their studies, Tristan and Isolt will be better positioned to manage the adverse circumstances in which they find themselves later.

Long before he meets Isolt and begins to instruct her, Tristan is already endeavoring to change things for the better with his acquired skills. An aborted kidnapping attempt by Norwegian merchants leaves him stranded on the coast of Cornwall. After coming upon a hunting party from Marke's court, Tristan dazzles one group of courtiers after another with his skills in hunting techniques, languages, and music. He demonstrates these in a series of successive *performances* before courtly audiences that include experts in the various respective fields of expertise. Tristan eventually performs before King Marke himself and the entire court, and the high standard he continues to achieve prompts the king to propose an exchange:

> Der künec sprach: "Tristan, hoere her:
> an dir ist allez, des ich ger.
> dû kanst allez, daz ich wil:
> jagen, sprâche, seitspil.
> nu suln wir ouch gesellen sîn,
> dû der mîn und ich der dîn.
> tages sô sul wir rîten jagen,
> des nahtes uns hie heime tragen
> mit höfschlîchen dingen:
> harpfen, videlen, singen,
> daz kanstu wol, daz tuo du mir.
> sô kan ich spil, daz tuon ich dir,
> des ouch dîn herze lîhte gert:
> schoeniu cleider unde pfert,
> der gibe ich dir swie vil du wilt.
> dâ mite hân ich dir wol gespilt."
> (3721–36)

"Tristan, listen to me," said the king, "you can do everything I want—hunting, languages, music. To crown it let us be companions. You be mine, and I will be yours. By day we shall ride out hunting, at night here at home we shall sustain ourselves with courtly pursuits, such as harping, fiddling, and singing. You are good at these things; do them for me. For you, in return, I will play a thing *I* know, which perhaps your heart desires—of fine clothes and horses I will give you all you want! With these I shall have played well for you."[64]

---

64. Ibid., 91–92; italics in original.

The new joyful standard of courtliness achieved by Tristan for Cornwall with his performances, along with the affection and generosity of King Marke that these performances earn him, are the first big *payoff* for the painful effort he previously invested in his studies and for the skill and poise with which he has performed before the critical audiences of Cornwall. The exchanges proposed by Marke also underscore the close relationship, and the comparable value, of the king's political power and the courtly *arts and sciences* so capably represented by Tristan. Tristan is already firmly positioned as Marke's "companion" when Rual, who has long sought him, comes to Cornwall and Marke's court, finally finds his foster-son, and publically divulges the whole story of Bansche-flur and Riwalin and of Tristan's birth, to the amazement of all. The talented young courtly companion of Marke has turned out to be the king's nephew. Given the close relationship visible in the above-cited verses and in the following ones, Marke's decision to remain unmarried and designate his nephew as heir to his kingdoms is perhaps not surprising (see vv. 5152–61).

From this point forward, Tristan engages himself with the formidable knowledge and skills he has obtained in his youth and beyond this as the designated heir of the kingdoms of Cornwall and England. One of the crucial differences between Tristan and Lanval with respect to the resources gained in love becomes evident here. Whereas the *riches* of love gained by Lanval are situated in and channeled through an otherworldly domain beyond Arthur's court to which he eventually returns to stay, the resources that are in play for Tristan largely overlap with those that have been designated to him as heir. Tristan's relationship to the rule over Cornwall and England (and possibly over Ireland, whose king Gurmun has no male heir) becomes less certain after he wins Isolt for Marke. But his interest in the love of Isolt remains inextricably connected to political and economic interests as long as she produces no heir for the king and as long as Tristan continues to prove himself to be the only one capable of overcoming threats to Marke's realm—as demonstrated in the case of Morold discussed below.

The love of Tristan and Isolt grows out of the enmity long plaguing the relationship between the Cornwall of King Marke and the Ireland of King Gurmun, Isolt's father. Tristan's moves in the direction of Isolt begin when he answers the challenge of Ireland's champion Morold, kills him in combat, and frees Marke's court from the painful tribute exacted by Ireland for many years. Soon thereafter Tristan must journey to Ireland to seek a cure to the poisoned wound inflicted upon him during the combat. Tristan will achieve this cure from his mortal enemy, the elder Isolt, queen of Ireland and sister of Morold, and known to be the only one capable of accomplishing this cure. Because he assumes the incognito identity of "Tantris," charms the people of Ireland with his many skills (as he had previously charmed the courtiers of Cornwall), and thus qualifies himself to be put to work as a tutor for the younger Isolt, Tristan succeeds in the seemingly impossible endeavor. In exchange for his tuition of Isolt, Tristan is healed by the queen, who remains ignorant of the cause of "Tantris's" wound. After returning to Marke's court, Tristan tells of the great beauty and courtly accomplishments of the younger Isolt, and pressure grows at court for Marke to seek to marry her and produce a male heir. Courtiers in Cornwall marvel at Tristan's accomplishments, but some clearly envy and fear him. The king first remains true to his promise to Tristan, but he ultimately relents to the pressure when begged to do so by his nephew. Likely fearing assassination by rivals or enemies at court, Tristan volunteers to return to Ireland and to attempt to win the younger Isolt for Marke. Again traveling incognito as "Tantris" to Ireland, Tristan *again* achieves his seemingly impossible goal, this time by slaying a dragon that has terrorized the kingdom and thereby winning the hand of Isolt as the proclaimed reward. As himself rather than Tantris—because Isolt has employed her sharpened intellectual faculties to put some clues together and arrive at the truth of his identity—Tristan eventually takes possession of the princess of Ireland on behalf of Marke.

At sea on route to Cornwall, where Isolt is to wed Marke and become his queen, the previous political enmity and strife between the realms of Gurmun and Marke has still not been put to rest. It remains prominent in the initial interaction between Isolt and Tristan, when the latter as ship's captain approaches the maiden to see if she is faring well during their journey at sea. Isolt's thoughts and feelings are still very much occupied with Tristan's killing of her uncle Morold and with the artful trickery with which he has been able—as "Tantris"—to deceive everyone in Ireland, win her as a prize largely under false pretenses, and take her away from her home and loved ones:

"lât stân, meister, habet iuch hin,
tuot iuwer arme hin dan!
ir sît ein harte müelîch man.
war umbe rüeret ir mich?"
"ei schoene, missetuon ich?"
"jâ ir, wan ich bin iu gehaz."
"saeligiu" sprach er "umbe waz?"
"ir sluoget mînen oehein."
"deist doch versüenet." "des al ein:
ir sît mir doch unmaere,
wan ich waere âne swaere
und âne sorge, enwaeret ir.

ir alterseine habet mir
disen kumber allen ûf geleit
mit pârât und mit kündekeit.
waz hat iuch mir ze schaden gesant
von Curnewâle in Îrlant?"
(11570–86)

"Enough, Captain," she said. "Keep your distance, take your arm away! What a tiresome man you are! Why do you keep on touching me?" "But, lovely woman, am I offending you?" "You are—because I hate you!" "But why, dear lady?" he asked. "You killed my uncle!" "But that has been put by." "Nevertheless, I detest you, since but for you I should not have a care in the world. You and you alone have saddled me with all this trouble, with your trickery and deceit. What spite has sent you here from Cornwall to my harm?"[65]

Love marks a new stage of the imaginary action of Gottfried's romance, but indications in these verses of continuing strife, of the intensity of negative emotion we first observed in the circumstances surrounding Tristan's birth, enable a view of love as something that emerges from or grows out of such conflict rather than as a radical break from it.

After Tristan and Isolt find and unknowingly drink a magic potion concocted by the elder Isolt to bring about a happy and loving relationship between her daughter and her future husband Marke, Lady Love makes a familiar entry into Gottfried's narration as an irresistible force:

ê sî's ie wurden gewar,
dô stiez s'ir sigevanen dar
und zôch si beide in ir gewalt.
si wurden ein und einvalt,
die zwei und zwîvalt wâren ê.
(11713–17)

Before they were aware of it she had planted her victorious standard in their two hearts and bowed them beneath her yoke. They who were two and divided now become one and united.[66]

Here as elsewhere, love—whether initiated by a potion or not—is something that *happens* to lovers. It is an overwhelming force or cataclysmic event over

---

65. Ibid., 193.
66. Ibid., 195.

which lovers have no control and to which they can seemingly only react. Lovers are *played* as in the case of Alexander and Soredamors in a previous section of this chapter, or *conquered* by love as in the case of Tristan and Isolt here (or that of Blancheflor and Riwalin before them). In the case of Isolt particularly, we observe that an emotion absolutely and forcefully directed toward the other as enmity (*haz*), suddenly becomes a love (*minne*) that is just as absolutely and forcefully directed. Here as elsewhere, as well, we observe in the ensuing verses that lovers *as players* tend to be in the best position to come to grips with the *force* of love and manage it to their advantage and enrichment.

The best medieval articulation of the *absolute* involvement with love as an opportunity or investment may be the response of Tristan to the disclosure by Isolt's maidservant Brangaene that the potion that has led to their love will also lead to their death:

> "nu walte ez got!" sprach Tristan
> "ez waere tôt oder leben:
> ez hât mir sanfte vergeben.
> ine weiz, wie jener werden sol;
> dirre tôt der tuot mir wol.
> solte diu wunneclîche Îsôt
> iemer alsus sî mîn tôt,
> sô wolte ich gerne werben
> umbe ein êweclîchez sterben."
> (12494–502)

"It is in God's hands!" said Tristan. "Whether it be life or death it has poisoned me most sweetly! I have no idea what the other will be like, but this death suits me well! If my adorable Isolde were to go on being the death of me in this fashion I would woo death everlasting!"[67]

"Death everlasting"—possibly Gottfried's most striking poetic move—takes the sweet suffering of love ubiquitous in court poetry *to another level*. As a courtly reiteration of the Christians' absolute investment in the heavenly kingdom, "death everlasting" is consistent with the absolute Christian parameters of love as developed by Gottfried here and elsewhere in his romance. Already in the prologue, Gottfried provocatively regards the story of the adulterous love of Tristan and Isolt as life-sustaining "bread" for the "noble hearts" among his

---

67. Ibid., 206.

audience, in what amounts to a courtly, poetic reiteration of the terms of the Holy Eucharist in the interest of adulterous love.[68] Here, in Tristan's "death everlasting," an *inversion* of the Christian sense (which nevertheless remains Christian, as things are left "in God's hands" and are expressed *everlastingly*) seems to become evident. Tristan's *êweclîchez sterben* seems to invert the infinite sense of the Christians' play for the heavenly kingdom—*infinite* insofar as its sense is toward the immeasurably great or large, something unbound by time or space—and makes of it a play that finds absolute value in something temporally and spatially limited, that is, another mortal self in this finite world. Tristan's total commitment to the joys of a "death everlasting" in love seems to establish a new benchmark in the general tendency throughout courtly culture to seek and find absolute value in temporal, perishable cultural goods. The ancient bishop Augustine of Hippo and the medieval abbot Bernard of Clairvaux would doubtless have considered the absolute investment of self in this kind of love to be utterly at cross-purposes with the Christian striving for the heavenly kingdom. But this is clearly not the case in the imaginary action of Gottfried's romance and in other narrative and lyric poetry at court involving love. At court, figures who manifestly understand themselves to be Christians are speculating that God will regard their absolute investments in love as an acceptable reiteration, elaboration, or variation of their absolute investment in the heavenly kingdom, rather than as something necessarily at cross-purposes with it.[69]

Tristan's words indicate love is both an overwhelming force and the lovers' latest and greatest difficult venture, in which they turn things to their advantage as they have always done before. Love *happens* to them as something beyond their control, but it also happens to *them* because of who they are and what they have been able to do. In Gottfried's imaginary action, no one other than Tristan and Isolt could be in a position to take the love potion in the particular time and place in which they take it. None other than Tristan and Isolt could find their way to each other in love as rapidly and adeptly despite the upheaval love is causing. Love happens to Tristan and Isolt and nobody

---

68. See vv. 233–40 in Gottfried von Strassburg, *Tristan* (Ranke).

69. Contrast the view of James A. Schultz, who writes: "If the theology of concupiscence was not widely known outside the church, the related distrust of all things sexual certainly was [...] At this historical moment, when vernacular literature was exploring new themes in the context of a courtly culture that was coming into its own and feeling a new confidence, Eilhart's refusal to ask why people make love and Gottfried's refusal to locate the beginning of love anywhere outside of love signal a refusal to engage these discourses." For Schulz, the love potion is the culturally significant "milestone" of this refusal: "This is a signal moment in the history of European sexuality, the moment when a self-conscious and sophisticated secular discourse on love declared its independence of the related theological and medical teachings on the subject" ("Why Do Tristan and Isolde Make Love?," 80).

else, because of the natural gifts, acquired skills, and successful strategies they have exhibited to this point. They soon begin to turn love to their advantage by employing these same faculties and abilities, as we see in the manner in which Gottfried varies the play on words between "love," "sea," and "bitter" in the exchanges between the lovers, whereby they are first able to ascertain their joint interest.[70] The lovers' exchanges in the passage below demonstrate the crucial transition Tristan and Isolt effect from love as irresistible force—associated with the turbulence of the sea by which they are surrounded and the bitterness associated with any difficult life-transforming challenge—to love as *opportunity,* as the way to the *other*:

> "ei schoene süeze, saget mir:
> waz wirret iu, waz claget ir?"
> Der Minnen vederspil Îsôt,
> "lameir" sprach sî "daz ist mîn nôt,
> lameir daz swaeret mir den muot,
> lameir ist, daz mir leide tuot."
> dô sî lameir sô dicke sprach,
> er bedâhte unde besach
> anclîchen unde cleine
> des selben wortes meine.
> sus begunde er sich versinnen,
> l'ameir daz waere minnen,
> l'ameir bitter, la meir mer.
> der meine der dûhte in ein her
> . . . .
> dô er des wortes z'ende kam,
> minne dar inne vernam,
> er sprach vil tougenlîche z'ir:
> "entriuwen schoene, als ist ouch mir,
> lameir und ir, ir sît mîn nôt.
> herzevrouwe, liebe Îsôt,
> ir eine und iuwer minne
> ir habet mir mîne sinne
> gar verkêret unde benomen,
> ich bin ûzer wege komen

---

70. We saw an earlier version of this play on words above in Chrétien de Troyes's *Cligès*. However, it seems Gottfried probably follows his stated source, Thomas, whose work also included the sea/bitter/love play on words, as indicated by the Carlisle fragment; see Grimbert, "*Cliges* and the Chansons," 128.

sô starke und alsô sêre:
in erhol mich niemer mêre.
mich müejet und mich swaeret,
mir swachet unde unmaeret
allez, daz mîn ouge siht.
in al der werlde enist mir niht
in mînem herzen liep wan ir."
Îsôt sprach: "hêrre, als sît ir mir."
(11982–12028)

"Come now, sweet, lovely woman," he whispered tenderly, "tell me, what is vexing you, why do you complain so?" "*Lameir* is what distresses me," answered Love's falcon, Isolde, "it is *lameir* that so oppresses me, *lameir* it is that pains me so." Hearing her say *lameir* so often he weighed and examined the meaning of the word most narrowly. He then recalled that *l'ameir* meant 'Love,' *l'ameir* 'bitter,' *la meir* 'the sea': it seemed to have a host of meanings [...] When he got to the bottom of the word and discovered 'Love' inside it, "Faith, lovely woman," he whispered, "so it is with me, *lameir* and you are what distress me. My dearest lady, sweet Isolde, you and you alone and the passion you inspire have turned my wits and robbed me of my reason! I have gone astray so utterly that I shall never find my way again! All that I see irks and oppresses me, it all grows trite and meaningless. Nothing in the wide world is dear to my heart but you." Isolde answered, "So you, sir, are to me."[71]

The lovers may be "utterly" lost in love at this moment, but we observe that in identifying what ails them and in finding the solution in each other, they are already beginning to find their way again. Thanks to their knowledge of the subtleties of linguistic meaning and their ability to reason things out by process of elimination—skills honed in their studies and life experience—Tristan and Isolt here begin to turn to their own advantage what is controlling them. Here they are no longer merely suffering a love that is happening to them but also taking initiative and making love happen—*as only they can*. The way is difficult for Isolt and Tristan at the beginning of their love, and it will continue to be so. This seems to be one of the main points Gottfried makes in this groundbreaking romance.

The romance's prologue had already anticipated the difficulty of the pioneering effort the principal lovers will have to make and prepared the way for the appropriate assessment of this effort:

---

71. Gottfried von Strassburg, *Tristan* (Hatto), 199–200.

Hei tugent, wie smal sint dîne stege,
wie kumberlîch sint dîne wege!
die dîne stege, die dîne wege,
wol ime, der si wege unde stege!
(37–40)

O Excellence! how narrow are thy paths, how arduous thy ways! Happy the man who can climb thy paths and tread thy ways![72]

Few courtiers will reach the high standard Gottfried holds forth here—perhaps just Tristan and Isolt in the imaginary action of his romance, and the "noble hearts" among the poet's audiences—but for them is reserved a high standard of accomplishment and a corresponding joy that remains unknown to others. Gottfried's romance is unfinished. It breaks off in the midst of Tristan's agonized quandary about whether he should marry Isolt of the White Hands, whom in his turbulent state of mind he confuses with his own beloved. Based on the surviving fragments of the romance by the Anglo-Norman poet Thomas, whose version of the story Gottfried tells us in his prologue that he favors, we know this love leads to death. Having received another poisoned wound, Tristan sends from his exile to Marke's court for his own Isolt, the only one who can heal him. After his wife Isolt of the White Hands falsely tells him the sails of the ship returning from Cornwall are black—the prearranged signal his beloved was unable to come—Tristan dies, and upon finding him, Isolt perishes shortly thereafter. However Gottfried might have ended his romance, we know the overarching narrative framework of the story is painful and sorrowful in contrast to the end of Marie's *Lanval* and the happy endings of romances such as *Érec et Énide* and *Parzival*. Within the limitations afforded by his subject matter, Gottfried nonetheless exploits the story's potential for the rare joy that comes from achieving the most impressive results under the most difficult circumstances.

The joy achieved in love, however qualified its full appreciation may be, has broader social implications, as we also saw in the case of Marie's *Lanval*. The lovers' standard of excellence, and the rewards in love that they acquire because of this standard, do not pertain to them alone. As we have seen, the steps leading toward love are simultaneously steps out of and away from the adversarial strife and pain visible in the circumstances of Tristan's birth and in many prior and subsequent episodes (Riwalin's attack on Morgan, Morgan's counterattack, Tristan's vengeance against Morgan, Tristan's battle with

---

72. Ibid., 41.

Morold, the enmity between Cornwall and Ireland, etc.). During the time in which love is pursued at Marke's court, it can even be seen as preventing or overcoming potential strife *there.* Love is joyful and enriching in enabling strife within unity, anger without hatred, as Gottfried illustrates with this description of the lover's relationship during the time at Marke's court when suspicion has not yet fallen upon them:

> ouch enwart niht under in verborn,
> dane waere ouch underwîlen zorn.
> ich meine zorn âne haz.
> und sprichet aber ieman daz,
> daz zorn ungebaere
> under sô gelieben waere,
> binamen dâ bin ich sicher an,
> daz der nie rehte liep gewan.
> wan diz daz ist der Minnen site,
> hie enzündet sî gelieben mite,
> hie mite sô viuret sî den muot.
> wan alse in zorn vil wê getuot,
> sô süenet sî diu triuwe,
> so ist aber diu liebe niuwe,
> und aber der triuwen mê dan ê.
> (13031–45)

> Nor did it fail to happen now and again that there was anger between them— anger without malice, I mean. And if anyone were to say that anger is out of place between such perfect lovers, I am absolutely certain he was never really in love, for such is Love's way. With it she kindles lovers and sets fire to their emotions. For as anger pains them deeply, so affection reconciles them, with the result that love is renewed and amity greater than ever.[73]

After the love of Tristan and Isolt has begun, the closest thing to the mortal hatred previously visible in their relationship—for example in Isolt's hostility toward Tristan at the beginning of their journey from Ireland to Cornwall— is the anger of lovers' quarrels, which only heightens their desire. Love enables a mitigation of aggression in the relationship between Tristan and Isolt, and it involves a similarly pacific negotiation of the potentially volatile relationship between the lovers and Marke's court. When cultivated as a *game,* as in the

---

73. Ibid., 212.

passage below from shortly after Isolt's successful withstanding of the ordeal,[74] love involves a kind of interaction with Marke's court in which Tristan and Isolt get what they need, desire, and merit, without causing any broader social or political upheaval:

> gespilen unde gesellen
> die ensulen niemer gewellen,
> daz in diu state widerseit,
> oder si wellent al ir leit.
> sô man enmac, der danne wil,
> daz ist ein harte unwaege spil.
> sô man wol müge, sô welle:
> daz ist guot spilgevelle,
> dane lît niht herzeleides an.
> die gespiln Îsôt und Tristan
> sô sî der state niht mohten hân,
> so liezen sî die state gân
> mit dem gemeinen willen hin.
> der wille der sleich under in
> lieblîchen unde suoze
> in micheler unmuoze.
> gemeine liebe, gemeiner muot
> die dûhten sî süeze unde guot.
> (16431–48)

Companions in love should never want what opportunity denies them, or they will want their sorrow. To desire when the means are lacking is a very impolitic game. When you have the means—that is the time for desiring. This game is rich in opportunities, it is not fraught with sorrow. When these partners Isolde and Tristan were unable to seize their opportunity, they let the occasion pass, content in their common will, which, never tiring, stole tenderly and lovingly from one to the other. A common desire and affection seemed sweet and good to them.[75]

Thus engaged in a game "rich in opportunities," the lovers pursue their love and find ways to defer to social and political necessities and practicalities as they do so. With discipline and restraint, and calling upon all their trained

---

74. I discuss Isolt's ordeal at the end of chapter 2.
75. Gottfried von Strassburg, *Tristan* (Hatto), 257.

faculties and life experience, the lovers do their best to make the right *moves* at the right times and places. These moves are indicative of a finer disposition of self that is able to situate the joy of love in "a common desire and affection," when finding a way to physical union would be "impolitic." Absolute love in Gottfried's romance has a clearly situational logic, and Isolt and Tristan have shown themselves to be masters of situations. In the verses preceding the above-cited passage, which describe the broader state of affairs at Marke's court subsequent to Isolt's Ordeal, Gottfried has already indicated that the successful moves of the lovers also have socially beneficial effects:

> Aber haete Tristan unde Îsôt
> überwunden ir sorge unde ir nôt
> und wâren aber des hoves wol.
> der hof was aber ir êren vol.
> ir beider lobes enwart niemê.
> si wâren aber heinlîch als ê
> ir beider hêrren Marke.
> (16403–9)

Once more Tristan and Isolde had surmounted their cares and perils, once more they were happy at court, which again overflowed with their honours. Never had they enjoyed such esteem. They were as intimate again as ever with Mark their common lord.[76]

At this moment, the lovers have each other, they have their position at court, and the court possesses the lovers as its most accomplished and capable representatives. Quite arguably, this is as good as things get in Gottfried's romance. The poet has already provided ample demonstrations of the alternatives to this courtly order based on love. Any frictions between love and politics at Marke's court have to be weighed against the anguish and fear associated with Morold's demands for tribute, or with Morgan's vengeful attacks to which Tristan's mother and father fell victim when he was born. The dissimulations with which Tristan and Isolt pursue their amorous interest enables joy for the lovers and—even if not at the same level—also for other courtiers, which is clearly preferable to the manifest alternative.

In his prologue, Gottfried is already preparing medieval and modern audiences to understand the benefits love brings to *everyone*. In the fourth chapter of this study, we considered the implications of these verses for the assessment

---

76. Ibid.

of Gottfried's own level of achievement as poet-performer. Here as there, love is supposed to have a beneficial social effect overall, even if the highest joys of love are reserved for a select few. I cite the relevant verses below at greater length, and now with specific reference to the proper appraisal of the lover's efforts in the imaginary action:

> Der guote man swaz der in guot
> und niwan der werlt ze guote tuot,
> swer daz iht anders wan in guot
> vernemen will, der missetuot.
> Ich hoere es velschen harte vil,
> daz man doch gerne haben wil:
> dâ ist des lützelen ze vil,
> dâ will man, des man niene wil.
> Ez zimet dem man ze lobene wol,
> des er iedoch bedürfen sol,
> und lâze ez ime gevallen wol,
> die wîle ez ime gevallen sol.
> Tiure unde wert ist mir der man,
> der guot und übel betrahten kann,
> der mich und iegelîchen man
> nâch sînem werde erkennen kann.
> (5–20)

We do wrong to receive otherwise than well what a good man does well-meaningly and solely for our good. I hear much disparagement of what people nevertheless ask for. This is niggling to excess, this is wanting what you do not want at all. A man does well to praise what he cannot do without. Let it please him as long as it may. That man is dear and precious to me who can judge of good and bad and know me and all men at our true worth.[77]

Gottfried's prologue is all about the accurate assessment of good things that are done for us. Looking forward to the subject matter of his romance, it is about understanding the benefits and growth that court society experiences by way of the interest in absolute love, even—indeed, *especially*—in *this* absolute love. Gottfried may well anticipate resistance to his conception of the absolute love of Tristan and Isolt as a benefit rather than detriment to court society in his endeavor to shape its assessment with these verses. Later audiences and

---

77. Ibid., 41.

readers, especially modern ones who view love anachronistically in subjective terms, will tend to assess the love of Tristan and Isolt as socially damaging or disintegrative. Nevertheless, we have observed in this chapter that the efforts of Tristan and Isolt deserve to be evaluated according to the terms the poet presents in his prologue—lest we "disparage" what we "nevertheless ask for," "niggle to excess," and fail in the end to "judge" people and their actions at their "true worth."

Gottfried's rendering of love arguably puts the finest point on a tendency we have observed in the romance poetry of some of the most famous poet-performers of the twelfth and thirteenth centuries. As an absolute investment in another perishable being, love involves a joy or pain that is experienced most directly and fully by lovers, but that is clearly of value for the entire court. By way of their different connections to love, courtiers stand to experience substantial individual and collective growth. As we have seen, diminishment and pain also remain possibilities in the difficult competitions associated with love. Despite their downsides, the absolute investments of self in love that we first observe in the court poetry of the High Middle Ages continue. European courts stay *bullish* on love, and the enthusiasm eventually spreads from courts to cities, and beyond. Love and adventure as we have observed them in this chapter and the last are conspicuous indications of the emergence of a culture of wagers and investments, of a medieval society based on risks and rewards in which the sacrifices of sufferers are being replaced by the ventures of entrepreneurs. Love and adventure are among the first global moves for perishable goods that will increasingly shape the cultural action of the later Middle Ages and modernity. As such they are *trendsetters*.

CHAPTER 7

The Modern Self in Play

THE GLOBAL AS INDIVIDUAL

St. Augustine's influential *City of God against the Pagans* helped shape the cultural action of the Middle Ages in terms of a bipartite city modeled on imperial Rome. In this influential patristic text, the heavenly city of the Christian faithful involves a longer-term dualist approach to things that finds absolute value in the eternal, spiritual-intellectual resources of the heavenly afterlife, while the worldly city—the pagan populace lacking the universal overview and disposition of things provided by faith—continues to establish the value of things much more immediately and discretely according to the characteristics and demands of different specific times and places. Augustine's speculation, as that of Paul before him, was that Christians would choose the creator over creation, the everlasting good of the heavenly afterlife over the perishable goods of this temporal life, and sacrifice themselves or "die to the world" in emulation of Christ. At the same time, in a manner that leaves room for Christians' free will as well as for God's omniscient and omnipotent capacity to establish perfectly just outcomes on the future Judgment Day, the heavenly and worldly parts of Augustine's bipartite city comingle indeterminately. It remains impossible for mortals—even one as authoritative as Augustine himself—to disentangle heavenly and worldly goods or determine their ultimate value. In this study, we have seen that the indeterminacy visible in Augustine's text—which with its imperial Roman dimensions is arguably the most expansive vision of the Christian faith bequeathed by antiquity to the Middle Ages—seems to have left room for if not inspired further speculations on the part of culturally *bullish* princes, poet-performers, and courtiers in the Middle Ages, particularly as of the twelfth and thirteenth centuries. In what *other, other* concerns might Christians legitimately invest themselves? Might the Christian global mobilization of self that has been accomplished in the interest of the heavenly afterlife be redirected to mutable perishable ends in ways that result in growth rather than perdition? As courtiers increasingly speculate on the value of temporal, transitory things—as strikingly visible in their poetry of adventure and love—we have observed that a society based on sacrifice is being replaced by one based on wagers and investments.

As long as the cultural action remains generally consistent with the imperial Christian parameters envisioned by Augustine in late antiquity, it seems primarily communal rather than individual or subjective in the modern sense. Even the literary and artistic achievements of Humanism and the Renaissance, however striking in their individual manifestations, do not seem to countervail the communal, imperial sense of the Christian cultural action. The accomplishments of the *uomo universale* lauded by Jacob Burckhardt as specifically Italian achievements may be seen as extending and elaborating the adventurous and amorous dispositions of self that are observable in court poetry north of the Alps in earlier centuries. *Popes* are among the principal patrons of Renaissance artists whose works, so dynamically, elegantly, and powerfully scaled to individual dimensions, help represent glory on an *imperial* scale. Already at the end of the thirteenth century, Dante's *Divina Commedia* takes us along with our guides Virgil and Beatrice through the teeming expanse of hell, purgatory, and heaven as imagined with unprecedented individual color and detail by *il sommo poeta*. When the poet comes across Marco Lombardo in Purgatory, the latter describes the bipartite imperial city in the same critical vein as Walther von der Vogelweide had done about a century earlier:

> Soleva Roma. che il buon mondo feo,
> due Soli aver, che l'una e l'altra strada
> facean vedere, e del mondo e di Deo.
> L'un l'altro ha spento, ed è giunta la spada
> col pastorale, e l'un con l'altro insieme
> per viva forza mal convien che vada;
> però che, giunti, l'un l'altro non teme.

Rome, that once kept the world good by her rod / was wont to have two suns, whose light made clear / both roads, that of the world and that of God. / One hath the other quenched; to crozier / hath now been joined the sword, and it must needs / be ill going, when the two together fare; / for, when joined, neither power the other dreads.[1]

In Dante's poetic rendering, the medieval world is still identifiably organized along bipartite imperial Christian lines, but it seethes with competitive energy, internal pressures, and rivalries to the point that it seems about to break apart in its myriad individual constituent elements. Religious figures such as John Wycliffe, Jan Hus, and Girolamo Savonarola question the Roman church's claims to cultural supremacy, more or less bluntly criticize it, and begin to place religious experience on a more individual footing, thus anticipating many of the moves that Martin Luther will later make.[2] The earlier critics and reformers underscore and add to the building pressures—borrowing from Dante's Marco Lombardo, we might say to the "ill-going"—within the imperial Christian church, without yet being positioned to effect a significant cultural shift. As objectionable or in need of reform as the Roman church may be, no widely embraced alternative to its directive force seems to exist before the sixteenth century. As long as the European cultural action still occurs mainly according to the parameters of the bipartite City of God originally envisioned by St. Augustine, it arguably remains medieval and communal according to the primacy of individuals' collective involvement in the City's universal Christian mission. Modernity and subjectivity could be seen to begin when the individual self—disengaged or *emancipated* from the bipartite imperial Christian church, but like it, aspiring to dispose *globally* of resources—becomes the new principal locus of cultural indeterminacy.[3] We first begin to

---

1. Text and translation from Dante Aligieri, *Divine Comedy*, 378–79. Placing these words in the mouth of Marco Lombardo, "whom Dante and his contemporaries apparently saw as a man of outspoken righteousness in a generally corrupt society" (Ruud, *Critical Companion to Dante*, 486), gives them legitimacy.
2. In many mystical writings produced as of the High Middle Ages, religious action is already occurring in very individual terms, to the degree it is disengaged from institutional religiosity in seeking the mystical *unio* directly. However, the mystical trend toward individualism does not seem to generate any broader cultural shift, even if it contributes to tensions.
3. I have noted that the earlier transition from a culture of sacrifice to a culture of wagers and investments needs to be regarded not as inevitable or *essential* (i.e., *given* in the nature of things), but rather as a shift in the preponderance of certain kinds of moves in the action. This transition of global religious authority from the imperial church to the individual self needs to be regarded in terms of a similar significant shift in the prevailing kinds of cultural moves that occurs especially in the more northern regions of western Europe.

observe such a broad and systematic *religious* disengagement of the individual from the imperial Christian church as a consequence of the writings of Martin Luther and their dissemination via the printing press that occurs in the early sixteenth century. By the time this occurs, it seems as though mutable, temporal, physical-material cultural resources have been so efficiently valorized over previous centuries that the individual self, for all its manifestly perishable characteristics, has nonetheless become *worthy* to take the place of the imperial church as the principal locus of religious cultural action.

In this concluding chapter, I follow through my global approach to the European cultural action and consider some especially pioneering and influential ways in which *individuality displaces the global parameters of the imperial Christian church as the principal locus of cultural indeterminacy.*[4] In the next two parts of this chapter, which deal with significant cultural moves made in the Reformation and Enlightenment, respectively, I focus on individualized or subjective articulations of the universal that are on the cutting edge of European cultural developments. In the penultimate section of this chapter, I return to the focal points of this study in examining courts, adventure, and love as rendered in the imaginary competitive action of Mark Twain's *A Connecticut Yankee in King Arthur's Court*. In this nineteenth-century romance, we observe how an absolutely empowered Gilded-Age Yankee—familiar with moves of the Reformation and Enlightenment—makes an all-or-nothing play to enlighten and modernize his medieval world. On the basis of the different cases considered in this chapter, and with the help of additional considerations by Hannah Arendt and Jean-François Lyotard, I conclude with some open-ended observations about emancipation and totalitarianism as global moves of (post)modernity.

REFORMATION MOVES

In the earliest years of what will come to be known as the Protestant Reformation, the Augustinian monk Martin Luther composes a brief treatise in German titled *Von der Freiheit eines Christenmenschen—On the Freedom of a*

---

4. "The key historical events in establishing the principle of subjectivity are the Reformation, the Enlightenment, and the French Revolution." In this chapter, I follow the course of modernity here staked out by Habermas. More specifically with regard to Luther—my starting point in this chapter—Habermas continues: "With Luther, religious faith became reflective; the world of the divine was changed in the solitude of subjectivity into something posited by ourselves" (*Philosophical Discourse*, 17).

Christian (1520).[5] According to the terminology employed in it, the principal purpose of this treatise is to provide more efficient Christian parameters for cultural action, and Luther achieves this purpose by shifting the parameters from imperial to individual dimensions.[6] This shift has become necessary, in Luther's view, mainly because of the false claims of papal representatives of the imperial Roman church to dispose of cultural resources that, by right, belong to worldly authorities (i.e., because of the mixing of crozier and sword lamented by Marco Lombardo in Dante's Inferno). These false claims on the part of the Roman *ecclesia* have resulted in the *waste* of cultural resources, both of spiritual-intellectual and of physical-material kinds (i.e., the souls lost based on belief in the efficacy of such human contrivances, the monies paid for indulgences of sins from Germany to Rome). In the open letter to Pope Leo X accompanying his treatise, Luther begins with reference to the ruin that has resulted from the papacy's disastrous *management* of cultural resources:

> Denn sag mir, wozu bist du doch nutz in dem Papsttum; denn je ärger und verzweifelter einer ist, desto mehr und stärker mißbraucht er deine Gewalt und Titel, die Leute zu schädigen an Gut und Seel, Sünd und Schand zu mehren, den Glauben und Wahrheit zu dämpfen.[7]

> For what happens in your court, Leo, except that, the more wicked and execrable any man is, the more prosperously he can use your name and authority for the ruin of the property and souls of men, for the multiplication of crimes, for the oppression of faith and truth, and of the whole Church of God?

---

5. Citations of Luther's German texts are from Martin Luther, *An den Christlichen Adel deutscher Nation, Von der Freiheit eines Christenmenschen, Sendbrief vom Dolmetschen*. (In the notes, I will reference only the single text among these three that I am quoting.) I cite English translations of Luther's "Dedicatory Letter of Martin Luther to Pope Leo X" and "On the Freedom of a Christian" from the online *Modern History Sourcebook*.

6. While the new reformed brands of Christianity starting with Luther will, of course, be closely associated with early modern communal developments (see, for example, the article of Peter Blickle, "Reformation and the Communal Spirit," 133–67), the focus of my reading of some of Luther's significant early writings is on the implications of the central position given to the individual self, which is mentioned by Habermas in the note above, and which Derek Wilson puts this way in his book, *Out of the Storm*: "Luther was undertaking the monumental task of creating a whole evangelistic system of theology and ethics. Moreover, he was making the individual conscience the sole arbiter in such matters. No other authority governing human conduct existed other than the word of God and no ecclesiastical or civil power could be placed above it" (179).

7. Luther, *Von der Freiheit eines Christenmenschen*, 115. For Luther's early modern German text, I will also refer the reader to von Clemens's edition of *Luthers Werke in Auswahl*; here "Ein Sendbrief an den Papst Leo X," 5.

In this letter to Leo, Luther implements an individualizing move that is consistent with the ideas he will develop in the treatise proper. We observe here that he disengages Leo as an individual—ostensibly even as a potentially sympathetic one—from the pope's institutional role as the chief official presiding over such disastrous ruin and waste. This is consistent with Luther's broader strategy to disengage individual Christians from the imperial Christianity of papal Rome. The move nevertheless remains largely rhetorical, because the Medici Pope Leo is very much in need of the sale of indulgences to underwrite his lavish living and is entirely invested in the current condition of the papal court that Luther wishes to expose and decry. The following description shows in greater vivid detail what the imperial church has become in Luther's view of it:

> Denn das ist dir selbst jedenfalls nicht verborgen, wie nun viel Jahre lang aus Rom in alle Welt nichts anderes denn Verderben des Leibs, der Seelen, der Güter, und aller bösen Dinge allerschädlichste Exempel gleichsam hineingeströmt und eingerissen sind. Welches alles öffentlich am Tage jedermann bewußt ist, wodurch Römische Kirche, die vorzeiten die allerheiligste war, nun geworden ist eine Mordgruben über alle Mordgruben, ein Hurenhaus über alle Hurenhäuser, ein Haupt und Reich aller Sünde, des Todes und der Verdammnis, so daß man sich nicht gut denken kann, wie die Bosheit hier noch zunehmen könne, wenngleich der Antichrist selber käme.[8]

> For many years now, nothing else has overflowed from Rome into the world—as you are not ignorant—than the laying waste of goods, of bodies, and of souls, and the worst examples of all the worst things. These things are clearer than the light to all men; and the Church of Rome, formerly the most holy of all churches, has become the most lawless den of thieves, the most shameless of all brothels, the very kingdom of sin, death, and hell; so that not even Antichrist, if he were to come, could devise any addition to its wickedness.

The once majestic Rome—the medieval incorporation of the heavenly City of God imagined by St. Augustine—has become for Luther the equivalent of a "Babylon or Sodom."[9] Luther's sordid picture of the cultural action associated with Rome underscores pernicious spiritual and material waste, the *perdition*

---

8. Luther, *Von der Freiheit eines Christenmenschen*, 113–14; "Ein Sendbrief an den Papst Leo X," (Clemens), 3–4.

9. Luther likens Rome to the Old Testament cities of sin in the paragraph preceding the above-cited passage. Similarly sharp and colorful criticisms, such as the still recent ones of Savonarola, were already in currency.

"of goods, of bodies, and of souls." Luther's language suggests that the dire situation lamented by Marco Lombardo in Dante's purgatory has reached a breaking point. The consequential move that Luther makes in view of this cultural ruin and waste is to reject the imperial Roman parameters for religious cultural action altogether, and to transpose the dualistic hierarchical ordering of spiritual-intellectual and physical-material resources as conceived by Paul and Augustine—along with the indeterminacy this ordering has always involved—to patently individual parameters.

The treatise's title—*On the Freedom of a Christian*—is programmatic. "Freedom" as understood and defined by Luther in this treatise and elsewhere is a scripture- and faith-based individual religiosity disengaged from any and every external guideline, restriction, or prohibition associated with the imperial Roman church. The emancipation of Christians from the ecclesiastical dictates of imperial Rome is the most significant aspect of a broader spiritual freedom of Christians from any and every *external* religious restriction or prohibition whatsoever, which follows from Luther's understanding of the supreme value of individual faith and his qualification of the value of works. With his rejection of the spiritual value of works to effect salvation, Luther gives a new *spin* to an ancient move—the Apostle Paul's rejection of the spiritual value of the laws of the Israelites—at a moment in the European cultural action when it serves to liberate individual Christians from the *laws* of the imperial Roman *ecclesia* that have shared in the governance of western European Christendom for more than a millennium. By insisting on a faith- and scripture-based religiosity of entirely *individual* dimensions, Luther effectively *streamlines* Christianity, in a manner analogous to Paul's streamlining of Judeo-Christian righteousness in the direction of faith in the early years of Christianity. Luther reiterates another ancient move as well, though on his systematically individualized scale:

> *ein jeglicher Christenmensch* [ist] von zweierlei Natur, geistlicher und leiblicher. Nach der Seele wird er ein geistlicher, neuer, innerlicher Mensch genannt, nach dem Fleisch und Blut wird er ein leiblicher, alter und äußerlicher Mensch genannt.[10]

> *Each single Christian* Man is composed of a twofold nature, a spiritual and a bodily. As regards the spiritual nature, which they name the soul, he is called

---

10. Italics have been added here and to the English translation to draw attention to the individuality of Luther's religious conception; Luther, *Von der Freiheit eines Christenmenschen*, 125; "Von der Freiheit eines Christenmenschen" (Clemens), 11.

the spiritual, inward, new man; as regards the bodily nature, which they name the flesh, he is called the fleshly, outward, old man.[11]

The dualist contest between higher spiritual-intellectual and lower physical-material (here: "fleshly") cultural resources—a flashpoint in the action of the imperial Christian church in the Middle Ages—is ongoing in Luther's conception of the individual Christian self. Correspondingly, the universal harnessing of resources that has occurred on an imperial level in the Roman church becomes with Luther a newly individualized sovereignty or power over all things, as indicated by the use of the individualizing modifiers of "Christian" in the above-cited passage—*Ein jeglicher Christenmensch*—"*each single* Christian"—and in another of the main theses with which Luther begins his treatise: "*Ein* Christenmensch ist ein freier Herr über alle Ding und niemand untertan"[12]—"*A* Christian is lord over all things, and subject to none" (italics added). As was previously the case in the Christian cultural action, this sovereignty is framed indeterminately in terms of a *sameness*, according to which spiritual-intellectual resources completely pervade physical-material ones (just as providence pervades the seeming randomness of events presenting itself to mortal humanity), at the same time as the latter resources are to be regarded by and subjected to the former as something absolutely and inimically *other*.

The freedom of the individual Christian as understood by Luther is supposed to be a strictly spiritual freedom that pertains to the individual Christian's posture toward all things physical, material, "fleshly." For Luther, the correct evaluation of and posture toward the things of this world cannot be imposed or regulated by any external agency such as the church, but comes about from within the individual as a consequence of faith. Having died to the world, the individual becomes lord over it, then freely serves it, as Christ served sinful humanity with his death and resurrection. Hence, the individual Christian self is not only "lord over all things" but also servant of one and all, as Luther states immediately after the above-cited pronouncement of the Christian individual's absolute sovereign freedom: *Ein Christenmensch ist ein dienstbarer Knecht aller Ding und jedermann untertan*[13]—"A Christian man is the most dutiful servant of all, and subject to every one." Despite the individualized scaling of the indeterminate dualist dynamics on which everything

---

11. "On the Freedom of a Christian" (Wace and Buchheim).
12. Luther, *Von der Freiheit eines Christenmenschen*, 125; "Von der Freiheit eines Christenmenschen" (Clemens), 11.
13. Ibid., 125; "Von der Freiheit eines Christenmenschen" (Clemens), 11.

continues to hinge, the *reward* to be experienced in Luther's version of Christianity still possesses universal, quasi-imperial dimensions:

> Wer kann nun ausdenken die Ehre und Höhe eines Christenmenschen? Durch sein Königreich ist er aller Ding mächtig, durch sein Priestertum ist er Gottes mächtig, denn Gott tut, was er bittet und will, wie da steht geschrieben im Psalter: "Gott tut den Willen derer, die ich ihn fürchten, und erhöret ihr Gebet"–zu welchen Ehren er nur allein durch den Glauben und durch kein Werk kommt.[14]

> Who then can comprehend the loftiness of that Christian dignity which, by its royal power, rules over all things, and, by its priestly glory, is all powerful with God; since God does what he seeks and wishes; as it is written: "He will fulfill the desire of them that fear Him: He also will hear their cry, and will save them"? (Ps 145:19). This glory certainly cannot be attained by any works, but by faith only.

In Luther's individualized conception of the Christian life, there is no longer *anything* other than the cultivation of scripture-based faith that one may do to bring oneself closer to heaven. The heavenly joy experienced already in this world—the all-powerful "loftiness" referenced by Luther—becomes an ongoing condition based on the continual effort on the part of the individual Christian to strengthen faith by means of scriptures. Nothing else one does, no mutable thing in this temporal world has any intrinsically superior value with regard to one's salvation, that is, everything is equally valuable or *exchangeable* in its subordinate status vis-à-vis the sovereign Christian self. In a world in which the values of things has been newly leveled, such sovereign faithful Christians freely serve others, sharing with them the endless bounty of the heavenly reward they receive via faith.

Luther's individualized gospel is disseminated by means of the still relatively recent European printing technology, developed by Johannes Gutenberg in the mid-fifteenth century, in a manner that illustrates this gospel's dynamism. The dynamics of the production of the ancient and medieval codex page had been relatively fixed and slow, as the letters had to be set down sequentially and could be changed only with great effort (i.e., as a palimpsest). Every single manuscript page resulting from these dynamics was unique (consider, for example, the image of the codex page featuring the illumination

---

14. Ibid., 136; "Von der Freiheit eines Christenmenschen" (Clemens), 18.

of the poet Marie de France at work that is included in the fourth chapter of this study). By contrast, the characteristics of book production with the new printing technology are highly fluid and rapid, corresponding to the different possible arrangements of individual types within the rectangular iron *forme* or frame, and to the almost instantaneous reproduction of entire pages once the desired types in the frame are in their proper place in the bed of the press. These technological characteristics reproduce identical copies of a given page, thus losing contact with the *absolutely unique* characteristics of the medieval codex page.[15] But they enable a speed, economy, and scale of production capable of making scriptures available to individual Christians everywhere, thus complementing and reinforcing the newly framed individuality of the (religious) cultural action.[16] Among the most significant of the many Lutheran writings soon flowing off the printing press is Luther's translation of the Bible into German, the widespread popularity and influence of which suggest how great the cultural value of the literary vernacular has become since the earliest forays of Otfried von Weissenburg.[17] In his *Sendbrief vom Dolmetschen* (1530)—"Open Letter on Translating"—that accompanies the publication of his Bible, Luther lingers on his use of the word *allein*—"alone"—in rendering Romans 3:28 (*Arbitramur enim justificari hominem per fidem sine operibus*

---

15. We have no problem today seeing the printing press as an inevitable, beneficial development. However, it is tempting to consider that the *lost quality of the original* might already have been negatively experienced in the early days of the printing press, much like what we today experience during a time when *real books* are being supplanted to a large degree by electronic devices. In the former instance, based on the findings of this study, the imperial church as communal *absolute* would be associated with the *uniqueness* of the manuscript page that has been lost or put behind, and lament concerning its passing would logically have been experienced most acutely by the priestly cast that was losing its control over the Word (efforts to criminalize the printing of vernacular bibles scarcely seem to have slowed this process down; see Flood, "Martin Luther's Bible Translation," 45–46). In the latter case, and other similar cases that we seem to experience ever more frequently in our own digitally and technologically enhanced cultural action as ever more bookstores go out of business, we may be reiterating this sense of loss (or of the putting behind) of an original communal absolute (which of course, seen inversely, is also an emancipation). I discuss the cultural significance of Luther's bible translation, in connection to Luther's *Sendbrief* and Walter Benjamin's conception of the artwork in the age of its mechanical reproduction, in my article, "Singularity of Aura and the Artistry of Translation."

16. Stephan Füssel writes: "Gutenberg's invention is as simple as it is ingenious: texts were broken down into their smallest components, i.e. into the 26 letters of the Roman alphabet, and from placing single letters in the right order, the new text would result time and time again. Texts had been copied over the centuries by writing them completely and sequentially, or by cutting them equally completely in wood [. . .], but now only the letters of the alphabet had to be cut and supplies cast, and they would always be available for setting up whatever text was chosen" (*Gutenberg and the Impact of Printing,* 15).

17. Otfried's forays were considered in the fourth chapter of this study.

legis—"We conclude that a man is justified by faith without the deeds of the Law") with the wording *allein durch den Glauben*—"by faith *alone*." Luther's critics had found "alone" objectionable because it seemed to involve an impermissible addition that was not justified by the original text, as the Latin equivalent of the German *allein* is not in the text of the Vulgate. This is Luther's famous reply to those critics:

> Man muß nicht die Buchstaben in der lateinischen Sprache fragen, wie man soll Deutsch reden, wie diese Esel tun, sondern man muß die Mutter im Hause, die Kinder auf der Gassen, den gemeinen Mann auf dem Markt drum fragen, und denselbigen auf das Maul sehen, wie sie reden, und darnach übersetzen.[18]

> We do not have to ask about the literal Latin for how we are to speak German—as these asses do. Rather we must ask the mother in the home, the children on the street, the common person in the market about this. We must be guided by their tongue, the manner of their speech, and do our translating accordingly.[19]

Luther's "alone" goes to the heart of the individualization of the religious cultural action that his writings are effecting. *Allein* underscores Luther's individualized conception of the religious action as independent from any external worldly agency or works, and beyond this, it designates the general sense of a newly fluid, individualized mode of experiencing God's word that is enabled and accelerated by the technological capacity of the printing press to deliver it to every single, solitary Christian, in the manner of speaking of those same single Christians, whoever and wherever they may be—mothers, children, common people—on streets, in homes, and at the marketplace.

Luther's typographically amplified moves help to mobilize individual Christians in a new cultural action in which the rules of play have become less clear, even those regarding the most basic questions of the Christian life. How far might the spiritual freedom of the Christian extend in the direction of potentially sinful engagements with this temporal world, such as the capabilities of the physical-material properties of the printing press or the colloquial turns of phrase of a vulgar language to render the word of God? At what point(s) do spiritual-intellectual and physical-material cultural resources

---

18. Luther, *Sendbrief vom Dolmetschen*, 159; "Ein Sendbrief vom Dolmetschen" (Clemens), 179–93, here 187.

19. The cited English translation of Luther's "An Open Letter on Translating" is from the online translation by Gary Mann in the *Internet Christian Library*.

overlap to a degree or in a way that makes the newly individualized religious action sinful, as the bipartite imperial city of the papacy had made itself sinful from the Lutheran perspective? Another early treatise of Luther disseminated along with *On the Freedom of a Christian* is his open letter *An den Christlichen Adel deutscher Nation*—"To the Christian Nobility of the German Nation"—in which Luther argues for the removal of all controls over desires and appetites of the flesh imposed by the Roman church. According to Luther, the faithful individual Christian has no need of such controls and an individual lacking faith will not benefit from them. Luther presses forward against all such external strictures to the point that he argues for dispensing with the requirement of celibacy for pastors, because forbidding a man and woman left alone together from succumbing to temptation is, as he puts it, like "putting fire and straw together and forbidding them to smoke and burn."[20] Luther has in mind the circumstances of pastors living among the town and village communities for which they provide. Advocating the removal of the requirement of celibacy in such cases seems practical and efficient. Nonetheless, by insisting people will inevitably succumb to temptations of the flesh, as if compelled by a force of nature, Luther opens up the ways in which the flesh is to be engaged by the spirit to arrangements other than the strict (i.e., celibate) subjugation of the former to the latter.

In the event the Bible provides no clear indications that might inspire faithful individual Christians to an accord, how will it be possible to determine whether celibacy or the arrangement proposed by Luther is righteous rather than sinful? A similar question might be posed about another passage in *On the Freedom of a Christian,* in which Luther warns Christians not to mistake their spiritual freedom for a release from responsibilities:

> Das ist die christliche Freiheit, der bloße Glaube, der da macht, *nicht daß wir müßig gehen oder übel tun können,* sondern, daß wir keines Werks bedürfen, um Frommsein und Seligkeit zu erlangen.[21]

> This is that Christian liberty, our faith, the effect of which is, *not that we should be careless or lead a bad life,* but that no one should need the law or works for justification and salvation.

---

20. The corresponding German is in Luther, *An den Christlichen Adel deutscher Nation,* 67. The English rendering here is from Luther, "To the Christian Nobility of the German Nation," 149–234, here 192.

21. Luther, *Von der Freiheit eines Christenmenschen,* 131; Clemens, 15; italics added to original quote and translation.

Albeit negatively or inversely, Luther here articulates the newly framed indeterminacy of the *individualized* cultural action that starts with the Reformation.[22] Who is to say, or how is one to determine, who or what is careless, slothful, or wicked? How are matters involving carelessness, sloth, or evil to be arranged when the authoritative imperial Christian church that previously regulated them has been discredited as a brothel? The cultural action is seemingly opened up to the possibility of carelessness, sloth, and evil, with no religious (i.e., religiously *legitimate*) mechanism or agency in place other than individualized faith to prevent or avoid lapses.

We have seen in the cases of the physical-material apparatus of the printing press and the vulgar colloquialisms of children, mothers, and common men at the marketplace that the cultural action is opened to new opportunities in the valuation of resources, novel risks, and rewards that are entirely in accord with faith according to Luther's understanding of it. Luther's turn to the German nobility in his open letter to them provides indications of how he thought the cultural vacuum left behind by the discredited bipartite imperial church should be filled. The German *principes,* acting on behalf of their Christian brethren, should call a council and undertake a thorough reform of religious, political, and social matters. In this text, Luther pragmatically calls upon the culturally best-positioned *players* to bring about the reforms he thinks are needed. However, the problem of the religious or spiritual legitimacy of arrangements in the newly individualized cultural action seems thereby only to be deferred rather than solved. Placing matters in the princes' hands, while politically expedient and crucial for the survival of Luther's Reformation, cannot guarantee that decisions in the newly reframed cultural action will be *righteous* or in accord with an individualized religiosity based on faith. The lack of certainty (i.e., the greater cultural indeterminacy) follows from the individualized scaling of the (religious) cultural action. As long as the religious action occurred imperially, the dictates of popes and emperors were necessarily in some way legitimate even when these authorities were at odds. When religion becomes a primarily or strictly individual matter, it no longer seems in the same way to provide interpersonal communal standards of evaluation.

---

22. There is another, similar passage, in which the indeterminacy of the newly framed individualized religious cultural action is put differently, though again *ex negativo:* "*Nicht, dass wir aller Ding leiblich mächtig wären, sie zu besitzen oder zu brauchen wie die Menschen auf Erden;* denn wir müssen sterben leiblich und kann niemand den Tod entfliehen" (italics added; Luther, *Von der Freiheit eines Christenmenschen,* 135; Clemens, 17)—"Not that in the sense of corporeal power any one among Christians has been appointed to possess and rule all things" ("On the Freedom of a Christian," Modern History Sourcebook).

The secular German princes will never wield *religious* authority in the same universal manner as medieval popes and emperors, but Luther's turn to them calls upon the best-positioned players in the newly defined European cultural action, those disposing of the skills and resources that will enable them to be most effective in the intense competitions to come. While there is no longer any way to demonstrate that the outcomes achieved by princes in their ongoing contests among each other and with the papacy are *religiously* correct or best in a cultural action evermore shaped by individualized faith, at the very least outcomes will be reached in competitions at the highest level, among the early modern cultural competitors best positioned to achieve maximal tangible results. In the above-mentioned open letter on translating that accompanies the publication of his vernacular bible, Luther provides indirect support for the notion that competition among the most resourceful people at the highest cultural levels is the best way to ensure optimal cultural outcomes. In response to papal critics of "his" Bible,[23] Luther challenges these critics to come up with a "better" one, thereby suggesting that the Bible itself—the foundation of faith-based individual religiosity—is contingent on the best efforts of its human renderers as competitors. In the same manner as one observes in the cultural action elsewhere, Luther describes his own efforts and those of his translating team figuratively as a physical, even athletic effort:

> Es läuft jetzt einer mit den Augen durch drei, vier Blätter und stößt nicht *ein*mal an, wird aber nicht gewahr, welche Wacken und Klötze da gelegen sind, wo er jetzt drüber hingehet wie über ein gehobelt Brett, wo wir haben müssen schwitzen und uns ängsten, ehe wir denn solche Wacken und Klötze aus dem Wege räumeten, auf daß man könnte so fein daher gehen.[24]

> One can now read three or four pages without stumbling one time—without realizing just what rocks and hindrances had once been where now one travels as if over a smoothly-cut plank. We had to sweat and toil there before we removed those rocks and hindrances, so one could go along nicely.

Luther's own efforts have cleared the way for something of no less import than the optimal rendering of the text upon which individual faith is based. If people can move with dispatch toward salvation, this is in part an outcome of Luther's individual investment of self, the toil he has invested in his translation and the superb level of this toil. The value of princes' engagements

---

23. As he calls it in his *Sendbrief vom Dolmetschen*, 153; Clemens, 180.
24. Luther, *Sendbrief vom Dolmetschen*, 158; Clemens, 183.

on behalf of the cultural reforms for which Luther is calling may need to be regarded in the same way that Luther here invites us to assess his own activity in the domain of translation. Here as there, the *moves* deemed to be in greatest accord with faith will be those perceived as *best* in the ongoing cultural action—those that best clear away hindrances so that one can "go along nicely." Trying to fashion a better, more efficient Christianity, Martin Luther inadvertently helps bring about a different, modern kind of global cultural action with individualized dimensions.[25] Not surprisingly in view of the Reformation moves we have considered above, the princes are at first best situated in the newly defined parameters of action to make consequential moves and experience cultural growth.

ENLIGHTENMENT MOVES

By 1714, nearly two centuries after Luther's early writings, princes in many parts of Europe will have become absolute sovereigns, combining in their persons and their offices religious and worldly dignities. In this year, the philosopher and mathematician Gottfried Wilhelm Leibniz, nearing the end of a distinguished career among the intellectual luminaries of the late seventeenth and early eighteenth centuries, publishes *La Monadologie*, a short text that explains the makeup and dynamics of the cosmos in terms of "monads." Leibniz's *Monadologie* provides us with views of yet another "city"—to go along with those we surveyed in the initial chapters of this study—and one that is definitively modern, even if there are some hints that it too follows in the tradition of Augustine's bipartite *civitas*. The city Leibniz places before us, writing in the courtly French of his era, consists of an infinite number of perfectly articulated, yet completely discrete, autonomous, individual building blocks called "monads." Each of these substances provides an absolutely unique perspective of the whole:

> Et comme une meme ville regardée de differens côtés paroist toute autre, et comme multipliée *perspectivement;* il arrive de même que par la multitude infinie des substances simples, il y a comme autant de differens univers, qui ne sont portant que las perspectives d'un seul selon les differens *points de veue* de chaque Monade. Et c'est the moyen d'obtenir autant de variété qu'il est possible, mais avec le plus grand ordre qui se puisse, c'est à dire, c'est le moyen d'obtenir autant de perfection qu'il se peut.

---

25. Richard von Dülmen elaborates this general idea in his essay, "The Reformation and the Modern Age."

And as one and the same town viewed from different sides looks altogether different, and is, as it were, *perspectively* multiplied, it similarly happens that, through the infinite multitude of simple substances, there are, as it were, just as many different universes, which are however only the perspectives of a single one according to the different *points of view* of each monad. And this is the way to obtain as much variety as possible, but combined with the greatest possible order, that is to say, it is the way to obtain as much perfection as can be.[26]

Every single monad constituting Leibniz's city is different from every other one, it contains all the characteristics and potential by which it functions (i.e., it receives no external influences, because it has no "windows"), and it constantly *strives* to realize its own specific individual potential or end.[27] A degree of the dualism that we saw in Augustine's bipartite city is manifested, as monads of a lower level live and strive in their own modest way without self-awareness, whereas only the monads functioning at a higher spiritual-intellectual level possess what Leibniz calls "apperception." Only these highest or *plus parfaite*—"more perfect"[28] monads can comprehend how a city constituted by such infinitely diverse individual building blocks, each with its own specific potential and striving, remains intact rather than falls apart. But the overriding sense in Leibniz's city is one of unified purpose(s), not of parts that are dualistically at odds. The unifying principle or master plan holding this city together, despite the infinite diversity of the discrete individual monads constituting it, is God's absolute power as the *Monarque de la Cité divine des Esprits*—the "Monarch of the Divine City of Spirits."[29] Leibniz's city, we discover, is also a heavenly city-state, and as such, it is necessarily the best of all possible worlds for him. This is because all the monads constituting it, though each one is a unique mechanism and none is influenced in any way by another, have all nevertheless been designed or *programmed* by God from the beginning to function in perfect harmony. Individual characteristics and striving have been arranged in them in such a way that they work together optimally in the manner of a perfectly fitted and finely tuned machine.

---

26. French text and English translation from Leibniz, *"Monadology"* (Rescher), here 200–201. In sections 85 and 86 of his *Monadologie*, where he discusses souls or spirits as the "group of monads of the highest level" (283), Leibniz reiterates key terms of Augustine's *City of God* according to his own early modern terms, most visibly in using the term *Cité de Dieu* with reference to the assemblage of all spirits (284).

27. Despite this, in the *Monadologie*, Leibniz never uses the terms "freedom, free agent, liberty of action, or the like," as Rescher observes (278).

28. Leibniz, *Monadologie*, 171.

29. Ibid., 286.

The monadic city placed in view by Leibniz is one of the important outcomes of early-modern enlightenment thinking.[30] As one of the principal cultural players of his time, Leibniz contends with Isaac Newton for the honor of having invented the infinitesimal calculus, one of the principal mathematical tools of modernity with which people have sought and acquired new values from what—in this study—I have been calling *mutable, temporal, physical-material cultural resources*.[31] He also contends with a mechanistic Cartesian view of the cultural action, according to which consciousness and the mental apprehension (and evaluation) of things occurs in ways consistent with Descartes's famous ontological move, *cogito ergo sum*. Descartes's dualist move radically valorizes the purely intellectual capacity and regards physical-material things as uniformly external and subject to intellectual consciousness.[32] To the degree the mechanistic Cartesian view of the cultural action assesses spiritual-intellectual goods as superior to and absolutely distinct from physical-material ones, it reiterates something akin to the foundational Judeo-Christian move that posits the ascendency of spiritual-intellectual over physical-material resources. With his monadic city, Leibniz advances an alternative global model that contrasts with Cartesian dualism.[33] Most important about Leibniz's city and every single monad constituting it is its indivisible unity, which outweighs any dualistic characteristic or tendency. As a totality, Leibniz's city is completely integrated in its infinite diversity on account of the divine master plan of the *Architecte de la Machine de l'univers*—"the Architect of the Mechanism of the Universe"[34]—that holds everything together in the

---

30. I occasionally capitalize "Enlightenment," for example in juxtaposition to "Reformation" or whenever a more limited and focused historical understanding of an eighteenth-century "Age of Enlightenment" seems appropriate. However, since my understanding of enlightenment tends to see it in terms of cultural *moves*, or in terms of an ongoing possible *approach* to things that is not necessarily specific to a particular period of time, I will typically use the more generic lower-case "enlightenment."

31. In her book *The Origins of the Infinitesimal Calculus*, Margaret E. Baron writes, "The infinitesimal calculus has been the principal tool in the exploitation of the earth's resources, the charting of the heavens and the building of modern technology. Applications occur wherever there exist measurable phenomena: gravitation, heat, light, sound, electricity, magnetism and radio waves" (1). Calculus as described by Baron is consistent with the trend I have been observing in this study, beginning in the High Middle Ages, toward finding absolute value in cultural resources understood to be finite. See also Ursula Goldenbaum and Douglas Jesseph, *Infinitesimal Differences*.

32. See Rosemond, *Descartes's Dualism*.

33. For example, see Leibniz's criticisms of "les Cartesiens" in the *Monadologie*: "This is where the Cartesians went badly wrong in taking no account of perceptions that are not apperceived. This led them to think that 'spirits' alone are monads, and that there are no souls of beasts or other entelechies" (75).

34. Ibid., 286.

optimal way. Leibniz's city is an early modern reiteration and elaboration of the imperial city of antiquity and the Middle Ages to the degree it is held together by the Christian God's providential master plan, but unlike its predecessors, it consists of the innumerable discrete *individuals* of which it is constituted. Each of these is utterly self-sufficient, a universe unto itself, and the best one it can possibly be.[35]

Apart from monads and calculus, Leibniz lays claim to the invention of the binary number system, and it would be appropriate to assume that the makeup of his monadic "city" would also include binary properties.[36] For Leibniz, binary numbers combine metaphysical and physical properties in their capacity to render quantities and even abstract notions as sequences of ones and zeros. In a letter composed in his native German to Prince Rudolph August von Braunschweig-Lüneburg-Wolfenbüttel in early 1697, Leibniz states that binary numbers reveal the mystery of creation in all its diversity and unity:

> Denn einer der Haupt-Punkten des christlichen Glaubens, und zwar unter denjenigen, die den Weltweisen am wenigsten eingegangen und noch den Heiden nicht wohl beizubringen, ist die Erschaffung aller Dinge aus nichts durch die Allmacht Gottes. Nun kann man wohl sagen, daß nichts in der Welt sie besser vorstelle, ja gleichsam *demonstriere,* als der Urprung der Zahlen, wie er allhier vorgestellet, durch deren Ausdrückung bloß und allein mit Eins und Null oder Nichts, und wird wohl schwerlich in der Natur und Philosophie ein bessers Vorbild dieses Geheimnisses zu finden sein.

> For one of the main points of Christian belief—something the worldly wise have grasped only poorly and that pagans cannot comprehend at all—is the

---

35. Morris Kline provides further specific illustration of Leibniz's conception of this world as the "best of all possible" ones, and, more generally, corroboration for the religious context in which I am placing Leibniz and some of his principal ideas: "The conviction that the world was mathematically designed derived from the earlier linking of science and theology. We may recall that most of the leading figures of the sixteenth and seventeenth centuries were not only deeply religious but found in their theological views the inspiration and conviction vital to their scientific work." Kline mentions Copernicus, Kepler, Descartes, and Newton in this context, and continues with respect to Leibniz: "Leibniz's explanation of the concord between the real and the mathematical worlds, and his ultimate defense of the applicability of his calculus to the real world, was the unity of the world and God. The laws of reality therefore could not deviate from the ideal laws of mathematics. The universe was the most perfect conceivable, the best of all possible worlds, and rational thinking disclosed its laws" (*Mathematical Thought,* 620).

36. See, for example, Leibniz, *Monadologie*: "So one can say that monads can neither come into being nor end save all at once; that is, they can begin only by creation and end only by annihilation" (57). This principle of creation is also at the heart of Leibniz's cosmological conception of binary numbers.

creation of all things out of nothing by God's absolute power. Now one can say that nothing in the world shows this better—one could even say *demonstrates* it—than the origin of numbers as I am introducing it here, by means of their expression exclusively with One and Zero or Nothing. There will scarcely be a better illustration of the mystery of creation to be found in nature or philosophy.[37]

According to Leibniz's understanding of the religious characteristics of binary numbers, everything can be seen as coming back to the duality of one and zero. The coming into being of One as the creation of everything (= 1) out of nothing (= 0) by a single omnipotent deity is describable as an early modern, post-Lutheran reiteration of the *dualist* global perspective explored in the initial chapters of this study.[38] In the Judeo-Christian cultural action of antiquity in chapter one of this study, we observed the emergence of new universal perspectives from which cultural resources can be considered and assessed uniformly. It is this perspective—as incomprehensible to the Roman pagans of Augustine's day as it continues to be to the "pagans" referenced by Leibniz in the cited passage—that is now advanced as the One of Leibniz's binary number system. The One and Zero, upon which binary numbers and arithmetic are based, are physical markers of God's metaphysical creation of everything out of nothing. Binary numbers tangibly reiterate the act of creation and, as such, function as the underlying ordering principle of the cosmos. In his essay "Explication de Arithmétique Binaire," Leibniz presciently observes that the binary number system, based on its interconnected physical (geometric) and metaphysical properties, might have practical applications. For example, it could enable "assayers to weigh all sorts of masses with few weights and could serve in coinage to give several values with few coins."[39]

We observed above that the properties of the mechanically printed page complemented the newly fluid disposition of cultural resources for

---

37. Leibniz, *Zwei Briefe*, 19. My English translation, and the italics are added.

38. In her article "Leibniz as a Lutheran" (169–92), Ursula Goldenbaum points out that Leibniz experienced his earliest intellectual formation in a strongly Lutheran household and his university studies occurred in the intellectual and religious milieu of Erfurt, not far from Luther's Wittenberg. Leibniz's positions in religious and philosophical matters are much too universal and eclectic to say that he ever takes an identifiably Lutheran stance. Nevertheless, the Lutheran *streamlining* of the individual's relationship to God in the direction of the faith of the single Christian *alone* can readily be seen as preparing the way for and facilitating Leibniz's numeric-mathematical view of the Christian cosmos in terms of zeros and ones, with no other extraneous considerations or instances being allowed to muddle the clarity of the dynamic dyadic relation.

39. The corresponding French text is in Leibniz, "Explication de Arithmétique Binaire," 224. I cite the online English translation by Lloyd Strickland, 224.

the individual (Christian believer), and their functioning had the effect of amplifying and accelerating the new (Christian) individuality throughout the cultural action. Now, Leibniz imagines binary numbers as a religious ordering principle underlying everything in an optimally ordered universe. These numbers are not merely a measure of things, but a tangible, physical, "geometric" manifestation of their origin and purpose. A physical-material apparatus designed to exploit the dynamic potential of binary numbers with their cosmological characteristics would seemingly have infinite potential to exploit resources and amplify and accelerate the cultural action. The potential of such an apparatus, in which binary numbers or their placeholders—such as the presence or absence of electrical currents in a microprocessor—are the functional equivalents of the moveable types of the printing press, seems to be limited only by the specific physical-material properties of the apparatus and the energy available to power it. In view of the momentum of the European cultural action, it seems inevitable that the means for constructing and powering such an apparatus will become available.[40]

Leibniz's speculation that an omnipotent God holds things together globally and individually in an optimal way is well suited to the absolutist era in which he lived, in which the absolute control of things by a *higher* power was the political norm. His "city" remains intact only as long as the absolutist faith undergirding it can be maintained.[41] In the penultimate decades of the eighteenth century, when princely absolutism begins to teeter, Immanuel Kant no longer believes one can know with certainty what Leibniz in the first decades of the same century was still quite sure about. In his *Critique of Pure Reason,* Kant employs his own reason to question some of the basic assumptions of thinkers of enlightenment before him, such as Descartes and Leibniz. Kant systematizes what he thinks human reason can reasonably know, and this does not include the divine

---

40. About this moment, in our own recent past and extending into our present, Friedrich A. Kittler writes: "One century was enough to transfer the age-old monopoly of writing in the omnipotence of integrated circuits" (*Gramophone, Film, Typewriter,* 18–19). Kittler's views here reinforce the idea of an expansion and acceleration of the cultural action, though his study's focus on recent technological developments causes the variety of ancient medieval and early modern moments of technological transition to receive short shrift, and thereby to appear monolithic. The transition from scrolls to codices, and from scribal codices to printed books, breaks up the "monopoly of writing" into different cultural stages that lead, however slowly by comparison, in the direction of the digital breakthrough. Kittler does not mention Leibniz, whose cosmological understanding of binary numbers provides what might be regarded as a kind of "symbolism" for the digital age.

41. If God as *Monarque de la Cité divine des Esprits* were not already indicative enough, the paternalistic, absolutist undergirding of Leibniz's city is made even more explicit in section 84 of his *Monadologie*: "[God] is in regard to [spirits] what an inventor is to his machine [...], but also what a prince is to his subjects, and even a father to his children" (278).

plan of "the master-builder of the universe" (just as it does not include being able to rule this out).[42] Enlightenment as understood by Kant can no longer be about the ongoing self-realization of the "best of all possible worlds" and the individual parts constituting it. Looking farther back than Leibniz, Kant's understanding of the cultural action seems almost like the inverse of Martin Luther's. Whereas Luther understood the world as good and meaningful only as the site of the free outpourings of the rewards of faith and as evil by virtue of its capacity to ensnare or entangle the flesh, Kant considers that an enlightened individual must endeavor to realize itself *fully* in *this* world. In order to do so, the individual must avail itself of its own reason and not let its course be decided by others, as we see in the definitive exhortation with which Kant begins his famous essay, "Beantwortung der Frage: Was ist Aufklärung?" (1784)—"Answer to the Question: What Is Enlightenment?": *"Sapere aude!" Habe Mut dich deines eigenen Verstandes zu bedienen! ist also der Wahlspruch der Aufklärung*—"'Sapere aude!' Have courage to use your own reason!—that is the motto of enlightenment."

The connection between Kant and Luther becomes closer and more complex upon greater scrutiny. On an individual level, the imperative to *enlighten* in the sense of to *liberate* oneself continues a century-long tendency in the cultural action. Having been emancipated from the dictates of the bipartite imperial church by Luther's moves in the early sixteenth century, the individual self is here urged by Kant near the end of the eighteenth century to free itself from any and every external dictate *whatsoever* that inhibits or impedes the individual's use of reason to bring about enlightenment. Seemingly free and solitary as never before, the individual, newly lacking any metaphysical certainties by virtue of the employment of its reason, now puts itself in play and endeavors to realize itself fully in a world to be assessed, possessed, and enjoyed for its own sake and via the exercise of reason. Banking on the integrative and stabilizing capacity of *faith,* Luther had called on the believing individual to free itself from all external hindrances in order to realize itself fully in a spiritual sense. Now, in the philosophical action of the late eighteenth century, the integrative and stabilizing capacity of faith is no longer available in the same way, and Kant banks on *reason* in calling upon the individual self to enlighten itself by freeing itself from any and every external controlling force. In their different ways, Luther and Kant—with Leibniz occupying an intermediary position—endeavor to fix or determine the value of the individual self in terms of some stable benchmark or standard.

The early modern cultural action observed thus far in this chapter suggests that if reason can take the place of faith on the cutting edge of cultural

---

42. See Grier, "Kant's Critique of Metaphysics."

developments—as the way to self-fulfillment, as the intrinsic principle that holds the individual in place or *stabilizes* its value—then the value of the early modern individual self is seemingly subject to the greatest possible fluctuation and potentially infinite or infinitesimal further qualifications. Now that the individual self is defined primarily by reason rather than by faith, one might pose versions of the question that we asked above in the case of Luther. How can reason succeed where religion has seemingly fallen short in the ongoing cultural action of modernity? How will individual reason—the presumptive new guiding principle of individuality in the modern cultural action—having been turned by Kant toward itself and having come to know it cannot know God as it once had, or rely on any other metaphysically *given* standard, continue in its ongoing functioning to be able to know itself, or know that the way in which the world has been arranged is *reasonable*?[43]

In the above-mentioned essay on enlightenment, Kant shows us the way in which he thinks the functioning of reason and the progress of enlightenment should proceed by reiterating a familiar cultural move:

Der öffentliche Gebrauch seiner Vernunft muß jederzeit frei sein, und der allein kann Aufklärung unter Menschen zustande bringen; der Privatgebrauch derselben aber darf öfters sehr enge eingeschränkt sein, ohne doch darum den Fortschritt der Aufklärung sonderlich zu hindern. Ich verstehe aber unter dem öffentlichen Gebrauche seiner eigenen Vernunft denjenigen, den jemand als Gelehrter von ihr vor dem ganzen Publikum der Leserwelt macht. Den Privatgebrauch nenne ich denjenigen, den er in einem gewissen ihm anvertrauten bürgerlichen Posten oder Amte von seiner Vernunft machen darf. Nun ist zu manchen Geschäften, die in das Interesse des gemeinen Wesens laufen, ein gewisser Mechanismus notwendig, vermittelst dessen einige Glieder des gemeinen Wesens sich bloß passiv verhalten müssen, um durch eine künstliche Einhelligkeit von der Regierung zu öffentlichen Zwecken gerichtet oder wenigstens von der Zerstörung dieser Zwecke abgehalten zu werden. Hier ist es nun freilich nicht erlaubt, zu räsonnieren; sondern man muß gehorchen.[44]

---

43. Many of the questions posed in the latter part of the volume *What Is Enlightenment?* are variations of the question I am posing here, for example that of Georg Picht: "If enlightened thinking posits standards for itself out of itself, if it is supposed to be its own tribunal, then the process of enlightenment itself invites the question who the subject of this thinking, the lawgiver of this tribunal, is supposed to be. The empirical individual cannot lay claim to this legislative role, for he is aware, precisely if he is enlightened, that by his drives and interests he is entangled in the world in manifold ways and subject to dependencies from which he cannot free himself for true autonomy" ("What Is Enlightened Thinking?," 372).

44. Kant, "Beantwortung der Frage," 171.

The *public* use of one's reason must always be free, and it alone can bring about enlightenment among human beings; the *private use* of one's reason may, however, often be very narrowly restricted without this particularly hindering the progress of enlightenment. But by the public use of one's own reason I understand the use which someone makes of it *as a scholar* before the entire public of the *world of readers*. What I call the private use of reason is that which one may make of it in a certain *civil* post or office with which he is entrusted. Now, for many affairs conducted in the interest of a commonwealth a certain mechanism is necessary, by means of which some members of the commonwealth must behave merely passively, so as to be directed by the government, through an artful unanimity, to public ends (or at least prevented from destroying such ends). Here it is, certainly, impermissible to argue; instead, one must obey.⁴⁵

Reason can and should be able to question *everything*, but to prevent its functioning from being politically and socially disintegrative, Kant here divides enlightenment and the individuals participating in it into two parts. We might consider these the *higher* part corresponding to the critical scholar and the reading public, and the *lower* part corresponding to political and social arrangements that may be in need of criticism and change (for which reason they are *lower*), but with which one must "artificially" or *virtually* conduct oneself as if one were in accord with them. Kant's *dualist* move has the effect of shielding reason from the potentially disintegrative effects of its own ongoing scrutiny of itself and the world. It does so by confining reason's actions to a scholarly domain, disengaged from the political, social, and economic structures (including society's physical-material *infrastructure*) upon which the pursuit of the ordinary ends of life—as well as of the more exalted ends of scholars and their reading publics—depends. Though it clearly has very different motives, the Kantian dualist move thus has patently Lutheran aspects. It seems the individual is completely and truly *free* only in a domain *above and beyond* its actions in the world of practical political, social, and economic relations. Following the Lutheran move, the individual becomes free in a higher domain (of scholars and the reading public), while it must continue to obey and conform to the dictates of authorities in the world (even if only "artificially").⁴⁶ Some of the same questions growing out of Luther's dualist

---

45. Kant, "An Answer to the Question: What Is Enlightenment?"; italics in original.

46. Another important theme linking Luther's Reformation and Kant's Enlightenment is the need for obedience to authority in the *lower* cultural domain; Luther had set forth his views on *obeying* in 1523 in his treatise *Von weltlicher Obrigkeit und Wieweit man ihr Gehorsam schuldig sei* (English edition in: *Luther and Calvin*).

arrangement of things based on individual faith arise here from Kant's different dualist arrangement of things in the Age of Enlightenment. How will it be possible to know that the world has been arranged or ordered in a manner consistent with the *higher* principle—previously faith, now reason? With more specific reference to Kant's dualism as expressed in his essay: how exactly is the enlightenment achieved *above* supposed to result in concrete changes *below*?

Kant's answer to these questions in his definitive essay on enlightenment reiterates another identifiably Lutheran move. Without going into the precise dynamics according to which enlightenment as the articulation of higher public and lower private cultural resources will proceed, Kant makes clear it should proceed *top down*. Kant calls upon individuals to obey when acting in the private domain near the beginning of his essay. Again, near the end of it, Kant reinforces the notion that enlightened individuals should privately conform to the political and economic status quo rather than question it, by invoking the authority of King Frederick II. The enlightened despot, patron of the *philosophe* Voltaire and sovereign over the Prussia in which Kant lived and worked, presumably can and will see to it that enlightenment will go forward and that the higher insights achieved by scholars among the reading public are implemented in the lower private sphere in a way and at a pace that is not overly disruptive to the political and social order. Like Luther before him, though consistently banking on reason rather than faith, Kant believes that optimal cultural outcomes will rely on the judicious exercise of princely power. In the end, it seems, one has to hope or have *faith* that the enlightened despot Frederick will remain committed to enlightenment and freedom, and allow the implementation of the best of the scholarly ideas in political, social, and economic practice.

With Kant as with Luther before him, the reliance on princely power defers rather than answers the question about the precise articulation of higher and lower cultural spheres. Enlightenment based on the individual's use of its own reason, independent of the guidance of others, shows itself in the end to be largely dependent on the power of a prince as judge or *referee* in the cultural action. It is better in Kant's view for people to move along slowly and steadily toward enlightenment, like toddlers learning to walk, with the arms of well-meaning princely guardians nearby to catch them if they fall, than risk *stumbling* by going too fast. Of course, Kant's is only one of many rival late eighteenth-century approaches to the realization of enlightenment. Between the slow, safe, and steady *top-down* approach to enlightenment espoused by Kant, and the explosive *bottom-up* dynamics of the enlightenment-inspired French Revolution that begins some five years later, a wide range of enlightened dispositions in the cultural action becomes visible. Those sympathetic to the Revolution will differ markedly from Kant's cautious view that the enlightened individual of this time, given too much freedom, would only be capable of making "an uncertain leap over even the narrowest ditch, since he would not be accustomed to free movement of this kind."[47] For the sympathizers with the Revolution, no jump could be sufficiently high or far, no pace sufficiently fast.

The ideals of *liberté, egalité,* and *fraternité* that were so prominent in the consequential penultimate decade of the eighteenth century in which Kant wrote his hallmark essay found a lasting poetic expression in Friedrich Schiller's poem dedicated to Joy, *An die Freude—Ode to Joy—*published a year after Kant's enlightenment essay and subsequently merged into the final movement of Beethoven's "Choral Symphony" in the following century. Space is made here for Schiller's ode because all the stanzas of this poem frame *joy* as the source and end of human striving, as we have observed in this study. Now as before, at that indeterminate locus where spiritual-intellectual and physical-material cultural resources are articulated, there is joy, albeit *not* as a preview of the fuller or fullest measure of joy to be experienced in another, better world:

> Freude heißt die starke Feder
> In der ewigen Natur.
> Freude, Freude, treibt die Räder
> In der großen Weltenuhr.
> Blumen lockt sie aus den Keimen,
> Sonnen aus dem Firmament,
> Sphären rollt sie in den Räumen,
> Die des Sehers Rohr nicht kennt.[48]

> Joy, in Nature's wide dominion,
> Mightiest cause of all is found;
> And t'is joy that moves the pinion,
> When the wheel of time goes round;
> From the bud she lures the flower,—
> Suns from out their orbs of light;
> Distant spheres obey her power,
> Far beyond all mortal sight.[49]

Schiller's *Ode to Joy* as later put to music might be regarded as the *anthem* of enlightenment, as a lyrical articulation of the joy experienced by emancipated

---

47. Kant, "What Is Enlightenment?," 17.
48. Schiller, *Werke,* 186.
49. Idem, *Works,* 26.

individuals and an emancipated world coming into its own for the first time in history. At the same time, Schiller's piece also poetically sets the course of the modern cultural action in a way that is consistent with the main concerns of the medieval romances. The solidarity with one's peers achieved via adventure and the absolute spiritual-physical relationship to another mutable mortal achieved in love is accomplished here by becoming *eines Freundes Freund*—"the friend of a friend" and by winning *ein holdes Weib*—"a lovely woman." In the chorus following the above-cited fourth stanza, the heroes of the Age of Enlightenment are urged to course joyfully and boldly forward toward their prize:

> Froh, wie seine Sonnen fliegen
> Durch des Himmels prächt'gen Plan
> Laufet, Brüder, eure Bahn,
> Freudig wie ein Held zum Siegen.
>
> As through heaven's expanse so glorious
> In their orbits suns roll on,
> Brethren, thus your proud race run,
> Glad as warriors all-victorious.[50]

How will the cultural athletes of modernity fare as they proceed along the track Schiller lays out for them? Pertinent answers to this question, which return us to the concerns of courts, adventure, and love, are provided by Mark Twain's *A Connecticut Yankee in King Arthur's Court*, composed one hundred years after the beginning of the French Revolution.

A GILDED-AGE CONNECTICUT YANKEE ADVENTURES FOR HIGH STAKES

Mark Twain's Arthurian narrative (1889) imaginatively returns us to the medieval action of romance poetry, but expands its parameters to include industrial modernity as represented by the "Connecticut Yankee" Hank Morgan. For much of Twain's novel, it seems that the superiority continually manifested

---

50. Rüdiger Safranski observes that Schiller's poem "An die Freude" grew out of moments in the young poet's life, when he was very much occupied by the idea and experience of love and friendship. Later on, the poet considered the poem so flawed that he was reluctant to include it in the edition of his collected poems (*Friedrich Schiller*, 202 and 218–19). Beethoven's employment of Schiller's Ode in his Ninth Symphony, mentioned in my text, suggests that noteworthy later readers did not share Schiller's critical view of the poem.

by the Yankee over his medieval rivals in their ongoing intense competitions, besides generating humor and entertainment for nineteenth-century audiences, might possibly lead to a happy final outcome for all that is generally consistent with the optimistic spirit of Schiller's above-cited verses.[51] The view of Twain's imaginary action to be presented in this chapter focuses not on the lengthy sections of Twain's narrative that are clearly designed to amuse and entertain, but rather on some of the Yankee's basic values and assumptions about how the world is supposed to work and on the cataclysmic final struggle between modernity and the Middle Ages that occurs in the Battle of the Sand Belt near the end of the novel, which may be viewed as a possible outcome of these values and assumptions when put into action.[52]

The Yankee first presents himself in a way that strongly suggests he would not have been an avid reader of Schiller's poetry or of the medieval romances:

> I am an American. I was born and reared in Hartford, in the State of Connecticut—anyway, just over the river, in the country. So I am a Yankee of the Yankees—and practical; yes, and nearly barren of sentiment, I suppose—or poetry, in other words. My father was a blacksmith, my uncle was a horse-doctor, and I was both, along at first. Then I went over to the great Colt arms-factory and learned my real trade; learned all there was to it; learned to make everything: guns, revolvers, cannon, boilers, engines, all sorts of labor-saving machinery. Why, I could make anything a body wanted—anything in the world, it didn't make any difference what; and if there wasn't any quick, new-fangled way to make a thing, I could invent one—and do it as easy as rolling off a log.[53]

---

51. Everett Carter writes, "In 1889, most readers, the illustrator Dan Beard among them, thought they were reading a book about a Yankee's praiseworthy attempt to make a better world [. . .] Hundreds of passages in the book support this premise, and dozens more document that the actions he takes have as their purpose the redesign of Arthurian England according to the American plan" ("Meaning of *A Connecticut Yankee*," 419); more recently, Railton writes, "It is worth quoting the contemporary reviews, because from teaching Connecticut Yankee I have learned that modern readers have difficulty seeing the novel as its original audience did. Regardless of whether they like the book, those readers assume Twain intends Hank to be an admirable hero who speaks for Twain himself" (*Mark Twain*, 82).

52. My approach is consistent with a more critical view of the Yankee and his modus operandi, which has not been lacking in the critical literature on this novel. In a look at the copious earlier scholarship in his book published in 1988, Hoffman presents these views of the Yankee: "daimonic entrepreneur," "an American individualist," "Manifest Destiny made flesh" (*Twain's Heroes*, 81). More recently, Messent suggests the Yankee represents "vulgar materialism and Gilded Age opportunistic enterprise," and later writes on the Yankee's attempt to remake the Middle Ages in a modern image: "Hank's late nineteenth-century American value-system has proved, in many ways, as flawed as the one it would replace" (*Cambridge Introduction*, 95).

53. Twain, *Connecticut Yankee*, 4.

In this introduction, the Yankee advances many of the values and interests he will advance in the medieval world in which he suddenly finds himself, which are those of the rapid industrialization occurring especially in northern Europe and North America in the century separating Twain from Kant and Schiller. For the nineteenth-century Yankee, the cultural action is about making things that control and manipulate the world in different, more or less destructive ways. He makes no distinction, beyond the successive order in which they are listed, between "guns, revolvers, cannon," on the one hand, and "boilers, engines, all sorts of labor-saving machinery," on the other. If the distinction doesn't "make any difference" for the Yankee, this may be because rapid industrialization in its convergence with enlightenment disposes of no clear extrasubjective criteria according to which the congruence of a given new technology with the course of enlightenment might be fixed. The Yankee's assumption seems to be that what may be dangerous or useless to some may have redeeming beneficial virtues for others and that it will always be possible to build another machine, "easy as rolling off a log," to counteract any damage caused by previous ones. In Twain's imaginary Middle Ages, the Yankee builds whatever the situation calls for, without wasting valuable time straying from his practical approach, waxing philosophical, poetic, or sentimental, or pondering the ethical implications of his machinery.

As Twain's Arthurian narrative progresses, it becomes evident that the Yankee's approach to the cultural action is indebted as much to an eighteenth-century idea of enlightenment as to the values and interests of nineteenth-century industrialization. As the Yankee becomes increasingly familiar with the hierarchical, undemocratic political and social structure of his medieval world, we see that he is driven by convictions similar to those of the enlightened critics of the inherited privileges and power of Church and nobility in the time leading up to Kant and the French Revolution. After he has gained some familiarity with the medieval world in which he finds himself, we observe the Yankee characterize and criticize it from a patently enlightened perspective:

> The truth was, the nation as a body was in the world for one object, and one only: to grovel before king and Church and noble; to slave for them, sweat blood for them, starve that they might be fed, work that they might play, drink misery to the dregs that they might be happy, go naked that they might wear silks and jewels, pay taxes that they might be spared from paying them, be familiar all their lives with the degrading language and postures of adulation that they might walk in pride and think themselves the gods of this world. And for all this, the thanks they got were cuffs and contempt; and so poor-spirited were they that they took even this sort of attention as an honor.

> Inherited ideas are a curious thing, and interesting to observe and examine. I had mine, the king and his people had theirs. In both cases they flowed in ruts worn deep by time and habit, and the man who should have proposed to divert them by reason and argument would have had a long contract on his hands.[54]

The power of "inherited ideas" is precisely the thing from which one must free oneself in order to become enlightened, according to Kant's above-discussed essay on enlightenment. Where things are not being done reasonably, there is an obligation to try to bring about change by way of criticism, argument, and persuasion. The Yankee shows himself here to be familiar with the imperative of enlightenment to use one's reason, but even his most forceful articulations, such as this one, reveal the complexity and difficulty of the particular challenge he faces. Not only would the effort to enlighten his world involve a "long contract," but the Yankee revealingly includes himself among those who would find it difficult to move out of "ruts worn deep by time." The Yankee here concedes that we may find him as inflexible as the unenlightened medieval people around him, which does not bode well for the future in view of how widely divergent the "ruts" in question are.

Corresponding to the passages cited thus far, the Yankee plays a role with two aspects. He is an advocate of nineteenth-century North American industrialization as well as of eighteenth-century European enlightenment. He wants to enlighten his medieval world and also to control it completely with his industrial technologies. The manner in which he first articulates his ambitions early in the novel suggests that the quest to control trumps the nobler mission to enlighten:

> I didn't want any softer thing: I would boss the whole country inside of three months; for I judged I would have the start of the best-educated man in the kingdom by a matter of thirteen hundred years and upwards. I'm not a man to waste time after my mind's made up and there's work on hand."[55]

One of the deeper "ruts" in which the Yankee apparently finds himself is the calling to be "boss." He soon realizes this ambition, obtaining an authority he joyfully trumpets as "enormous" and "colossal" (for our purposes we might also say *absolute*), but for the continuing power of "the Church"

---

54. Ibid., 65.
55. Ibid., 17.

as his ultimately indomitable rival.[56] With the power he has achieved, the Yankee—"not a man to waste time"—proceeds expeditiously with his dual aim of enlightening and industrializing the dark ages. Only a few years later, the Yankee provides this status report on his civilization-in-the-making:

> My works showed what a despot could do, with the resources of a kingdom at his command. Unsuspected by this dark land, I had the civilization of the nineteenth century booming under its very nose! It was fenced away from the public view, but there it was, a gigantic and unassailable fact—and to be heard from, yet, if I lived and had luck. There it was, as sure a fact, and as substantial a fact as any serene volcano, standing innocent with its smokeless summit in the blue sky and giving no sign of the rising hell in its bowels. My schools and churches were children four years before; they were grown-up now; my little shops of that day were vast factories, now; where I had a dozen trained men then, I had a thousand now; where I had one brilliant expert then, I had fifty now. I stood with my finger on the button, so to speak, ready to press it and flood the midnight world with intolerable light at any moment. But I was not going to do the thing in that sudden way. It was not my policy. The people could not have stood it; and, moreover, I should have had the Established Roman Catholic Church on my back in a minute.
>
> No, I had been going cautiously, all the while. I had had confidential agents trickling through the country some time, whose office was to undermine knighthood by imperceptible degrees, and to gnaw a little at this and that and the other superstition, and so prepare the way gradually for a better order of things. I was turning on my light one-candle-power at a time, and meant to continue to do so.[57]

The construction of this "hidden" civilization that the Yankee would like eventually to institute throughout his medieval world takes about five years. This provides a rough imaginary criterion for assessing how much faster the accelerated cultural action of the Yankee is occurring than that of his medieval *contemporaries*. Taking the year 528 CE—the year of the solar eclipse that saves the Yankee at the beginning of the novel—as our starting point,[58] and 1889—the year of publication of Twain's novel—as an arbitrary date approximating the time of the Yankee's industrial Connecticut, we ascertain that the representative of enlightened industrial modernity accomplishes in less than five years

---

56. Ibid., 62–63.
57. Ibid., 82–83.
58. Ibid., 15.

what will take the better part of fourteen hundred years for his contemporaries and their descendants to accomplish in the course of history. Exemplifying the acceleration and amplification of the cultural action of modernity, the Yankee lays out a modern industrial world—albeit one still kept secret—alongside the medieval one, and the imaginary "Middle Ages" of Twain's narrative is thereby made larger, richer, and vastly more complex.

The amplified cultural action brought about by the Yankee involves a huge speculation. Aware of the volatility of the divided world he has created, the Yankee wagers he will have enough time to close the cultural gap between the dark ages and the mechanical apparatus of modernity he has created. This gap corresponds to the outstanding enlightenment of his future civilized, modernized workforce, and the Yankee proposes to close the gap in a manner reminiscent of the approach we observed above with Kant: better to move in slow, careful steps, keeping fundamental political and social structures intact, than risk moving too fast and thereby causing his medieval protégés to stumble, which in the Yankee's mind would occur most dangerously as a reaction on the part of the Church. The Yankee banks on being able to bring enlightenment to medieval people where they live and work. Proceeding "by imperceptible degrees" and employing "confidential agents," the Yankee hopes medieval people will be persuaded to abandon their medieval world and assume positions in the modern industrial one he is creating for them. As an enlightened "despot" disposing of the material resources of his whole world, both the medieval and modern parts of it, the Yankee exercises a regulatory function similar to that which Kant proposed for Frederick II of Prussia in the latter eighteenth century, though the similarity is superficial. For Kant and Frederick II, enlightenment could easily happen too fast. For the Yankee, as we soon see, it really cannot happen fast enough.

The kind of enlightenment on which the Yankee speculates leads in the direction of the industrial infrastructure—the factories, along with the schools and churches preparing the workforce to power them[59]—which he has created. The Yankee's hope is that medieval people will become enlightened as they freely, knowledgably, peacefully, and smoothly assume positions in his industrial apparatus. For the eventuality that medieval people do not become enlightened in due time, or that some other major obstacle presents itself, the Yankee appears to have no backup plan, but his thinking on the French Revolution reveals a possible future course of events for which he manifests sympathy:

---

59. The Yankee's religious approach is clearly informed by Reformation moves of the kind that we observed earlier in this chapter: "Everybody could be any kind of a Christian he wanted to; there was perfect freedom in that matter" (Ibid., 81).

There were two "Reigns of Terror," if we would but remember it and consider it: the one wrought murder in hot passion, the other in heartless cold blood; the one lasted mere months, the other had lasted a thousand years; the one inflicted death upon ten thousand persons, the other upon a hundred millions; but our shudders are all for the "horrors" of the minor Terror, the momentary Terror, so to speak; whereas, what is the horror of swift death by the axe, compared with lifelong death from hunger, cold, insult, cruelty, and heart-break? what is swift death by lightning compared with death by slow fire at the stake?[60]

The Yankee has selected an approach to enlightenment that proceeds by small increments, but here he shows signs that he might not be averse to a very different and much faster approach to enlightenment and modernity that would proceed along a bloodier track. In view of the Yankee's thoughts about the "ever-memorable and blessed Revolution, which swept a thousand years of such villainy away in one swift tidal wave of blood,"[61] his characterization of the industrial apparatus that he has created as a "rising hell" in the "bowels" of the medieval world sounds more ominous. In the Yankee's somewhat ambivalent notions about the best way forward to enlightenment, his thoughts about the bloodshed of the French Revolution represent the closest thing he has to an alternative plan of action, in the event his slower, incremental approach to enlightenment falls short. If it came to this, one might ask what role the Yankee's "labor-saving machinery" will play? What exactly will it mean to "flood the midnight world with light"? How might the "horror of swift death by the axe" be enhanced by the Yankee's nineteenth-century technological knowhow?[62]

As Twain's narrative brings us ever closer to the resolution of the question concerning how enlightenment is to be achieved in this case, the Yankee engages himself to the best of his ability in the pursuit of adventure and love. Love is a modest concern at best, probably as a consequence of the Yankee's practical and unsentimental approach to things. He wins his wife Alisande ("Sandy") in the joint adventure that he undertakes with her, despite the communication gap between her medieval, magical view of things and his own realistic, pragmatic one. Few details are provided: the Yankee and Sandy marry, have children, and enjoy a private domestic bliss that belongs more to

---

60. Ibid., 111–12.
61. Ibid., 111.
62. I elaborate these considerations in connection to the critical theory of Theodor Adorno and Max Horkheimer in my essay, "Revolutions and Final Solutions: The Dialectic of Enlightenment in Mark Twain's *A Connecticut Yankee in King Arthur's Court*."

the nineteenth century than to the "sixth century" of this imaginary Arthurian world. Greater and more revealing is the Yankee's interest in adventure. In view of his generally speculative bent, it is consistent to see him regard knight errantry correspondingly:

> A successful whirl in the knight-errantry line—now what is it when you blow away the nonsense and come down to the cold facts? It's just a corner in pork, that's all, and you can't make anything else out of it. You're rich—yes, suddenly rich—for about a day, maybe a week: then somebody corners the market on *you,* and down goes your bucket shop.[63]

Knight errantry in Twain's narrative might well be termed *ad-venture* capitalism, not only according to the Yankee's view of it as a medieval chivalric practice but also according to the specific uses to which the Yankee puts it. One such use is the Yankee's production of Persimmon's Soap, with which he hopes to *cleanse* the medieval world and which he advertises by using errant knights as traveling billboards.[64] Near the end of Twain's narrative, the role played by *ad-venture* capitalism has become much more significant. The Yankee's incremental approach to enlightening and modernizing the medieval world has brought about significant innovative changes, including a willingness on the part of the most important knights of Arthur's court to collaborate with the Yankee in the transformation of the Round Table to a stock board, on which knights now sit as shareholders and speculators. Predictably, Launcelot is president of the board.

The Yankee's effort to enlighten, civilize, and modernize his medieval world ultimately falls short, and the collapse of his high stakes speculation grows out of turmoil in the marketplace. Amplifying the action from Malory's account of the downfall of Arthur's court, Twain adds a preface to the traditional account of the trap set by Mordred and Agravaine to catch Launcelot and Guenever. In a conversation between the Yankee and his enlightened medieval assistant Clarence at the outset of the chapter titled "War!," we discover Launcelot has cornered the market of the London-Canterbury-Dover railroad line by buying up vast quantities of cheap stocks deemed a "wildcat."[65] Mordred and Agravaine are "among the flayed," forced to redeem stocks they sold to Launcelot "at fifteen and sixteen and along there" for two hundred eighty-three when "the Invincible One" comes calling. The downfall of Arthur's court, in Twain's

---

63. Twain, *Connecticut Yankee,* 177.
64. Ibid., 138–41.
65. Ibid., 413.

account, thus grows out of stock market speculations gone bust. With Arthur and his familiar chivalric retinue gone from Twain's novel, a power vacuum results. The Yankee, as "the Boss," tries to fill it by declaring a Republic, but the Church declares the Interdict and thereby brings the twenty-five or thirty thousand remaining knights of England back under its control as the implacable enemy of the Yankee. Positions polarize and events accelerate, leaving no more time for the Yankee's incremental approach. The endeavor to enlighten in slow short steps has been overtaken by events.

In the ensuing action, the "Terror" of the French Revolution shows the way forward, as we had reason to believe it might. In defense of his Republic, the Yankee engages the "insurgent chivalry of England" in the Battle of the Sand Belt, resolved to destroy superstition, tyranny, and the inherited privileges of nobility with his nineteenth-century industrial version of the guillotine. With the cohort of fifty-two enlightened boys he has managed to bring over to his side, the Yankee takes a position in Merlin's cave, which he has surrounded with a minefield and electric fences. Water has been diverted from a nearby brook to flood a ditch that will be created by detonating the mines. Knights proceeding through this perilous terrain will also face withering machine gun fire. Elsewhere in the kingdom, the industrial civilization that the Yankee hoped would be occupied by his newly enlightened workforce has been rigged with explosives and set to explode when a button is pushed at the command-and-control center in Merlin's cave. When the forty thousand knights of the chivalry of England move forward into this battleground, the full destructive potential of the Yankee's technological know-how becomes evident. He sets off the explosives rigged to his distant schools and factories to prevent them from falling into the hands of his enemies. Then he "floods the midnight world"—in a manner quite different from the ambition to enlighten that formed the original context of this phrase—with water and electricity directed into the ditch and fences where the masses of knights have tried to take cover. The Yankee's prepared *battleground* shows itself to be a technological apparatus capable of producing death on a mass scale. The Yankee's wonderment over the destructive potential of the devices he has made, presumably "as easy as rolling off a log," is clear as he examines what the explosion has left behind:

> As to destruction of life, it was amazing. Moreover, it was beyond estimate. Of course, we could not *count* the dead, because they did not exist as individuals, but merely as homogeneous protoplasm, with alloys of iron and buttons."[66]

---

66. Ibid., 432.

We discover by the end of Twain's Arthurian romance that this horrific destruction may be no more that the ravings of a shattered, dying man, perhaps hallucinations that could scarcely be believable to the kind of practical, nineteenth-century man as whom the Yankee first introduces himself. It is as if the destruction he has wrought among his chivalric adversaries has revisited the Yankee, leaving little or nothing that could be said to "exist as individuals," and leaving the veracity of his detailed account of his medieval adventures and the reliability of his judgment in question. The modern subjective self here, at the end of Mark Twain's *A Connecticut Yankee in King Arthur's Court*, is either an incoherent madman—not really an individual self anymore and scarcely more substantial than the "homogeneous protoplasm" produced by the war machines in his crazed mind—or he is perhaps the shattered remnant of the omnipotent, all-conquering spirit of European modernity, which the Yankee has turned against the medieval past, though to his ultimate demise and that of thousands of others. The Yankee's approach anticipates the kind of individualized, yet *global* totalitarian moves that will largely shape the cultural action of the next century.

EMANCIPATION, TOTALITARIANISM, AND THE (POST)MODERN CULTURAL ACTION

Endeavors to "stabilize" the modern subjective self[67]—a concern addressed at the beginning this study—have continually sought to reiterate an experiential integrity and existential assurance imagined in the Middle Ages,[68] while screening out its perceived tyrannical and oppressive aspects, such as those excoriated by the Connecticut Yankee. Positing any kind of trans-subjective scheme or *master plan* that is not arbitrary, oppressive, and ultimately destructive—as, for example, the master plan of the Connecticut Yankee turns out to be—has nevertheless proven difficult. Looking back in this study, we have observed that any presumed cultural stasis, any integrity of experience and existential assurance attributed to the Middle Ages in modernity, may be illusory. From a modern perspective characterized by the rapid acceleration and expansion of the European and global cultural action, selves

---

67. With "stabilize" I return to the term used by Habermas that I also cited in the first chapter of this study; see Habermas, *Philosophical Discourse*, 20.

68. See for example Ulrich Beck, *Risk Society*, which connects modernization with a "*removal* from historically prescribed social forms and commitments in the sense of traditional contexts of dominance and support," and with a related "*loss of traditional security* with respect to practical knowledge, faith, and guiding norms" (italics in original; 128).

and things in the European Middle Ages might wrongly seem to have been stationary. In much the same way as modern people, medieval people had to achieve and maintain their relative positions in competitions—ongoing competitions involving risks and rewards. We have observed that religion and empire, more than being forces that held medieval people in place, were parameters according to which they engaged in the action and sought rewards for themselves and their own. As global parameters, religion and empire—by way of adventure and love, as considered in this study—eventually become defining features of the emancipatory, individualized cultural action of modernity, in which individuals potentially become worlds to themselves and others.

In the transition from medieval to modern, the autonomous subjective self does not so much disengage or liberate itself from the medieval religious and imperial self upon which this study has focused, as reiterate it in new ways, as one sees nowhere more clearly than in the early theological writings of Martin Luther. Global, imperial parameters as a *potential* of the early modern individual self, rather than as external constraints holding the individual in place, subsequently enable Leibniz to put forth the One of his binary number system as an absolute, as the mathematical equivalent to and proof of the Christian God's creation of everything out of nothing. Kant is later able to call upon the modern self to avail itself of this global potential in a very different way, in the interests of an enlightenment that empowers the individual self absolutely and in a manner devoid of the religious trappings with which absolute power was previously associated. In different ways but to similar effect, Luther, Leibniz, and Kant—in *cutting edge* cultural moves of Reformation and Enlightenment—empower or emancipate the individual One absolutely and set it loose in a new cultural playing field. The result is new kinds of action in which the rules of the game are understood to be in the individual players themselves, and by extension in different individual cultural domains, such as "science, morality, art in general."[69] Still, each of the above-mentioned figures also has recourse to princely power to regulate the newly defined and increasingly dynamic if not volatile cultural action, in which every single self has become, potentially, an emperor. In the examples from Luther, Leibniz, and Kant, the ongoing deference to princely power might account for the fact that the aspect of *competition* among the newly conceived autonomous individuals virtually disappears from view. In the imaginary action of Mark Twain's *Connecticut Yankee*, this aspect comes to the fore with full force. We behold an

---

69. Compare Zygmunt Baumann's *Freedom*: "In the absence of one all-powerful, overwhelming current, individual ships must have their own gyroscopes to keep them on course" (41). The quotation in text, also cited in my first chapter, is from Habermas, *Philosophical Discourse*, 20.

everyman Yankee wielding the technological power of industrial modernity against his medieval adversaries, desiring to do so in the interests of an identifiably Kantian enlightenment and becoming *himself* an absolute despot, who regulates the cultural action with the best of intentions albeit to a disastrous end.

The constitution of the religious-imperial self of the Christian Middle Ages is not left behind or overcome, but rather becomes part of the vastly faster and more resourceful modern self by which it is extended and varied. The Connecticut Yankee's *revolutionary* modus operandi in Mark Twain's imaginary action is demonstrative of the reiteration of older cultural moves in new and different ways. Hannah Arendt's concluding words on Fascism and Communism in her *Origins of Totalitarianism* (1949) are worth citing here, because they similarly draw attention to totalitarianism as a *new* global form of government, and with a terminology of *potentiality* that is consistent with the one I have employed in this study:

> There remains the fact that the crisis of our time and its central experience have brought forth an entirely new form of government which as a potentiality and an ever-present danger is only too likely to stay with us from now on, just as other forms of government which came about at different historical moments and rested on different fundamental experiences have stayed with mankind regardless of temporary defeats—monarchies, and republics, tyrannies, dictatorships and despotism.[70]

Since the mid-twentieth century when Arendt wrote on totalitarianism, the parameters of the action have been increasingly shaped by moves of radically different dimensions and technological characteristics, though with similar underlying features. Integrated circuits and microprocessors have realized, and in ever new ways continue to realize, the potential of binary numbers to—as Leibniz put it—"weigh all sorts of masses with few weights" or "give several values with few coins." Whereas the imperial or totalitarian move continues to render things globally or *infinitely* according to an absolutely *other* perspective, idea, or master plan, microprocessors shape the cultural action according to a seemingly *infinitesimal* version of the same principle, with the cosmological One of Leibniz's binary number system standing in for the absolutely Other. Invested in multitudinous interests, ranging along the political spectrum from emancipation to totalitarianism, the electronically enhanced absolute One of Leibniz is set in play via the myriad digital moves that have

---

70. Arendt, *Origins of Totalitarianism*, 478.

come to pervade the contemporary cultural action. Individuals' ability to avail themselves of these moves seems to be limited only by the cultural resources of which they dispose overall. The status of self in Lyotard's *Postmodern Condition* (1979) is worth citing at this point for its descriptive value in this regard:

> A *self* does not amount to much, but no self is an island; each exists in a fabric of relations that is now more complex and mobile than ever before. Young or old, man or woman, rich or poor, a person is always located at "nodal points" of specific communication circuits, however tiny these may be. Or better: one is always located at a post through which various kinds of messages pass. No one, not even the least privileged among us, is ever entirely powerless over the messages that traverse and position him at the post of sender, addressee, or referent.[71]

In this study, the "mobility" of self to which Lyotard refers has been regarded in different terms. We have observed that the individual self, however "tiny," possesses an absolute, *global* potential. In view of the absolute characteristics of binary numbers as conceived by Leibniz, the increasingly minute moves of our electronically enhanced, digitized cultural action can be seen as consistent with and potentially embellishing or merging with global moves of grander dimensions. Following upon and elaborating its ancient, medieval, and early modern precedents, the postmodern *condition* on which Lyotard reports seems to show itself as *positions,* postmodernity as *spins* on modernity. A "grand narrative" that remains, however increasingly broken into infinite and infinitesimal perspectives, is the global, imperial, or—to use Arendt's designation—*totalitarian* one.[72]

Corresponding to the ongoing cultural action as I have endeavored to view it, this study must remain open ended. Its final words and final cited source might most aptly be the last lines of Hannah Arendt's *Origins of Totalitarianism,* which follow immediately upon the previously cited ones and somewhat qualify the dangers of totalitarianism by laying out the emancipatory characteristics of the potentiality underlying it.[73] Instead, I conclude here with

---

71. Lyotard, *Postmodern Condition,* 15.

72. Immediately before the above-cited passage, Lyotard had used the term "grand Narratives," more specifically, "the breaking up of the grand Narratives," to describe the status of the principal strategies for the legitimation of knowledge in modernity.

73. The paragraph at the end of Arendt's *Origins of Totalitarianism* reads: "There remains also the truth that every end in history necessarily contains a new beginning; this beginning is the promise, the only 'message' which the end can ever produce. Beginning, before it becomes a historical event, is the supreme capacity of man; politically, it is identical with man's freedom.

a similar but more elaborate passage from Arendt's *The Human Condition* (1958), with a prefatory reiteration of my suggestion that what is at stake in this potentiality might be not so much a *condition* as *positions*. Arendt's words here, as those at the end of her earlier book, fittingly return us to St. Augustine and are consistent with my view of culture as action:

> To act, in its most general sense, means to take an initiative, to begin (as the Greek word *archein*, "to begin," "to lead," and eventually "to rule," indicates), to set something into motion (which is the original meaning of the Latin *agere*). Because they are *initium*, newcomers and beginners by virtue of birth, men take initiative, are prompted into action. *[Initium] ergo ut esset, creatus est homo, ante quem nullus fuit* ("that there be a beginning, man was created before whom there was nobody"), said Augustine in his political philosophy. This beginning is not the same as the beginning of the world; it is not the beginning of something but of somebody, who is a beginner himself. With the creation of man, the principle of beginning came into the world itself, which, of course, is only another way of saying that the principle of freedom was created when man was created but not before.[74]

Initium ut esset homo creatus est—'that a beginning be made man was created,' said Augustine. This beginning is guaranteed by each new birth; it is indeed every man" (478–79).

74. Arendt, *Human Condition*, 177.

BIBLIOGRAPHY

PRIMARY SOURCES

St. Augustine of Hippo. *Avrelii Avgvstini Opera, De Civitate Dei Libri I-X, Corpus Christianorum—Series Latina.* Vol. 47. Tvrnholti Typographi Brepols Editores Pontificii, 1965.

———. *Avrelii Avgvstini Opera, De Civitate Dei Libri XI-XXII, Corpus Christianorum—Series Latina.* Vol. 48. Tvrnholti Typographi Brepols Editores Pontificii, 1965.

———. *Avrelii Avgvstini Opera, De Doctrina Christiana, Corpus Christianorum—Series Latina.* Vol. 32. Tvrnholti Typographi Brepols Editores Pontificii, 1962.

———. *The City of God, Books I-VII.* Translated by Demetrius B. Zema and Gerald G. Walsh. New York: Fathers of the Church, Inc., 1950.

———. *The City of God, Books VIII-XVI.* Translated by Gerald G. Walsh and Grace Monahan. New York: Fathers of the Church, Inc., 1952.

———. *The City of God, Books XVII-XXII.* Translated by Gerald G. Walsh and Daniel J. Honan. Washington, DC: Catholic University of America Press, 1954.

———. *The Confessions of St. Augustine.* Translated by Warren W. Wiersbe. Grand Rapids, MI: Baker Book House, 2005.

———. *On Christian Doctrine.* Translated by D. W. Robertson, Jr. Indianapolis, IN: Liberal Arts Press, 1958.

Bernard of Clairvaux. "In Praise of the New Knighthood." In *The Templars, Selected Sources Translated and Annotated,* translated by Malcolm Barber and Keith Bate. Manchester: Manchester University Press, 2002. 215–27.

———. "Liber ad Milites Templi: de laude novae militia." *Sancti Bernardi Opera, Vol. 3: Tractatus et Opuscula.* Edited by J. LeClercq and H. M. Rochais. Rome: Editiones Cistercienses, 1963. 3:222.

Biblia Sacra Vulgata, 2001. http://www.drbo.org/lvb/ (accessed July 2014).

Chrétien de Troyes. *Cligès*. Edited and translated by Peter F. Dembowski. In *Chrétien de Troyes: Oeuvres completes*, edited by Daniel Poiron, Anne Berthelot, Peter F. Dembowski, Sylvie Lefèvre, Karl D. Uitti, and Philippe Walter. Paris: Gallimard, 1994. 173–336.

———. *Cligès*. Translated by William W. Kibler. In *Chrétien de Troyes, Arthurian Romances*. London: Penguin Classics, 1991. 123–205.

———. *Erec and Enide*. Translated by Carleton W. Carroll. In *Chrétien de Troyes, Arthurian Romances*, translated by William W. Kibler and Carleton W. Carroll. London: Penguin Classics, 1991. 37–122.

———. *Érec et Énide*. Edited and translated by Peter F. Dembowski. In *Chrétien de Troyes: Oeuvres completes*, edited by Daniel Poiron, Anne Berthelot, Peter F. Dembowski, Sylvie Lefèvre, Karl D. Uitti, and Philippe Walter. Paris: Gallimard, 1994. 3–169.

———. *The Knight of the Cart (Lancelot)*. Translated by William W. Kibler. In *Chrétien de Troyes, Arthurian Romances*. London: Penguin Classics, 1991. 207–94.

———. *Lancelot ou le Chevalier de la Charrette*. Edited and translated by Peter F. Dembowski. In *Chrétien de Troyes: Oeuvres completes*, edited by Daniel Poiron, Anne Berthelot, Peter F. Dembowski, Sylvie Lefèvre, Karl D. Uitti, and Philippe Walter. Paris: Gallimard, 1994.

———. *The Story of the Grail*. Translated by William W. Kibler. In *Chrétien de Troyes, Arthurian Romances*. London: Penguin Classics, 1991. 381–494.

Codex Manesse. Die Minaturen der Großen Heidelberger Liederhandschrift. 5th ed. Frankfurt am Main: Insel Verlag. 1992.

Dante Aligieri. *The Divine Comedy: Text with Translation in the Metre of the Original by Geoffrey L. Bickersteth*. Oxford: Blackwell, 1981.

Die Lieder Neidharts. Edited and translated by Siegfried Beyschlag. Darmstadt: Wissenschaftliche Buchgesellschaft, 1975.

Gottfried von Strassburg. *Tristan*. Edited by Friedrich Ranke. Translated by Rüdiger Krohn. 2 vols. Stuttgart: Reclam, 1981.

———. *Tristan*. Translated by Arthur T. Hatto. London: Penguin Classics, 1960.

Hartmann von Aue. *Erec*. Edited and translated by Thomas Cramer. Frankfurt am Main: Fischer Taschenbuch Verlag, 1972.

———. *Erec*. Translated by Kim Vivian. *Arthurian Romances, Tales, and Lyric Poetry: The Complete Works of Hartmann von Aue*. University Park: Pennsylvania State University Press, 2001. 51–163.

———. *Iwein: Eine Erzählung von Hartmann von Aue*. Edited by G. F. Benecke and Karl Lachmann. 7th ed. revised by Ludwig Wolff. Berlin: De Gruyter, 1968.

———. *Iwein*. In *Arthurian Romances, Tales, and Lyric Poetry: The Complete Works of Hartmann von Aue*, translated by Richard H. Lawson. University Park: Pennsylvania State University Press, 2001. 235–321.

———. *Iwein*. Translated by J. W. Thomas. Lincoln: University of Nebraska Press, 1979.

Heinrich von Veldeke. *Eneasroman: Die Berliner Bilderhandschrift mit Übersetzung und Kommentar*. Edited by Hans Fromm. Frankfurt am Main: Deutscher Klassiker Verlag, 1992.

———. *Eneit*. Translated by J. W. Thomas. New York: Garland, 1985.

The Heliand: The Saxon Gospel; A Translation and Commentary. Translated with commentary by G. Ronald Murphy. New York: Oxford University Press, 1992.

Hêliand: Text and Commentary. Edited and Translated by John E. Cathey. Morgantown: West Virginia University Press, 2002.

The Holy Bible: Authorized King James Version. Grand Rapids, Michigan: World Publishing, 1989.

Homer. *The Iliad*. Translated by Robert Fagles. London: Penguin Books, 1990.

Kant, Immanuel. "An Answer to the Question: What Is Enlightenment?" In *Immanuel Kant, Practical Philosophy*, edited and translated by Mary J. Gregor. Cambridge: Cambridge University Press, 1996. 17–22.

———. "Beantwortung der Frage: Was ist Aufklärung?" In Vol. 4, *Immanuel Kant: Schriften.* Edited by Arthur Buchenau and Ernst Cassirer. Berlin: Cassirer, 1922. 169–76.

Leibniz, Gottfried Wilhelm. "Explanation of Binary Arithmetic." In *Leibniz Translations.com*, translated by Lloyd Strickland. http://www.leibniz-translations.com/binary.htm (accessed July 1, 2015). 224.

———. "Explication de Arithmetique Binaire. " In Vol. 7, *G. W. Leibniz: Mathematische Schriften.* Edited by C. I. Gerhardt. Hildesheim: Olms, 1971. 223–27.

———. *G. W. Leibniz's "Monadology": An Edition for Students.* Translated by Nicholas Rescher. Pittsburgh, PA: University of Pittsburgh Press, 1991.

———. *Zwei Briefe über das binäre Zahlensystem und die chinesische Philosophie.* Edited by Renate Loosen and Franz Vonessen. Stuttgart: Belser, 1968.

Luther, Martin. *An den Christlichen Adel deutscher Nation, Von der Freiheit eines Christenmenschen, Sendbrief vom Dolmetschen.* Stuttgart: Reclam, 1962.

———. "Dedicatory Letter of Martin Luther to Pope Leo X" and "On the Freedom of a Christian." In *First Principles of the Reformation,* translated by Henry Wace and C. A. Buchheim. London: John Murray, 1883; cited from *Modern History Sourcebook,* http://www.fordham.edu/halsall/mod/luther-freedomchristian.asp (accessed July 1, 2015).

———. "Ein Sendbrief an den Papst Leo X: Von der Freiheit eines Christenmenschen." In Vol. 2, *Luthers Werke in Auswahl: Unter Mitwirkung von Albert Leitzmann.* Edited by Otto von Clemens. Bonn: A. Marcus & E. Weber's Verlag, 1912. 1–27.

———. "Ein Sendbrief vom Dolmetschen." In Vol. 4, *Luthers Werke in Auswahl: Unter Mitwirkung von Albert Leitzmann.* Edited by Otto von Clemens. Bonn: A. Marcus & E. Weber's Verlag, 1913. 179–93.

———. *Luther and Calvin: Secular Authority.* Edited by Harro Höpfl. Cambridge: Cambridge University Press, 1991.

———. "An Open Letter on Translating." Translated by Gary Mann. *Internet Christian Library.* http://www.iclnet.org/pub/resources/text/wittenberg/luther/luther-translate.txt (accessed July 1, 2015).

———. "To the Christian Nobility of the German Nation." In *German Humanism and Reformation,* edited by Reinhard P. Becker. New York: Continuum, 1982. 149–234.

Marie de France. *Lais de Marie de France.* Edited and translated by Alexandre Micha. Paris: Flammarion, 1994.

———. *The Lais of Marie de France.* Translated by Glyn S. Burgess and Keith Busby. London: Penguin Books, 1989.

———. *The Lais of Marie de France.* Translated by Robert Hanning and Joan Ferrante. New York: Dutton, 1978.

Otfried von Weissenburg. *Otfrids Evangelienbuch.* Edited by Oskar Erdmann. 3rd ed. revised by Ludwig Wolff. Tübingen: Niemeyer, 1957.

———. "Ohtfrid's Letter to Liudbert." Translated by James Marchand. http://ftp.sunet.se/pub/etext/wiretap—classic-library/Latin/Malin/ohtfrid.txt (accessed July 1, 2015).

Otto I, Bishop of Freising. *The Deeds of Frederick Barbarossa: By Otto of Freising and His Continuator, Rahewin.* Translated by Charles Christopher Mierow. New York: Columbia University Press, 1953.

———. *Gesta Friderici Imperatoris: Monumenta Germaniae Historica—eMGH.* http://clt.brepolis.net/emgh/pages/Toc.aspx?ctx=668680 (accessed July 1, 2015).

———. *Ottonis Episcopi Frisingensis Chronica sive Historia de Duabus Civitatibus.* Edited by Adolf Hofmeister. Impensis Bibliopolii Hahniani: Hanover and Leipzig, 1912.

———. *The Two Cities: A Chronicle of Universal History to the Year 1146.* Translated by Charles Christopher Mierow. New York: Columbia University Press, 1966.

Schiller, Friedrich. *Schillers Werke.* Vol. 2. Edited by Norbert Oellers. Weimer: Böhlau, 1983.

———. *The Works of Friedrich Schiller.* Translated by E. P. Arnold Forster and Percy E. Pinkerton. Edited by Nathan Haskell Dole. Boston: Wyman-Fogg, 1902.
Thomasin von Zirclaria. *Der Welsche Gast.* Edited by Heinrich Rückert. Quedlinburg: Basse, 1852.
———. *Der Welsche Gast (The Italian Guest).* Translated by Marion Gibbs and Winder McConnell. Kalamazoo, MI: Medieval Institute Publications, 2009.
Twain, Mark. *A Connecticut Yankee in King Arthur's Court.* Edited by Bernard L. Stein. Berkeley: University of California Press, 1979.
Virgil. *The Aeneid.* Translated by Robert Fitzgerald. New York: Random House, 1990.
Walther von der Vogelweide. *The Single-Stanza Lyrics.* Edited and translated by Frederick Goldin. New York: Routledge, 2003.
Wolfram von Eschenbach. *Parzival.* Edited by Karl Lachmann. Translated by Wolfgang Spiewok. 2 vols. Stuttgart: Reclam, 1981.
———. *Parzival.* Translated by Arthur T. Hatto. London: Penguin Classics, 1980.

SECONDARY SOURCES

Aho, James. *Confession and Bookkeeping: The Religious, Moral, and Rhetorical Roots of Modern Accounting.* Albany: State University of New York Press, 2005.
Allard, Jean-Paul. *L' initiation royale d' Erec, le chevalier.* Paris: Archè, 1987.
Arendt, Hannah. *The Human Condition.* Chicago: University of Chicago Press, 1958.
———. *Love and Saint Augustine.* Edited by Johanna Vecchiarelli Scott and Judith Chelius. Chicago: University of Chicago Press, 1996.
———. *The Origins of Totalitarianism.* New York: Harcourt, 1951.
Arnold, Benjamin. *German Knighthood 1050–1300.* Oxford: Oxford University Press, 1985.
Bakhtin, Mikhail. "Epic and Novel." In *The Dialogic Imagination: Four Essays by M. M. Bakhtin,* edited by Michael Holquist and translated by Caryl Emerson and Michael Holquist. Austin: University of Texas Press, 1981. 3–40.
Baron, Margaret E. *The Origins of the Infinitesimal Calculus.* New York: Dover, 1969.
Bauman, Zygmunt. *Culture as Praxis.* London: Sage Publications, 1999.
———. *Europe: An Unfinished Adventure.* Cambridge: Polity Press, 2004.
———. *Freedom.* Minneapolis: University of Minnesota Press, 1988.
Baumgartner, Emmanuèle. "Chrétien's Medieval Influence: From the Grail Quest to the Joy of the Court." In *A Companion to Chrétien de Troyes,* edited by Norris J. Lacy and Joan Tasker Grimbert. Cambridge: D. S. Brewer, 2005. 214–27.
Beck, Ulrich. *Risikogesellschaft: Auf dem Weg in eine andere Moderne.* Frankfurt am Main: Suhrkamp, 1985.
———. *Risk Society: Towards a New Modernity.* Translated by Mark Ritter. London: Sage Publications, 1992.
BeDuhn, Jason David. *Augustine's Manichaean Dilemma, Volume 1: Conversion and Apostasy.* Philadelphia: University of Pennsylvania Press, 2010.
Blickle, Peter. "Reformation and the Communal Spirit: The Reply of the Theologians to Constitutional Change in the Late Middle Ages." In *The German Reformation,* edited by C. Scott Dixon. Oxford: Blackwell, 1999. 133–67.
Bloch, R. Howard. *The Anonymous Marie de France.* Chicago: University of Chicago Press, 2003.
Bowery, Anne-Marie. "Plotinus, The Enneads." In *Augustine through the Ages: An Encyclopedia,* edited by Allan D. Fitzgerald. Grand Rapids, MI: Eerdmans, 1999. 654–57.
Bruckner, Matilda. "Chrétien de Troyes." In *The Cambridge Companion to Medieval French Literature,* edited by Simon Gaunt and Sarah Kay. Cambridge: Cambridge University Press, 2008. 79–94.

Bumke, Joachim. *Courtly Culture. Literature and Society in the High Middle Ages.* Berkeley: University of California Press, 1991.
———. *Wolfram von Eschenbach.* 8th ed. Stuttgart: Metzler, 2004.
Burgess, Glyn S. *Chrétien de Troyes: Érec et Énide.* London: Grant & Cutler, 1984.
———. *The Lais of Marie de France: Text and Context.* Athens: University of Georgia Press, 1987.
Bynum, Carolyn Walker. *Metamorphosis and Identity.* New York: Zone Books, 2001.
Carter, Everett. "The Meaning of *A Connecticut Yankee.*" *American Literature* 50 (1978): 418–40.
Chinca, Mark. *Gottfried von Strassburg: Tristan.* Cambridge: Cambridge University Press, 1997.
Classen, Albrecht, ed. *Discourses on Love, Marriage, and Transgression in Medieval and Early Modern Literature.* Tempe: Arizona Center for Medieval and Renaissance Studies, 2004.
Cormeau, Christoph, and Wilhem Störmer. *Hartmann von Aue: Epoche-Werk-Wirkung.* Munich: Beck, 1985.
Curtius, Ernst Robert. *European Literature and the Latin Middle Ages.* Translated by Willard R. Trask. Princeton, NJ: Princeton University Press, 1983.
Dahmus, Joseph. *Seven Medieval Kings.* New York: Doubleday, 1967.
Dallapiazza, Michael. *Wolfram von Eschenbach: Parzival.* Berlin: Erich Schmidt, 2009.
Davies, Philip R. *On the Origins of Judaism.* London: Equinox Publishing, 2011.
Dinzelbacher, Peter. "Über die Entdeckung der Liebe im Hochmittelalter." *Saeculum* 32 (1981): 185–208.
Dixit, Avinash K., and Barry J. Nalebuff. *The Art of Strategy: A Game Theorist's Guide to Success in Business and Life.* New York: Norton, 2008.
von Dülmen, Richard. "The Reformation and the Modern Age." In *The German Reformation,* edited by C. Scott Dixon. Oxford: Blackwell, 1999. 193–219.
Dunning, Eric, with Norbert Elias. *Quest for Excitement: Sport and Leisure in the Civilizing Process.* Oxford: Blackwell, 1986.
Ehlers, Joachim. "Die Reichsfürsten." In *Heiliges Römisches Reich Deutscher Nation 962 bis 1806: Von Otto dem Grossen bis zum Ausgang des Mittelalters,* edited by Matthias Puhle and Claus-Peter Hasse. Dresden: Sandstein, 2006. 199–209.
Eichberger, Jürgen. *Game Theory for Economists.* San Diego: Academic Press, 1993.
Elias, Norbert. *Über den Prozess der Zivilisation: Soziogenetische und psychogenetische Untersuchungen.* Basel: Verlaghaus zum Falken, 1939.
Fleckenstein, Josef. "Friedrich Barbarossa und das Rittertum: Zur Bedeutung der großen Mainzer Hoftage von 1184 und 1188." In Vol. 2, *Festschrift für Hermann Heimpel.* Göttingen: Max Planck Institut, 1972. 1023–41.
Flood, John L. "Martin Luther's Bible Translation in its German and European Context." In *The Bible in the Renaissance,* edited by Richard Griffiths. Sydney: Ashgate, 2001. 211–20.
Fowler, Jeaneanne. *Perspectives of Reality: An Introduction to the Philosophy of Hinduism.* Brighton: Sussex Academic Press, 2002.
Fox, Nili. "Concepts of God in Israel and the Question of Monotheism." In *Text, Artifact, and Image. Revealing Ancient Israelite Religion,* edited by Gary M. Beckman and Theodore J. Lewis. Providence, RI: Brown Judaic Studies, 2006. 326–45.
Frasetto, Michael. "History of Emperors and Empire, c. 750–c. 1350." In *A Companion to Middle High German Literature to the 14th Century.* Leiden: Brill, 2002. 1–25.
Füssel, Stephan. *Gutenberg and the Impact of Printing.* Translated by Douglas Martin. Burlington, VT: Ashgate, 2003.
Gentry, Francis G. "Gahmuret and Herzeloyde: Gone but Not Forgotten." In *A Companion to Wolfram's "Parzival,"* edited by Will Hasty. Rochester, NY: Camden House, 1999. 3–11.
———. "German Literature to 1160." In *A Companion to Middle High German Literature to the 14th Century,* edited by Francis. G. Gentry. Leiden: Brill, 2002. 53–115.

Gibbs, Marion E. "Ideals of Flesh and Blood: Women Characters in *Parzival*." In *A Companion to Wolfram's "Parzival,"* edited by Will Hasty. Rochester, NY: Camden House, 1999. 12–34.

Goldenbaum, Ursula. "Leibniz as a Lutheran." In *Leibniz, Mysticism, and Religion*, edited by Allison P. Coudert, Richard H. Popkin, and Gordon M. Weiner. Dordrecht: Kluwer, 1998. 169–92.

Goldenbaum, Ursula, and Douglas Jesseph. *Infinitesimal Differences: Controversies between Leibniz and His Contemporaries*. New York: De Gruyter, 2008.

Gransden, K. W. *Virgil: The Aeneid*. Edited by S. J. Harrison. 2nd ed. Cambridge: Cambridge University Press, 2004.

Green, D. H. *The Beginnings of Medieval Romance: Fact and Fiction, 1190–1250*. Cambridge: Cambridge University Press, 2002.

Gregerson, Linda, and Susan Juster, eds. *Empires of God: Religious Encounters in the Early Modern Atlantic*. Philadelphia: University of Pennsylvania Press, 2011.

Grier, Michelle. "Kant's Critique of Metaphysics." *The Stanford Encyclopedia of Philosophy*. February 2004. Revised April 2012. http://plato.stanford. edu/entries/kant-metaphysics/ (accessed July 2015).

Grimbert, Joan Tasker. "*Cliges* and the Chansons: A Slave to Love." In *A Companion to Chrétien de Troyes*, edited by Norris J. Lacy and Joan Tasker Grimbert. Cambridge: D. S. Brewer, 2005. 120–36.

Groos, Arthur. *Romancing the Grail: Genre, Science, and Quest in Wolfram's Parzival*. Ithaca, NY: Cornell University Press, 1995.

Habermas, Jürgen. *Der philosophische Diskurs der Moderne: Zwölf Vorlesungen*. Suhrkamp: Frankfurt am Main, 1985.

———. *The Philosophical Discourse of Modernity: Twelve Lectures*. Translated by Frederick Lawrence. Cambridge, MA: MIT Press, 1992.

———. *Strukturwandel der Öffentlichkeit: Untersuchungen zur Kategorie der bürgerlichen Gesellschaft*. Darmstadt: Luchterhand, 1980.

Hamburger, Henry. *Games as Models of Social Phenomena*. San Francisco, CA: Freeman, 1979.

Harf-Lancer, Lawrence. "Chrétien's Literary Background." Translated by Amy L. Ingram. In *A Companion to Chrétien de Troyes*, edited by Norris J. Lacy and Joan Tasker Grimbert. Cambridge: D. S. Brewer, 2005. 26–42.

Harris, Nigel. "God, Religion, and Ambiguity in *Tristan*." In *A Companion to Gottfried's "Tristan,"* edited by Will Hasty. Rochester, NY: Camden House, 2003.

Hasty, Will. "Bullish on Love and Adventure: Chivalry as Speculation in the German Arthurian Romances." *Arthuriana* 20.3 (2010): 65–80.

———. "Revolutions and Final Solutions: The Dialectic of Enlightenment in Mark Twain's *A Connecticut Yankee in King Arthur's Court*." *Arthuriana* 24.2 (2014): 21–42.

———. "The Singularity of Aura and the Artistry of Translation: Luther's Bible as Artwork." *Monatshefte* 101.4 (2009): 457–68.

———. "Theorizing German Romance: The Excursus on Enite's Horse and Saddle in Hartmann von Aue's *Erec*." *Seminar* 43.3 (2007): 253–64.

Hatto, Arthur T. "An Introduction to a Second Reading." In *Wolfram von Eschenbach: Parzival*. New York: Penguin Books, 1980. 412–38.

Hauck, Albert. "Innocent III Desired to Rule the World." In *Innocent III: Vicar of Christ or Lord of the World?* Edited by James M. Powell, 2nd ed. Washington, DC: Catholic University of America Press, 1994. 15–18.

Haug, Walter. *Die höfische Liebe im Horizont der erotischen Diskurse des Mittelalters und der Frühen Neuzeit*. Berlin: De Gruyter, 2004.

———. *Vernacular Literary Theory in the Middle Age: The German Tradition, 800–1300, in Its European Context*. Translated by Joanna M. Catling. Cambridge: Cambridge University Press, 1997.

Heer, Friedrich. *The Holy Roman Empire*. Translated by Janet Sondheimer. London: Weidenfeld & Nicholson, 1968.
Hoffmann, Andrew J. *Twain's Heroes, Twain's Worlds: Mark Twain's Adventures of Huckleberry Finn, A Connecticut Yankee in King Arthur's Court, and Pudd'nhead Wilson*. Philadelphia: University of Philadelphia Press, 1988.
Huber, Christoph. *Gottfried von Strassburg: Tristan and Isolde*. Munich: Artemis, 1986.
Huizinga, Johan. *Homo Ludens: A Study of the Play Element in Culture*. Boston: Beacon Press, 1955.
Jackson, W. H. *Chivalry in Twelfth-Century Germany: The Works of Hartmann von Aue*. Cambridge: D. S. Brewer, 1994.
Jaeger, C. Stephen. *Ennobling Love: In Search of a Lost Sensibility*. Philadelphia: University of Pennsylvania Press, 1999.
———. *The Origins of Courtliness: Civilizing Trends and the Formation of Courtly Ideals*. Philadelphia: University of Pennsylvania Press, 1985.
Kaeuper, Richard. *Chivalry and Violence in Medieval Europe*. Oxford: Oxford University Press, 1999.
Kay, Sarah. *Courtly Contradictions: The Emergence of the Literary Object in the Twelfth Century*. Stanford, CA: Stanford University Press, 2001.
Kittler, Friedrich A. *Gramophone, Film, Typewriter*. Translated by Geoffrey Winthrop-Young and Michael Wutz. Stanford, CA: Stanford University Press, 1999.
Kline, Morris. *Mathematical Thought from Ancient to Modern Times*. New York: Oxford University Press, 1972.
Kratz, Dennis M. "Waltharius." In Vol. 148, *Dictionary of Literary Biography: German Writers and Works of the Early Middle Ages: 800–1170*. Edited by Will Hasty and James Hardin. Detroit: Gale Research, 1995. 287–94.
Kratz, Henry. *Wolfram von Eschenbach's "Parzival": An Attempt at a Total Evaluation*. Bern: Francke, 1973.
Kuhn, Hugo. "Erec." *Dichtung und Welt Mittelalter*. Stuttgart: Metzler, 1969. 133–51.
Küng, Hans. *Great Christian Thinkers*. New York: Continuum, 1994.
———, ed. *Yes to a Global Ethic*. New York: Continuum, 1996.
Lachmann, Karl. *Kleinere Schriften zur Philologie*. Berlin: Reimer, 1875.
Lawrence, C. H. *Medieval Monasticism*. London: Longman, 2001.
Lewis, Brenda Ralph. *Ritual Sacrifice: An Illustrated History*. Gloucestershire: Sutton, 2001.
Liddell and Scott's Greek-English Lexicon. Oxford: At the Clarendon Press, 1984.
Louden, Bruce. *The Iliad: Structure, Myth, and Meaning*. Baltimore: The Johns Hopkins University Press, 2006.
Lyotard, Jean-François. *The Postmodern Condition*. Translated by Geoff Bennington and Brian Massumi. Minneapolis: University of Minnesota Press, 1991.
Maddox, Donald. *Structure and Scaring: The Systematic Kingdom in Chrétien's Érec et Énide*. Lexington, KY: French Forum Publishers, 1978.
Maddox, Donald, and Sara Sturm Maddox. "*Érec et Énide*: The First Arthurian Romance." In *A Companion to Chrétien de Troyes*, edited by Norris J. Lacy and Joan Tasker Grimbert. Cambridge: D. S. Brewer, 2005. 103–19.
Mailath, George, and Larry Samuelson. *Repeated Games and Reputations: Long Run Relationships*. Oxford: Oxford University Press, 2006.
Mar, Raymond A., and Keith Oatley. "The Function of Fiction is the Abstraction and Simulation of Social Experience." *Perspectives on Psychological Science* 3:3 (2008): 173–92.
McCarty, Nolan, and Adam Meirowitz. *Political Game Theory: An Introduction*. Cambridge: Cambridge University Press, 2007.

McNeely, Ian F., with Lisa Wolverton. *Reinventing Knowledge: From Alexandria to the Internet.* New York: Norton, 2008.

Ménard, Philippe. *Les Lais de Marie de France: Contes d'amours et d'aventures du Moyen Age.* Paris: Presses Universitaires de France, 1979.

Messent, Peter. *The Cambridge Introduction to Mark Twain.* Cambridge: Cambridge University Press, 2007.

Mohr, Wolfgang. "Parzival's Knightly Guilt." In *Perceval/Parzival: A Casebook,* edited by Arthur Groos and Norris J. Lacy. Routledge: New York, 2002. 139–53.

Murphy, G. Ronald. *Gemstone of Paradise: The Holy Grail in Wolfram's "Parzival."* Oxford: Oxford University, 2006.

Murray, K. Sarah-Jane. *From Plato to Lancelot: A Preface to Chrétien de Troyes.* Syracuse, NY: Syracuse University Press, 2008.

Niehr, Klaus. "Herrscherliche Architektur." In *Heiliges Römisches Reich Deutscher Nation 962 bis 1806: Von Otto dem Grossen bis zum Ausgang des Mittelalters,* edited by Matthias Puhle and Claus-Peter Hasse. Dresden: Sandstein, 2006. 159–71.

Nykrog, Per. *Chrétien de Troyes: Romancier discutable.* Geneva: Droz, 1996.

Pagden, Anthony. *Peoples and Empires: A Short History of European Migration, Exploration, and Conquest from Greece to the Present.* New York: Random House, 2001.

Passerini, Luisa. *Love and the Idea of Europe.* New York: Berghahn, 2009.

Picht, Georg. "What Is Enlightened Thinking?" Translated by Garrett Green. In *What Is Enlightenment? Eighteenth-Century Answers and Twentieth-Century Questions,* edited by James Schmidt. Berkeley: University of California Press, 1996. 368–81.

Pietarinen, Ahti-Veikko, ed. *Game Theory and Linguistic Meaning.* Oxford: Elsevier, 2007.

Pincikowski, Scott E. *Bodies of Pain: Suffering in the Works of Hartmann von Aue.* New York: Routledge, 2002.

Railton, Stephen. *Mark Twain: A Short Introduction.* Malden, MA: Blackwell, 2004.

Reith, Gerda. *The Age of Chance: Gambling in Western Culture.* London: Routledge, 1999.

Robinson, I. S. *The Papacy 1073–1198: Continuity and Innovation.* Cambridge: Cambridge University Press, 1990.

Rorty, Richard. *Contingency, Irony, and Solidarity.* Cambridge: Cambridge University Press, 1989.

Rosemond, Marleen. *Descartes's Dualism.* Cambridge, MA: Harvard University Press, 1998.

Rossi, Andreola. *Contexts of War: Manipulation of Genre in Virgilian Battle Narrative.* Ann Arbor: University of Michigan Press, 2004.

de Rougemont, Denis. *Love in the Western World.* New York: Pantheon, 1956.

Rubenstein, Richard E. *Aristotle's Children: How Christians, Muslims, and Jews Rediscovered Ancient Wisdom and Illuminated the Middle Ages.* Orlando: Harcourt, 2003.

Ruud, Jay. *Critical Companion to Dante: A Literary Reference to His Life and Work.* New York: Facts on File, 2008.

Safranski, Rüdiger. *Friedrich Schiller oder Die Erfüllung des Deutschen Idealismus.* Munich: Hanser, 2004.

Samuelson, Larry. *Evolutionary Games and Equilibrium Selection.* Cambridge, MA: MIT Press, 1997.

Schausten, Monika. *Erzählwelten der Tristangeschichte im hohen Mittelalter: Untersuchungen zu den deutschsprachigen Tristanfassungen des 12. und 13; Jahrhunderts.* Munich: Fink, 1999.

Schieffer, Rudolf. "Konzepte des Kaisertums." In *Heilig—Römisch—Deutsch: Das Reich im Mittelalterlichen Europa,* edited by Bernd Schneidmüller and Stefan Weinfurter. Dresden: Sandstein Verlag, 2006.

Schnell, Rüdiger. "Kirche, Hof, und Liebe: Zum Freiraum mittelalterlicher Dichtung." In *Mittelalterbilder aus neuer Perspektive,* edited by Ernstpeter Ruhe. Munich: Fink, 1985. 75–111.

Schulz, James A. *Courtly Love, the Love of Courtliness, and the History of Sexuality.* Chicago: University of Chicago Press, 2006.

———. "Why Do Tristan and Isolde Make Love? The Love Potion as a Milestone in the History of Sexuality." In *Visuality and Materiality in the Story of Tristan and Isolde,* edited by Jutta Eming, Ann Marie Rasmussen, and Kathryn Starkey. Notre Dame, IN: Notre Dame University Press, 2012. 65–82.

Silk, M. S. *Homer: The Iliad.* 2nd ed. Cambridge: Cambridge University Press, 2004.

Speer, Nicole K., Jeremy R. Reynolds, Khena M. Swallow, and Jeffrey M. Zacks. "Reading Stories Activates Neural Representations of Perceptual and Motor Experiences." *Psychological Science* 20 (2009): 989–99.

Starkey, Kathryn. *Reading the Medieval Book: Word, Image, and Performance in Wolfram von Eschenbach's "Willehalm."* Notre Dame, IN: University of Notre Dame Press, 2004.

Taylor, Jamie K. *Fictions of Evidence: Witnessing, Literature, and Community in the Late Middle Ages.* Columbus: The Ohio State University Press, 2013.

Vitz, Evelyn Birge. Orality and Performance in Early French Romance. Rochester, NY: D.S. Brewer, 1999.

Warrior, Valerie M. *Roman Religion.* Cambridge: Cambridge University Press, 2006.

Wenzel, Horst. *Höfische Repräsentation: Symbolische Kommunikation und Literatur im Mittelalter.* Darmstadt: Wissenschaftliche Buchgesellschaft, 2005.

Whalen, Logan E. *Marie de France and the Poetics of Memory.* Washington, DC: Catholic University Press, 2008.

Wilson, Derek. *Out of the Storm: The Life and Legacy of Martin Luther.* New York: St. Martin's Press, 2007.

Wynn, Marianne. "Parzival and Gâwân: Hero and Counterpart." In *Perceval/Parzival: A Casebook,* edited by Arthur Groos and Norris J. Lacy. Routledge: New York, 2002. 175–98.

Yarkoni, T., Nicole K. Speer, D. A. Balota, M. P. McAvoy, and Jeffrey M. Zacks. "Pictures of a Thousand Words: Investigating the Neural Mechanisms of Reading with Extremely Rapid Event-Related fMRI." *NeuroImage* 42 (2008): 973–87.

Ziegler, Vickie L. *Trial by Fire and Battle in Medieval German Literature.* Rochester, NY: Camden House, 2004.

INDEX

Aachen, Charlemagne's court at, 46
Abraham, 17, 20–23, 26, 30
Abram, 30
Absalom, 144
Achilles, 16–19, 21, 30, 30n43, 125
Aeneas, 18, 23–25, 25n38, 30–32, 68–69, 104
Aeneid, 2, 23, 23n35, 25n38, 68, 82, 104
Agamemnon, 16–18, 21
Ajax the Great, 17–18
Ajax the Lesser, 18
Alexander (Chrétien's Cligès), 171–172, 172n30, 173, 195
Alexander the Great, 64, 144
Alisande—"Sandy" (Twain), 236
Anfortas, 152, 155–156
An Answer to the Question: What is Enlightenment?, 5, 225, 226n43
Antichrist, 210
Antikonie, 128–129, 129n20, 130, 130n23
Antony, Saint, 127
Aphrodite, 17–18
Apollo, 18, 31, 86
Apollo and the Muses, 86
Arator, 89
Arc of the Covenant, 21, 26

Arendt, Hannah, 5, 163n7, 208, 241–242, 242n73, 243
Aristotle, 78n52
Arthur. *See* King Arthur
Ascanius, 14, 25
Augsburg, meeting of German princes to discuss deposition of Henry IV, 75
Augustine. *See* St. Augustine of Hippo
Augustus Caesar, 25, 58, 82, 178
Avalon, Isle of, 187

Babylon, 210
Bearosche, 128
Beatrice, 206
Beethoven, Ludwig van, 229
Benjamin, Walter, 214n15
Beowulf, 92
Bernard of Clairvaux, 123, 137–139, 149, 151, 156, 158, 167–168, 196
binary numbers, 5, 222, 222n36, 223, 223n38, 224, 224n40, 240–242
Blancheflor, 170–171, 188–189, 195
Bligger von Steinach, 87
Blumenberg, Hans, 13
Boccaccio, 95n36

Brangaene, 54, 195
Briseis, 16
Brobarz, 165
Brunhilt, 82
Burckhardt, Jacob, 206
Byzantium, 46

Calculus, 221, 221n31, 222, 222n35
Canossa, 75
Carduel, 176–177
Carlisle Fragment, 197n70
Carnant, 147
Carolingian, 46–47, 73, 82, 89, 91, 93–94
Castle of Marvels, 152n60
Charlemagne, 46–47, 47n40, 71–73, 73n36, 92–93
Chaucer, 95n36
Chernobyl, 15n18
Choral Symphony (Beethoven), 229, 230n50
Chrétien de Troyes, 1, 66, 66n19, 67–69, 88, 95, 99, 99n41, 100–102, 102 n46–47, 103–104, 106–107, 109–110, 110n61, 112–113, 113n66, 118, 122n10, 123, 127, 128n18, 130, 133, 134n30, 139–145, 145n49, 146–147, 147n53, 148–149, 149n56, 150–151, 151n58–59, 155, 157, 157n70, 158, 160, 168, 171, 173, 187
Christ, 3, 26–27, 55, 74, 89, 92–93, 94n34, 153, 165–166, 212
Chronicle of Two Cities (*Chronica de duabus civitatibus*), 47–50, 61, 71n33, 73
City of God (*Civitas Dei*), 3, 33–36, 36n3, 37–42, 42n31, 43–47, 59, 73, 94, 122, 205, 207, 210, 220n27
Clamide, 151n59, 165, 165n12, 166, 166n14, 168, 171, 185
Cligès, 131, 133, 171, 171n27, 173–175
Cligès, 131, 133, 171–175
Clinschor, 152n60
codex (as technology), 38, 39n15, 213–214, 224n40
Codex Manesse, 79, 79n2, 80–81
Columbus, Christopher, 15n18
Concordat of Worms, 76
Condwiramurs, 151n59, 157, 165–166, 166n14, 168, 171, 185
A Connecticut Yankee, 5, 208, 230–240
Copernicus, 222n35
Corinth, 29
1 Corinthians, 29, 125
2 Corinthians, 26
Cornwall, 188, 191–194, 199–200
Critique of Pure Reason (*Kritik der reinen Vernunft*), 224

Cundrie, 152n60, 154, 157
Curvenal/Kurvenal, 54, 111–112

Dame World, 70
Dante Alighieri, 206–207, 209, 211
Davidson, Donald, 13
Deeds of Emperor Frederick (*Gesta Friderici Imperatoris*), 47, 70–71
Descartes, René, 221, 222n35, 224
Der arme Heinrich, 108n59
Dice, game of, 13, 108, 123, 127–128, 130, 137, 159, 169, 169n19, 172
Dido, 25, 30
Diomedes, 18
The Divine Comedy, 206, 207, 209, 211
Dollenstein, 129–130
dualism, dualist, 5, 21–23, 26, 27n40, 28, 37–40, 40n22, 48–49, 52, 55–56, 61, 61n11, 70, 75, 123, 125, 139, 158, 162, 205, 211–212, 220–221, 223, 227–228
Duke of Cornwall, 185–186
Duke of the Saxons, 131–133

Ecclesiastes, Book of, 61
Eilhart von Oberge, 196n10
Einhard, 47, 72, 92
England, 188, 192
Enide (Chrétien), 66, 103, 118, 142–144, 144n45, 145, 145n49, 146, 146n50, 147, 147n52, 148, 152, 155, 160, 187
Enite (Hartmann), 103, 103n49, 104, 106–107, 110–111, 134, 137n34
Enlightenment, to enlighten, 5, 208, 208n4, 219, 221, 224–226, 226n43, 227, 227n46, 228–230, 232–236, 236n62, 237–238, 240–241
Ephesians, Book of, 25–26
Erec (Chrétien), 66, 101, 118, 140–141, 141n40, 142, 142n43, 143–145, 145n49, 146, 146n50, 147, 147n52, 148, 152, 152n60, 155
Erec (Hartmann), 104, 122n10, 134–136, 136n33, 137n34
Erec (Hartmann), 103–106, 110, 134–136
Érec et Énide (Chrétien), 66, 100–103, 110, 112, 123, 126, 139–151, 160, 168, 199
Eucharist, 196
Evangelienharmonie, 89–91
Exodus, Book of, 20, 22
"Explanation of Binary Arithmetic" ("Explication de Arithmetique Binaire"), 223

Fables (Marie de France) (illumination), 96
Feirefiz, 50–53, 53n55, 56, 152, 157–158
Fenice, 171n27, 173–175, 183

financial markets, 10, 237–238
Franks, 71, 89–90, 91n28
Frau Ava, 94
Frederick, Duke of Swabia, 67–68
Frederick I "Barbarossa" (Hohenstaufen), 47, 67–72, 76, 80, 82, 83n7, 85, 119
Frederick II (Hohenstaufen), 76, 76n45
Frederick II of Prussia, 228, 235
French Revolution, 208n4, 228–229, 235–236
Freud, Sigmund, 13
Fukushima, 15n18
Functional Magnetic Resource Imaging (fMRI), 4, 119–120

Gahmuret, 151n59, 153n63
Galatians, Book of, 25–26
games of chance, 5, 10, 123
Gauvain, 113n69, 127–128, 128n17, 140, 142–143, 149
Gawain, 122n10, 127
Gawan, 113, 128–130, 152, 152n60, 154–155
Gawein, of Hartmann von Aue, 128, 131–134; of Marie de France, 186
Ginover, 111
gnomic poetry, 62, 64, 88n24
Gospels, 26, 42, 89–93
Gottfried von Strassburg, 1, 50, 53–55, 55n60, 78n51, 79, 79n2, 80–81, 85–88, 88n24, 95, 103, 107, 109–115, 115n69, 116, 116n70–71, 117, 165, 169, 171n26, 188, 188n59–60, 189–190, 194–196, 196n69, 197, 197n70, 198–200, 202–204
Grail, 121, 151n59, 152, 155–158
Grail castle, contingent, company, 151n59, 152, 154–156, 159–160
Gregory VII, 72, 74–77
Guenievre, 141–142
Guivreiz, 104
Guivret, 145n49, 146
Gurmun, 192
Gurnemanz, 151n59, 152n59
Gutenberg, Johannes, 213, 214n16

Halberstädter Bischofschronik, 63n15
Habermas, Jürgen, 3, 6, 12–14, 14n15, 34, 44n36, 57, 57n1, 208n4, 209n6, 239n67
Hartmann von Aue, 67–69, 69n28, 86–88, 103–108, 108n57, 109–110, 110n61, 111–113, 118, 122n10, 123, 123n11, 124, 125n14, 126, 131–132, 132n28, 133–134, 134n30, 137n34, 139, 146
Hebrews, Book of, 25, 28, 33
Hector, 19, 30, 125

Heinrich von Veldeke, 68–69, 82, 83n7, 87
Helen of Troy, 16
Heliand, 92–93, 93n30, 94
Henry III, 74
Henry IV, 72, 74–76
Henry VI, 67–68, 76
Hera, 17
Herzeloyde, 107–108, 130, 151n59, 153
Hildebrandslied, 92
Holy Scriptures, 21, 38, 39n15, 91–92
Homer's Iliad/Troy, 2–3, 16–17, 17n22–23, 18, 18n25–26, 19–20, 20n32, 23, 23n35, 31–32, 35, 104, 172
The Human Condition (Arendt) 5, 243
Humanism, 206
hunt, hunting, 140–141, 141n40, 142–143
Hus, Jan, 207

In Praise of the New Knighthood (*De Laude Novae Militiae*), 137–138, 149
Industry, Industrialization, 230, 232–236, 238, 241
Innocent III, 74, 76–78
Ireland, 192–193, 200
Irene Angelina, Princess of Byzantium, 61–62
Isaac, 26
Isolt, 53, 53n56, 54–56, 78n51, 114–116, 115n72, 116, 165–166, 169, 188, 190–201, 201n74, 204
Isolt, the elder Queen, 190, 192
Isolt of the White Hands, 199
The Italian Guest (*Der Welsche Gast*), 59, 122n10
Ither, 151n59, 154
Iwein, 122n10, 131–134
Iwein (Hartmann von Aue), 67, 69, 108n59, 110, 124, 126, 131–132

Jericho, 16, 20–23, 25–26, 28–29
Jerusalem, 16, 25, 27–28, 35, 40, 40n23
Jeschute, 151n59, 152n59, 154
Jethro, 20
Joshua, 21
Joshua, Book of, 20–21
joy, 4, 11, 20, 28, 56, 59, 63, 67, 67n21, 69–70, 86, 88, 88n24, 95, 98n39, 115, 118, 123, 134, 137n35, 152, 152n59, 154, 160, 163, 168, 171, 179–180, 186, 189, 192, 196, 199–200, 202–204, 213, 229–230, 233
Joy of the Court (*Joie de la curt*), 134, 134n30, 136, 136n33, 137n34, 146–147
Judas Iscariot, 92, 165–166, 185
Judgment Day, 43–45, 125, 205

Judith, the Reverend Lady, 90, 92
Juno, 24, 31–32, 32n46, 104
Jupiter, 24, 31–32, 32n46, 104
Juvencus, 89

Kalogreant, 124, 125n14, 126–127, 131–133, 136, 142n43, 159
Kant, Immanuel, 5, 224–227, 227n46, 228–229, 232–233, 235, 240–241
Karnant, 137n34
Karsnafite, 111
Keie, 112, 152n60
Kepler, Johannes, 222n35
King Arthur, 5, 67–69, 82–83, 110–112, 119, 122n10, 123–124, 127, 133–134, 140–141, 143–144, 145n49, 147, 151n59, 152, 152n59, 155, 159, 173, 176–177, 180–188, 192, 231n53, 236n62, 237–239
Kingrimursal, 129
Klingsor von Ungarland, 80n2
knight errantry, 126–127, 237
Konrad III, 47
Kyot, 112, 112n63–64, 150

Lachmann, Karl, 116
Lais (Marie), 95, 95n36, 97, 99–100
Lancelot (Chrétien), 127
Lancelot (Chrétien), 127
Lanval, 176–177, 177n37, 177–188, 192
Lanval, 165, 176, 176n34, 177–188, 199
Launcelot (Twain), 237
Lavinia, 23–25, 69
Leibniz, Gottfried Wilhelm, 1, 5, 219–220, 220n27, 221, 221n33, 222, 222n35–36, 223, 223n38, 224, 224n40–41, 225, 240–242
Leibzig, 223
Leo III, 73–74
Leo X, 209–210
Liutbert, Archbishop of Mainz, 89–91
Lohengrin, 160n67
love lyrics, 88n24
love potion, 194, 194n69, 195–196.
Lucan, 89–90
Luther, Martin, 5, 77, 77n48, 207–208, 208n4, 209, 209n6, 210, 210n10, 211, 211n11, 212–213, 214n16, 215–219, 223, 223n38, 225–228, 240
Luther's Bible, 214, 218
Lyotard, Jean-François, 208, 242

Mabonagrin, 134

Magdeburg, Christmas Day Procession in 1199, 61–63, 65
Magyars, 94
Mainz, court festival in 1184, 67–69, 71, 80, 83n7, 85, 119
Marco Lombardo, 206–207, 207n1, 209, 211
Marie de France, 1, 88, 95, 95n35, 96–98, 98n39, 99, 99n41, 100–103, 106–107, 109, 117–118, 165, 176–177, 177n36, 178, 179n40, 180, 183–184, 186n55, 187–188, 188n60, 199, 214
Marke, King of England and Cornwall (in Gottfried's *Tristan*), 53, 111, 114, 188, 190–194, 199–201
Mary. See The Virgin Mary
matière de Bretagne, 99
Meleagant, 127–128
Menelaus, 16, 18
The Monadology (*La Monadologie*), by Gottfried Leibniz, 219–220, 220n27–28, 221, 221n33
monads, 5, 219–220, 220n27, 221, 221n33
monist, monism, 40n22
monolatry, 22
Morgan, 188, 199, 202
Morholt, 143, 192–194, 200, 202
Moses, 20, 22
mout bele conjointure, 123, 139–140, 148
mysticism, mystical writings, 207n2

Nantes, 147
Neidhart, 58n4
Neoplatonism, 40
Nestor, 18, 125
Neurological simulation of narrative events, 4, 119–122
New Testament, 2, 147–148
Newton, Isaac, 221, 222n35
Nibelungs, 82
Nietzsche, Friedrich, 13
noble hearts (*edele herzen*), 115–116, 195, 199

"Ode to Joy," 229–230, 230n50
Odysseus, 17–18, 125
Octavian, 178
Old Testament, 2, 147–148
On Christian Doctrine (*De Doctrina Christiana*), 1, 42, 82n5, 137, 161–162
On the Freedom of a Christian (*Von der Freiheit eines Chrisstenmenschen*), 208–209, 211–213, 216, 217n22

INDEX • 259

Open Letter on Translating (*Sendbrief zum Dolmetschen*), 214–215, 218–219
Orgeluse, 152
The Origins of Totalitarianism (Arendt), 5, 241–242, 242n73
Orilus, 151n59, 152n59
Otfried von Weissenburg, 89–91, 91n28, 92–94, 97–98, 102, 214
Otherworldly Lady (Marie's *Lanval*), 177, 177n37, 178–188
Otto, Bishop of Freising, 47–50, 61n12, 70–71, 71n33, 73
Otto I, 47, 71–72
Otto of Brunswick, 76
Otto of Wittelsbach, 70n29
Ovid, 89–90, 164n11

pain, 4, 11, 28–29, 29n41, 63, 70, 114–115, 123, 125, 123n11, 152n59, 154, 158, 160, 167–168, 171–173, 188, 190, 192, 198–200, 204
Paris (Iliad), 18, 125
Parzival, 50–52, 107, 110–113, 118–119, 122n10, 130, 151, 151n59, 152, 152n59–60, 153, 153n63, 154, 154n64–65, 155, 155n66, 156–157, 157n70, 158–160, 165, 165n12, 166, 166n14, 168, 171
Parzival (Wolfram), 50–52, 53n55, 84, 107, 107n53, 108n55–56, 109, 109n59, 110, 110n61, 111–113, 113n66, 116, 123, 128, 139, 149, 149n55–56, 150, 152–159, 159n76, 160, 165–169, 199
Patroclus, 18
Perceval, 113n69, 157, 157n70, 158
Perceval (Chrétien), 112, 128n18, 149
Philip of Swabia, 61–62, 64–65, 67, 69–70
Pietà, 167
Plotinus, 40
Pontius Pilate, 165–166
The Postmodern Condition (Lyotard), 242
potential(ity), 4, 14, 14n16, 15–16, 28, 35, 45, 56, 78, 82, 102, 106, 110, 133, 148, 159, 176, 199, 224, 240–243
Prester John, 160n76
Priam, 17, 19, 31
printing press, 208, 213–214, 214n16–17, 215, 217, 224
Priscian, 97, 98n40
Prudentius, 89
Psalms, 11

Queen (Marie's *Lanval*), 181–186

race, racing, 9–10, 16, 19, 29–30, 33, 125–126, 138, 230
Rahewin, 83n7
Reformation, 5, 34, 78, 208, 208n4, 209n6, 217, 219, 227, 227n46, 235n59, 240
Reign of Terror (French Revolution), 236, 238
Reinmar, 88n24
Renaissance, 206
Repanse de Schoie, 51–53
repeated game, 2, 11, 142
representative Öffentlichkeit (representational public), 3, 57
Richard I "Lionheart," 65–66
Riwalin, 169–171, 188, 192, 195, 199
Romans, Book of, 27, 32, 214–215
Rome, 16, 19, 23–25, 25n38, 29, 31–33, 35–36, 39–40, 42–43, 46, 48–49, 73, 77, 80, 82, 89–90, 205–207, 209–210, 210n10, 211
Rorty, Richard, 13, 29n41
Rual, 188, 190, 192
Rudolph August von Braunschweig-Lüneburg-Wolfenbüttel, 222
Rudolf von Ems, 58n4

Sagramor, 152n59
Saints Lives (Hagiography), 5, 121–122, 126–127
Saladin, 65
Sand Belt, Battle of the, 231, 238
Sarpedon, 18
Savonarola, Girolamo, 207, 210n9
Saxons, 62, 72, 93, 93n30, 94
Schiller, Friedrich, 229–232
Sekundille, 51
Semiramis, 178
Schionatulander, 151n59, 166–168
Shrovetide, 129–130
Siegfried, 82
Sigune, 130, 151n59, 152n59, 166–168
Sodom, 210
Solomon, 144
Soredamors, 171, 171n27, 195
St. Augustine of Hippo, 1–3, 33–50, 54, 56, 59–60, 73–74, 80, 82, 82n5, 82n6, 90, 94, 121–122, 125–126, 135, 137, 137n35, 161, 162n2, 163, 163n7, 164, 169, 196, 205–207, 210–211, 220, 220n27, 223, 242n73, 243
St. Paul, 3, 25–26, 26n39, 27–29, 32–33, 35, 40, 125, 205, 211
Strukturwandel der Öffentlichkeit (*Structural Transformation of the Public Sphere*) (Habermas), 3, 57

"Tantris," 192–193
Thisbe and Pyramus, 104
Thomas of Britain, 197n70, 199
Thomasin von Zirclaria, 59n6, 122n10
To the Christian Nobility of the German Nation (*An den Christlichen Adel deutscher Nation*), 216
Trevrizent, 152n60, 155–158
Tristan (Gottfried), 53–54, 56, 78n51, 85–87, 111, 114–115, 115n69, 116, 169, 182, 184, 188, 190–204
Tristan (Chrétien), 143
Tristan (Gottfried), 50, 53–55, 85–87, 113–116, 116n71, 165, 169–171, 188, 188n59, 189–203
Troy, 16–24, 29–32, 35, 104, 125, 172
Turnus, 23–24, 25n38, 69
Twain, Mark, 5, 208, 230–231, 231n51–52, 232, 234–241
Typology, 147–148

Umbriz, 104, 110, 112
universities, 78n52
uomo univerale, 206

Vergulaht, 128, 130
vernacular, 4, 68, 69n28, 82–83, 85–86, 88–95, 97, 99–100, 102, 113n66, 117, 196n69, 214, 214n18, 218

Vikings, 94
Virgil's Aeneid, 2–3, 23–25, 25n38, 30–32, 68, 82, 104
The Virgin Mary, 62, 153
Visigoths' sack of Rome 410 CE, 36, 39, 46
Vulgate Cycle, 102n48

Wagner, Richard, 116
Waltharius, 94
Walther von der Vogelweide, 61–67, 69–70, 76, 76n46, 77, 87n22, 88n24, 206
Widukind, 72
Wolfram von Eschenbach, 1, 50–53, 53n55, 55, 84, 84n10, 87–88, 107, 107n53, 108, 108n56, 109–110, 110n61, 111–112, 112n63–64, 113, 113n66, 114, 116–119, 122n10, 123, 127–128, 128n18, 129–130, 139, 149, 149n55–56, 150–151, 151n58–59, 152, 152n59–60, 153, 155, 157–160, 165–169
Wycliffe, John, 207

Yankee (Hank Morgan), 230–239, 241
Yder, 143
Yvain (Chrétien), 110, 139.

Zero-Sum Game, 126, 133, 136
Zeus, 17, 19
Zurich, 80

INTERVENTIONS: NEW STUDIES IN MEDIEVAL CULTURE
Ethan Knapp, Series Editor

Interventions: New Studies in Medieval Culture publishes theoretically informed work in medieval literary and cultural studies. We are interested both in studies of medieval culture and in work on the continuing importance of medieval tropes and topics in contemporary intellectual life.

The Medieval Risk-Reward Society: Courts, Adventure, and Love in the European Middle Ages
WILL HASTY

The Politics of Ecology: Land, Life, and Law in Medieval Britain
EDITED BY RANDY P. SCHIFF AND JOSEPH TAYLOR

The Art of Vision: Ekphrasis in Medieval Literature and Culture
EDITED BY ANDREW JAMES JOHNSTON, ETHAN KNAPP, AND MARGITTA ROUSE

Desire in the Canterbury Tales
ELIZABETH SCALA

Imagining the Parish in Late Medieval England
ELLEN K. RENTZ

Truth and Tales: Cultural Mobility and Medieval Media
EDITED BY FIONA SOMERSET AND NICHOLAS WATSON

Eschatological Subjects: Divine and Literary Judgment in Fourteenth-Century French Poetry
J. M. MOREAU

Chaucer's (Anti-)Eroticisms and the Queer Middle Ages
TISON PUGH

Trading Tongues: Merchants, Multilingualism, and Medieval Literature
JONATHAN HSY

Translating Troy: Provincial Politics in Alliterative Romance
ALEX MUELLER

Fictions of Evidence: Witnessing, Literature, and Community in the Late Middle Ages
JAMIE K. TAYLOR

Answerable Style: The Idea of the Literary in Medieval England
EDITED BY FRANK GRADY AND ANDREW GALLOWAY

Scribal Authorship and the Writing of History in Medieval England
MATTHEW FISHER

Fashioning Change: The Trope of Clothing in High- and Late-Medieval England
ANDREA DENNY-BROWN

Form and Reform: Reading across the Fifteenth Century
EDITED BY SHANNON GAYK AND KATHLEEN TONRY

How to Make a Human: Animals and Violence in the Middle Ages
 KARL STEEL

Revivalist Fantasy: Alliterative Verse and Nationalist Literary History
 RANDY P. SCHIFF

Inventing Womanhood: Gender and Language in Later Middle English Writing
 TARA WILLIAMS

Body Against Soul: Gender and Sowlehele *in Middle English Allegory*
 MASHA RASKOLNIKOV

www.ingramcontent.com/pod-product-compliance
Lightning Source LLC
Chambersburg PA
CBHW021837220426
43663CB00005B/281